COOPERATIVE SYSTEMS DESIGN

Frontiers in Artificial Intelligence and Applications

FAIA covers all aspects of theoretical and applied artificial intelligence research in the form of monographs, doctoral dissertations, textbooks, handbooks and proceedings volumes. The FAIA series contains several sub-series, including "Information Modelling and Knowledge Bases" and "Knowledge-Based Intelligent Engineering Systems". It also includes the biannual ECAI, the European Conference on Artificial Intelligence, proceedings volumes, and other ECCAI – the European Coordinating Committee on Artificial Intelligence – sponsored publications. An editorial panel of internationally well-known scholars is appointed to provide a high quality selection.

Series Editors:
J. Breuker, R. Dieng, N. Guarino, J.N. Kok, J. Liu, R. López de Mántaras,
R. Mizoguchi, M. Musen and N. Zhong

Volume 137

Recently published in this series

ISSN 0922-6389

Cooperative Systems Design

Seamless Integration of Artifacts and Conversations –
Enhanced Concepts of Infrastructure for Communication

Edited by

Parina Hassanaly

Université Aix Marseille III Paul Cezanne, France

Thomas Herrmann

Ruhr-Universität Bochum, Germany

Gabriele Kunau

Ruhr-Universität Bochum, Germany

and

Manuel Zacklad

Université de Technologie de Troyes, France

IOS
Press

Amsterdam • Berlin • Oxford • Tokyo • Washington, DC

ISBN 1-58603-604-1
Library of Congress Control Number: 2006924056

Publisher
IOS Press
Nieuwe Hemweg 6B
1013 BG Amsterdam
Netherlands
fax: +31 20 687 0019
e-mail: order@iospress.nl

Distributor in the UK and Ireland
Gazelle Books Services Ltd.
White Cross Mills
Hightown
Lancaster LA1 4XS
United Kingdom
fax: +44 1524 63232
e-mail: sales@gazellebooks.co.uk

Distributor in the USA and Canada
IOS Press, Inc.
4502 Rachael Manor Drive
Fairfax, VA 22032
USA
fax: +1 703 323 3668
e-mail: iosbooks@iospress.com

Cooperative Systems Design
P. Hassanaly et al. (Eds.)
IOS Press, 2006
© *2006 The authors. All rights reserved.*

From the Editors

COOP'06 is the 7th International Conference on the Design of Cooperative Systems. The conference aims at bringing together researchers who contribute to the design of cooperative systems and their integration into organizational settings. The challenge of the conference is to advance:

- Understanding and modeling of collaborative work which is mediated by technical artifacts;
- Design methodologies for cooperative work analysis and cooperative systems design;
- New technologies supporting cooperation;
- Concepts and socio-technical solutions for the application of cooperative systems.

The COOP conferences are based on the conviction that cooperative systems design requires a deep understanding of the cooperative work of groups and organizations, involving both artifacts and social practices. This is the reason why contributions from all disciplines contributing to/related to the field of cooperative systems design are considered as relevant, including computer science (CSCW, HCI, Information Systems, Knowledge Engineering, etc.), organizational and management sciences, sociology, psychology, anthropology, ergonomics, linguistics, etc.

Various approaches and methodologies are considered, theoretical contributions as well as empirical studies reports or software development experiences on topics such as:

- Analysis of collaborative work situations;
- Conceptual frameworks for understanding cooperative work;
- Guidelines for designing cooperative systems;
- The influence of new technologies (mobile Computing, ubiquitous computing, etc.) on cooperation;
- Expertise sharing and learning in cooperative work;
- Communities and new forms of organization;
- Innovative technological solutions and user interfaces;
- Methods for participatory design of cooperative systems.

In 2006, COOP puts a special emphasis on the issue of the "seamless integration of artifacts and conversations – enhanced concepts of infrastructure for communication". The emergence and distribution of cooperative systems has been accompanied by an increased communication workload. This is characterized by increased information exchange, message overflow, numerous interruptions of work, cognitive overload, or a dominance of virtual context. To alleviate and improve the situation, greater integration of conversational acts (e.g. message exchange) and documents is clearly required.

43 long papers were submitted for COOP'06; from these 18 were selected to be presented in the conference and published in this book. An additional set of approx. 20 short papers is also presented at the conference and published in a supplementary

booklet. The conference program is completed by a workshop programme and a doctoral consortium.

The papers included in the proceedings draw from a rich empirical background including studies in healthcare, homecare, software-development, architectural design, marine insurance industry, and learning in university settings. They integrate different theoretical foundations and conceptual frameworks to further the understanding of cooperative work, build advanced conceptual frameworks, derive design implications for information systems, and present new technological concepts for cooperative systems.

Michael Buckland is the keynote speaker of COOP'06; and an abstract of his talk is included in this book. Michael Buckland comes from the School of Information Management & Systems which is part of the University of California and located in Berkeley. He has contributed to renew the approach of documents particularly by going back to the foundational work of the French archivists like Suzanne Briet. His famous papers "What is a "document"?" and "Information as Thing" are surprisingly relevant in the context of the CSCW debate about the importance of the materiality of coordinative artefacts.

The papers in this book are presented in alphabetical order. We hope that you will find them interesting to read and that they will inspire further discussions and further research on cooperative system design.

Acknowledgements

Many persons and institutions helped to make the conference and the publication of this book possible. We would like to thank them for their great efforts. Our special thanks go to the members of the program committee who took the responsibility for selecting the papers to be presented on the conference and to be included in the proceedings; they fulfilled their task with great care and provided helpful comments to the authors. We also want to thank the helpers behind the scenes: Michael Prilla (Ruhr-Universität Bochum) for configuring and maintaining the conference tool in the internet; L'Hedi Zaher (Université de Technologie de Troyes) for designing and maintaining the conference web page in the internet; Alexandra Frerichs (Ruhr-Universität Bochum) for the quality assurance of all camera ready papers.

We are indebted to the CONSEIL GENERAL DES BOUCHES DU RHONE for supporting us at the conference site in Carry-le-Rouet.

Bochum, February 2006

The editors
Parina Hassanaly, Thomas Herrmann, Gabriele Kunau and Manuel Zacklad

Conference Committee

Program Committee Co-Chairs

Thomas Herrmann
Ruhr-Universität Bochum,
Germany

Manuel Zacklad
Université de Technologie de Troyes,
France

Conference Chair

Parina Hassanaly
Université Aix Marseille III Paul Cezanne,
France

Proceedings Chair

Gabriele Kunau
Ruhr-Universität Bochum,
Germany

Workshop Chair

Myriam Lewkowicz
Université de Technologie de Troyes,
France

Doctoral Consortium Chair

Carla Simone
Università di Milano Bicocca,
Italy

Short Paper Interactive Session Chair

Andrea Kienle
Fraunhofer Integrated Publication and
Information Systems Institute (IPSI),
Germany

Organisation Chair

Patrick Fournier
Université Aix Marseille III Paul Cezanne,
France

Program Committee

Program Committee Co-Chairs

Thomas Herrmann
Institute of Applied Work Science, Ruhr-University Bochum

Manuel Zacklad
Tech-CICO/Dpmt GSIT, Université de Technologie de Troyes

Scientific Committee

Mark Ackermann, *USA*
Alexandra Agostini, *Italy*
Liam Bannon, *Ireland*
Susan Bodker, *Denmark*
Dominique Bouiller, *France*
Jean-Francois Boujut, *France*
Geof Bowker, *USA*
Béatrice Cahour, *France*
Angela Carell, *Germany*
Françoise Darses, *France*
Elisabeth Davenport, *UK*
Bertrand David, *France*
Francoise Decortis, *Belgium*
Wolfgang Deiters, *Germany*
Alain Derycke, *France*
Francoise Detienne, *France*
Rose Dieng-Kuntz, *France*
Monica Divitini, *Norway*
Gerhard Fischer, *USA*
Geraldine Fitzpatrick, *UK*
Alain Giboin, *France*
Tom Gross, *Germany*
Andrea Kienle, *Germany*
Michael Koch, *Germany*

Gabriele Kunau, *Germany*
Kaari Kutti, *Finland*
Myriam Lewkowicz, *France*
Christian Licoppe, *France*
Jacques Lonchamp, *France*
Paul Luff, *UK*
Gloria Mark, *USA*
Giorgio De Michelis, *Italy*
Keiichi Nakata, *Japan*
Bernard Pavard, *USA*
Volkmar Pipek, *Germany*
Wolfgang Prinz, *Germany*
Dave Randall, *UK*
Pascal Salembier, *France*
Marcello Sarini, *Italy*
Walt Scachi, *USA*
Kjeld Schmidt, *Denmark*
Carla Simone, *Italy*
Jean-Luc Soubie, *France*
William Turner, *France*
Ina Wagner, *Austria*
Niels Windfeld Lund, *Norway*
Volker Wulf, *Germany*
Pascale Zaraté, *France*

Contents

Invited Speaker

Cooperative Systems Design
P. Hassanaly et al. (Eds.)
IOS Press, 2006

Collaboration:
Bad Words and Strong Documents

Michael BUCKLAND
School of Information Management & Systems[1]
University of California, Berkeley, CA 94720-4600
(510) 642 3159 buckland@sims.berkeley.edu
http://www.sims.berkeley.edu/~buckland
Co-Director, Electronic Cultural Atlas Initiative

Keynote - Abstract

The use of communications technologies and artifacts in cooperative systems and the integration of cooperative systems in organization settings can be seen as a special case of the broader use of communications and artifacts in society. The broader system is of interest to those concerned with the documents and documentation. In this talk we will address two themes:

1. **Language is cultural and evolves within communities of discourse.** Every little community evolves its own dialect through metaphor and negotiation. Collaboration between individuals from different communities necessarily involves some dissonance, both in terms of what words mean (denote) and what they imply (connote) and, therefore, what words will be effective and socially acceptable. These issues extend broadly across the classification, categorization, and naming practices which form an important part of the infrastructure of collaborative activities.

2. **Documents have enormous social power.** My passport is more powerful than I am: It can cross frontiers without me, but I cannot cross frontiers without it. Analysis of the character and role of documents leads to an expansive functional definition of document which converges with the notion of artefact in the design of cooperative systems. These two related issues will be examined from the perspective of the study of documents and documentation.

---

[1]Correspondence: University of California, Berkeley, CA 94720-4600, (510) 642 3159, buckland@sims.berkeley.edu

Papers

Cooperative Systems Design
P. Hassanaly et al. (Eds.)
IOS Press, 2006

Beyond Electronic Patient's File: Assisting Conversations in a Healthcare Network

Valérie BENARD, Myriam LEWKOWICZ, Manuel ZACKLAD
ICD – FRE CNRS 2848 – Université de Technologie de Troyes, BP 2060,
10010 Troyes Cedex, France[1]

Abstract. Healthcare networks have been created to meet new health requirements. This new mode of organization gives healthcare professionals with different competences overall patient coverage. The aim of this study was to define tools supporting cooperation between these professionals. An ethnographic study on a healthcare network carried out during a period of one year has helped to understand how these networks function and what their requirements are. In this paper, we present the network studied, and describe a theoretical framework which can be used to analyze its activities; we focus in particular on the transactions taking place during face-to-face meetings, and we conclude that in order to cooperate efficiently, professionals need a coordination tool which is more than just an electronic patient file. We end this paper by suggesting guidelines for computer-supported cooperative activities in the field of healthcare networks.

Keywords: Healthcare network, CSCW, ethnographic study, conversation

Introduction

The growing specialization of health professionals has given rise to an increasing need for cooperation between the various healthcare professionals dealing with the same patient [1]. To meet these needs for integrated, coordinated teamwork, a new mode of organization is emerging: the healthcare network. However, integrated patient coverage involves more than simply coordinating the contributions of medical, psychological and social specialists working side by side. Coherence is required in order to give patients really relevant overall coverage. The electronic patient's file, which is often the first step in computer-supported medical work, makes it possible to share data about patients and their treatment .It promotes coordination between several health professionals by allowing each of them, for instance, to know what the others have done for a patient. But pooling patient files does not make it possible for professionals to communicate with each other and therefore does not promote cooperation between all the disciplines dealing with a patient at the same time. The aim of our present research is to define tools for computer-supported cooperation in healthcare networks. We are particularly interested in collective coverage, which goes beyond data and information sharing. This joint approach to healthcare is one of the goals of the RPM network (Réseau Pôle Mémoire in French, which means Memory Pole Network),

---

[1] Research funded by Conseil Général de l'Aube (district grant) and the European Social Fund.

which we studied for one year. In this paper, after briefly presenting the RPM network, we describe the Theory of Symbolic Communicational Transactions, which is the theoretical framework adopted to analyze its activities. We then present our analysis of the network and our initial results, before suggesting some design principles for computer-supported RPM activities. Lastly, we describe how our work links up with other research on computer-supported medical activities.

1. Case Description: the RPM network

The term "Healthcare network" involves being "centered on populations, on the scale of a district or of a city. These networks developed at the same time a medico-psycho-social coverage of people, and a public health or community health activity. They associate the local public utilities, health professionals and associations in projects of diagnosis, prevention, and training. They are generally not-for-profit associations"[2]. The ageing of the population in industrial countries the failure to detect cognitive disorders in the early stages, and the wish to treat these pathologies in a cooperative way involving different professions were the main reasons for creating this network. The main objective of RPM is to improve the medico-psycho-social coverage of people suffering from memory disorders. Its members are now negotiating with URCAM (Union Régionale des Caisses d'Assurance Maladie in French, which means Regional Union of Health Insurance Funds) to obtain funds for the network. Other initiatives have also been launched to find money to help the network.

RPM is a non-for-profit association composed of 190 members who are all health professionals interested in setting up the network. According to the statutes of this association, "including mainly private health professionals, as well as hospital workers and other actors in the medical and social fields the objective of the association is to promote and carry out all activities such as prevention, care, services, training and research for the benefit of elderly people suffering from cognitive disorders inhabiting Troyes and the surrounding area" (translated from the French statutes*). The specialties of these 190 health professionals were as follows: 4 Neurologists, 3 Psychiatrists, 12 Gerontologists, 98 General practitioners, 20 Speech therapists, 13 Psychologists, 2 Nurses, 1 Auxiliary, 10 Institutional representatives, 4 Users representatives, 23 Others (social centers, mutual insurance company, local information and coordination center representatives). One of the main roles in the network is that of the coordinator: the present coordinator is a neuropsychologist who plays her own professional role as well as role of coordinator, which consists in supervising the patients' follow-up.

The objective of improving the medico-psycho-social coverage of people suffering from memory disorders can be defined more specifically as follows:

- First, the network members want to reduce the time taken to reach a diagnosis in order to be able to act fast and thus to slow down the progression of the disease as early as possible; this point is particularly critical in the case of Alzheimer's disease.

---

[2] CNR (Commission Nationale des Réseaux in French, which means National Networks Commission) - http://www.cnr.asso.fr/presentationCnr/presentation.htm

- The network plans to provide complete coverage of patients, so that they can benefit from full medico-psycho-social assistance.
- Finally, the assistance of those close to the patient is very important in mental diseases of this kind, and the network also wishes to help families having to cope with the problems involved when these pathologies occur in their midst.
- Training is another network commitment because health professionals must be able to update their knowledge and improve their practices.

One of the more implicit but necessary objectives for the successful functioning of the network is to abolish all hierarchical barriers between the various members. Efficient communication and cooperation between members will only be possible if everyone is listened to in the same way, whatever their skills and their role in dealing with patients.

In activity theory terms ([2], [3]), RPM can be depicted as in figure 1.

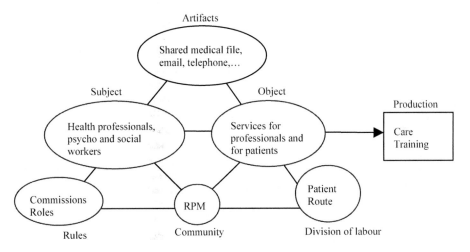

Figure 1. The activity system for RPM

Activity Theory framework clearly defines the various concepts mobilized by the RPM network. However, although this theory provides a general analytical framework, none of the underlying models can be used to perform a close analysis focusing on the interactions between members, which are "sense -creative" within a collective. We therefore now propose a more fine-grained theoretical framework.

2. Issues and theoretical framework

2.1. Issues

Upon observing RPM meetings, we noted that in many cases the conversations were not task-centred. Designers defining Information Systems often ignore exchanges of this kind and focus on information management functions relating directly to the ongoing task. What is produced during these conversations is therefore generally neglected. In fact, if we are interested in the provision of services, since all conversations are value–creative, they must be taken into account when analyzing collectives [4]. In order to identify and qualify these conversations, we used the Theory of Symbolic Communicational Transactions, according to which transactions are by definition sense-creative. This analytical framework includes a model distinguishing between the four different modes of regulation involved in transactions, which are presented below.

2.2. Theoretical framework: Theory of Symbolic Communicational Transactions

Symbolic Communicational Transactions have been defined by Zacklad [5] as "interactions between actors cognitively interdependent allowing them to create new meanings to reduce their mutual uncertainty in their activity management. Creating meaning consists in sharing knowledge to develop representations, attitudes or affects which the value is cemented by a mutual grip of commitment" (translated from [6]). Creating new meanings is a major step in RPM. The exchanges between its members allow each of them to become aware of various aspects of the pathologies in question. They can then develop common or shared representations. In addition, the actors have to define cooperative practices, which are not yet existent because the network is still in the early stages. We have classified interactions between RPM members as Symbolic Communicational Transactions.

According to Dewey et al [7], transactions, which differ from interactions, characterize creative meetings at the end of which a new production is achieved and each actor has been transformed (in other words, interactions do not lead to original production or the transformation of the actors). In the present study, we will not use "interactions" with this particular connotation because this does not fit the meaning of symbolic interactionism, for example[3]. We will use the term "interactions" to denote behaviour associated with the exchanges which take place at meetings without the creative suggestions.

Moving away from this terminology, we now oppose routine transactions and creative transactions. Unlike the production of routine transactions, which is largely standardized, creative transactions involve the production of both an original (semiotic or material) "work" and "selfs" (Figure 1 in [4]). Selfs can be either individual or collective, and the producers of transactions can be either different people or the same person engaged in an internal dialogue. Symbolic Communicational Transactions become effective in the context of transactional situations, which are made up of different constituents, as described in the RPM context by the example shown in figure 2.

---

[3] Dialogue is here largely considered. Indeed, preparing oneself a good meal is a transaction too.

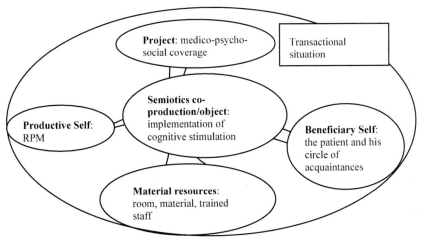

Figure 2. An example of an RPM transactional situation: the implementation of cognitive stimulation

The modes of regulation involved in transactions are defined by crossing the transaction focus (on work or on self) with the degree of reflexiveness of the transactions (introspective or extrospective) (table1). The extrospective degree of reflexiveness is that occurring in quite concrete actions, such as the way people get organized to work together. For instance, the patient route (figure 3) is an extrospective function which tells RPM members who does what and in what order; here we could speak about coordination. The introspective degree of reflexiveness is much more abstract. It relates for example to ethics and people's interest in working together. Focusing on the work or on the self means focusing on care or on the members of the group.

Table 1. Four modes of regulation- SEPI matrix (new version of OSIR matrix [5])

	INTROSPECTIVE	EXTROSPECTIVE
SELF	Socio - Relational Regulation centered on explicitation of the conditions of relations' development between productive self(s) and beneficiary(ies) in the structural and personal dimensions	Politico - Organizational Regulation centered on explicitation of the relations between selfs (productive and beneficiary) towards the collective functioning allowing the semiotic production
WORK	Epistemic Regulation centered on the conditions of realization of the semiotic production from the points of view of the explicitation of the common necessary representational basis, required instruments, and functioning rules	Instrumental Regulation centered on the explicitation of measure criteria for the evaluation of the semiotic production

In other words, the socio-relational mode of regulation deals with understanding others and their needs; the politico-organizational mode concerns the way people share out work; the epistemic mode of regulation relates to definition and coverage in healthcare network settings, and the instrumental mode of regulation concerns pooling patients' data.

Table 1 suggests that we could define the information management functions corresponding to each mode of regulation. Analyzing the interactions between RPM members in the framework of these modes of regulation will therefore make it possible to identify more quickly the functions of a tool supporting RPM activities. In designing an Information System for a healthcare network, it is necessary to fulfill at the same time needs related to each of the modes of regulation, and needs in terms of flexibility, so that the members of the network quickly and easily reconfigure their workspace according to the current mode of regulation. Taking all possible types of transactions types into account in Information System design makes it possible not to neglect conversations which are not directly connected to the task in hand.

The Theory of Symbolic Communicational Transactions is an analytical framework which can be used to define and identify the various interactions occurring in the RPM Network. This analysis includes the conversations which constitute the main observable cooperative activity of the network. It is now proposed to present the RPM analysis.

3. RPM Analysis

We conducted an ethnographic study, which "describes a social setting as it is perceived by those involved in the setting" [8]. In addition, we contributed considerably to setting up the network by being present at the actors' side when they needed support, especially computer support. Furthermore, we actively participated in the IT commission by proposing a method enabling the participants to specify their needs exactly. In this way, although we joined the network simply as observers, we were also involved in designing the Information System in order to support their cooperative work. However, this was rather a difficult position, because we are not the usual actors: only health professionals or social professionals normally take part in the network.

The aims of the network, as well as the way it works, are defined by its members at meetings of various kinds:
- "Staff" meetings, which are attended by fifteen people or so on average, give participants an opportunity of presenting complex cases. Depending on their specialties, the other participants ask questions and suggest solutions or give advice about care and patient coverage. The composition of the staff can change at each meeting.
- Commission meetings:
  - The practical commission, which includes fourteen people, meets once a month. This commission is attempting to define good practices so that professionals can refer to specific documents and act accordingly. These practices can evolve with time and experience.
  - The assessment commission consists of four people responsible for defining quantitative and qualitative assessment criteria, as well as procedures for

collecting the information needed for assessments. This commission has not yet met.

- The IT commission, which meets once a month, consists of six people. It is responsible for drafting the functional specifications of the Information System. The requirements are determined via the patient route.

Whatever the agenda of these meetings may be, the aims of the network, its role and its limitations are also often discussed.

Members of the RPM also meet each other at training sessions. For example, twenty-seven participants are taking part in a scheme to train speech therapists and psychologists to use methods of neuropsychological assessment. Three training meetings for general practitioners have also taken place, each of which was attended by ten general practitioners on average. At these training sessions, participants learn how to perform three simple tests. These tests make it possible to rule out possible pathologies, depending on the signs observed, and to confirm certain fears or intuitions. A general practitioner trained in this way will be able to decide whether his patient should undergo further investigations. In this case, the patient can consult the network and follow five steps (figure 3):

1. The first step, named "detection", is an initial filter. It sorts out patients who require a detailed assessment and those who do not.
2. If the patient needs a more detailed assessment, the patient can choose which of the neuropsychologists will carry out this test.
3. Depending on the test results, the patient will then choose one of the specialists, who can be a neurologist, a gerontologist or a psychiatrist.
4. The specialist diagnoses the pathology exactly and prescribes an appropriate treatment. The patient's regular doctor, who will follow the patient, will be free to adapt this treatment as required.
5. At the end of these steps, the patient is examined by a team of health professionals. If the diagnosis is psychopathology, the team will be composed of the regular doctor, a social worker or a coordinator of a CLIC ("Centre Local d'Information et de Coordination" in French, which means Local Information and Coordination Center), the RPM coordinator, and maybe a psychiatrist or a psychologist. If the diagnosis is neurodegenerative pathology, the team will be composed of the regular doctor, a specialist, a speech therapist, a psychologist, a social worker, a gerontological psychologist, the RPM coordinator, and possibly other network partners. If the diagnosis is intermediate, the team will consist of the regular doctor, a specialist, a neuropsychologist, the RPM coordinator, and maybe a psychiatrist. In the case of an undefined condition, the patient's situation is discussed at a staff meeting.

This patient route implemented in the network reduced by four months the time elapsing between the first contact with the patient and the treatment of this patient. In order to act fast during the first few steps on the route, neuropsychologists and specialists reserve slots in their schedules. Patients can therefore obtain appointments much more quickly than is normally the case. Thanks to the five-step procedure described above, professionals in the network meet only people with real needs.

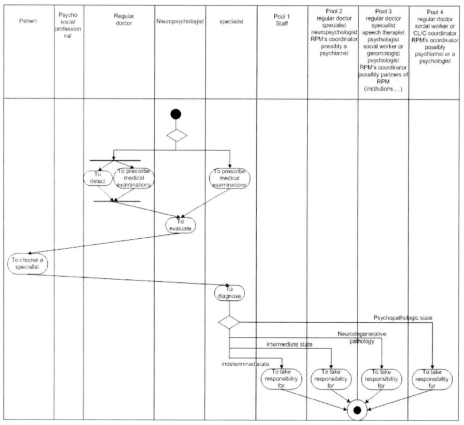

Figure 3. Patient route in RPM

On the above patient route (figure 3), it can be noted that a patient often changes health professionals. These professionals, especially those working together in pools, need more than just sharing access to patients' data; communication is essential, and conversations are necessary for RPM to function well. In fact, the first steps on the patient route could be assisted by a workflow, since the procedure has been well defined. Some information exchanges take place between professionals: for example, the assessment report is sent to the patient's regular doctor and to a specialist, when it is necessary to pursue investigations. But once they have been integrated into the healthcare network, patients are followed by the whole team of professionals (called the pool), which becomes responsible for them. The pooling of data does not suffice here. In fact, each case is quite different, and professionals have to cooperate to treat each patient without being able to follow a pre-defined procedure (such as that available in the early stages, before diagnosis). Actually, the only means at their disposal are the telephone and email, which do not satisfy the need for effective cooperation and properly processing the questions which arise while treating a patient.

3.1. Corpus collection and analysis

In order to understand exactly how the RPM functions, we decided to attend all the meetings listed above. During one year, we therefore watched and filmed most of these meetings. The assessment commission has not yet met and the IT commission does not deal with medical or organizational issues. It therefore did not seem to be relevant to film the meetings of the latter commission. Ten meetings, lasting around one hour and a half each, were filmed and now being retranscribed. In addition, retranscriptions of ten meetings which took place during previous years before the RPM association was officially set up were incorporated into the corpus.

We processed the corpus using the NVivo[4] software tool, which makes it possible to manage a set of independent documents in the context of the same project. It gives overall results on the whole project, aggregating the analysis carried out on all or some of the documents associated with the project. We coded the corpus according to the theoretical framework adopted: modes of regulation (cf. SEPI matrix in table 1) from the Symbolic Communicational Transactions Theory.

From the operational point of view, RPM activities can be classified as follows: cooperative activities correspond to socio-relational, epistemic and instrumental modes of regulation, and coordination activities correspond to the politico-organizational mode of regulation. It was then proposed to identify the various modes of regulation in the corpus, noting which modes occurred most frequently, and to note any changes from one mode to another. Here we present the initial results obtained, which focus on the identification of the modes of regulation. To handle this corpus, we needed to define how to identify the modes of regulation encountered. It was decided to associate each mode with types of face to face interactions, as illustrated in table 2.

Table 2. The SEPI matrix applied to RPM activities

Reflexiveness degree / Focus	Introspection	Extrospection
Self	**Socio-relational** *(reaffirming the network objectives, creating a collective identity)* to join to describe an experience	**Politico-organizational** *(establishing how to work together)* to define good organizational practices
Work	**Epistemic** *(defining care within RPM)* To define good health care and ethical practices	**Instrumental** *(defining the global patient coverage)* to describe a situation (a patient case) to ask for additional description of the situation to suggest a solution

---

[4] NVivo (2002). QSR's software. http://www.qsrinternational.com, July © 2002 QSR International

In the socio-relational mode of regulation, "to join" refers to the interactions which lead to re-defining the objectives of the network, or creating a collective identity within the RPM. "To describe an experience" corresponds to a professional helping others by explaining a way of handling a problem. In the epistemic mode of regulation, "to define good health care and ethical practices" means attempting to define new practices making for better healthcare. In the instrumental mode of regulation, "to describe a situation" corresponds to professionals explaining patients' cases to give an overall picture of the problem. "To ask for additional description of the situation" always occurs after a "to describe a situation" interaction and helps professionals who do not know the patient to understand the case. "To suggest a solution", which is also an interaction which occurs after "to describe the situation", generates the giving of advice. In the politico-organizational mode of regulation, "to define good organizational practices" means defining the distribution and organization of work. To illustrate these categories, we quote the following three corpus extracts.

Table 3. Corpus extracts and their qualitative definitions.

Corpus extracts	Qualitative definition
He's an 80-years-old patient, who suffers from Alzheimer's disease. He's diabetic and suffers from hypertension.	**To describe a situation**
Why did he arrive here?	**To ask for additional description of the situation**
It's a familial reconciliation. He has his children here.	**To describe a situation**
Advising him to go to Arcades for example? Could we make him do any activities?	**To suggest a solution**
In a few words, take time to do tests and we'll not need the network…	**To join**
So the network has to be here. It's going to say « let's do this or that, we have to hurry up, etc… »	**To join**

3.2. Initial results

Thirteen meetings have been retranscribed so far, forming a written corpus. Table 4 gives a break-down of this corpus. It indicates the number of speech turns/written characters devoted by each professional to each activity. Table 5 gives the distribution of these transactions according to the modes of regulation.

Table 4. Number of speech turns / Number of characters according to the activity and the profession

Profession Activity	Regular doctor	Neuro-logist	Psycho-logist	Speech therapist	Geria-trician	Social worker	IS or management consul-tant	total
to define good organizational practices	41 / 2176	80 / 5567	63 / 5525	13 / 1115	5 / 286	0	184 / 24798	386 / 39467
to join	54 / 10320	40 / 8849	15 / 2472	1 / 22	4 / 742	11 / 1938	45 / 8156	170 / 32499
to describe the situation	84 / 16200	81 / 12998	49 / 8234	91 / 15429	0	0	0	305 / 52861
to ask for a complement of description of the situation	5 / 224	61 / 2702	14 / 603	7 / 239	0	0	7 / 304	94 / 4072
to suggest a solution	4 / 595	25 / 3718	14 / 1893	6 / 542	0	0	6 / 875	55 / 7623
to define good health care and ethical practices	29 / 3696	48 / 9981	33 / 6696	42 / 4963	3 / 505	0	17 / 2893	172 / 28734
to describe an experience	15 / 6083	14 / 7289	7 / 284	8 / 1534	0	0	1 / 69	45 / 15259
Total	232 / 39294	349 / 51104	195 / 25707	168 / 23844	12 / 1533	11 / 1938	260 / 37095	1227/ 180515

Table 5. Number of speech turns / Number of characters according to the modes of regulation (SEPI matrix)

Degree of reflexiveness Focus	Introspection	Extrospection
Self	Socio-relational mode of regulation 215 / 47758 (18% / 26%)	Politico-organizational mode of regulation 386 / 39467 (31% / 22%)
Work	Epistemic mode of regulation 172 / 28734 (14% / 16%)	Instrumental mode of regulation 454 / 64556 (37% / 36%)

Based on this analysis, it can be concluded that:

- 37 % of the speech turns were in the instrumental mode of regulation, that is to say, they were devoted to working out patients' global coverage. They amounted to 36 % of the whole corpus,
- 31 % of the speech turns corresponded to defining organizational practices, They amounted to 22 % of the corpus,
- 18 % of the speech turns or 26 % of the corpus corresponded to the socio-relational mode of regulation,
- 14 % of the observed speech turns, amounting to 16 % of the corpus, corresponded to the epistemic mode of regulation.

These results support the idea that even conversations which are not directly related to problem-solving play a relevant role in the life of the RPM; they should therefore not be neglected and must, on the contrary, be taken into account in designing a tool favoring cooperation within the network.

For instance, in the case of pool work, professionals have to follow up patients in the course of their everyday practice. They also have to decide together whether it is necessary to change the treatment and whether the patient needs psycho-social advice. This type of activity cannot be reduced to a formula, since each case is unique. Professionals therefore have to define new cooperative practices. During a staff meeting, a psychologist speaks about this problem in these terms: "at a more general level, I would like to speak about this… Well, about the treatment given by the neuropsychologist or speech therapist (those belonging to the pool)… What are we going to do?" Not only conversations, but also transactions are creative, since they have effects on the actors and on the situation, which are both changed as a result. We intend to support these same processes by providing a new medium other than the telephone and email. Supporting these activities by providing a computer tool seems absolutely necessary to enable health professionals, who are often remotely located and not always available, to follow up their patients in an asynchronous way. Besides, it would certainly be interesting to be able to trace previous exchanges in order to make full use of the information available and to be able to assess the efficiency of the work carried out by the network.

Furthermore, interactions between RPM members depend on various activities being organized and carried out. We therefore propose to develop a flexible Information System for the RPM, enabling its members to interact according to the four SEPI modes of regulation, and to shift from one mode to another. In table 6, we suggest some features characteristic of each of the four modes. For instance, global patient coverage requires collective decision-making and the pooling of patient data. Training requires learning activities to be organized, and defining good practices can require the cooperation of editorial staff and document sharing activities. Dialogue functions as well as document sharing and coordination functions both seem to be necessary for the network to function efficiently. The re-defining of the network identity, which was a recurrent theme in discussions between professionals, could be supported by tools facilitating dialogue. However, dialogue may not suffice to deal with the identity issue. This is a broader issue, in our opinion; it has been dealt with by Wenger [9], who introduced the idea of "communal identity" or "belonging and relationship" which make the stable functioning of networks possible. This point has also been discussed in the field of healthcare [10].

Table 6. Information management features related to the SEPI matrix

Reflexiveness degree Focus	Introspection	Extrospection
Self	**Socio-relational mode of regulation** Communication features	**Politico-organizational mode of regulation** Coordination features
Work	**Epistemic mode of regulation** Collaborative documents drafting Sharing of documents	**Instrumental mode of regulation** Patient data sharing Collective decision-making Learning

We now intend to collect all these features together to create a coherent set. However, it is important to keep in mind healthcare professionals' current attitudes, and to wonder whether they are willing to change their working habits. Would they be satisfied with completely computer-mediated relationships when they have chosen professions dealing with human beings? Some of them may be open-minded to technological change and be willing to adapt their practices to more efficient tools, but the risk has to be faced that others may feel less like becoming involved in these systems and even completely refusing to have anything to do with them. We must therefore find a balance, when it comes to introducing technologies which are essential to networking. Innovations such as the shared medical file or the workflow and the shared diary might be more acceptable, since they would obviously save a considerable amount of time without fundamentally changing professional practices, which already include filling in individual patient files. The issue of mediating meetings is still an open question: mediating them technologically would allow a larger number of professionals to participate, but this would mean making radically changing current practices. The question therefore arises as to how to support key meetings without risking a loss of motivation on the part of the professionals involved.

In this study, the specificity of the collective on which we focused led us to use the SEPI matrix originating from the Theory of Symbolic Communicational Transactions. It is now proposed to see how our research links up with other developments in the field of computer-supported medical activities.

4. Related work

Several analyses of activities in a healthcare network setting have been published, which help to understand occupational situations involving professionals with various competences. For instance, Bossen [11] has developed an analytical framework based on seven parameters forming a "common information space". Wolf et al [12] have defined a procedure which consists in answering eight questions, to guide the analysis and to show up possible interactions with other tasks. Four other questions can be used in which individual work is viewed as being integrated into a collective process. However, these analytical frameworks focus on existing situations. In the case of the RPM network, these cooperative situations do not exist for the moment, because the network is in the preliminary phase, where the rules are still being defined by its members.

Concerning the involvement of the final users, we agree with Ruppel et al [13], who suggest that strong involving the end users makes for a better-quality final application, and better acceptance, particularly in the case of collaborative systems. In fact, the RPM members already participate actively in the definition of their Information System by explaining their needs and expectations. Our own contribution is restricted to giving advice and technical support. The RPM members will have to manage on their own the implementation of the system in collaboration with the firm developing the software program.

Another key point about cooperation and coordination between distributed professionals is knowledge sharing. Kindberg et al [14] suggest distinguishing between several types of knowledge: data, domain (specific vocabulary and particular competence), other people (their knowledge, their competences, their needs). The professionals in the RPM network want to share the data they have on their patients, and to exchange specialized knowledge, mainly by referring to specialists to improve their practice. They try to continue learning from others by inquiring about their profession and their tasks. They therefore know what to expect of their colleagues and who possesses the information they need to be able to deal with their patients. Kindberg et al [14] have also insisted on the value of knowledge, which can vary depending on the moment, or the professional involved. The effort required obtaining or transfering knowledge can be measured, and decisions can be made accordingly.

As far as the technologies used by health professionals are concerned, we have observed that many of them, whether they are private or hospital practitioners, use electronic files individually to record information about their patients. For the moment, apart from some hospitals where research activities are conducted, most of the files which are used collectively are paper based. This was pointed out in a paper [15] where the authors explain that hospital professionals use many collective paper documents. In order to improve this practice, these authors suggested introducing a documentary approach, and were particularly interested in developing means of annotating the electronic patient files. Several tools have been developed with a view to meeting the need for professionals to work on cooperative lines on each patient's case. Kindberg et al [14] have suggested implementing a "timeline view" giving good visibility as to who does what, and when. We intend to integrate this feature into the future RPM system. Bardram [1] proposed a tool called the "patient scheduler", consisting of four modules, each associated with one kind of cooperative activity: (1) an organizational module, (2) a module handling communications, (3) a module handling planning and scheduling, and (4) a sharing module. Calde et al [16] suggested producing a tool centered on roles, where each role corresponds to a personalized module based on a filter on the patient's data. This seems to be an interesting approach; we have already analyzed the various profiles occurring in the network, and we could possibly design interfaces dedicated to each profile.

Finally, the issue of supporting interactions has been discussed by Hardstone et al [10]. These authors mention that numerous informal discussions take place between health professionals and that they constitute necessary steps towards caring for patients and organizing the caring process. This was also found to be the case in the RPM, where a quarter of all the conversations recorded subscribed to the socio-relational mode of regulation.

5. Conclusion

We observed the RPM during a period of one year and analyzed its activities, using the Theory of Symbolic Communicational Transactions. This method was used to classify the transactions occurring in this healthcare network on the basis of four modes of regulation: the socio-relational, epistemic, politico-organizational and instrumental modes. We observed that a quarter of all the face-to-face exchanges occurring during RPM meetings belonged to the socio-relational mode. Their content did not relate directly to healthcare or organizational tasks, but these exchanges seem to be essential because they create a common sense of identity between all the members having different professions, and enable them to get to know each other better. We therefore feel it is necessary to support these transactions in order to promote cooperation and integrated care in the everyday activities of the network. Another point worth noting was the fact that switches between modes of regulation occur commonly at meetings.

We can then conclude that an Information System for this healthcare network must also make provision for conversations, and that it must be sufficiently flexible to allow professionals to re-configure their interface, depending on the modes of regulation and the switches occurring between them.

We are also involved in another network, Addica, which is in a much more advanced stage because it exists officially since the year 2001. Addica deals with addictive practices (drug, alcohol and food abuse). Based on these parallel analyses on two networks, which differ in their age, their size, and the field of interest, it will be possible to check whether the findings made in our analysis of the RPM network are applicable to another network. We could then define generic principles for designing flexible Information Systems to support these particular communities, namely healthcare networks.

References

[1]   Bardram, J. E. (1998). Collaboration, Coordination, and Computer Support, An Activity Theoretical Approach to the Design of Computer Supported Cooperative Work. *PhD thesis*, University of Aarhus, Denmark, May, 264 p.

[2]   Kuutti, K. (1995). Activity Theory as a potential framework for human-computer interaction research. Published in Nardi (ed.): *Context and Consciousness: Activity Theory and Human Computer Interaction, Cambridge: MIT Press, pp 17-44.*

[3]   Engeström, Y. (1999). Expansive Visibilization of Work: An Activity-Theoretical Perspective. *Computer Supported Cooperative Work Journal*, February, Volume 8, Issue 1-2, p. 63-93. Kluwer Academic Publishers, Norwell, MA, USA.

[4]   Zacklad, M. (2005-a). Transactions communicationnelles et actes de langage dans l'économie de services. In: M. Chabrol, C., Olry-Louis, I. & Najab, F. (Eds.) *Interactions communicatives et psychologies.* Paris: Presses de la Sorbonne Nouvelle.

[5]   Zacklad, M. (2003). Communities of Action: a Cognitive and Social Approach to the Design of CSCW Systems. In : Schmidt, K., Pendergast, M., Tremaine, M., Simone, C. *Proceedings of the 2003 international ACM SIGGROUP conference on Supporting group work, GROUP'03,* 2003, Sanibel Island, Florida, USA. New York: ACM Press, 2003, p.190-197.

[6]   Zacklad, M. (2005-b). Transactions communicationnelles symboliques et communauté d'action : réflexions préliminaires. In: Lorino, P., Teulier, R. *Entre la connaissance et l'organisation, l'activité collective*, Maspéro, Paris, 2005.

[7]   Dewey, J., Bentley, A. F. (1949). *Knowing and the known.* Boston: Beacon.

[8]   Hughes, J. A., O'Brien, J., Rodden, T. et al (1997). Designing with ethnography: a presentation framework for design. In: Coles, S. *Proceedings of the conference on Designing interactive systems: processes, practices, methods, and techniques*, 1997, Amsterdam, The Netherlands. New York: ACM Press, 1997, p.147-158.

[9]   Wenger, E. (2001). *Supporting communities of practice: a survey of community-oriented technologies.* [On-line]. Report to the Council of CIOs of the US Federal Government. Self-published at www.ewenger.com/tech.

[10] Hardstone, G., Hartswood, M, Procter, R. et al (2004). Supporting informality: team working and integrated care records. In: Herbsleb, J., Olson, G. *Proceedings of the 2004 ACM conference on Computer supported cooperative work,* 2004, Chicago, Illinois, USA. New York: ACM Press, 2004, p. 142-151.

[11] Bossen, C. (2002). The Parameters of Common Information Spaces: the Heterogeneity of Cooperative Work at a Hospital Ward. In: Churchill, E. F., McCarthy, J., Neuwirth, C., Rodden, T. *Proceedings of the 2002 ACM conference on Computer supported cooperative work*, CSCW'02, November 16-20, New Orleans, Louisiana, USA. New York: ACM Press, 2002, p.176-185.

[12] Wolf, C. G., Karat, J. (1997). Capturing What is Needed in Multi-User System Design: Observations from the Design of Three Healthcare Systems. In: Coles, S. *Proceedings of the conference on Designing interactive systems: processes, practices, methods, and techniques, DIS'97,* 1997, Amsterdam, The Netherlands. New York: ACM Press, 1997, p.405-415.

[13] Ruppel, C., Konecny, J. (2000). The role of IS Personnel in Web-based Systems Development: The Case of a Health Care Organization. In: Prasad, J., Nance, W. *Proceedings of the 2000 ACM SIGCPR conference on Computer personnel research*, 2000, Chicago, Illinois, USA. New York: ACM Press, 2000, p.130-135.

[14] Kindberg, T., Bryan-Kinns, N., Makwana, R. (1999). Supporting the shared care of diabetic patients. In: Hayne, S. C. *Proceedings of the international ACM SIGGROUP conference on Supporting group work*, 1999, Phoenix, Arizona, USA. New York: ACM Press, 1999, p. 91-100.

[15] Bringay, S., Barry, C. and Charlet, J. (2004). Annotations: a new type of document in the Electronic Health Record [On-line]. In: Proceedings of The Document Academy, DOCAM'04, 2004, San Francisco, USA. http://thedocumentacademy.hum.uit.no/events/docam/04/program.html

[16] Calde, S., Goodwin, K., Reimann, R. (2002). SHS Orcas: The first integrated information system for long-term healthcare facility management. In: Dykstra-Erickson, E. *Proceedings of Conference on Human Factors in Computing Systems*, Minneapolis, Minnesota, USA. New York: ACM Press, 2002, p.2-16.

Cooperative Systems Design
P. Hassanaly et al. (Eds.)
IOS Press, 2006

On a Mission without a Home Base: Conceptualizing Nomadicity in Student Group Work

Cristian BOGDAN, Chiara ROSSITTO, Maria NORMARK, Pedro JORGE (Adler)
and Kerstin SEVERINSON EKLUNDH
*IPLab, HCI Group, School of Computer Science and Communication, Royal Institute
of Technology (KTH), Stockholm, Sweden*
{cristi,chiara-1,adler,kse}@nada.kth.se
maria.normark@sh.se

Abstract. We are observing that the current body of CSCW research is focusing
either on stable workplaces with a single cooperative unit or on mobile work, with
highly mobile professionals. We are attempting to fill the gap between workplace
and mobile with a field study of student work, which we regard as exhibiting a
high degree of nomadicity. After comparing student work with centres of
coordination and mobility work, we unpack the notion of nomadicity as a work
condition, constituted by a complex of discontinuities, leading to work partitioning
and re-assembly. We draw design and methodological implications.

Keywords: mobility, nomadicity, discontinuity, partitioning, re-assembly

Introduction

Conceptualization of work in the field of Computer Supported Cooperative Work
(CSCW) has seen many transformations with regard to the workplace, working time
and the nature of work. Whereas workplaces have been a constant concern, and places
like centres of coordination [1] and small offices [2] have been typical sites for CSCW
researchers to study and design for, an increasing interest in communities (e.g. [3]) and
mobility (e.g. [4]) can be regarded as a shift of focus towards settings that do not
assume stable working hours or working places.

Expanding the notions of workplace and working hours is partially determined by
the latest changes in the technologies available to users. Phone facilities and Internet
connections, available on the move, together with high capacity Internet connections at
home enable work outside traditional workplaces and work hours, thus separating it
from the rest of the cooperative ensemble. Traditionally, both conceptualizations of
cooperative work and the cooperative systems designed tended to assume a single
'cooperative unit': a group, a generic activity and the supporting technologies.
Nevertheless, it is well-understood that work involves partitioning and re-assembly of
subgroups, subtasks, and use of the technology at hand. As mobile and portable
technology is increasingly available, more tools are likely to be at hand at all times. As
a consequence, travelling time, previously considered off-work, acquires new
meanings: phone calls can be made, documents can be modified or shared, and

interactions can take place [4]. As broadband technologies become more pervasive, work gets a more prominent role in the home and the place for work is not necessarily the only workplace [5]. We are thus moving away from a single cooperative unit, and work is composed of various configurations of subgroup and individual work, carried out in various subspaces of the workplace, both at home and in other places.

Work has surely been characterized as such even before any digital support was available. However, with the advent of mobile and broadband technology, group work partitioning and its corresponding re-assembly can now be *enabled* by modern technology. We are approaching a stage where almost any task or group decomposition can be bridged by the availability of pervasive technology, as different digital artefacts are accessible at every stage of a group activity. *What does that imply for CSCW design?* To answer this question we need a re-conceptualization of work which encompasses the different levels at which work partitioning takes place. In this regard CSCW research tends to look at two extremes: a group at the traditional worksite at one end [6], and mobile workers at the other end [7]. Indeed, little research is being done in the middle of this spectrum, on people who have traditional workplaces, but also work on the move, or at home; or on groups that morph in and out of various subgroups because of different tasks.

In this paper, we attempt to address this focus gap between workplace and mobility. We have chosen student group work as a perspicuous instance of partitioned cooperative work. Although student groups working on university projects generally lack a fixed workplace within the university boundaries, their intense combination of home and university work, along with their openness to using modern technologies, made them a suitable setting to study such partitioned work features and their methodological and technology design implications.

An increasing body of work related to more design oriented research areas, such as Mobile Networks and Applications [8] or Ubiquitous Computing[9], seems to address similar concerns under the name of "nomadicity" [10]. While the term is not well defined, nomadicity seems to imply users moving in and out of network connection hotspots, of various speeds and natures. Moving between connectivity of various speeds is precisely what happens when a user is in transit from work to home, from a location to another one, or when moving from a group meeting to an individual workplace, hence the similarity with the above issues of work discontinuity. However in such studies, the understanding of people's activities and the related needs seem to be intuitively derived, from researchers' personal experience.

With this paper, we try to inform this type of work and, on the way, adopt and adapt the notion of nomadicity to work carried out: (i) in different places and on the move; (ii) individually, with the whole group or just a part of it; (iii) by using different types of tools, from pen and paper to smart-phones, laptops tablet and stationary PCs. In order to express and combine different types of variability, such as work variability, place variability, work duration variability and group attendance variability; we will attempt to inform a definition of nomadicity as a work condition, by looking at the different facets of work and the tools supporting it. We believe that it is necessary to understand such a work condition to be able to properly design nomadicity-aware technologies.

In the remainder of this paper, we review related work, and then we present our method and a case study. We then compare our results with previous work in workplaces and mobile settings. We end with a discussion, including implications for design and methodology and draw conclusions.

1. Related Work

1.1. Nomadicity in technology design

In most technology design work that we reviewed it is assumed that there is a need to support nomadic work. Nevertheless, very little is said about the type of work, while the underlining notion of nomadicity seems to be based on intuition and personal experience. We can mention, as an example, the *Nomadic Radio* [11], a wearable platform for managing voice, text-based messages, personal calendars and events. This application is built on the main idea of engaging users in audio-based interactions, so that managing communication can take place synchronously with other tasks. Despite its technical richness, very little is said about the context and the type of mobile work the radio has been designed for.

An active proponent of "nomadicity", Kleinrock [12], mentions independence of location, motion and of platform as the main requirements when designing for nomadic technologies, his main concern being the possibility to connect, anytime anywhere, to a network.

As nomads, we own computers and communication devices that we carry about with us in our travels. Moreover, even without carrying portable computers or communications, there are many of us who travel to numerous locations in our business and personal lives, and who require access to computers and communication when we arrive at a destination. Indeed, a move from my desk to a conference table constitutes a fundamentally nomadic move, since the computing platforms and communication capability may be considerably different [at the two ends].

Furthermore, by examining the wide range of new portable devices (laptops, notebooks, personal digital assistants, wrist watch computers, mobile phones etc.), Kleinrock envisions the opportunities, offered by these technologies, to work on the move. Indeed nomadic computing is a question of access anytime, anywhere.

The combination of portable computing with portable communication is changing the way we think about information processing [reference to [13]]. We now recognize that access to computing and communications is necessary not only from one's ``home base'', but also while one is in transit and/or when one reaches one's destination. Indeed, anytime, anywhere access.

Drawing on these assumptions, Kleinrock describes the technological challenges to design and develop nomadic-aware applications: they must work whether a connection is available or not, adjust to what connection is available and in a transparent manner for users. This perspective is also shared by other researchers [14] who, stressing the opportunities enabled by technology, identify connectivity, both to networks and desktop applications, as the main requirements for nomadic technology. Based on Kleinrock's idea of nomadic work, such efforts focus on how technology can be adapted to different environments by, for example, connecting to local instead of global networking services [15]; they discuss different modes of connectivity (connected, disconnected and ad-hoc) [16] and how to technically adapt to them, without an active human intervention (e.g. [15]). In these, more technical research communities (e.g., IEEE, ACM SIGSOFT, ACM SIGCOMM), the expression "nomadic computing" is often used interchangeably with "mobile computing", while the terms nomadicity and mobility are often used as synonyms.

1.2. Mobility in CSCW

Despite the richness and the diversity of different types of mobile work, most of the research efforts in HCI/CSCW have been technology centred, focusing on investigating the opportunities offered by technology to working on the move. The concept of mobility involves the way people interact with each other, and affects the kind of interactions they perform. In this sense, Kakihara and Sørensen [17] state that interactions between people are becoming *mobilized*. This shift of focus expands the concept of mobility by including three main aspects of people's interactions: spatial, contextual and temporal mobility. Spatial mobility refers to the movement of people, together with objects and symbols (information in different forms) they use. Temporal mobility refers to the fact that the usage of various asynchronous communication tools, allows for multi-tasking and the opportunity to explain a set of interactions without framing them in a linear and sequential temporality. Finally, contextual mobility refers to the situated nature of human activities, and to the way different contexts affect the interactions people are engaged in.

Both theoretical and empirical efforts (e.g. [4], [18], [19] and [20]); are being made in order to understand mobile workers, the type of work they carry and what technology would better support it. Luff and Heath [21], for example, based on observation of mobile work in three different settings, raise the issue that requirements for mobile technology should go beyond the too generic principle of availability. In their analysis, they discuss how the replacement of an old paper allocation sheet (used to record the time spent by each worker on a given task), with an electronic notebook, actually hindered some important collaborative aspects of the work carried out in a building site. Whereas the paper sheet was filled out *in situ*, the new electronic tool ended up being used off site, as a stationary machine. The new technology did transform the way people used to work by, among other things, hindering on-site meetings between the foreman and the workers, useful opportunities to discuss work related problems. Criticism has also been raised [4] towards the ideal of "access, anytime, anywhere". In fact, different tasks might require different types of access to information; they might not be performed at just any time (it could be inappropriate to call someone on the mobile phone out of working hours) and not all the places are functionally equivalent (because of social norms, it could be inappropriate to talk on the phone in some places). These terms being too general, the design for mobile work should be supported by empirical studies aiming at understanding the nature of mobile work and the challenges imposed by different environments in terms of resources and constraints on communication and collaboration [20]; by an understanding of how mobile workers associate activities to different places and how they transform a given location into their own workplace [19].

Mobility is therefore not a matter of people travelling around, independently from physical and spatial constraints. It is rather a dimension of work bound to different places and whose understanding is also related to the way work practices change places [22] and the way places change work [4]. Brown and O'Hara [22], give an example of how *hotdeskers*, office workers who do not have a fixed desk location, configured place on a day-by-day basis. Every morning a hotdesker has to book a desk to work at. This selection is usually done so that it will be possible to sit close to colleagues working in the same team. The location of the desk chosen takes into account the social organization of the workplace. Furthermore, Brown and O'Hara show examples of how non-traditional workplaces, such as cafés, bars and restaurants are transformed into working environments by mobile workers, as it is feasible to meet colleagues or carry out individual work in such places; and how access to resources, both in paper and digital format, is well planned in advance and connections to the office are still maintained by the use of e-mail or mobile telephones.

As it emerges from these two last paragraphs, the terms nomadic and mobile are related and often used as synonyms. But is there a substantial difference between being mobile and being nomadic? As it has been suggested [23], the term mobile emphasises individual work as opposite to stationary; the term nomadic refers to work as a collaborative ensemble, and it includes transitions between work situations and technology use. We will delve more into this difference in this paper.

2. Field Study: The UCPD Setting

Our field study focuses on technological support for learning and collaboration in student groups. The UCPD project course that we followed during two intensive months is open to several universities and one goal of the course is to make students work together over program and/or university boundaries. That means that engineering students as well as psychology and art students are welcome in the course and are expected to collaborate in project work. This course was well suited for our interest in project work of "nomadic" character, i.e. without established workplace and scheduled workdays. The topic of the UCPD course was User-Centred Program Development. The aim of the course was to design a new tool in a given context. In order to report on the project work, the students were required to produce a mock-up, a report, a web page, a six minutes video and an oral presentation. Each group comprised about eight students. Many of the groups set up sharing spaces in Yahoo!® Groups or handcrafted equivalents on the Web.

2.1. Methodological Approach

To follow the nomadic character of student project work presents a challenge to the researcher. It is certainly a difficult task to keep track of what happens in whole group meetings, of work in smaller groups and of the individual work as well. In the UCPD study, our aim was to understand how the students coped with their situation and to explore the activities that took place in relation to coordination and technology use. We were inspired by the ethnographic approach [24], a method that is suitable to study how members of a setting make sense of their everyday activities, and which is often employed in CSCW to characterize work and work conditions, such as the ones we are interested in. The main technique we used was the observation of activities, which we complemented with other qualitative data collection techniques such as interviews and gathering work artifacts, such as different versions of the group deliverables. We have got extensive data, from about 30 observations and 10 interviews, and we also have some of the group's email conversations. Four of the authors followed one group each, and participated in as many of their meetings as possible. The fact that we could not participate in all meetings is, we later realized, a feature of the very kind of work conditions we were seeking to understand.

3. Analyzing Nomadic Characteristics based on the UCPD Setting

We will comment on our field data by means of two comparisons. On the one hand, we will illustrate how our UCPD setting is different from a single cooperative unit in a traditional workplace, such as the classical 'centre of coordination' [25]. The UCPD study is contrasted with data collected in earlier studies in air traffic control and emergency dispatch (see e.g. [26]). On the other hand, we will show the differences we have observed between our setting (for a wider review of our data see [27]) and what is commonly understood in CSCW as mobile work. In Figure 1 we therefore list a set of work characteristics that enable us to compare student group work with centres of coordination and professional mobile work, respectively.

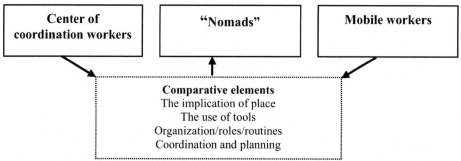

Figure 1: Contrasting and comparing nomadic work with other kinds of work familiar to the CSCW area.

The student work setting is different from what we usually see in CSCW research. Usually, important issues like professional skills and routines, experience, organization and work practice, to a large extent structure the way an activity is performed. There is also usually continuity in the work, tasks are reoccurring during the time of the study or at least people have stories to tell about other similar experiences and unexpected occurrences [28]. In most traditional work settings there are activities that can be considered as ordinary. Ethnographers often try to understand normal practices and, the related, out of the ordinary occurrences. In this study we have a more complicated setting. There is one part of the students' activities that can be considered as ordinary: the school practices: going to class, writing reports, etc. But what we are mostly interested in are the activities surrounding the project, given that our informants are non-professional. As such, they do not rely on established project practices, organizational routines, articulation work [29].

We noticed that one of the main characteristics of their work is the lack of a stable and exclusive location where students, from the same group, can be met and work can be done jointly. How do they cope with this? How does it influence their ability to work? In which way do they differ from centres of coordination and from other mobile workers? In the following sections, we point out some of the main differences.

3.1. Comparison between Centres of Coordination and Student Group Work

Much about work, collaboration and technology in the field of CSCW has been learned through studies of control rooms and similar centres of activities [1], [6], [25], [30],

[31]. Such settings will be important for us in making a contrast with the less 'stable' settings discussed in this paper. Control rooms are sometimes called centres of coordination. Suchman [25] writes:

"Centres of coordination are characterizable in terms of participants' ongoing orientation to problems of space and time, involving the deployment of people and equipment across distances, according to a canonical timetable or the emergent requirements of rapid response to a time-critical situation." (p. 42)

Our experiences in these contexts mainly refer to two types of settings; air traffic control (e.g.[32]) and emergency dispatch (e.g. [33]).

The implication of place: In centres of coordination, place is usually designed ad hoc for a given activity. In most of the cases, it is a control room with numerous supporting tools. The organization of the physical space is essential for the performance of tasks. In the case of the student group work, no physical space was assigned to their nomadic collaboration and work could take place virtually anywhere and at anytime. The meeting places, such as group rooms, cafeterias, museums, varied with the task but were seldom adjusted to the one at hand. As these places were often patronized by other students, and people as well, there were no facilities to keep working material and tools.

The use of tools: In environments such as control rooms, tools are numerous and specially made for the tasks. They are usually also adjusted by the users to fit the professionals' needs better. They are provided by the organization and available all the time. For the students, tools were gathered in an ad hoc fashion; the closest computer room happened to be a Mac room - then let's use Macs! Private tools (such as mobile phones) and public tools (such as the university computers) were intertwined and not necessarily compatible. The students we observed did not rely on a common availability of technology and tools (such as common operating systems, communications programs, digital cameras, mobile phone functions, etc.). The tools available were not enough to support adequately the many needs of their work:

But then... those crucial decisions, they weren't really in all those emails and notes. If one were to follow every decision one should have been there live so to speak...

Organization, roles and routines: In centres of coordination, the work is strictly organized by rules and regulations and, in many cases, supervised with scrutiny. The work is often managed by teams, or by shifts of people. The essence of the work in centres of coordination is routines. In order to be able to trust and predict other's parts of the work process, routines are heavily relied on. For the UCPD students, work was organized as well, however the lack of formally assigned roles made it difficult to know what to do and when. The variability of place, duration and attendance, hindered the emergence of routines. Only a few could be expected, but they were mainly related to general expectances on people, such as that they were expected to read email and be reachable through telephone. This is for example, one of the students' descriptions of how work was carried out within the group:

We stopped planning and started to do something. In the beginning we tried to keep everyone in the loop but then I think it was individuals in the project that started to do things so that things actually got done.

Coordination and planning: Coordination in centres of coordination is routinized, organized and, to a large extent, predictable and often synchronous. The lack of routines in a student project enhanced the need for coordination. Not only must work be planned, organized and performed, it must also be coordinated for those who are not present. For our students, coordination was of two different kinds: general updates (asynchronous through email and Yahoo Groups), and reciprocal advising (synchronous through mobile phones or chat, MSN/ICQ). However, because of the lack of time, at the end of the project, most of the other group members' work was accepted, almost without checking it out. This is how another student describes the practice of exchanging comments on the report:

> *We sent out stuff all the time so that everyone could comment. However I don't think that many people were so interested in what the rest did. I read through the report and commented. But it's like…if you don't have this in the project plan, like this day everyone should read through the report and comment…well then there are few who do it…*

At most centres of coordination there are time-critical and/or safety-critical tasks. This means that while working, people need to be 100% committed to the tasks at hand. The place and setting makes it very clear when on duty and when not on duty. In contrast, students had other tasks to take care of simultaneously during the project span. That is why their attention, to a varying extent, zoomed in and out of the project. The lack of formal organization made it easier to ignore responsibilities, but it also suggested (see 3.1.2) constant availability.

3.2. Comparison of Mobile Workers and Student Group Work

Despite the theoretical and empirical attempts to provide a comprehensive understanding of mobile work, the cultural, social and task characteristics, typical of different settings, call for a specific analytical attention. In a study of seventeen mobile workers, for example, Perry et al. [4] point out that, despite some similarities, the very nature of the work the participants engaged in was heterogeneous. Mobility included, in fact, cases of working at multiple, but stationary locations; cases of travelling to other locations and working in hotel rooms; moving around in the same environment, and so forth. In all the cases, workers used travelling time to accomplish work or keep contacts with the office; phone calls were made to people back in the office, asking them to read aloud pieces of information, send a fax to a client, etc.. E-mails and mobile phones where used in order to keep track on what was going on in the workplace.

The implication of place: As mentioned, the very meaning of the concept of mobility can vary, depending on different work settings. Workers can thus be mobile in different ways: they can move around in the same site; travel within the same city; travel from a city to another, etc. The UCPD students used to move around within the relatively small city area (university campus, downtown, museum, etc.); moving from home to the university, to a cafeteria, or to a project field site, constituted a short term travelling. That has implications for the work done while on the move. Long distance travelling makes it possible, for professional mobile workers, to work on the move and accomplish different types of task, such as connecting to and coordinating with the office [22], prepare presentations, read the latest report. Travelling by bus, underground or commute trains is, on the other hand, usually quick and short. Only small tasks can be accomplished, often depending on the availability of seats. Among our students, we have not observed many cases of work being done while on the move, which cannot therefore be considered as a part of the work itself. However, in some cases, an informal discussion on the underground train was a good opportunity to discuss and comment on the results of the previous meeting.

On the contrary, a more anchored meeting place was selected for two reasons: it provided a space to work and an opportunity to coordinate with other members of the group. The library cafeteria was also a nice place in which to hang out and wait for others to come. Despite the possibility to choose among several locations, finding and agreeing on a place to meet was a main concern for the UCPD students. Furthermore, places such as meeting rooms, classrooms, and cafeterias were also used by other student groups. That made it impossible to store prototypes, paper copies, or any other kind of working material, in a common working place. This is actually a feature that the UCPD students share with the *hotdeskers* [22] who were discouraged from keeping paper copies or other artefacts in their offices.

Under other circumstances, when the use of computers was required, the students found their way towards a solution. In this case, for example, two students were supposed to work together, but only one of them had his own laptop.

I sat at the computer [in the library cafeteria where internet connection is available] and Ann sat at the lab and we talked via MSN. Then I moved to the lab when there was a computer available.

Moreover encounters in corridors or other places, like the canteen or a computer lab, were opportunities to meet up with group members and discuss project details, or decide about issues. As noticed in other contexts, short encounters [34] and local mobility [21], [35] play an important role in coordinating work.

The use of tools: Differently from some professional mobile workers, who often use expensive technology provided by their companies (e.g. WAP, Bluetooth, 3G, GPRS), students use what is available personally to them or at school in order to manage their group work. E-mails and mailing lists were extensively used to arrange meetings, to share working files with all the group members, and to keep the others updated on what had been done most recently. For example, in one case e-mail was used to plan and to write the project report. The two co-writers being in different locations, e-mail was used to send versions of the documents, exchange comments, to agree on writing strategies and to coordinate with each other. However the mere use of e-mail for such a complex task was quite problematic.

I wrote a skeleton, with headlines only, just to get an idea of what to write. I sent it to Katy and asked if it was ok, but she didn't reply...I don't know why [...] I thought I started writing [...] and then I got an e-mail from her, and we're working on the same part.

Another example is the use of generic groupware like Yahoo!® Groups both for communicating between group members and to store working files. In other cases, a self-made website was used in the same way as the groupware, in order to exchange project information, such as meeting agenda and minutes, project documents, task descriptions, etc. Instant messengers, such as ICQ and MSN, were used when working online. Another tool used by the UCPD students was SubEthaEdit, a software for collaborative writing and programming which allows users to work synchronously on a file, from different locations.

Organization/roles/routines: Professional mobile workers share a social understanding of "work time" that would make a phone call about work related issues late at night inappropriate. The importance of these type of social conventions is one of the arguments [4] on which criticism to access anytime (anywhere) is based. On the contrary, in students' life the boundaries between working and non-working hours were blurry. It seemed to be proper to make a phone call after dinner to communicate a change in the ongoing work. Especially when the project deadline was approaching, students were likely to work at late hours and they were not bothered by receiving a project-related e-mail, or a SMS late at night.

Once one member sent an email at 1 AM and got 4 replies in a very short time.

It seemed natural to move, in the late evening, from a fast-food restaurant, where a decision about the prototype had been taken, to the closest home in order to start working on the prototype. Examples like these ones reveal the differences between professional and student working hours, less easily separated from private-life time.

It is very hard for everyone to meet at the same time; someone is always missing [...]. We met on Sunday and then I did the PowerPoint in the evening, based on the idea we had. Then on Monday evening we had a meeting when we revised the PowerPoint and then I did the new version.

Coordination and planning: Considering group work, for the UCPD students, the main reason to be mobile was to meet other group members, in order to plan and manage collaborative activities. Similarly to professional mobile workers [4], [21], [35], meeting face-to-face was, therefore, an important moment to get some work done and to decide, all together, upon the different tasks that needed to be done. For example, in one of the subgroups, a meeting was arranged in order to plan the final presentation of the project. The meeting, which took place at the university library, had two main goals. On the one hand participants were to jointly decide how the presentation should be and what it should contain. On the other hand, the meeting was an opportunity to meet a 'third party', the other subgroup, who handed over the video scenario to be included in the presentation.

Mobile workers, as observed in CSCW, engage in careful planning before the trip [4]. This planning has to do mostly with considering what to bring on business trips and timing of meetings. For UCPD students planning had a different main goal: the division of work. As the students were attending other courses, had different schedules and were not sure that they would meet each other, it was important to decide in advance who will be doing what. Although this type of planning played an important role, improvisation was a key feature as well. The case of moving from a fast-food restaurant to someone's house, to work on a deliverable, is an example of this. Spontaneous encounters (e.g. in corridors, during other course lectures) did happen and had a strong impact on the way work was carried out. During an interview, a student told us about a group member who, at the university, bumped into a subgroup meeting and decided to stop by, discuss and take decisions about the project work.

Being aware of the actual planning was not always easy due to the different schedules and availability of each member. For instance, a group member missed one of the group meetings and had no time to check her e-mail afterwards. As a result she did not know what happened in the meeting. In fact, she said:

I'm not sure of who is working on the report, Robert and maybe the other person is Elias, and I don't know if they have started already. I really do not know what other people are doing right now.

Having emphasized the main points of difference between student work as we observed it and mobile work, as it has been described in the literature review, we will now move to further analysis.

4. Discussion

Throughout our data commentary, we emphasized the 'intermediate' character of the student work: such work is different from both work in traditional offices and centres of coordination, and it is also different from what CSCW understands by mobile work.

On further analysis, it is interesting to note that "mobile work" as described in e.g. [4] and [22] exhibits many of the differences from "office work" that we show in our first comparison: lack of assigned physical space, opportunistic use of resources, lack of routines, etc. That is, from the perspective of the 'traditional' workplace, student work is not easy to delimit from mobile work. However, as we are showing in our second comparison, many differences exist between student work and mobile work.

Such differences help us establish our 'middle focus' for CSCW, i.e. a focus in between 'workplace' and 'mobility' which we are detailing under the adopted name 'nomadicity'. We will reconsider the concept of nomadicity and we will show how nomadicity, as we regard it, tends to be less pronounced in more 'traditional' CSCW workplaces such as centres of coordination, more pronounced in "middle settings" like student work settings, and differently pronounced in what is currently viewed as mobile work. In other words, by conceptualizing nomadicity, we are attempting to shed more light on the widely accepted statement that "there are many kinds of mobility" [5].

4.1. Nomadicity as a Group Work Condition

We regard nomadicity as a work condition: it can affect any work, be it in a traditional workplace or in a mobile situation. We are thus not looking into a specific type of work, such as focusing on "mobile work" would do. We are focusing on a condition which we believe is important to consider in CSCW research and design along with other specifics of the work in question. In what follows, we will unpack some of the characteristics of work affected by nomadicity. Later on, we will begin to consider specific ways in which nomadicity can be addressed in both research and design.

Throughout these considerations, it is important to re-iterate that we are referring to collaborative, not to individual work. We are thus interested in nomadicity as a group work condition which applies to the whole group and, consequently, to individual members as well.

4.1.1. Discontinuities in Work

We will begin to unpack nomadicity as a group work condition by considering the ubiquitous mobility in the physical space. From a nomadicity standpoint, we suggest to regard such movement as a *spatial discontinuity*. As a choice of term, discontinuity emphasizes the endpoints of the movement, as different from the whole movement. For example, in a travel with a vehicle, discontinuity denotes embarking and disembarking, more than the whole trip. This is important from a work standpoint, because work is affected more at those ends than it is affected during the trip itself. Indeed, the physical conditions of work will tend to stay the same during the trip. It is at the discontinuity points (embarking and disembarking) that work is affected, most probably by interruption, due to attending to the 'operations' needed to be made in the physical space. Students, for example, configure their work in terms of collaborative tasks, either in advance, before moving to the chosen location, or once they meet. Furthermore, another practice observed, among the UCPD students, was to gather up in public and in an easily reachable place, such as the library, cafeteria or the university hall, and to decide, either afterwards or while waiting for the others, on a group room or a classroom where to work.

As such, by discontinuity we denote a *significant change in the group work organization or conditions,* such for example the abrupt interruptions occurring, on a plane, during landing procedures. This is, for example, what happened to a group of students who had to interrupt their project planning, once the underground train arrived to the stop where they had to split up.

With regard to spatial discontinuity, it is important to note that work of different *duration* is appropriate to be held in different physical spaces. Corridors will typically imply short durations before a discontinuity is needed (either breaking e.g. an impromptu meeting, or moving it into a more appropriate space for a longer meeting), and so will airport boarding lounges. At the other end, we find meeting rooms that imply longer work duration, etc. Several places in the home will probably have a different meaning in regard to work duration before a discontinuity is needed. Such meanings will be known in common by the home dwellers.

Spatial discontinuities often bring *technology support discontinuities.* Simply put, by moving to another place, the static technology available may change. Under a circumstance, for example a student decided to move from the library cafeteria, where a member of the group was working with his laptop, to one of the computer labs. This implied the opportunity for her to use a computer, and the need to use instant messaging for communication issues related to the task at hand.

This also affects portable technology: after a spatial discontinuity it may become more appropriate or comfortable to use a certain mobile technology (paper included, see e.g. [21]). But spatial discontinuities and technology support discontinuities are not strictly interrelated. Consider the airplane trip example: technology support discontinuities in terms of being able to use e.g. laptops occur after the spatial one (at take-off) and before the spatial discontinuity (at landing) due to regulations related to radio interference. Further, discontinuity of network coverage (losing or gaining coverage or other significant variation of bandwidth), besides showing an example of no-relation with the spatial discontinuities (as different from the actual movement in space!) offers an example of *hazard discontinuity* i.e. a discontinuity that one cannot control and is not easy to anticipate, thus resulting in *unpredictability* and practices of back-up such as bringing on physical or digital document copies just in case they cannot be accessed online [5].

We can note at this point that people tend to consciously control various kinds of discontinuity in their relations to the other group members. Erickson [34] introduces the concept of "interaction trajectory" to denote movements in space and other forms of discontinuity (e.g. opening and closing communication channels) to move between individual and group work in telecommuting or in more co-located work. In an illustrative example, apparently random corridor strolls are actually scheduled to plan the possibility of meeting co-workers. A further form of planning discontinuity, spatially-induced technology support discontinuity in this case, is to deliberately move away from the place where e-mail can be checked. This is referred to as "availability modulation".

More such group-related, longer-term, consciously organized discontinuities can be suggested. Discontinuities in *group work attendance* by an individual member depending on other obligations have been illustrated by students "zooming in and out" of the group work, as a consequence of their participation in other courses, or being away for holidays or illness. *Discontinuities in group and structure* can be observed in groups re-organizing their sub-groups for various tasks. At a limit, we can consider *discontinuities in the group existence*, by the group being formed for a certain task, and disbanded afterwards, like our student groups were. Group *ephemerality*, the group being constituted and discontinued over a relatively short period, like it happens to student groups, and many others, can thus be viewed as a form of group work nomadicity.

4.1.2. Partitioning and Re-assembly

Group structure discontinuity is particularly important to consider. It usually leads to *partitioning of work* and to *re-assembly* at later stages. The term re-assembly is so chosen to suggest closure of the work process. We can, at this point, consider the *symmetry* of partitioning. In much of "mobile work" described in CSCW such as [4], partitioning is asymmetrical: a number of travelling workers are on business trips towards the 'resource' (customers, etc) while others, such as secretaries, stay at the 'home base' and provide backup services such as access to documents, composition of new documents, etc. This group partitioning into "catchers and pitchers" [5] is not something that we can observe with students. Indeed, their group partitioning is much more independent on the mobility condition. They are, in that sense, mobile workers without a group-wise 'home base'.

Partitioning of work is not necessarily induced by group structure change, it can also be induced by technological discontinuities, as e.g. observed in student group work when a deliverable or parts of a deliverable needed to be produced using another technology. This sometimes led to spatial discontinuity: in one of our observations, a film editing platform was located in a special room, requiring re-organization of work to suit this arrangement, including room booking, etc.

4.1.3. Features of Nomadicity

Let us now re-visit some of the themes introduced and view them through the lens of nomadicity as we started to conceptualise it. First it is now a bit clearer why *centres of coordination are workplaces with low nomadicity*. There is very little discontinuity in such workplaces. Spatial discontinuity is not much of an issue as space is rarely reconfigured. The same goes for technology support, plus, the centres are well prepared for accidental discontinuities in technology support (e.g. air traffic control without radar). Discontinuities in co-worker attendance are often life threatening (as accidents in e.g. air traffic control have shown). Discontinuities in subgroup and task allocation are very rare: tasks are well-partitioned in centres of coordination, yet that partitioning rarely changes, and such changes are well-marked. It does happen though that operators move to help their colleagues, however, the main task they are responsible for stays the same.

Second, *nomadicity is an everyday occurrence*. A significant body of CSCW research [4], [36] and [22] regards mobility as organized around "business trips", which, in our perspective, are high-nomadicity periods of activity. However, nomadicity can be a *quotidian* condition. It can thus capture less 'nomadicity-burst', yet nomadicity-intensive settings such as student work groups. Indeed, *nomadicity does not always imply mobility* as understood in the CSCW literature, i.e. movement in the physical space. While such movement will of course always exist in work, it will only be important from a nomadicity perspective if and when it constitutes an important discontinuity, and that discontinuity will be taken into account on equal footing with discontinuities of e.g. technology support, group and task partition, etc.

Third, the conceptualisation of nomadicity that we are proposing accounts for the ambitions of technology designers such as Kleinrock [10] and others. Looking back at Kleinrock's description we can recognize what [21] and [35] have called micro-mobility, local mobility or remote mobility. Nomadicity as the technology designers view it is, in our perspective, an attempt to address *technological support discontinuity* by technology design. That is not to say, however, that addressing such discontinuities is not desirable, as e.g. [4] would propose. While technology support "anytime anywhere" may indeed sometimes be too ambitious and vague in its focus, such discontinuity-resilient technology designs can be regarded as giving their users more than they sometimes need. Taking more than one needs is not unusual while on the move: in order to circumvent the uncertainty of their availability, or to anticipate "unused time" during travel, mobile workers would bring along more material than needed (e.g. paper documents). Besides, we should also consider the plethora of unused features we already carry in mobile phones. What is essential, we believe, is that while partitioning, re-assembly and other points of work discontinuity used to imply that technology support begins or ends, i.e. used to assume technology support discontinuity, mobile and broadband technologies come to reduce these discontinuities. The way they do so can be better informed by studies of nomadicity-affected work.

4.2. Implications

In terms of *design implications*, our upcoming conceptualisation suggests a special design attention to discontinuities of different kinds. Besides the *network connection discontinuity* already being addressed by technologists, *technology nature discontinuity* (e.g. having to move from one system or device to another, including paper) will certainly need to be addressed. In other words, we acknowledge that one device (even connected anytime, anywhere) cannot fit all needs. *Integration at the points of discontinuity* is then an important challenge in technology design. It is sometimes difficult to integrate content kept on paper with e.g. the content of a work-related phone call. However, the availability, in the system, an inventory of such non-digital artefacts is already a beginning in supporting such technology diversity.

Awareness of discontinuity is another important implication. Co-workers should be made aware that their peers face a certain type of discontinuity. Translucency [37] is a feature of technology that can help in this endeavour. We have already begun to address this issue in a pre-study [38].

Implications on methodology can be introduced by referring to our difficulties in applying ethnographic techniques that were previously successfully applied in low-nomadicity settings. It is hard to follow a group through a large number of discontinuity boundaries, while it is easier to observe e.g. work in a centre of coordination. It appears that much of CSCW investigation and design is typically centred on a low-nomadicity setting, with a small number of "collaboration units", i.e. with little discontinuity. We are currently looking into techniques such as diaries, e.g. [39] to follow discontinuities during field study.

5. Conclusions and Future Work

We have introduced the concept of nomadicity as a group work condition through a study of student group work. We propose this work condition as a more suitable alternative for the research and design of cooperative work support than earlier considerations of "mobile work". In characterizing nomadicity, we observed the importance of discontinuities, partitioning and re-assembly. "Discontinuity" is not aiming at *explaining* the character of the activities but is used as an umbrella term for the different aspects that we have noticed in nomadic work compared to the traditional work settings. We are currently involved with, or planning to work on, a more thorough exploration of research methods suitable for high-nomadicity settings, and planning more studies employing those methods. We are also considering a more detailed mapping of nomadicity-affected settings, through re-visiting CSCW work studies, with the goal to refine concepts such as micro-, local or remote mobility, as well as spatial or temporal mobility using our perspective centred on discontinuities as an essential ingredient of nomadicity. Finally, we are involved with the design of prototypes that we want to evaluate in highly-nomadic work settings such as student groups.

6. Acknowledgements

The research presented was carried out as part of a project supported by the Swedish Research Council (Vetenskapsrådet). Thanks to John Bowers for the observation on nomadicity as a work condition. We are grateful to our student informants.

References

[1]   Suchman L. Centers of Coordination: A Case and some themes. Presented at the NATO Advanced Research *Workshop on Discourse, Tools and Reasoning*, Lucca, Italy, 1993.
[2]   Rouncefield M., Viller S., Hughes J.A., Rodden T. Working with "Constant Interruption": CSCW and the Small Office. *The information society*, 11 (1995), 173-188.
[3]   Bogdan, C. *IT Design for Amateur Communities*, PhD thesis, Royal Institute of Technology, ISBN: 91-7283-44467, http://www.diva-portal.org/kth/theses/abstract.xsql?dbid=3470, Stockholm, Sweden, 2003.
[4]   Perry M., O'Hara K., Sellen A., Brown B., Harper R. Dealing with Mobility: Understanding Access Anytime, Anywhere. *In ACM Transactions on Computer-Human Interaction*, Vol. 8, n°. 4 (2001).
[5]   Churchill, E., Munro, A., Work/place: mobile technologies and arenas of activity, *In ACM SIGGROUP Bulletin*, Vol. 22, Issue 3 (2001), ACM Press, 3-9.
[6]   Hughes, J.A., Shapiro, D.Z., Sharrock, W.W., Anderson, R. The Automation of Air Traffic Control. *Lancaster Sociotechnics Group*, Department of Sociology, Lancaster University, 1988.
[7]   Nilsson, M., Hertzum, M. Negotiated rhythms of mobile work: time, place, and work schedules. *In Proc. of ACM GROUP*, ACM Press, 2005, 148-157.
[8]   Chlamtac, I., Journal of the Mobile Networks and Applications, Vol. 10, 1-2 (2005), Kluwer, Dodrecht
[9]   Thomas, P. Journal of Personal and Ubiquitous Computing, Vol. 9, 2, (2005), Kluwer.
[10] Kleinrock, L., Nomadic Computing - An Opportunity, *In ACM SIGCOMM Computer Communication Review*, Vol. 25, No. 1 (January 1995), ACM Press, 36-40.
[11] Sawhney, N., Schmandt, C., Nomadic Radio: Speech and Audio Interaction for contextual messaging in Nomadic Environments, *In ACM Transactions on Computer-Human Interaction*, Vol. 7, Issue 3 (2000).
[12] Kleinrock, L., Nomadicity: Anytime, Anywhere In A Disconnected World, Invited paper, *In Mobile Networks and Applications*, Vol. 1, No. 4 (1996), 351-357.
[13] Weiser, M. Some computer science issues in ubiquitous computing. *In Communications of the ACM*, Vol. 36 (1993), ACM Press, 75-84.

[14] La Porta, T.F., Sabnani K. K., Gitlin R. D. Challenges for Nomadic Computing: Mobility management and wireless communications, *In Mobile Networking and Applications*, Vol. 1, No. 1 (1996), Kluwer Academic Publishers, 3-16.

[15] Kindberg, T., Barton, J. A Web-based nomadic computing system. *In Computer Networks: The International Journal of Computer and Telecommunications Networking*, Vol. 35, Nr. 4 (2001), Elsevier North-Holland, Inc., 443-456.

[16] Reif, G., Kirda, E., Gall, H., Piccoz, G. P., Cugolaz, G. Fenkam, P. A Web-based Peer-to-Peer Architecture for Collaborative Nomadic Working, *In Proc. of IEEE WETICE*, IEEE, 2001, 334-339.

[17] Kakihara, M., Sørensen, C., Expanding the "Mobility" Concept. *In SIGGROUP Bulletin*, Vol. 22, No.3 (December 2001), ACM Press, 33-37.

[18] Bardram, J. E., Bossen, C. Mobility Work: The Spatial Dimension of Collaboration at a Hospital. *In Computer Supported Cooperative Work*, 3, Nr. 14 (2005), 131-60.

[19] Ciolfi, L., Bertolucci, I., Murphy, D. Meaningful Interactions for Meaningful Places: Investigating the Relationship between Nomadic Work, Tangible Artefacts and the Physical Environment. *In Proc. of EACE 2005*, 2005.

[20] Brodie, J., Perry, M J. Work and Collaboration in Mobile Settings, Epsrc. Progress Report, Deliverable 1.1, *Designing for Mobile and Distributed Work: Technology Use in Remote Settings*. 2001.

[21] Luff P., Heath, C. Mobility in Collaboration, *In Proc. of ACM CSCW'98*, 1998.

[22] Brown, B. and O'Hara, K., Place as a practical concern for mobile workers. *Environment and Planning A.*, Vol. 35, Nr. 9, 2003, 1565-1587.

[23] Bødker, S., Kristensen, J., Sperschneider, W., Technology for Boundaries, *In Proc. of ACM GROUP*, 2003, 311-320.

[24] Blomberg, J., Burrell, M., Guest, G. An ethnographic approach to design. *In The Human Computer Interaction Handbook - Fundamentals, Evolving Technologies, and Emerging Applications*. Lawrence Erlbaum, 2003. 964-986.

[25] Suchman L. Technologies of accountability: On lizards and airplanes. In Button G. (ed.) *Technology in Working Order. Studies of work, interaction, and technology*, Routledge; 1993, 113-126.

[26] Normark, M. *Work and Technology Use in Centers of Coordination: Reflections on the relationship between situated practice and artifact design*, PhD thesis, Royal Institute of Technology, ISBN: 91-7178-184-6, http://www.diva-portal.org/kth/theses/abstract.xsql?dbid=462, Stockholm, Sweden, 2005.

[27] Normark, M., Bogdan, C., Jorge, P. , Rossitto, C. and Severinson Eklundh, K. The UCPD study: On nomadic coordination and technology use in student projects. *Technical report TRITA-NA-P0509*, NADA, Royal Institute of Technology, August 2005.

[28] Orr, J.E. *Talking about machines: An ethnography of a modern job*, Ithaca, N.Y.: ILR Press, 1996.

[29] Gerson, E.M., Star, S.L. Analyzing due process in the workplace. *In ACM Transactions on Computer-Human Interaction*, 4, 3 (1986), 257-270.

[30] Heath, C., Luff, P. Collaboration and control: Crisis management and multimedia technology in London Underground control rooms. *Journal of CSCW*, Vol. 1, 1-2 (1992), 69-94.

[31] Bowers, J., Button, G., Sharrock, W. Workflow from within and without: Technology and cooperative work on the print industry shopfloor, *In Proc. of the ECSCW*, Kluwer, 1995. 51-66.

[32] Berndtsson J, Normark, M. The Coordinative Functions of Flight Strips: Air Traffic Control Revisited. *In Hayne SC, editor.*, Phoenix, Arizona, USA. 1999, 101-110.

[33] Normark, M. Sense-making of an emergency call - possibilities and constraints of a computerized case file. *In cooperation with ACM/SIGCHI and the Nordic HCI organisations*, 2002.

[34] Erickson, T. Here and There, Now and Then: A Long-Distance Teleworker's Reflections on 'Workplace. *In ACM SIGGROUP Bulletin*, Vol. 22, Nr. 3, (2001), ACM Press, 5-10.

[35] Bellotti V., Bly S., Walking Away from the Desktop Computer: Distributed Collaboration and Mobility in a Product Design Team. *In Proc. of ACM CSCW,* ACM Press, 1996, 209-218.

[36] Brown, B. Perry, M., Of Maps and Guidebooks: designing geographical technologies, *In Proc. DIS: processes, practices, methods, and techniques*, ACM, 2002.

[37] Dourish, P., Button, G., On 'technomethodology': foundational relationships between ethnomethodology and system design, *In Human-Computer Interaction*, 13 (1998), 395-432.

[38] Bogdan C., Severinson Eklundh, K. FingerPrint: supporting social awareness in a translucent sensor-mediated cue-based environment, *In Proc. of ACM CHI*, ACM Press, 2004, 1263-1266.

[39] Palen, L., Salzman, M. Voice-Mail Diary Studies for Naturalistic Data Capture under Mobile Conditions, *In Proc. of ACM CSCW*, ACM Press, 2002.

Cooperative Systems Design
P. Hassanaly et al. (Eds.)
IOS Press, 2006

Annotations: A Functionality to support Cooperation, Coordination and Awareness in the Electronic Medical Record

Sandra BRINGAY[a], Catherine BARRY[a], Jean CHARLET[b]

a LaRIA, University of Amiens (France), {bringay, barry}@laria.u-picardie.fr
b STIM/DSI/AP-HP, Paris (France), Jean.Charlet@spim.jussieu.fr

Abstract. The interest of the Electronic Medical Record EMR is from now on obvious. However, Health Professionals still not have at their disposal tools allowing them to support their cooperative practices. In the French DocPatient project, we try to improve practitioners' cooperation when they use the medical documents by implementing a document-based EMR. Our assumption is that a best integration of the way they use these medical documents in the EMR design will improve its utility, its use and its acceptance. In this paper, we show that annotations practices must be transposed in the EMR to reinforce collaboration, coordination and awareness.

Keywords: CSCW, Electronic Medical Record, Annotations, Cooperation, Coordination, Awareness

Introduction

Since 2002, we were part of the DocPatient project. We work on the problematic of a document-based Electronic Medical Record EMR [1]. This project of the University of Amiens is financed by the Picardy region (France). It gathers a multi-field team composed of sciences for the engineer (data-processing) and social sciences (law, management, psychology). We work in collaboration with a pilot site[1] and an industrial partner[2]. We develop documentary functionalities making easier the manipulations of the electronic documents and the collaboration between Health Professionals HPs.

The evolution of the Information Systems is one of the stakes of the system of health. Indeed, the more the number of HPs around the patient increases, the more the flow of data, information and knowledge must be fast and coherent to provide collaboration to all the HPs. The Medical Record MR is the main support to all this knowledge. We were inspired by the definition of a corporate memory [2], to describe in [3] the MR as a memory which represents all the medical data, information and knowledge, relative to a patient and which is produced and used by a medical organisation. The representation of this information must be *persistent* (constant and durable in time), and *explicit* (not ambiguous for HPs' interpretation). Thanks to this memory, the HPs can store and retrieve all the information they need during their collaborative activities.

---

[1] The hospital ward of paediatric intensive care and neonatal medicine of Amiens
[2] The company UNI-MEDICINE http://www.uni-medecine.com/

Traditionally, HPs use a Paper Medical Record PMR. From now on, this record shows its limits, in particular for the sharing of medical information between all the HPs in an hospital and in the city (care network, homecare...). The EMR must be a transposition of this record on the electronic medium. It must allow at least the same collaborative practices than the PMR. However, recent studies on HPs' work practices with the EMR [4-9] reveals important gaps between the presumptions of the EMR role and the ways in which practitioners actually use it. Systems have failed in a wide variety of medical organisations (medical offices, hospitals...). These failures cause frustrations for the practitioners and important costs for the medical organisations. For example, in our pilot site, HPs use both a PMR and a EMR. They still prefer to use the PMR to collaborate. This observation can be extended to others wards. We can doubt that EMR as it is actually presented to the HPs can deliver their promised benefits.

How can we explain this series of failures? To our mind, developers are confronted with numerous problems which are related to the scale of the medical organisations. For example, the hospital organisations are *particular organisations*, since they offer services (the care) and manage knowledge thanks to the MR. The *stakeholders* are all the *"persons who have an interest or a stake which can be affected by the system"* [10]. They are not inevitably the users of the MR. In a hospital, many stakeholders have activities relative to the MR: medical units (physicians, fellows...), technical units (pharmacy, laboratories...), administrative staffs, researchers, patients... For all those actors, the MR plays a key role and a strong collaboration is needed between all of them. Those actors use the MR for very *varied tasks*: medical activities (diagnoses, therapeutic decisions...) or others (control, planning, education...). The MR must represent *varied data, information and knowledge* (weight, hospitalisation reports, images...) on *varied mediums* (paper or electronic documents, images, databases...). The memory, its users and its managers are distributed in heterogeneous geographical places. To conclude, it is very difficult to build an EMR. Although the technical meadows are now available, the developers do not succeed in providing HPs tool adapted to the scale of their organisation and to their intercorrelation of practices. For example, in the ward we work with, HPs complain about the problems of data capture, time-consuming (need of adapted interfaces), the lack of incentives coming from the medical authorities, their fear of the transparency provided by the system (need of communication about the deontology linked to the EMR)... They still wait for an EMR which will provide them more benefits than the PMR.

In this paper, we use the concepts coming from CSCW researches, to describe the collaborative activities of the HPs observed during the DocPatient project. We show why the electronic medical documents do not allow reproducing some practices of collaboration carried out with the PMR. We focus our attention on one particular practice: annotations which are used as support for the collaboration, coordination and awareness in the PMR and which are lacking in the EMR. To finish, we present the test of our annotations tool realised with the potential users in our pilot site.

1. Documents of the MR as support to the cooperation, coordination and awareness

The study presented is the result of the multidisciplinary observations and reflections realised during the DocPatient project, in the Paediatric Unit of Amiens, to understand why and how practitioners use the documents of the MR. We will apply the theoretical frameworks widely used in the CSCW community, Distributed Cognition [11,12], Situated Action [13], Activity Theory [14] (among others) to the problematic of the EMR. Indeed, CSCW studies have generated a set of useful concepts to help thinking the collaborative nature (and functional requirements) of human activities. In particular, they consider that the introduction of a new technology modifies the performances of the system, redistributes the activities of the workers, modifies their practices and also impacts on their social interactions... Consequently, the future performances of a new technology depend on these reconfigurations and on their acceptance by the workers. According to them, the design of the tools must be related to uses studies because understanding how workers use a system in situation helps to provide them tools adapted to their activities. In this section, we stress the intercorrelation of the medical activities and the needs in term of coordination and awareness, and we show why the documents are the privileged supports for these activities.

1.1. Tasks interdependences of the actors in medical collaborative work

Actors invested in a collaborative work aim at realise a common task. They are linked by social relations. In a hospital ward, HPs work for the patient. They have a common project: the patient's recovery, but they also have their own projects. The physician wants to find the treatments the more adapted to the state of the patient and the nurse wants to carry out the better the care for the patient. For Schmidt [15], the cooperative work is, in essence, distributed. The actors share the tasks which must be carried out to achieve their common goal. Work is distributed in the sense that "*decision making agents are semiautonomous in their work in terms of contingencies, criteria, methods, specialties, perspectives, heuristics (...)*". The nurse and the physician are free to organise their own tasks as long as their activities merge to care the patient.

Bricon-Souf et al. [16] according to the Hoc's model [17,18] distinguish three types of coordination:

- *Cooperation in action* (goals and procedures management activities, in the course of task execution, in real time and in the short term) : the physician who interacts with the nurse at the patient's bedside to carry out a care...
- *Cooperation in planning* (elaboration or maintenance - in the medium term) : the staff meeting which allows to coordinate the action of the medical team, to allot the practitioners to the patients...
- *Meta cooperation* (high level of abstraction activities producing useful support for other activity levels): the use of an implicit terminology understandable by all the members of the medical team...

Actors engaged in such a cooperative work are "*mutually dependent*" [19]. Workers depend on the quality, efficiency and repartition in time of the tasks of others workers. The nurse cannot begin the administration of a drug as long as the physician did not carry out the regulation. There are "*interferences*" [17,18] between the activities of the workers. These interferences can be positive i.e. the work of an actor helps positively another actor to carry out his task and to achieve his goal. The observations of the nurse noted in her book help the physician to build his diagnosis. On the contrary, the interferences can be negative. The nurse must wait until the physician finished his visit to carry out a care. Many researchers [5,19,20] stress the importance to take into account these interdependences and these interferences to design systems.

1.2. Need of coordination

These activities must be articulated, coordinated. Indeed, the coordination is not limited to the sharing of the same resources in a particular environment but these one appears when workers negotiate in order to allot a task to the most competent worker, to prevent two workers from doing the same activity, to manage the repartition in time of the dependent tasks... It is well-recognised that a good coordination of the actors who work in a cooperative way is an essential element in the success of their common task. It is also well recognised that such a coordination is essential for quality health care, particularly when different structures have to organise themselves to treat a patient in a cooperative way [16].

To coordinate their activities, the workers need a form of agreement. They must negotiate to have shared knowledge, beliefs and representations. Bricon-Souf et al. [16] uses the concept of Common Frame of Reference (COFOR) introduced by Terssac et al. [21]. COFOR is "*the sharing of competencies to prepare and perform an action; this sharing of competencies at the same time complements each individual representation of the task, and enables the adjustment of each individual decision, considering the other's knowledge*" [16 translation]. For example, the physician who writes a prescription does not have the same concerns than the pharmacist who manages all the drugs of the hospital. Fortunately, during their direct interactions, they will use a common representational ground (on the patient, on medicine, on their activities) as well as their own competences in order to disambiguate the communication. These direct interactions are not sufficient. To support this COFOR, the actors need shared artefacts. For example, in the wards, we find several material artefacts such as the whiteboards which lists the tasks to do, the MR which sums up the things done for a patient and the things to do... We find also immaterial artefacts such as the rules, the protocols... that regulate the activities of care. Although the importance of the COFOR is well known, supports dedicated to the coordination are often neglected during the design of new electronic settings [6,23] and it is the case in the EMR.

1.3. Documents as a support to the coordination

Traditionally, practitioners developed a significant culture of writing words. In order to keep the most traces of their exchanges and of their acts, they transcribe or record them on a perpetual medium, the paper or electronic documents of the MR. So, practitioners can handle (complete, annotate, read) this knowledge. It is reactivated in various contexts and will be the support of new interactions. Considering the number and the complexity of the situations of interactions, the hospital units organise a real process of "*documentarisation*" [24]. The heads of department designed the architecture of the record and the organisation of the documents. So, the management of the documents is easier: in the PMR, we know where to retrieve the surgical report. Likewise, their physical manipulations are easier: thanks to the predefined outline of the patient discharge summary, a writer knows where to look for the paragraph he wants to fill in and a reader knows where to retrieve the paragraph with the required knowledge. "*The Medical Record is a tool (...) it does not 'represent' the work, but it feeds into it, it structures and transforms it in complex ways: it structures that communication between healthcare personnel, shapes medical decision making, and frames relations between personnel and patients.*" [25]

Several creators can produce a document and several beneficiaries can read it. For example, the "fellows' synthesis", built collectively and daily update, is written for all the practitioners tacking care of the patient. However, most of the documents are written for precise beneficiaries. The physician writes the patient discharge summary for the specialists who take part into the patient's recovery when he leaves the hospital. However, these documents can be the support of non foreseeable exchanges, when unexpected beneficiaries take advantage of the knowledge stored in them. A teacher-physician incites his students to read an imagery report in the MR. The intentionality of the document moves. A document written with a particular aim can satisfy a need of communication not envisaged during its design. The reader distorts the initial intentionality of the document. He "*recontextualises*" the knowledge in the document according to his reading objectives. Berg et al. [26] affirm that this way of using and re-using the MR is linked to the contextual nature of the medical knowledge. "*Medical information is entangled with the context of production: medical data are tied to the purpose of their generation and they are part of an evolving array of medical data which continually reshapes their meaning (...) Physicians are aware of the constantly evolving nature of the data they produce and they generate their data accordingly*".

In order to "*documentarise*" the record, the head of department (designer) have organised the documents in the record and the knowledge in the document. In the PMR, there are two types of documents:

- The *forms written in real time*, at the bedside, contain primarily raw data related to the care. The designer structures the forms finely and uses the fields' headings to specify the knowledge to be captured. The writer interprets these indications to fill in the fields. These two authors have a joint project: to keep traces of the knowledge used during stereotyped transactions. They have also their own project. The designer wants to codify knowledge in the forms to re-exploit it easily. The writer wants, as fast as possible, to keep the most traces of the medical events in which he took part. In these structured forms, we can identify easily small semiotics productions and the precise links relating them. The writers' works (their captures are limited to some words or sentences) and the readers' works (they learned how to retrieve knowledge in such forms) are easier. An example is the administrative document of entry.

- The *documents of synthesis written after the medical acts* contain practitioners' interpretations. There are also two authors. The designer uses the outline of the document to structure the document into paragraphs (and not into fields as for the forms). He also gives indications on the contents of the paragraphs. The writer remains free of the knowledge he captures. Generally, he uses the natural language. According to Bachimont [27], only this linguistic layout allows the expression of the various levels of information (the factual, the potential and the intentional), necessary to the knowledge contextualisation. The two authors have a joint project: to consign the most knowledge resulting from an analysis. They have also their own project. The designer, with the outline, wants to organise the writing to make it exploitable. This outline cannot be as precise as the forms outline because it is impossible to predefine the knowledge resulting from a reflection. The writer wants to keep traces of his analysis which will help him during the care. These documents are semi-structured. So, important semiotics productions and the links relating them can be identified easily. An example of document is the patient discharge summary.

Of course, there are also documents written without a predefined model, such as the diagram improvised by the surgeon to explain his operation to the patient. However, these documents are rare. Finally, we can oppose these two categories of documents by the type of knowledge captured (predefined knowledge vs unforeseeable knowledge), by the type of writing (a rigid writing vs a free writing) and by the level of structure of the document (structured documents vs semi-structured documents). Bachimont [27] affirms that the predefined textual types fix the rules of reading and writing. These rules allow readings in distant contexts in time and space from the creation and consequently offer an efficient support to the coordination. Indeed, the documents allow to build the COFOR necessary to the understanding of the patient's state and to the perception of the activities realised to improve his state.

1.4. Need of awareness

Awareness is an understanding of the others' activities and the perception of the environment. Détienne [19] explains that awareness *"refers to practices, through which cooperating actors, while engaged in their respective individual activities and dealing with their own local urgencies and troubles, manage to pick up what their colleagues are doing or not doing and to adjust their own individual activities accordingly."* Awareness is critical to successful collaboration. A lot of studies have shown that coordination increases when people can actively produce and maintain the idea of what happen around them (synchronous mode) or what have happened (asynchronous mode) [18, 18-35]. Without awareness, a worker can repeat an action carried out by another worker. He can look for information because he does not know that another worker has this information. He can hamper the work of another actor because he is not aware of his presence in the environment...

When people work in a synchronous way, face-to-face, awareness is provided by their direct interactions and their mutual observations. For example, when the nurse and the physician collaborate in the room of the patient, they are conscious of each others. During an asynchronous work, awareness needs a support. It is more difficult to fill the lack of information between periods of working activities [23]. However, actors must be aware of the activities in which they could not take part and thus of the existence of information in themselves. *"Awareness support must include facilities for monitoring, directing attention, and handling over tasks at different levels of obtrusiveness and persistence"* [37]. For example, the physician uses the "placard" at the bedside as a support to be aware of the nurses' activities. In electronic distributed environments, awareness is more difficult to achieve than in the real world. Indeed, workers have to not only locate themselves in time but also in space. To conclude, actors' collaboration can become efficient only if actors can perceive traces or signs of the presence and activities of the others. As for the COFOR, authors as Pankoke-Babatz et al. [23] underline the *"considerable lack for the support of awareness in electronic environments"* and it is the case in the EMR

1.5. Documents as a support to awareness

As we said before, during the process of care, as in any collaborative activity, the actors need awareness. The direct interactions, as the conversations between a physician and a nurse at the bedside, support awareness. *"Without such interactions, it would be difficult for the physician to ascertain which patients are of most concern to the nurse, or for the nurse to know which orders are the most important*" [4]. But, these direct interactions are not sufficient and the documents of the MR will also play a key role for awareness. The documents do not provide only information on the patient's health but also enable HPs to be informed of the others' activities allowing them to coordinate effectively their activities. Reddy et al. [35] showed "*that users often were not looking for information about the patient per se, but rather for information about the activities of other health-care workers regarding that patient*". For example, the physician, just by looking at the nurses' book, is aware of the nurses' activities. If a nurse writes in the margin of the MR, the duration of a care whereas she never does it, the physician understands that the care was longer than usual because there was a problem. The use of the PMR ensures that HPs stay aware of each other's activities and can prioritise theirs tasks due to his flexibility. They can add any information they want in the documents (in annotations) and they can add any document they find important for patient's care.

1.6. Synthesis: recommendation for the building of a relevant document-based EMR

We see in this section how documents play a key role for the storage of the medical knowledge, and for the cooperation, coordination and awareness of the practitioners. In most of the actual EMR, we do not find sufficient functionalities to support these mechanisms. Consequently, these tools are often perceived as organisational and cultural obstacles by the HPs. These latter are frustrated because they find no sufficient benefit which would justify them to use the EMR rather than the PMR. Indeed, there is a contradiction between the institutions' needs (they want electronic standardised data for their activities of management, research and teaching) and the HPs' needs (they want a relevant support to help them to cooperate). In the current EMR, the documents presented to the HPs are standardised to answer the medical authorities' needs. The HPs who tend to adjust the categories of the MR to answer their needs for coordination and awareness cannot any more do it in these rigid structures. "*In summary, there is evidence that communication problems in health-care settings are significant, collaborative work around documents is not well supported by informatics systems, and that there are insufficient in-depth, observational studies of real world communication behaviours in health care*" [30]. However, HPs are the main collectors of knowledge. Designers of new EMRs are likely to think of these added functionalities which will help practitioners to maintain cooperation, coordination and awareness.

2. Annotations of the MR as support to the cooperation, coordination and awareness

Among all the practices of cooperation of the HPs, we will now focus our attention on one of them: annotations. Our assumption is that annotations are a relevant support for the cooperation, coordination and awareness which is not provided by the standardised documents we find in the EMRs. We went out into the field to analyse this particular practice. We discussed with the HPs during individual semi-structured interviews to understand how and why they annotate. We studied the literature concerning this activity and mainly the authors as [24, 36-40]. We also took part in a workshop

"Annotations" of the French Thematic Multidisciplinary Network dealing with documents (RTP Doc[3]). Thanks to those works, we give in [3] the following definition:

> *An annotation is a particular note linked to a target. The target can be a collection of documents, a document, a segment of document (a paragraph, a group of words, an image, and a part of image ...), and another annotation. Each annotation has a content, materialised by an inscription. It is the trace of the mental representation elaborated by the annotator about the target. The content of the annotation can be interpreted by another reader. The anchor links the annotation to the target (a line, a surrounded sentence ...).*

In this section we show why annotations take part in the cooperation, coordination and awareness of the care activities, before giving specifications about the implementation of such a functionality of annotations in an EMR.

2.1. Analyse of cooperation practices around the annotations

In spite of the "*documentarisation*" effort of the medical authorities to simplify the writing and the reading of the medical documents, those documents are not sufficient to allow the practitioners to really work on all the knowledge they create. The change of medium from paper to electronic medium stresses these difficulties. Informal annotations can solve a part of these problems because as the documents, the annotations will play a key role for the storage of knowledge, coordination and the awareness of the medical practices.

Some difficulties encountered by practitioners are related to the type of the documents (too rigid and standardised for writers' writing) and to the unpredictability of medical knowledge. Where practitioners can consign the knowledge not envisaged by the designers and which emerge during the writing and the reading? On paper, practitioners currently use informal annotations to complete their capture in the forms and to keep traces of their readings. Indeed, even if the designer leaves textual fields for non foreseeable knowledge, the writers will prefer to annotate the rigid forms. With a graphical way (an arrow, an underlined part), they connect the comment and the part of the document having caused the comment. We do not find annotations written by writers in the documents of synthesis, less rigid, because they have sufficient freedom to write in the paragraphs. *A posteriori*, whatever the type of the document is, readers leave traces of their comprehension in annotations. The annotations thus allow contextualise the knowledge not envisaged by the designer of the documents, produced during the writing and the reading. The reader enters in the constitutive process of the document. With the annotation practice, he can re-appropriate the document, rewrite it according to the desired use. Consequently, he becomes the "author of his reading" [41]. Currently, this knowledge (not envisaged by the designer of the document) is annotated on paper and not written in the predefined electronic documents because there is no means to extend the electronic forms.

In addition, as we discuss in the second part of this paper, informal interactions, most of the time oral, are very important within the framework of the medical collaborative activities to provide cooperation and coordination. Thanks to these interactions (communications), practitioners exchange knowledge often partial,

---

[3] http://rtp-doc.enssib.fr/

speculative, provisional, incremental... Due to the work organisation in the wards, they need asynchronous ways of communicating when they cannot meet each others. They do not want to consign this knowledge in the documents of the MR which have a statute too much "public" (all the practitioners working with the patient consult the documents of the MR) and too much "formal" (the practitioners consign knowledge according to writing rules' fixed by the documents designers). Therefore, annotations are a relevant support, less "official" for all their interactions. Practitioners know that annotations will be read as incomplete and subject to revision, contrary to the predefined documents of the MR. The passage to the electronic medium accentuates this way of thinking of the practitioners. Indeed, they often consider that all things captured in a computer must be finalised because they can be distributed to a wide audience. We could observe a particular behaviour of the practitioners, writers of documents, in our pilot site. A data base equips this service. Practitioners often delay the data-processing capture in this data base until the moment they validate collectively information. But in the first step, they consign knowledge in their personal notes or in the annotations added to the documents of the paper record.

From this study, we can conclude that a person annotates because:

- *She cannot*, without annotations, add her semiotic production to the document because most of the data captures do not allow the writer to enter the desired data. It is the case of the medical forms too rigid for allowing the writer to add knowledge not envisaged by the designer. Therefore, an annotation is an escape clause if there is no current method to extend forms.

- *She does not want* to add her semiotic production to the document because this one is written with an intention of communication different from the initial intention of the annotated document. In so doing, the annotator is adding meta-information, i.e. information about the document rather than information that belongs in the document itself. It is the case when a reader annotates to keep traces of his reading, when a person wants to build a new document using her readings or when several practitioners collaborate by taking as support the documents they annotate. Consequently, an annotation is also an escape clause if there is no means to code the comments about the documents.

For each scenarios presented before, we have studied more precisely the content of the annotations. The table 1 synthesises these different types of annotations and their functional roles for storage of knowledge, coordination and awareness. We deduced that an annotator can have two types of objectives when he annotates:

- He writes the annotation for himself but he can communicate it to the others members of the organisation according to the needs (memos, personal notes, reports/ratios of actions, bonds);

- He writes the annotation directly for one (or several) targeted reader(s) (instructions, daily transmissions, requests for information, development of information and circulation of information).

We now want to focus your attention on the fact that the use of the annotation during the collaborative activities depends on the role of the reader in the organisation. For example, a physician writes « blood gas in 2 hours ». A nurse reads this message, she detects the interference with her own care (she has to delay the child's bath) and she understands that she must prepare the child and the material for the blood gas. A fellow analyses this comment from another point of view and consequently, this note induces others collaborative activities.

Table 1: Annotations: definition, example and functional role

Personal annotations possibly published		
Definition	**Example**	**Functional role**[4]
To write a memo note we write of something we do not want to forget. These notes allow to remind an action to do for ourselves or for a group.	The nurses write memos as: to think of sending of the results of the electrocardiogram, to think of making sign the document by the parents, to think of not giving an injection in the arms, clothing lent to the child…	- **Storage of knowledge:** HPs write what they must do in the short-term. We find these memos on supports as post-it or personal notes (not in the documents of the MR) because once the action is carried out, the experts want them to disappear. - **Coordination:** memos (in particular memos for the group), are important for implicit tasks' allocations. Indeed, although the name of the agent who has to carry out the action is not often specified, the HPs use their common knowledge about the role of each worker in the organisation to determine who must carry out the action. - **Awareness:** the HPs retrieve in memos traces of the realised and future activities of the medical team in the short-term.
To write their personal notes: note we take of something to keep a trace of our reasoning: not confirmed information, hypothesis…	The physicians use these notes for their assumptions, when they still have doubts: "The mother is undoubtedly a depressive woman".	- **Storage of knowledge:** HPs write traces of their reasoning **Coordination:** the personal note helps to build the COFOR. Indeed, the possible readers are aware that as long as the information is not consigned in the final documents, there still forms part of the process of reasoning. **Awareness:** the personal note helps the HPs to know what is the annotator's point of view about the controlled process (the patient's state) and the controlled activity (the way the medical team cares the patient).
To write a report of action: note we write to preserve a trace of the actions (stereotyped or not) carried out.	The nurses who have in charge the majority of the care often note near the prescriptions "done/not done".	- **Storage of knowledge:** HPs write what they did and this information is kept in the MR in the long-term. **Coordination/Awareness:** the report of action helps the medical team to know what task has been done for the patient and consequently, when there is no report of action, what still to be done.
To link documents: personal note used to keep a trace of the link between 2 documents.	To justify his argumentation in an imagery report, an expert writes "cf. thorax radio. n°2".	- **Storage of knowledge:** HPs keep traces of a part of their reasoning when they read documents. **Coordination/Awareness:** the HPs can appropriate the reading roads of others users.
Annotations written directly to be published		
To pass an instruction: to tell someone to do something.	To give his consign to the fellow, the physician writes "Control the electrocardiogram in two hours".	- **Storage of knowledge:** HPs write their orders (what can be useful *a posteriori* in the case of problem with the law). **Coordination:** an instruction is important to allot a task to someone and to manage the time. **Awareness:** the HPs retrieve the tasks they have to do (if the annotation is for them) and of the tasks their colleagues have to do (if the annotation is not for them).
To update the daily transmissions: to support the daily transmissions between the various medical teams	To ensure the care continuity, the fellows write for their colleagues in rest, notes about the patients.	- **Storage of knowledge:** HPs write synthesis of the most important information about the patient. **Coordination/Awareness:** the synthesised information about the patient's sate is important to build the COFOR and the HPs retrieve traces of the realised tasks and future activities.

---

[4] Before its publication, these personal notes do not impact on the coordination and awareness because the annotator is the only one who can read them.

To ask for information: to ask someone (or a group of persons) some information.	A HP asks for the specialist's opinion and keeps his answer in personal post-it/notes.	- **Storage of knowledge:** in his answer, an expert writes the knowledge he wants to transmit to the medical team. His answer does not form part of the MR. - **Coordination/Awareness:** the COFOR is enriched with new information coming from the experience of the specialist.
To draw the attention: to emphasise information in documents.	By highlighting a value in blood gases, the physician draws the attention of his fellows to a possible diagnosis.	- **Storage of knowledge:** HPs underline the most important information according to their point of view. **Coordination:** this note allows the HPs to prioritise the information they find the most important. **Awareness:** with this note HPs understand what is the most important for the annotator's activities.
To make circulate information: to distribute knowledge to all the medical actors working with the patient.	The administrative agents receive a lot of information (telephone, fax...) redistributed thanks to annotations.	- **Storage of knowledge:** HPs write information dedicated to a large number of persons - **Coordination/Awareness:** with this note HPs contact the largest number of persons.

All these examples show how the practitioners use annotations to act: either to enrich the annotated document or to be the transitory support of knowledge used to create new knowledge (recorded or not in a document). Therefore, annotating is already an action which enables HPs to store knowledge but which will also help HPs to maintain a certain level of coordination and awareness.

2.2. Our tool of annotations dedicated to the EMR

As we said in section 1, designers of new EMR are likely to think of these added functionalities which will help practitioners to maintain cooperation, coordination and awareness. Providing a functionality which allows users to write comments in the documents can be used for that. But we can go further. In our tool, we have exploited these annotations to improve the use of the EMR.

HPs need functionalities of hypertextual navigation because they have readings problem in the EMR (cognitive overload, noise, no global vision...). As we find in annotations traces of their readings, we can reuse them to build documents of navigation. It is a new document added to the MR, which allows to retrieve the initial documents of the MR (as a summary, index). Such a document of navigation contrived from annotations corresponds to a list of items leading to annotations, selected by the user according to one or more criteria (annotator's name, date, topic). From these annotations, a reader retrieves the annotated documents. So, we offer him new reading roads. We can also use annotations to have particular point of view on the document. During the creation of an annotation, the annotator can specify the recipients of his annotation with access rights: himself, a group of users, all the readers. During the consultation of the record, there is an automatic filtering of these annotations. Consequently, a reader visualises only the annotations he has the right to see. In addition, during his reading of the record, the reader can filter manually the annotations and choose to visualise only a collection of annotations selected according to criteria. For example, a nurse can retrieve all the annotations dealing with the tasks she has to carry out. These three functionalities will help the readers to build their own vision of the MR by appropriating the common base of knowledge constituted by this MR.

HPs need aids to build synthesis used for exchanging the most important knowledge they need during the care. These syntheses are very important for coordination and awareness. To build a new document editable, we place the contents of the annotations selected by the user the ones after the others. Then, he can rewrite the generated document, add knowledge and a page setting. For example, a practitioner writes the patient discharge summary. He reads the record, selects and comments some parts with annotations intended for this document. Gathering all these annotations in a new document gives him a base to write this report. The reader becomes a "reader-writer" [41] because he carries out two tasks: the reading of the documents used for the writing of the new document.

HPs need aids to exchange information for maintaining coordination and awareness. A user can send an annotation to one or more recipients. The message can have content (a comment) or not. There are several kinds of messages:

- a message can be produced in connection with an element of a record. For example, a practitioner reads an analysis and detects an anomaly. He comments the document and decides to indicate it to all the practitioners concerned by the record. When a recipient receives this message, he must be able to retrieve the annotated document.

- a message can be produced in connection with a patient and thus in connection with a record taken as a whole. For example, a practitioner encounters difficulties to establish a diagnosis. He decides to ask his opinion to a colleague. He sends him a message linking the annotation to the record of the patient. When the recipient receives this message, he must be able to retrieve the record of the patient.

- a message can be produced in response to another message. When the recipient receives this message, he must be able to retrieve the previous message, as well as the source, if it exists, at the origin of the first message.

We built a first tool in collaboration with our industrial partner according to these specifications. We describe it in detail in [1]. On the Figure 1, a user annotated a document. He highlighted in yellow in the document and attached a comment and a link up to another document of the record (a thorax radiograph).

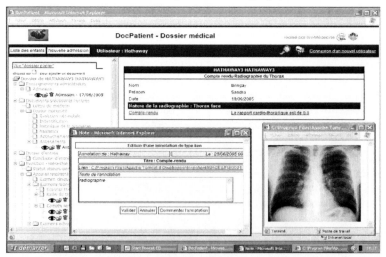

Figure 1: Our tool of annotations

3. Utilisability test: to reinforce our specifications

We undertook a semi-realistic utilisability study of our tool to check with the potential users the interest of adding annotations in the EMR as well as their reuse. We have chosen 20 users representative of the end-users: 5 senior physicians, 5 fellows, 5 nurses and 5 administrative agents. To limit their investment in time, we carry out the tests in the Paediatric Unit. Each interview lasts approximately two hours. At the beginning of the test, we invite the user to fill in a pre-evaluation form. With this form, we can identify his profile, his data-processing competences and his current use of paper annotations. Then, we carry out a brief demonstration of the tool. We want him to discover by himself the functionalities. For this reason, we ask him to carry out some tasks. The head of department helped us to build 10 scenarios adapted to the 4 professional categories. In so doing, the user handles the various annotations functionalities as he could do for his work. We use 10 fictitious documents created for the scenarios. During the test, an observer guides the user and observes the way he uses annotations. A second observer notes the information given orally by the user, his reactions and his mimicries. At the end of the test, the user fills in a post-evaluation form. With the form, we collect his point of view about the relevance and the user-friendliness of all the functionalities.

A pre-evaluation of the observations, pre-evaluation form and post-evaluation form has been done in [43]. The users' comments were very positive. Practitioners value to retrieve the practices they have with the PMR and they enjoy the new functionalities. The system matches with their current collaborative activities. They felt that it could avoid some waste of time, and could make coordination and awareness easier, in particular thanks to the sending messages module. The main interest they perceive is that knowledge can be in full view in the context of the document, thanks to annotations. Consequently, they can quickly alarm their colleagues. For example, a senior physician said that annotations are a relevant medium to encourage the fellows he supervises to read the documents containing rough knowledge (radiographs, examinations results) and to retrieve his conclusions in his own annotations. Moreover, those positive comments came from users whose jobs are different. The navigation through the interface seems to be intuitive. Required improvements concern some ergonomic points and could be easily modified in a future version. To conclude, these first results justify the presence of annotations in the EMR. Indeed, the criticisms collected are mainly related to the way we present the new functionalities in our model. These criticisms are not related to the interest of these functionalities. We will take into account these criticisms to refine the adaptation of the functionalities to the EMR context. Annotations correspond to a real demand of the practitioners.

Two future directions may be noted:
- Improvement of the visualisation of the annotations in the document. We plan to develop a system to help the reader to construct a part of the annotation creation and reading context without having to read the comment (for example a system of colour for the anchor to known the profession of the user, a system of icons to underline the urgent information…).
- Improvement of our policy of access right on the annotations content. For the experimentation, we define three predefined spheres: public annotations – every body can read them, private annotations – the annotator is the only one who can read them and annotations for the group – annotations are visible only for the group in charge of the patient. These three spheres must be more

precise to support the collaborative practices (sphere by profession, sphere built during the creation of the annotation...)

4. Conclusions et Prospects

In this paper we argued for the need of cooperation, coordination and awareness in the EMR. We affirm that even if sometimes neglected, the cooperation of the medical team is essential for the acceptance of this tool. The MR is the privileged partner of the medical practice. Its computerisation has many consequences on the medical actors and their organisation. As the study of their practises show that documents are the most adapted support to handle medical knowledge during the care, we affirm that a documentary approach is adapted to build interfaces in adequacy with the various uses. In addition, we propose the integration of a particular documentary functionality: annotations. Indeed, from now on, the tools of annotation are common. Most of the word processing software and the collaborative software include functionalities of annotations. Moreover, practitioners already annotate the paper documents of the MR. Consequently, such functionality in the EMR seems natural. The originality of our work comes from the way we exploit these annotations to make easier the handlings of the electronic documents and the communications. The tests realised by the practitioners on the tool developed by our team, validate our assumption that an annotation tool is useful for their care mission. About the theoretical prospects, we foresee to generalise our definitions with contexts broader than the MR because experts use annotations in many others fields as genetics, architecture... We also need to study more precisely the impact of the change of medium on this practice, by considering the fact that it is possible to make non-linguistic annotations (diagrams, video, audio...) in the complex multimedia documents.

Acknowledgements

We thank Physician G. Krim, in charge of the Unit of pediatric intensive care and neonatal medicine (CHU of Amiens), for his hospitality.

References

[1] S. Bringay, C. Barry and J. Charlet, Annotations for managing knowledge in the Electronic Health Record, In Proceeding Workshop Knowledge Management and Organizational Memories IJCAI-2005, Edinburgh (Scotland), July 30 - August 05 (2005).
[2] A. Rabarijaona, R. Dieng, O. Corby and R. Ouaddari, Building a Xml-based Corporate Memory, IEEE Intelligent Systems Special Issue on Knowledge Management and Internet (2000), 56-63.
[3] S. Bringay, C. Barry and J. Charlet, The Health Record: Kernel of a Medical Memory. In Proceeding of the Workshop Knowledge management and organisational memories ECAI-2004, Valencia (Spain), August 23-27 (2004).
[4] W. Pratt, M.C. Reddy, D.W. McDonald, P. Tarczy-Hornoch and J.H. Gennari, Incorporating ideas from computer-supported cooperative work, Journal of Biomedical Informatics 37 (2004), 128-137.
[5] M. Hartswood, R. Procter, M. Rouncefield and R. Slack, Making a Case in Medical Work: Implications for Electronic Medical Record, Computer Supported Cooperative Work 12 (2003), 241-266.

[6] B. Fields and E. Duncker, Articulating Resources: The Impact of Electronic Health Records on Cross-Professional Healthcare Work, Technical Report of the Interaction Design Centre: IDC-TR-2003-002, December (2003). http://www.cs.mdx.ac.uk/research/idc/papers/IDC-TR-2003-002.pdf

[7] D.A. Travers and S.M. Downs, Comparing the user acceptance of a computer system in two pediatric offices: A qualitative study, In American Medical Informatics Association Symposium AMIA-2000, Los Angeles (USA), November 4-8 (2000), 853-7.

[8] BL. Goddard, Termination of a contract to implement an enterprise electronic Medical Record system, Journal of the American Medical Informatics Association 7(6) (2000), 564-8.

[9] JG. Lenhart, K. Honess, D. Covington and K. Johnson, An analysis of trends, perceptions, and use patterns of electronic Medical Records among US family practice residency programs. Family Medecine Journal 32(2) (2000), 109-14.

[10] R. Dieng-Kuntz, O. Corby, F. Gandon, A. Giboin, J. Golebiowska, N. Matta and M. Ribière, Méthodes et outils pour la gestion des connaissances : une approche pluridisciplinaire du Knowledge Management, 2ème Éditions Dunod, ISBN 2 10 006300 6, (2001).

[11] Decortis, F., Noirfalise, S., Saudelli, B. (2000) Distributed cognition as framework for cooperative work.

[12] Hollan, J., Hutchins, E., Kirsh, D. (2000) Distributed cognition: toward a new foundation for human-computer interaction research. ACM Transactions on Computer-Human Interaction , 7 (2), 174-196.

[13] Suchman, L.A. (1987). Plans and Situated Actions: The Problem of Human-Machine Communication. Cambridge: Cambridge Press.

[14] Bannon L., Bødker S. Beyond the interface: Encountering artifacts in use. In: J.Carroll (ed.): Designing Interaction: Psychology at the Human-Computer Interface. Cambridge: Cambridge University Press 1991, pp. 227-253.

[15] K. Schmidt, Cooperative work and its articulation: requirements for computer support, Le Travail Humain 57 (1994), 345-366.

[16] N. Bricon-Souf, F. Anceaux, N. Bennani, E. Dufresne and L. Watbled, A distributed coordination platform for home care: analysis, framework and prototype, International Journal of Medical Informatics 74 (2005), 809-825.

[17] F. Détienne, Collaborative design: managing task interdependencies ad multiple perspectives, Interacting with computers, In press (2005), 1-20.

[18] J.M. Hoc, From human-machine interaction to human-machine cooperation, Ergonomics 43 (2000), 833-843.

[19] J.M. Hoc, Towards a cognitive approach to human-machine cooperation in dynamic situations, International Journal of Human-Computer Studies 54 (2001), 509-540.

[20] K. Schmidt and L. Bannon, Taking CSCW Seriously: Supporting Articulation Work. Computer Supported Cooperative Work: The Journal of Collaborative Computing 1(1), 7-40.

[21] G. de Terssac and C. Chabaud, Référentiel opératif commun et fiabilité, in J. Leplat, G. de Terssac (Eds.), Les Facteurs Humains de la Fiabilité Dans les Systèmes Complexes, (1990).

[22] L. Bannon and S. Bødker, Constructing Common Information Spaces. In European Conference on Computer Supported Cooperative Work ECSCW'97, September 7-11 (1997).

[23] U. Pankoke-Babatz, W. Prinz and L. Schaffer, Stories about Asynchronous Awarenes, In F. Darses, R. Dieng, C. Simone, M. Zacklad (Eds.): Cooperative Systems Design - Scenario-Based Design of Collaborative Systems, IOS Press (2004), 23-38.

[24] M. Zacklad, Documents for Action (DofA): infrastructures for Distributed Collective Practices. Proceedings of the workshop Distributed Collective Practice: Building new Directions for Infrastructural Studies CSCW-2004, Chicago (USA), November 6-10 (2004).

[25] M. Berg, C. Langenberg, IVD. Berg and JK. Kwakkernaat, Considerations for socio-technical design: experiences with an electronic patient record in a clinical context. International Journal of Medical Informatics 52, (1998), 243-51.

[26] M. Berg and Els. Goorman, The contextual nature of medical information, International Journal of Medical Informatics 56, (1999), 51-60.

[27] B. Bachimont, Dossier et lecture hypertextuelle : problématique et discussion : Exemple autour du dossier patient. Les cahiers du numérique, special issue of the revue Information médicale numérique 2/2, P. Le Beux et D. Boullier, (2001), 105-123.

[28] C. Gutwin and S. Greenberg, Workspace awareness for groupware, CHI-96, Companion Proceedings of the ACM SIGCHI-96 Conference on Human Factors in Computing System, Vancouver (Canada), ACM Press, New York, April 13–18 (1996), 208-209.

[29] M. Reddy, W. Pratt, P. Dourish and M. Shabot, Socio-technical requirements analysis for clinical system methods, Methods of Information in Medicine, 42 (2003), 437-444.

[30]   J. H. Gennari, C. Weng, J. Benedetti and D. W. McDonald, Asynchronous communication among clinical researchers: A study for systems design, International Journal of Medical Informatics 74 (2005), 797-807.

[31]   E.T. Diamadis and G.C. Polyzos, Efficient cooperative searching on the Web: system design and evaluation, International Journal of Human-Computer Studies 61, (2004), 699-724.

[32]   M. Divitini, and B.A. Farshchian, Collaboration and coordination through basic internet tools: a case study. CSCW-98, Workshop on Internet-based Groupware for User Participation in Product Development, Seattle (USA), November 14-18 (1998).

[33]   K.M. Everitt, S.R. Klemmer, R. Lee and J.A. Landay, Two worlds apart: bridging the gap between physical and virtuel media for distributed design collaboration CHI-2003, Ft. Landerdale USA, April 5-10 (2003).

[34]   P.H. Carstensen and K. Schmidt, Computer supported cooperative work: new challenges to systems design. In Kenji, I. (Ed.), Handbook of Human Factors/Ergonomics, Asakura Publishing, Tokyo (Japon), (2003), 619-636.

[35]   M. Reddy, P. Dourish and W. Pratt, Coordinating Heterogeneous Work: Information and Representation in Medical Care. In European Conference on Computer Supported CooperativeWork ECSCW-01, Bonn (Germany), (2001), 239-58.

[36]   F. Chahuneau, C. Lécluse, B. Stiegler and J. Virbel, Prototyping the Ultimate Tool for Scholarly Qualitative Research on Texts. Proceedings of the 8th Annual Conference New Oxford English Dictionary, Waterloo (Canada), October 18-20 (1992).

[37]   E. Churchill, J. Trevor, S. Bly, L. Nelson and D. Cubranic, Anchored Conversations. Chatting in the Context of a Document. Proceedings of Conference on Humans Factors in Computing Systems CHI-2000, The Hague (Netherlands), April 1-6 (2000), 454-461.

[38]   L. Denoue, P. Chiu and T. Fuse, Shared Freeform Input for Note Taking across Devices. Proceedings of Humans Factors in Computing Systems, Fort Lauderdale (Florida), April 5-10 (2003), 794-795.

[39]   G. Golovchinsky, Emphasis on the relevant: Free-form Electronic Ink as a mechanism for relevance feedback, Proceedings of RIAO2000 Recherche d'Information Assistée par Ordinateur (Computer-Assisted Information Retrieval), Paris (France), April 12-14 (2000), 180-1995.

[40]   M.R. Koivunen and R. Swick, Metadata Based Annotation Infrastructure offers Flexibility and Extensibility for Collaborative Applications and Beyond. Presentation for the WorkShop K-CAP International Conference on Knowledge Capture, Victoria B.C (Canada), October 21-23 (2001).

[41]   B. Bachimont, Arts et sciences du numérique : ingénierie des connaissances et critique de la raison   computationnelle.   Habilitation   report,   (2004). http://www.utc.fr/~bachimon/Livresettheses_attachments/HabilitationBB.pdf

[42]   B. Stiegler, Annotation, navigation, édition électronique : vers une géographie des connaissances, Ec/arts, n°2, (2000).

[43]   S. Bringay, C. Barry and J. Charlet, Evolution of a functionality of annotations in an electronic health record, DocPatient project report, August (2005).

Cooperative Systems Design
P. Hassanaly et al. (Eds.)
IOS Press, 2006

Pair programming and the re-appropriation of individual tools for collaborative software development

Sallyann BRYANT, Pablo ROMERO and Benedict DU BOULAY
IDEAS Laboratory, University of Sussex, United Kingdom

Abstract. Although pair programming is becoming more prevalent in software development, and a number of reports have been written about it [10] [13], few have addressed the manner in which pairing actually takes place [12]. Even fewer consider the methods used to manage issues such as role change or the communication of complex issues. This paper highlights the way resources designed for individuals are re-appropriated and augmented by pair programmers to facilitate collaboration. It also illustrates that pair verbalisations can augment the benefits of the collocated team, providing examples from ethnographic studies of pair programmers 'in the wild'.

Keywords: Pair Programming, Collaboration, Artifacts, Software development.

Introduction

Collaborative programming is common in the commercial world, a fact that is borne out if one considers the regularity with which more than one programmer is seen at a computer terminal working on a debugging problem, assisting in design or simply providing 'another set of eyes'. One form of collaborative programming has been formalised as 'pair programming', one of the twelve core practices of the eXtreme Programming (XP) methodology. XP is classed as an 'agile' methodology, explained [4] as valuing:

> "Individuals and interactions over processes and tools
> Working software over comprehensive documentation
> Customer collaboration over contract negotiation
> Responding to change over following a plan."

In pair programming, "all production code is written with two people working at one machine, with one keyboard and one mouse" [3]. Two roles have been identified, the "driver", who is currently using the peripherals to manipulate the computer, and the "navigator", who contributes to the task verbally (and more subtley in other ways, as shown later). Typical reports by practitioners talk about these roles in two ways. First, the navigator is seen as providing a 'constant design and code review' [36] by observing the work of the driver (see also [37] and [38]). Second, the navigator is considered to be thinking at a higher level of abstraction than the driver, considering strategic issues, such as 'how the code that is being written fits in with the overall design' [37] while the driver is involved in the tactical process of writing the code (see also [3]). These two themes are also seen in some of the academic pair programming literature. For example [33] talks of the navigator 'looking for...defects' and claims that he/she is the 'strategic, long-range thinker' while the driver 'is typing at the computer'. These reports also assume that a pair will work together for the whole of an assigned task or for a pre-determined amount of time.

A number of studies have considered the costs and benefits of pair programming [7] [18] [21] [22], and several experience reports have suggested that working collaboratively assists in producing better quality software, improving communications, facilitating knowledge transfer and increasing enjoyment [33]. Some studies have considered why this might be; Flor and Hutchins [12] suggest that when collaborating on software maintenance it is more likely that the correct plan will be chosen.   Williams, Kessler et al. [33] suggest 'pair pressure' assists in focusing developers. However, none of these studies have closely considered how the roles of driver and navigator are dynamically realised and facilitated by the artifacts, environment and language used by the pair.

This paper uses the results of four, one-week studies of pairs of commercial programmers. It draws on a detailed ethnographic account to highlight how pair programming is practically accomplished, in particular focusing on how tools are re-purposed and used alongside dialogue to facilitate role management and communication.

The first part of this paper discusses the existing literature on representations and artifacts in software development, considers the methodology used in the studies and gives an overview of the teams observed. Peripheral awareness is discussed and it becomes clear that the benefits generally attributed to collocation are further facilitated by the transparency provided as a result of pair programmers verbalising. The paper then focuses in on the pair. In particular we consider the phenomenon by which tools explicitly designed for individual use are re-appropriated by the programming pair and instead used to assist collaboration. The conclusion then situates this work and suggests future directions.

1. Representations and Artifacts in Software Development

There is evidence that external representations and artifacts play an important role in software development. At a general level, Ackerman and Halverson [1] suggest that any organisation's memory is constructed and maintained by both people and artifacts and Schmidt and Simone [40] highlight the use of artifacts for coordination. More specifically, Gilmore and Green [14] suggest that external elements play an important role in a software developer's mental model. Similarly Davies [9] shows that experts often rely on their tools to compensate for the limitations of working memory. This approach may go some way to explaining why the role of tools and artifacts may be an important one in ensuring "accurate and effective communication about a product no-one can see" [24]. Work by Grinter [34] and de Souza and Redmiles [35] among others has considered the challenges and tools required for team coordination of software development, however we consider the commercial programming pair and the special role of representations and artifacts with regards to communication and role management.

Comparing self-ratings of pair programming ability with those of peers and managers from pre-assessment questionnaires from the studies reported here suggests that these skills are far from obvious to the practitioner [39]. In fact, experienced pair programmers were more likely to under-rate their ability to work in pairs and those who are inexperienced were likely to be over-confident about their ability to work collaboratively.

2. Study Methodology

The methodology used for this work is ethnographically informed, based on observational studies supplemented with informal interviews, photographic and video evidence of artifact use and the verbal protocol analysis of transcribed sessions. As an experienced commercial software developer, the lead author feels that this facilitated acceptance in the field, however she is also aware that her own experience may lead to different focus than, for example, a social anthropologist may have had (similar issues are reported in Sharp, Robinson et al [29]). In addition, although disruptions were kept to a minimum, the developers were being recorded in order to further analyse their interactions, therefore one should consider the impact of this on their behaviour.

An opportunistic sampling method was used, as there are only a limited number of companies available for study, however only sessions with programmers of at least six month's commercial pair programming experience are considered in this report as a pilot study [6] indicated that pair programmers without this level of experience behave somewhat differently. The data gathered for this paper originates from field notes, informal interviews, photographs, recorded sessions and observations during the studies.

The method used was inspired by the work of Grinter [41] and based on Grounded theory [15]. Grounded theory helps to ensure a solid foundation for hypotheses by basing them on observational studies in the real world. The methodology has also been greatly influenced by the work of Chi [42] who puts forward a compelling argument for analysing qualitative data in a quantifiable manner as a method of integrating the two approaches. Instances reported below relate to themes consistently seen in the data unless otherwise specified. In addition, all of the sessions were recorded in digital audio and three captured on video. These recordings were transcribed and combined with the field notes, informal interviews and photographs to create a rich picture of the interactions from each session. Where possible, examples of actual occurrences are given.

3. Teams Observed

The data was collected from four, one-week studies of pairs of experienced programmers (those with at least six month's continual commercial experience of pairing) in four different companies. All the companies used an agile approach [4], and several of them used eXtreme Programming [3]. The studies took place in the workplace, with the programmers working on typical tasks. The profiles of the sessions are shown in Table 1.

Table 1. Profiles of sessions observed

	Number of projects considered	Number of pair programming sessions considered	Agile/XP development approach?
Banking	1	3	Yes
Banking	4	12	Yes
Entertainment	2	10	Yes
Mobile communications	2	11	Yes

36 sessions were observed, transcribed and analysed. Each session was an hour long and a total of 45 programmers participated in the studies. As pair composition switched frequently and the organization of pairs and their work was not impacted by the studies, some individuals were observed in more than one pair. However, any particular pair was observed working together for 2 one-hour sessions and any individual a maximum of four times. In total 18 different pair combinations were observed.

4. A Typical Pair Programming Session

This section describes a typical pair programming session. The day begins with a stand-up meeting. Each pair gives an overview of what they worked on yesterday and any issuesthey encountered. Areas where one task might impact on another are identified. The pairs in the team consider the outstanding tasks and decide which to work on next. A task will usually take about one full 'ideal' programming day to complete. In some cases this will mean continuing to work as a pair on a task not yet completed, but in other cases there may be some negotiation. Here, John and Mary continue working on yesterday's unfinished task.

Once the meeting is finished, they agree to work at John's desk. As the team all pair program, the desks are set out with room for two chairs to fit side by side in front of the large screen. They spend some time discussing progress and decide that now that they have completed writing the automated test script that will prove their code works once it is done, they can get on with the writing the code itself. Mary remembers that there was an outstanding issue and they have a discussion with the allocated business 'customer' in order to clarify the requirement. Once resolved, John pushes the keyboard over to Mary and suggests "you drive". Mary starts up the Integrated Development Environment that the team use and it opens up two initial views. One view shows the suite of automated tests, including the one that they wrote yesterday. The second view shows the system source code, organized into classes and their methods. It is here that the new code will be written.

As they start working, they discuss the approach they are going to take on each sub-task together before continuing. Often they draw informal sketches, type a piece of example code or point at something on the screen. They switch seamlessly between views and often transfer the keyboard and mouse between them, sometimes with utterances like 'show me what you mean' and sometimes simply indicating their intention to change roles with a gesture. Occasionally, whoever is navigating picks out a typing mistake or syntax error. At one stage Peter, who is working nearby, overhears them discussing an issue that they are having problems solving. Peter knows about this area and they have a three-way discussion. Occasionally one of the pair overhears their name being mentioned by another pair and gets involved in another issue. When there are short breaks in the development task, perhaps while the test suite is running or completed code is being integrated, they take the opportunity to have a break, a social chat or check their email.

Once the code is complete and the test suite runs successfully, Mary picks up a fluffy toy from on top of the integration machine and places it on top of their terminal to show that they are integrating their code with the most recent version of the whole system. This signals to the rest of the team that they should not be making changes at the same time. Once the code is copied across, a full set of integration tests are successfully run, and they place a green sticker on their paper task card and stick it back on the progress chart.

5. Role Management, Communication and Transparency

As shown in the previous section, a typical pair programming session has many subtleties beyond the formal 'driver' and 'navigator' roles described in the XP literature. In fact, the pair programming session takes place in the context of a rich environment of artifacts and talk. Although 'artifacts have been in use for coordination purposes...for centuries' [40], here tools for individual software development are re-appropriated and combined with verbalization to assist in fluid resource and role management and the communication of complex technical issues. Conversations between the pair and specially assigned tokens with mutually agreed meanings provide transparency to the rest of the project about what the pair are doing as a means of highlighting any dependencies or potential areas for knowledge sharing. These issues are addressed individually in detail below.

6. Pair Utterances Assisting Peripheral Awareness

All of the teams studied worked in open-plan environments. This approach to team collocation has been seen to be highly effective. For example Teasley et al. [32] found this approach doubled productivity in terms of function points produced, and took only one third of the time to get to market. This type of layout allows a team to 'overhear' each other and pick up on useful or relevant information. This phenomenon is similar to that reported between journalists [17] but is facilitated by the fact that pair programming demands a high level of verbal communication and therefore renders transparent much information which might be hidden in a more traditional software development environment. In fact, through verbal protocol analysis of one of the four studies included in this paper, pair programmers were shown to produce more than 250 verbal interactions per pair programming hour [6].

This paper also shows that experienced pair programmers produced 27% fewer interactions per hour than those with less pairing experience. Observation suggests that with experience one might become more selective about interactions, better able to make assumptions about ones partner, more successful at using the environment and better able to negotiate a mutually agreeable way forward. Preliminary findings also suggest that, contrary to the XP literature, a pair work at the same level of abstraction, irrelevant of role.

'Overhearing' a pairs verbalizations not only allows a third party to tune in to relevant conversations from surrounding pairs (see Figure 2), but also allows a developer to highlight information that might be relevant to others (see Figure 1). Figures 1 and 2 below provides anonymised examples from different pair programming sessions where Zoe is used as the name of the project member who is external and Andrew and Betty are the names used for members of the pair.

Andrew: Because it'll fail won't it?
Betty: Yeah…that was in…(sighs)…package one wasn't it? And it's not here, so it needs to
              go into package two I think.
Andrew: OK, so that's something we can make (raises voice) Zoe aware of.
Zoe: What's that?
Andrew: Ummm…something which was, I think in (package name), which has just
              been abolished.
Zoe: Right, yeah. It's going to be constantly evolving unfortunately, isn't it?

Figure 1. Example of proximity facilitating peripheral awareness through name-dropping

Andrew: Reporting requirements…oh yeah.
Betty: Whenever he's free we're…
Zoe (overhearing): He's free now.
Andrew: Is he?!

Figure 2. Example of proximity facilitating peripheral awareness through over-hearing

On occasions overhearing triggers episodes where a third party joins the pair. In some cases, where the problem required specialist knowledge that the pair did not have, a pair change is negotiated. This allows the developer who had overheard to become part of the pair working on that problem. This fluid re-pairing is contrary to the static, formal nature of pair allocation typically described in the pair programming literature.

7. The Re-appropriation and Augmentation of Solo Software Development Artifacts

This section identifies a number of artifacts, designed for and usually used by individuals, which are re-appropriated or augmented for collaborative use and play an intrinsic role in pair programming. In particular, these artifacts assist in the dynamic negotiation of driver and navigator roles, assist within-pair communication, render work visible and help assure that the programming pair are maintaining a common mental model of the task at hand.

7.1. Keyboard

The keyboard, designed as a solo data input device, consistently became the primary token for 'floor control' - possession of the keyboard signalled who was in the 'driver' role and who was 'navigating'. This is an example of constraints being built into the tools [20] as complications from having both programmers simultaneously editing code are avoided. The keyboard was often used to indicate intention of role change: the driver might slide the keyboard over to the navigator to suggest an exchange of roles, sometimes with an accompanying utterance (see Figure 3 for an example). Interestingly, although relinquishing control of the keyboard in this way seemed acceptable, initiating control of the keyboard was rare. That is, the keyboard was often 'offered and accepted' but very rarely 'taken without offering'.

> **Andrew:** If you...go to...
> **Betty:** (sliding the keyboard over to him) (You) drive...it's easier.

Figure 3. An example of dialogue during keyboard hand-over.

As well as being used for both it's traditional role and as a token for 'floor control', the keyboard also assisted intra-pair verbal communication. One of the methods by which the object of conversation might be highlighted is by use of the keyboards cursor keys. This seemed to take place for a number of reasons including: avoiding the overhead for the driver of switching to another medium; overcoming difficulties with mouse control/dexterity; ensuring accuracy of communication and allowing multi-modal pointing (one partner could highlight with the keyboard while the other used her finger).

7.2. Mouse

Despite also being designed as a solo data-entry device, the mouse was used as a collaborative resource. Control of the mouse was less formal than the keyboard and while in the majority of cases, the driver would control the mouse and the keyboard, in three of the sessions this was not at all the case. It was not uncommon across sessions for the navigator to lean over and use the mouse to 'point' at something on the screen, rather than pointing with their finger or describing the target of interest verbally (see Figure 4 for an example). Presumably this was to avoid both the physical inconvenience of finger-pointing and the time and cognitive load associated with verbally describing.

> **Andrew:** ...just test it...and that means you don't have to start faffing about with this...
> (uses mouse to point at screen)
> **Betty:**   Yeah...I know.

Figure 4. An example of navigator use of the mouse for pointing
(Betty is driving and Andrew is navigating)

In two cases, a wireless mouse was placed on the desk between the two programmers and used as a communal resource to point at and highlight code during discussions, and to position the cursor. This was possible because the pair were close enough to easily reach the mouse with the appropriate hand. Interestingly, neither pair had any difficulty coordinating mouse or cursor control although this was never discussed or mentioned during observations.

7.2.1. Surrogate mouse

In one session a small ball of paperclips was used as a very informal role control mechanism. Assume the programmer using the paperclips is called B and his pairing partner is A. When A was the driver, B (currently the navigator) would take up the paperclips and make movements and finger-twitches similar to those that the driver was making with the actual mouse. When B wished to assume the role of driver he would let go of the paperclips as a signal to A, who would then relinquish control of the mouse (and keyboard). Once finished as the driver, B then let go of the mouse and once more picked up the paperclips, at which point A almost immediately took up the driver role (and the mouse) once more. Use of the surrogate mouse can be seen in Figure 5.

Figure 5. The surrogate mouse

7.3. Interactive Development Environment (IDE)

The code itself played an important role in communication and did not seem to be merely the driver's 'translation' of the collaborative effort. For example, on occasions a period of silence did not indicate the end of an interaction. Sometimes verbal communication between the two programmers would trail off and the interaction would be continued by the driver typing at the keyboard. This was clearly the case where the navigator interjected using agreement protocols normally reserved for conversations (e.g. Uttering "mmmn' or' yes' or 'uh huh'). Examples of this type of interaction are shown in Figure 6.

Andrew:	A slightly different side. That's got a…(types code)
Betty:	Uh huh
(later)	
Betty:	Yeah, I think so. Yeah it makes it easier to write accessor methods as well, I think, if you do…(types code)
Andrew:	Yeah
Betty:	OK, so that's cool

Figure 6. Examples of the code being used to continue conversation

Often the target piece of code being referred to would be identified via pointing as previously discussed. In such cases, the distributed cognition afforded by this representation often led to underspecified statements, as reported elsewhere [12]. An example of this is given in Figure 7, where '*this*' and '*that*' are used to refer to parts of the code being pointed at in a variety of manners (emphasis added).

Andrew:	Err…get *this* version of *that*….so *that*'s got *that*….so it's come through *there* now.
Betty:	So if you try and run *that* through *there* now.
Andrew:	Is *this* a problem?
Betty:	*That* should be included in the project.
Andrew:	Yeah

Figure 7. An example of the code being used to supplement verbalisation

The Interactive Development Environment (IDE) that was being used facilitated this form of interaction by providing a readily visible and comprehensible representation of the program for both parties. The physical layout of the screen and the programming pair ensured that this representation could be easily read by both and referred to by gesturing either using the mouse or keyboard, or by physically pointing at the screen. On occasions the IDE actually initiated a 'conversation'. This was particularly evident when, for example, the programmers' attention was drawn to an error that had been introduced by a 'red light' appearing next to a particular automated test. This representation would trigger a conversation between the programmers and often initiate a new episode of problem solving.

8. Other Artifacts in New Roles

The role of diagrams and other paper-based external representations in software development is well-documented and key to many development methodologies. The documented benefits of diagrams are many, including their ability to "show complexity in a simple, retainable form" [11], to disambiguate mental representations [8] and to assist in offload, ease problem solving and provide constraints [28].

One of the core values of agile projects is the focus on working software rather than documentation. In particular, the XP methodology downplays the role of system architecture diagrams. Each of the projects observed had some communal representations posted up either in the physical project space (in three of the four companies) or on the intranet (in one of them). The role of these representations seemed to be in allowing the wider implications of a pair's work to be visible and to provide a means of facilitating communication across pairs and ensuring an understanding of the system as a whole.

In addition to these 'project representations', a form of informal, paper-based representation was produced or used during nearly every session observed. These were either informal sketches or lists. Sketches were widely used, they featured in 20 of the 36 sessions observed. These sketches were highly informal (e.g. Figure 8) and in some cases near illegible. This was considered preferable to using more formal or communal diagrams. For example, one programmer suggested "if it's pre-drawn you feel like there's nothing you can contribute", and another that "it feels more comfortable than an official document".

While the representations appeared useful in facilitating communication, the extent to which the non-sketching partner engaged differed widely. On some occasions these representations seemed to be produced to clarify the thoughts of the programmer doing the sketching, and in one particular case, the 'sketch' was merely traced on the table with a finger. In an informal interview, one programmer referred to these diagrams as "like a brain-dump" and another stated "If I scribble it down I can find out if I'm thinking absolute rubbish". This implies that such sketches may at best be playing a highly ephemeral role in communication with the partner, or be used as part of the pragmatics of the interaction (for emphasis, say), or may simply be acting as a cognitive aid for one member of the pair. If this is the intention, then their role may be simply to lower the load on working memory and assist in discovering inferences as documented in [31] or to attempt to externally work with very rich, multi-dimensional models [25].

Where both parties appeared to engage with the representation, its role seemed to be to highlight structure or logic regarding how things related to each other. In one session a timeline was drawn to show the relationship between three conceptual dates and in another a diagram was produced to show how one code method called a number of other sub-routines. Interview data suggests that these were used to assist communication: "It helps communication better than just talking", "Some things are hard to articulate…so it gives you a common diagrammatic language". See Figure 9 for an example of a verbal exchange about creating an informal representation. However, the usefulness of diagrams was considered limited, with comments such as "Between a pair it's easier to just whack out a piece of code" or "You work in small mini-steps, so you can keep it all in your head".

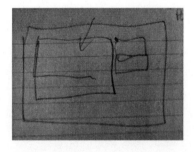

Figure 8. An example informal external representation

Andrew: Oh god (laughs)…Shall we draw the hierarchy?
Betty: Mmn.
Andrew: Because it's…it's more than just one.
Betty: It's loads isn't it.

Figure 9. An example exchange about creating an external representation

Lists were mainly produced as an aide memoire. They were produced in mutual view and both partners often contributed, either at the time the list was produced, or when additional items required adding later. Usually these lists were created in a programmer's personal 'day book' (a kind of diary for each day) or on a separate sheet of paper. In one case items were noted on post-it notes and stuck to the screen. This fits findings by Adelson and Soloway [2], who found that experienced software engineers tend to work in a roughly hierarchical manner, taking notes if something comes to their attention which is not at the current level of detail.

Figure 10 shows an example of the type of list produced. As is obvious from the degree of informality, these lists do not seem to be produced for anyone other that the pair who produce them. Informal interview data shows that they represent more of a check-list, for personal assurance that all the necessary sub-tasks are complete before a piece of work is deemed finished. However, in one case a programmer claimed that they would be useful for another pair who might later work on the same or a similar task. Interestingly, while a number of these lists were produced, they were rarely referred back to and 'checked off' in the sessions that were observed, and never seen to be transferred from one pair to another. This implies that their value might lie more in their creation than in their persistence. Perhaps their very existence was enough of a 'memory jog' without a need to refer to them.

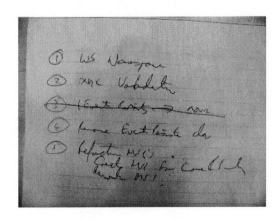

Figure 10. An example list

8.1. Toys

On three of the projects, soft toys were used as tokens. A programming pair would collect the token toy and place it on top of their computer terminal to indicate that they were currently loading new code onto the integration machine. Essentially these tokens were an informal 'locking mechanism' for integration. In fact they were so informal that their effectiveness relied entirely on members of the project understanding and conforming to their rules of use. This is interesting as a more formal, technology based locking mechanism might just as easily have been put in place. It is also contrary to an example in Rogers and Ellis [26], showing that software developers were inconsistent in using a manual whiteboard system for file locking as this was extraneous to their work activities.

In keeping with a number of studies, the physical presence of the toy and the manner by which it is manipulated may play an important role in alerting others to peripheral events which might be of interest (in this case use of the integration machine). This is consistent with studies of news rooms, police operations, traffic control centres and operating theatres, by Heath, Sanchez, Svensson et al. [17] in which participants were seen to "design and produce actions to render features of their conduct selectively available to others" and "encourage another..without interrupting what they are doing, to...notice something..which may have to be dealt with". Robertson [27] stresses the human ability of peripheral awareness as particularly pertinent to this phenomenon. In the pair programming teams, each team member is given the opportunity to notice the change in integration machine control by the action of the developer retrieving the toy. If this is not attained, the toy's placement on top of the developer's monitor is still continually available to the team.

9. Discussion

The account above has given a rich picture of how pair programming is practically achieved. In particular we have focused on the augmented role of artifacts and talk with regards to role management and communication within and outside of the programming pair.

9.1. Role Management

Whereas the XP literature suggests that the roles of 'driver' and 'navigator' have specific properties regarding focus and level of abstraction, little has been written about the management of these roles. The observational studies discussed have shown that the roles not only do not appear as formal in nature as is suggested, but also that they are managed in a number of subtle ways, and practically realised via the interplay of verbalizations and the re-appropriation of traditional software development tools. The keyboard in particular has an important role to play in managing the relationship between driver and navigator. While it might be considered preferable to provide a separate keyboard for each programmer, in fact the use of a single shared keyboard facilitates role management by enforcing a method of floor control and providing an informal means of negotiating role change-over. It also becomes a common reference, embodying a set of social rules for changing role. For example, one can now relinquish the role of driver but not take it without being offered simply by following a known social protocol for physical items - one is not accustomed to 'snatching' an item that is being used by someone else. More subtly, alternative tokens like the 'surrogate mouse' might be used to facilitate role change by implying a request to drive in a socially acceptable manner.

9.2. Within Pair Communication

Software development is a taxing task. One might consider that the overhead of communicating at the same time as producing software would be cognitively exhausting. The studies considered show that a mixture of verbalizations and artifacts work together to lessen this cognitive load, and in fact, produce tools that not only assist pair communication, but may also help an individual programmer.

The manner in which the programming pair combine verbalizations, gestures, the use of mouse, keyboard, the code and the IDE, external representations and other tokens and seamlessly weave these many artifacts together as a means of communication is nothing short of amazing. In addition to using this rich array of 'props', the pair programmers observed had an implicit understanding of the role and appropriateness of each item and it's role as a method of communication. Only on one occasion, where a partner was less able to physically manipulate the mouse, was this management of resources explicitly discussed.

9.3. Extra-Pair Communication

One of the additional benefits of the verbalizations required to successfully program in a pair is the transparency this lends to the work the pair is engaged in. Traditionally, the work of an individual programmer has little visibility to the rest of the team. However, where a pair is actively discussing their work in an open-plan environment they can easily be overheard by others. This provides opportunities to easily identify potential dependencies, conflicts or areas where assistance might be provided. Where additional attention needs to be drawn to an issue, a pair may raise their voices, or 'name drop' the person whose attention they wish to gain. On occasions a more formal mechanism for gaining attention is required. For example, when integrating new code onto the existing code base, three out of the four projects observed used a soft toy to indicate control of the integration machine.

These studies show pair programmers interacting seamlessly within a rich environment, using artifacts and verbalizations to assist in collaboration within the pair and provide transparency outside the pair. Most interestingly, a number of the tools used to assist with collaboration were initially created for individual use and have been re-appropriated to embody additional constraints or skills which are now required. Perhaps the key to understanding expertise in pair programming lies in acknowledging the skills required to actively situate oneself and interact with fluency within this rich environment.

Conclusion

The analysis draws on ethnographic data in the form of field notes, photographs, video sessions, audio tapes and transcriptions to begin to describe an ecology within which pair programming takes place in four organisations observed. It focuses on the use of artifacts and speech as a mean of easing some of the challenges faced by the pairs, particularly regarding role management and the communication of technical information.

It highlights some of the ways pair programmers facilitate collaboration by re-appropriating or augmenting existing 'solo' tools or by using everyday artifacts in novel ways. It shows some of the rich and subtle ways in which pair programmers communicate and indicates that the verbalisations produced can make activities more transparent and accentuate the benefits of the 'war-room' type environment. Further verbal protocol analysis work is currently being done to analyze these verbalizations with regards to their level of abstraction, the contribution of new information by each partner and the decision making process.

The table below is a summary of the artifacts in question, and the activities they appeared to facilitate:

Table 2. Summary of the roles of artifacts and the activities they facilitate

	Role management	Within pair communication	Extra-pair communication
Verbalisation	√	√	√
Keyboard	√	√	
Mouse		√	
Code		√	
ERs		√	
Tokens	√	√	√
IDE		√	
Gestures	√	√	

The analysis described above should help provide a clearer understanding of pair programming for those inexperienced in its use. The re-appropriation and augmentation of tools designed for individual use also suggests that programming pairs have some very specific extra requirements from their environments. While this 're-purposing' shows ingenuity and flexibility on the part of the programmers, it suggests that there is scope for the design of more specialised tools for use in collocated pair programming. To the authors' knowledge this has so far only been considered in distributed pair programming environments (e.g. the Additional hand cursor [16] and the Transparent Video Facetop [30]). One must question whether it would be more appropriate to provide specifically tailored tools for collocated collaborative software development rather than shoe-horning existing resources into collaborative use.

In addition, focus should be given to the skills involved in coordinating and manipulating the variety of tools and artifacts required when considering how to characterize an experienced pair programmer. Perhaps the lack of focus in this area provides some insight into the difficulties described in the introduction that have been seen in assessing ones own and others level of pair programming competence.

Acknowledgements

This work was undertaken as part of DPhil research funded by the EPSRC. The authors would like to thank the participating companies: BBC iDTV project, BNP Paribas, EGG and LogicaCMG.

References

[1] Ackerman, M. S. and Halverson, C. (1998). 'Considering an Organization's Memory'. *Proceedings of the 1998 conference on Computer supported cooperative work*, Seattle, Washington, United States: 39-48.

[2] Adelson, B. and E. Soloway (1988). A model of software design. *The nature of expertise*. M. Chi, R. Glaser and F. MJ. Hillsdale, New Jersey, Lawrence Erlbaum Associates: 185-208.

[3] Beck, K. (2000). *Extreme programming explained: Embrace change*, Addison Wesley.

[4] Beck, K., M. Beedle, et al. (2001) The Agile Manifesto. http://agilemanifesto.org

[5] Blackwell, A. (2002). 'What is programming?' 14th workshop of the Psychology of Programming Interest Group, Brunel, Middlesex, UK. J Kuljis, L. Baldwin & R. Scoble (eds): 204-218.

[6] Bryant, S. (2004). "Double trouble: Mixing quantitative and qualitative methods in the study of extreme programmers" Visual languages and human centric computing, Rome, Italy. IEEE Computer Society.

[7] Cockburn, A. and L. Williams (2001). 'The costs and benefits of pair programming'. *Extreme programming examined*. G. Succi and M. Marchesi, Addison Wesley: 223-243.

[8] Cox, R. (1999). 'Representation construction, externalised cognition and individual differences.' *Learning and instruction* 9: 343-363.

[9] Davies, S. (1993). 'Expertise and display-based strategies in computer programming'. *People and Computers VIII* - HCI '93 conference: 411-423.

[10] Dick, A. and B. Zarnett (2002). 'Paired programming and personality traits'. Third International Conference on eXtreme Programming and Agile Processes in Software Engineering, Alghero, Sardinia, Italy.

[11] Dogan, F. and N. Nersessian (2002). 'Conceptual diagrams: Representing ideas in design'. Second Internation Conference on Diagrammatic Representation and Inference, Callaway Gardens, GA, USA, Springer: 353-355.

[12] Flor, N. and E. Hutchins (1991). 'Analyzing distributed cognition in software teams'. *Empirical studies of programmers: Fourth workshop*, J. Koenemann-Belliveau, T. Moher and S. Robertson (eds). Ablex publishing corporation: 36-64.

[13] Gallis, H., E. Arisholm, et al. (2002). 'A transition from partner programming to pair programming - an Industrial Case Study'. Workshop: "Pair programming installed" at Object-oriented programming, systems, languages and applications (OOPSLA) 2002, Seattle, USA.

[14] Gilmore, D. and T. Green (1984). 'Comprehension and recall of miniature programs. *International Journal of Man-Machine Studies* 21(1): 31-48.

[15] Glaser, B and A. Strauss (1967). The discovery of grounded theory: Strategies for qualitative research. Hawthorne, New York, Aldine de Gruyter.

[16] Hanks, B. F. (2002) "Tool support for distributed pair programming". Workshop "Distributed pair programming, extreme programming and agile methods" at XP/Agile Universe 2002 , Chicago, USA.

[17] Heath, C., M. Sanchez Svensson, et al. (2002). 'Configuring awareness.' *Computer Supported Collaborative Work* 11: 317-347.

[18] Heilberg, S., U. Puus, et al. (2003). 'Pair-programming effect on developers productivity'. Fourth International conference on extreme programming and agile processes in software engineering. Springer-Verlag: 215-224.

[19] Holy, L. (1984). Theory, methodology and the research process. *Ethnographic research: A guide to general conduct*. R. Ellen (ed.). San Diego, CA, Academic Press: 12-34.

[20] Hutchins, E. (1995). *Cognition in the wild*. Cambridge, MA, The MIT Press.

[21] Jensen, R. (2003). 'A pair programming experience.' *The Journal of Defensive Software Engineering* 16(3): 22-24.

[22] Lui, K. and K. Chan (2003). 'When does a pair outperform two individuals?' *Fourth international conference in Extreme Programming and Agile Processes in Software Engineering.* Springer-Verlag: 225-233.

[23] Navrat, P. (1996). 'A closer look at programming expertise: critical survey of some methodological issues.' *Information and software technology* **38**: 37-46.

[24] Perry, D., N. Staudenmayer, et al. (1994). 'Understanding software development: Processes, organisations and technologies.' *IEEE software* **11**(4): 36-45.

[25] Petre, M. and A. Blackwell (1999). 'Mental imagery in program design and visual programming.' *International Journal of Human-Computer Studies* **51**: 7-30.

[26] Rogers, Y. and Ellis, J. (1994). 'Distributed cognition: an alternative framework for analysing and explaining collaborative working'. *Journal of Information technology* **9(2)**: 119-128.

[27] Robertson, T. (2002). 'The public availability of actions and artefacts'. *Computer Supported Collaborative Work* **11 (3-4)**, Kluwer Academic Publishers: 299-316.

[28] Scaife, M. and Y. Rogers (1996). 'External cognition: How do graphical representations work?' *International Journal of Human-Computer Studies* **45**: 185-213.

[29] Sharp, H., H. Robinson, et al. (2000). 'Using ethnography and discourse analysis to study software engineering practices'. *Twenty-second International conference on software engineering*, Limerick, Ireland.

[30] Stotts, D., J. McC.Smith et al (2004). "Support for distributed pair programming in the transparent video facetop". XP/Agile Universer 2004, Calgary, Canada. Springer Verlag.

[31] Suwa, M. and B. Tversky (2002). 'External representations contributing to the dynamic construction of ideas'. *Diagrammatic representation and inference.* M. Hegarty, B. Meyer and N. Narayan (eds): 341-343.

[32] Teasley, S., Covi, L., Krishnan, M.S. and Olson, J.S. (2000). 'How does radical collocation help a team succeed?', *Proceedings of the 2000 ACM conference on Computer supported cooperative work.* Philadelphia, Pennsylvania, United States: 339-346.

[33] Williams, L., R. Kessler, et al. (2000). 'Strengthening the case for pair programming.' *IEEE software* **17**(4): 19-25.

[34] Grinter, R. E. (1995). 'Using a configuration management tool to coordinate software development'. Proceedings of conference on Organizational computing systems: 168-177, August 13-16, 1995, Milpitas, California, United States.

[35] de Souza, C. R. B., Redmilles, D. F. and Dourish, P. (2003) 'Breaking the code', Moving between private and public work in collaborative software development'. Proceedings of the 2003 International ACM SIGGROUP conference on Supporting group work, November 09-12, 2003, Sanibel Island, Florida, USA.

[36] Wake, W. (2002). 'Extreme Programming Explored', Addison-Wesley, Boston, USA: 63.

[37] McBreen, P (2003), 'Questioning Extreme Programming', Addison-Wesley, Boston, USA: 80.

[38] Auer, K. and Miller, R. (2002), 'Extreme Programming Applied: Playing to win', Addison-Wesley, Boston, USA: 171.

[39] Bryant, S. (2005), 'Rating expertise in collaborative software development', 17th workshop of the Psychology of Programming Interest Group, Brighton.

[40] Schmidt, K. and Simone, C. (1996), 'Coordination mechanisms: Towards a conceptual foundation of CSCW systems design'. Computer Supported Cooperative Work: The Journal of Collaborative Computing. 5 (2-3). Kluwer Academic Publishers: 155-200.

[41] Grinter, R. (2001) From local to global coordination: Lessons from software reuse. International acmsiggroup conference on supporting group working.

[42] Chi, M. Quantifying qualitative analyses of verbal data: A practical guide. The journal of the learning sciences 6(3): 271-315. (1997).[18],

Cooperative Systems Design
P. Hassanaly et al. (Eds.)
IOS Press, 2006

Memetic:
An Infrastructure for Meeting Memory

Simon BUCKINGHAM SHUM [a1], Roger SLACK [b], Michael DAW [c], Ben JUBY [d],
Andrew ROWLEY [c], Michelle BACHLER [a], Clara MANCINI [a],
Danius MICHAELIDES [d], Rob PROCTER [b], David DE ROURE [d], Tim CHOWN [d],
Terry HEWITT [c]

[a] *Knowledge Media Institute, The Open University, UK*
[b] *School of Informatics, University of Edinburgh, UK*
[c] *Access Grid Support Centre, Manchester Computing, University of Manchester, UK*
[d] *Intelligence, Agents, Multimedia Group, School of Electronics and Computer Science*
University of Southampton, UK

Abstract. This paper introduces the Memetic toolkit for recording the normally ephemeral interactions conducted via internet video conferencing, and making these navigable and manipulable in linear and non-linear ways. We introduce two complementary interaction visualizations: argumentation-based concept maps to elucidate the conceptual structure of the discourse using a visual language, and interactive event timelines generated from the meeting metadata. We discuss in detail the affordances of Memetic's tools, in particular the *Compendium* hypermedia mapping tool, and the *Meeting Replay* tool that renders the semantic navigation indices into the videoconference replays. Additionally, with respect to methodology and evaluation, we describe how we are engaging diverse end-user communities in the process of designing and deploying these tools.

Introduction

'Meetings are where organizations come together. (They) remain the essential mechanism through which organizations create and maintain the practical activity of organizing. They are, in other words, the interaction order of management, the occasioned expression of management-in-action, that very social action through which institutions produce and reproduce themselves.'[1]

The meeting is a pervasive feature of everyday work life and, not surprisingly, there have been numerous attempts to support meeting activity with technology. Examples of previous work in this area include: Bush's [2] Memex – with its 'associative indexing' of texts and artifacts; Engelbart's [3] NLS /AUGMENT[2], which enabled navigation through 'complex information structures' and conceptual mapping; Stefik et al's [4] Colab, which focused on collaborative problem solving and documentation; and the myriad of video whiteboard systems. For the Memetic[3] project, the core issue is getting a sense of what has been achieved in the meeting, how

---

[1] Corresponding Author: Simon Buckingham Shum, Knowledge Media Institute, The Open University, Walton Hall, Milton Keynes, MK12 5AY, UK; E-mail: sbs@acm.org
[2] Engelbart's demonstration is available at: http://sloan.stanford.edu/mousesite/1968Demo.html
[3] JISC Memetic VRE Project: www.memetic-vre.net

decisions have been made and by whom. This is not meant in a normative sense, rather the aim is to provide a 'natural history' of the meeting and the decisions made therein and to make these visible to participants in a manner which written minutes often occlude. Centrally, the aim is to use the tools developed within Memetic to realize a shared understanding of meetings' work and to map the dimensions of issues raised therein.

Many teams now use video conferencing as an indispensable part of their daily work. It is fair to say that the 'teething troubles' of early internet video conferencing have been largely resolved by improved bandwidth and video conferencing technologies such as the Access Grid (although even state of the art systems can be perceived at times as unstable, so sensitive are people to disruptions in face-to-face discussion).

In contrast, relatively little progress has been made on delivering robust, accessible tools for creating and flexibly navigating records of videoconferences. Whilst not considered useful or even desirable in some contexts (e.g., for reasons of privacy, litigation, intrusiveness, etc.), in the many situations where it would be useful, there is a need for functionality that goes beyond simply replaying/skimming a digital movie.

This paper introduces a toolkit for transforming the normally ephemeral character of video conferencing interactions into persistent records which can be navigated in linear and non-linear ways, and which, as interactions spanning multiple meetings, can be traced and manipulated.

The contributions which this paper seeks to make are twofold. First, with respect to meeting tools, we will introduce two complementary interaction visualizations: argumentation-based concept maps to elucidate the conceptual structure of the discourse using a particular interactional language, and multiple event timelines generated from the meeting metadata. These become semantic navigation indices into a digital video rendered in an advanced form of 'movie player' called Meeting Replay, the design of which is discussed. Second, with respect to methodology and evaluation, we describe how we are engaging diverse end-user communities in the process of designing and deploying these tools.

Section 2 gives an overview of the tools we are developing and these are described in more detail in Section 3. In Section 4, we discuss our methodology for designing, developing and refining the tools. In Section 5, we review related work. We conclude by considering in Section 6 the lessons we have learnt to date and how this work might be developed in the future.

1. Overview of Approach

The goal of the Memetic project is to create a toolkit for meeting support. Specifically, this involves:

- Developing tools to record all or selected video streams in a meeting;
- Investigating the scope for *automatically* indexing the video stream timeline with potentially significant events (such as slide changes, visits to websites, progression through agenda items, or changes in speaker), whilst *manually* indexing other significant events which are too complex for automated system detection (such as the raising of arguments and making of decisions).

The critical bottleneck in creating such accounts of meetings is, of course, the overhead of manual indexing. However, the effort required is minimized in Memetic through the use of a concept mapping approach to capturing discussions, mediated via a hypermedia tool called Compendium. While requiring someone to map ideas, these maps are displayed for all to see and validate, and so justify the effort by adding value to the meeting by virtue of the shared focus of attention to the unfolding of decisions that they bring.

Our approach to creating the Memetic toolkit is to take a number of existing tools for meeting support and to refine and integrate them. We now introduce the Memetic tools.

1.1. Access Grid Video Conferencing

The Access Grid (AG) is an open collaboration and resource management architecture for video conferencing based on the metaphor of persistent virtual venues.

Figure 1. Participating in an Access Grid (AG) videoconference from a personal computer. The enlarged central video window shows participants at a 'venue' in a full AG 'Node' (see text).

A team of researchers collaborating in, for example, a laboratory would expect to find there a set of tools available to help their work; so in a virtual venue, as well as video and audio feeds of all participants, applications and services to aid a specific virtual organization to work together remotely can also be accessed. The philosophy underlying AG is that each group of collaborators has their own virtual venue in which they can store shared objects such as documents and data, together with shared applications, perhaps to aid access to a physical resource such as a radio telescope or electron microscope.

An AG meeting can be attended via a single personal computer (Figure 1) or by going to a full AG 'Node', a designed space with very large display, multiple video cameras and high quality audio system. An intermediate solution is to have a desk-based AG node, consisting of three aligned PC displays and echo-canceling microphones, which provides a richer environment than can be achieved using a single PC desktop with webcam and microphone headset.

AG supports the recording of meetings that can be played and stopped as digital video streams. Our task in the Memetic project is to implement and evaluate extensions to this replay by improving the video replay functionality, and indexing it using Compendium and the Meeting Replay tool.

1.2. Compendium

Compendium is hypermedia software tool for authoring and publishing issue-based Dialogue Maps: concept networks that structure Issues, Ideas and Arguments in a discussion, linked as required to supporting and background multimedia documents and internet resources. Compendium is best thought of as a knowledge management environment for supporting personal/group deliberations and memory, combining hypermedia, modelling and mapping [5].

Compendium uses an approach called Conversational Modeling [10], which extends the technique developed by Conklin [7] termed Dialogue Mapping, which in turn derives from the formative public policy planning work of Horst Rittel [9]. Rittel characterized the concept of "wicked problems", which can only be solved by all stakeholders striving to define the problem and being willing to explore issues dialogically, in what he termed argumentative design. He proposed the Issue-Based Information System (IBIS) as a notation to mediate discourse. Software-supported Dialogue Mapping has been under development since the late 1980s, resulting in a large body of knowledge about the craft, process skills [7], and since 1993, the skills of Conversational Modeling are being analyzed (e.g., [10]). We return to Compendium's affordances as a tool for recording interactions within meetings below.

Figure 2 shows an extract from a Dialogue Map created over several meetings, both face-to-face and virtual. As part of a large scale NASA Mars exploration field trial [11], which deployed and evaluated the tools now being extended in the current project, co-located field geologists at a desert site (a Mars simulation) arranged rock sample photos for analysis. Colleagues (simulating a remote science team back on Earth) reviewed this on the internet and raised queries, linking them into the map as new ☜ Questions, ♀ Ideas and ✚ / ➖ Arguments. The Mars crew then responded (highlighted nodes). In other maps, discussions include links to voice annotations and web datasets. Compendium provided a shared visual focus on the contributions as they were made (particularly useful in the absence of other shared visual referents in virtual meetings), and a group-validated memory of how contributions connected. The Dialogue Map became the group's evolving, shared picture of their problem.

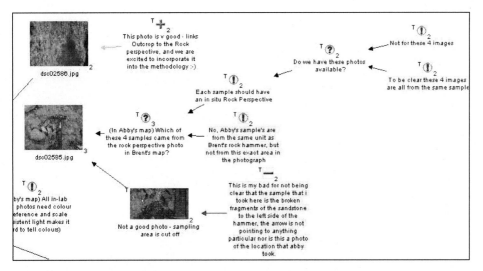

Figure 2. A Dialogue Map created in the Compendium software tool, illustrating its capabilities for integrating media resources with analysis and argumentation from different stakeholders (in both co-present and virtual meetings).

The content of maps may be driven entirely by issues raised by participants, or at the other extreme, discussion can be driven by working through predefined Issue Templates that specify the issues to be tackled, and possibly the options available and the criteria by which they should be judged. The approach can be particularly powerful by blending freeform and predefined maps. In all of the above cases, maps are created by people as an aid to thinking. However, maps can also be automatically generated and read by a software agent (e.g., [11]). The maps then provide hypertext functionality for navigating and linking data elements, and can be combined with any of the above modes of use.

As a semantic, visual hypertext system, Compendium provides several ways to manage the connections between ideas: drawing optionally labeled graphical links between nodes (connections in a given context); transclusion (tracking occurrence of the same node across different contexts); metadata tagging (enabling harvesting of nodes with common attributes across different contexts); and catalogues (managing libraries of nodes and template structures). See [5] for details.

Several significantly-sized case studies have documented the value of rendering real-time interactions as visual maps, whether co-present or online meetings [5] [12] [13]. The approach has also been used to model and interpret the key issues and arguments in an extended, asynchronous discourse, rendering a corpus of documents around a controversy such as the Iraq debate as interactive IBIS maps on the Web [14].

1.3. Meeting Replay

The Meeting Replay interface (Figure 3) integrates the Access Grid videos, Compendium database and other indices into the meeting. The meeting can be navigated via the interactive event timelines shown in bottom frame, or from any node in a Compendium client (e.g., to play the video at the point when a particular argument was made). The richness of the video record thus compensates for the terseness of the Compendium maps; in turn, the maps and event timelines provide hyperlinked indices into the video.

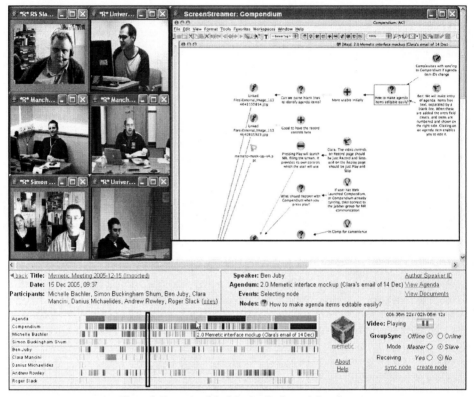

Figure 3. Example of the Meeting Replay web interface

All of the above are integrated within, and launched from, a Meeting Manager website which enables users to book, record, replay and annotate meetings. We have not detailed the technical implementation of the tools, since this is not of primary interest for this paper. Our concern is to focus on the affordances of these tools as a specific form of manipulable record of meeting interactions.

2. Affordances of Memetic tools

What do we know about the affordances of the tools as a resource for recovering and working with past discourse?

2.1. Access Grid video replay

Prior to the Memetic project, the video streams from an AG meeting could be simply played or stopped. Our work improves on this firstly, with a tool called Arena, which adds conventional video player controls to pause, fast forward and rewind. This is further augmented by another new tool called ScreenStreamer which adds a video stream from participants who choose to share the video output from their computer screens. The affordances of video replay are as one would expect of this familiar metaphor: participants know that what they say and do is being recorded, and adjust their behavior accordingly. If they want their presentations to be recorded then they are no longer restricted to AG-aware software, but can opportunistically share anything via ScreenStreamer. With Arena alone, however, when seeking to replay a point in the meeting users must recall or guess the offset from the start time, or simply browse to find the desired moment. Arena has subsequently been embedded in the Meeting Replay tool's upper frame, which as discussed below, expands the medium's affordances considerably.

2.2. Compendium Maps

The key affordances of such maps are summarized in Figure 4. Notational affordances are to some extent intrinsic to the approach, available to anyone who is 'literate' in reading Compendium maps (e.g., Figure 2) and interpreting the cues highlighted in Figure 4 below. But the way in which the notation is used in an interaction can determine its success. The key affordances of the Dialogue Mapping/Conversational Modeling dynamic can be summarized as follows.

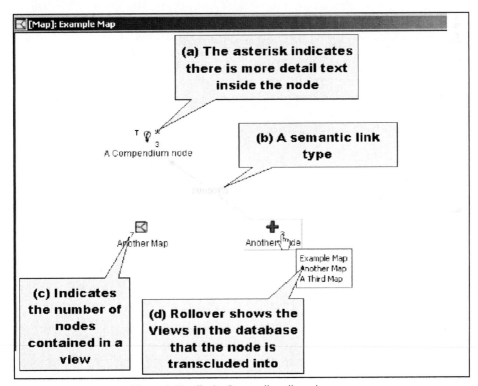

Figure 4. 'Reading' a Compendium discussion map.

The Compendium mapper functions as "technographer", actively crafting structures on a shared display screen that both capture the meanings and ideas of the group and reflect back to it the larger implications of their thinking [16].

2.3. Advantages of Compendium Mapping

Based on the studies cited earlier, and over a decade's experience with the approach in real organizational contexts, we are able to identify a number of affordances of the Compendium's issue-based, highly visual, real time mapping in meetings, physical and virtual (for details see Conklin [7]):

- *Beneficial slowing down.* A complaint sometimes heard when argument/discourse mapping is first introduced to meetings, is that it disrupts the flow of the meeting. When done appropriately, however, we find that it can be extremely beneficial to focus attention on a feature of the hypertext map: potential sources of conflict in the ongoing interaction can be topicalized and conflict can be defused. After a while, people become noticeably unhappy when their contributions are not mapped, but if these are captured on screen, they know that their view has been heard, correctly recorded, and will be harder to ignore when the map is assessed at decision time.

- *A visual trace of the analysis.* The graphical IBIS notation has a number of properties which can 'talk back' [15] to participants to show them when the quality of an analysis can be strengthened. These cues can be learnt implicitly through use (rather like learning how to format a document through experience), or explicitly through training. A workshop can teach participants how to raise effective issues, spot weak or irrelevant positions, and question implicit assumptions. While these are skills offered by a good meeting chair or facilitator, newcomers can use the structure of the IBIS map as a cognitive scaffold to develop these skills.

- *Depersonalization of conflict.* When ideas and concerns are mediated via a shared display, challenges to positions assume a more neutral, less personal tone. We cannot of course claim that this technique resolves all conflicts, but in ill-structured situations where there are competing agendas, it helps participants to clarify the nature of their disagreement (e.g., the definition of 'the problem'; understanding different criteria of 'success'). We have seen Compendium defuse meetings which otherwise looked to be polarized, and bring together parties who were unable to work together.

- *Flexible rhythmic review.* To a surprising degree, collaborative knowledge work can be characterized as 'group list processing'. Whether the list is a set of requirements, budget items, or action items, a common activity is group review of a list of potentially complex elements. While some items draw little comment, others can lead into deep discussions and even debate. With Compendium, the facilitator and the group establish a 'call and response' rhythm during these exercises, creating a sense of shared purpose and momentum. When occasional elements lead to intense discussions about meaning, or spark disagreement among group members, the Compendium practitioner can open a new map and keep facilitating, mapping or modeling the new interaction. With the new issues captured in the shared display, the group can return to the previous review task without losing momentum.

- *Incremental mediation of interaction.* We are discovering a variety of strategies for introducing Compendium to a new group, strongly determined by the context. Some of us simply start to capture the normal discussion in a meeting and, at appropriate points, use it to reflect back to the meeting personal insights gleaned. Curiosity about what one is doing often leads to natural opportunities to introduce the tool. If the shared display is used from the start, again, there is a spectrum of how strongly discourse is mediated via this display (cf. the continuum in Buckingham Shum and Hammond, [17]). It may be used to punctuate discussion to reflect on progress, but at its most powerful, the discussion and the map shape each other.

It may be argued that the need to be skilled in the use of Compendium is a fundamental weakness of the approach: someone has to become fluent with it, before beginning to take advantage of its affordances. In contrast, our view is that like any other tool that takes time to learn, Compendium yields greater benefits with practice. Mapping ideas in IBIS during a meeting is unquestionably an acquired ability, but one which can be learnt (there is an international Compendium user community, and project members use it to map meetings). We discuss the important issue of cognitive overhead, and strategies for overcoming it, in [5], while other work is beginning to articulate the skills displayed by experienced knowledge mappers [10].

2.4. Meeting Replay

Whereas Compendium is a relatively mature approach to interaction capture and visualization, semantically indexed Meeting Replay of videoconferences is new territory. However, it is possible to begin articulating the affordances of this representation for 'reading' an interaction from a videoconference.

2.4.1. Event Stream Visualization

The key additions to Arena's video replay functionality that the Meeting Replay tool brings are:

- *interactive event timelines* provide a visual index to get an overview of the video, and navigate around it by clicking on an event (Figure 5);
- *integration with Compendium* enables the user to click on a node in a Compendium map to navigate the Meeting Replay to the point in the meeting just before that node was created.

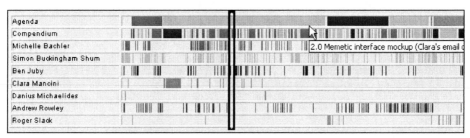

Figure 5. Meeting Replay's interactive event timelines.

The key question is what kinds of information this display can, or should, afford. Taking firstly the event timeline visualization, the following information not normally accessible from a video can be read from the display:

- When an agenda item was discussed (e.g. Figure 5 shows that the second item, in green, was returned to after item 3). Details for a given event are displayed on a mouse rollover.
- Who spoke when, and about which agenda items
- Who spoke a little or a lot.
- Who was speaking when a given Compendium node was created, highlighted, tagged, or a hyperlink followed to an external application or website; this node might be an Issue, Idea or Argument, or a Reference node to an external document such as a spreadsheet, website, photo or slide (see Figure 2).
- What the distribution of Compendium node types is (again, they are color coded by type).
- Combining the above, for instance, one can see at a glance which agenda items or Compendium nodes provoked a lot of discussion, amongst whom, and with an approximate indication of whether there was much argumentation (presence or Pro, Con and Argument nodes)

There is an additional cue provided during navigation around the replay, e.g., on clicking a timeline event or Compendium node. When one jumps into the middle of a video recording, for someone who was not at the meeting or who has forgotten the details, there is an orientation phase while one establishes the context. The Meeting Replay interface offers the user an often reliable cue to the context by displaying the 'current' (most recently created) Compendium node (e.g. see Figure 3: *"How to make agenda items editable easily?"* is displayed as the current node, and can be highlighted in the Compendium map on request, as shown). Thus, although a slide or photo may be on the main display as a context cue to the subject of discussion, the user is also provided with a cue to the particular Issue, Idea, or Argument. The user is, however, left to disambiguate whether this motivated inspection of the slide/photo, arose from it, or indeed, pertains to another topic altogether.

Finally, Meeting Replays can be further annotated in Compendium by anyone in the project, to add missing material that might be useful, or to construct completely new navigational maps around the video, an affordance that we are now investigating to support distributed video data analysis.

2.4.2. Navigating Interactions Spanning Multiple Meetings

An affordance that we have yet to implement in Meeting Replay, but which we are beginning to consider, is navigation of interactions spanning multiple meetings. This is already possible in Compendium, whereby maps from discussions going back years can be retrieved (based on keyword, date, node type, author or metadata), pasted into a current discussion, or even actively cued by the interface by providing auto-completions of a new node's label as the user types it, based on matches to existing nodes (which might come from years back). Once these nodes are linked into a Meeting Replay archive, it will be possible for the user to select from multiple possible Meeting Replays in which a given node has arisen. Similarly, a search on the Compendium database will in effect be a search across multiple videoconferences.

Finally, to represent the contents of meetings, the Meeting Replay semantic web architecture uses an RDF triplestore, from which the Meeting Replay interface is generated. This opens up further possibilities for reasoning over multiple interactions and providing meeting memory services that mine, or act upon, the memory traces.

3. End-User Participatory Design

Meetings are central to the conduct of organizations often with the participation of persons over a number of sites via video conferencing. However, in part because meetings have become part of the fabric of everyday life, there is a sense in which their organization is, to use Garfinkel's [19] term, 'seen but unnoticed'. This obviously has implications for the design of a set of technologies and tools that support records of meetings. The work of participants in making meetings run is often not explicitly formulated or examined but is, nevertheless, a vital resource in the design of technologies for recording interactions. How, then, to get at this stock of practical methods for making meetings work in order to use it as a resource for the design of tools to enhance and possibly transform them?

Following the pioneering work of the Participatory Design (PD) community (Greenbaum and Kyng [20]), the involvement of end-users in the design of technologies and tools has become accepted practice within the world of Information Technology. There are numerous variations on PD and the one that we have followed in the Memetic project goes by the name of 'co-realization'. The aim of co-realization is to develop technologies and tools in co-operation with those who will use them, and to do so over time. Following Trigg, Blomberg, and Suchman [21], co-realization strives to create a situation where "... co-development of CSCW [Computer Supported Collaborative Work] technologies ... means more than engaging prospective users in the design of new computer systems to support their work. It requires that we as designers engage in the unfolding performance of their work as well, co-developing a complex alignment among organizational concerns, unfolding trajectories of action, and new technological possibilities."

Co-realization's orientation to design and development conceptualizes design as a co-operative and situated practice involving end-users and designers of technology as equal partners (Hartswood et al. [22]; Buscher et al. [23]). Design and development work is grounded in the lived experience of end-users as they come to use technologies and to appropriate their functionalities and affordances into their work practices and relations.

3.1. Methodology

Our methodological approach takes a twin track: first, workshops with end-users and developers; second, a series of site visits to observe meetings 'in the wild', linked with an ongoing commitment to observe meetings over time via Access Grid and to discuss issues arising from these meetings with developers and end-users. The initial workshop meetings were fora for developers and end-users to interact, discuss the potential of Memetic technologies, and understand how these might be deployed within each organization in order to afford work. Each technology within the Memetic project was demonstrated to users and a workshop discussion allowed users and developers of each technology to discuss the ways that the technologies might a) be used within end-user organizations; b) the potential for enhancements based on site-specific experiences and needs.

The aims of the user requirements workshops were as follows:

a)   To provide familiarity with the potential of the technologies and their uses;
b)   Predicated on (a), to develop on the day an emergent 'wish list';
c)   Discussion of this 'wish list' in plenary sessions
d)   A series of 'core' requirements based on (b) and (c);
e)   A series of action items based on (d)[4].

The second track of our approach involves a series of site visits. These involve Memetic researchers in observing the conduct of meetings via Access Grid. The value of these observations lies in the familiarization of the researchers with the setting and the issues that users within each organization face – both in terms of getting meetings organized and in using Memetic technologies within the fabric of these meetings. Site visits also allow the end-users to develop what we might think of as in vivo requirements, i.e., requirements that occur during the meeting and which may have not been envisaged in the workshop.

An example is useful here. During one site visit, an Access Grid meeting involved the use of a shared PowerPoint presentation; collaborators at a remote site were unable to navigate consistently through the presentation and had to be prompted by the presenting site. Presenters interrupted their presentations with utterances such as "could you click onto the next slide [centre name], please" and "click again [site name] yes, that's it". Such interruptions also led to the partner centre moving too far ahead and having to track back over slides with consequent disruption of the narrative of the presentation. After the meeting, one attendee who had been at our user requirements workshop commented to the Memetic representatives that he had "really thought that, yes, there's a place where they could use Screen Streamer, but I couldn't get [remote centre] to set it up. Next time I'll suggest that to them". Such in vivo realizations as to the ways that Memetic technologies could be used are invaluable in both designing systems that afford the work within the user organization and enable buy-in to the project.

In line with the aims of co-realization, our aim is to build upon these partnerships over time as the project unfolds.

4. Related Work

There is a considerable amount of research on capturing physical meetings, to offer a meeting record, but not much on Internet videoconferences (which ironically, are easier to capture since everything is digitally mediated). Some of these are investigating advanced technologies that are not yet widely available within the mainstream environments we are seeking to augment. Speech recognition technologies are being trialed by Pallotta et al. [24] who are also experimenting with IBIS as the basis for a schema to model the output of speech recognition tools. Face recognition cameras are prototyped by Cutler et al. [25] who then generate event timelines. Abowd et al. [26]

---

[4] We used Compendium to analyze the materials from the workshops and thereby to capture requirements. This also functioned as a demonstration of the utility of Compendium for participants.

and Moran et al. [27] have demonstrated how activity around digital whiteboards can be indexed and replayed.

The key difference of our work, is that we are working with an infrastructure that is widely available and supported, and our use of real-time IBIS conceptual mapping provides a notation for capturing a wide variety of discourse moves, and an open ended way to generate meaningful event timelines for different user communities, simply by defining different combinations of nodes and metadata as indices into the video.

4.1. Emergent Research Questions

The tools are about to deployed with end-user partners. Ultimately, our question is to what extent participants report that the tools improve their work (following a five-month evaluation phase). Specific research questions can be summarized as follows:

- How far does the technology support naturally occurring interactions: where can it be seen to augment these and where does it just get in the way?
- What is the relationship between naturally occurring references to the technology made by end-users during meetings, and their more 'official' accounts when asked by us as researchers (we are helped here because all meeting interactions are recorded)?
- Which parts of the toolkit that we provide will be used, and in what (possibly unexpected) ways?
- What requirements emerge for 'meeting memory services'? Memetic models semantics in discussions (Compendium maps), within the RDF store (People, Agenda items, Meetings, Venues, etc), and within Meeting Replay (Events, Documents, People, etc); these provide a platform for experimenting with services to support projects.

5. Conclusions

In this paper we have described the toolkit which we are developing and integrating: video of participants and shared presentations, hypermedia Dialogue Maps, and interactive event timelines. Each of these has specific affordances for navigating and 'reading' off information about what happened in the meeting. Future papers will report the results of the participatory design engagements with our end-user partners, and the results of the deployment and evaluation of the tools in use.

Acknowledgements

We would like to thank our user groups for their time and contributions to the work reported here. The Memetic project is funded by the UK Joint Information Systems Committee *Virtual Research Environments* program.

References

[1]   Boden, D. (1994). *The Business of Talk.* Cambridge: Polity.
[2]   Bush, V. (1945) As We Might Think. *Atlantic Monthly* 176 (1), 101-108
[3]   Englebart, D. and English, W. K. (1968). A Research Center for Augmenting Human Intellect. *Proc. Fall Joint Computing Conference*, San Francisco, CA. AFIPS: Reston, VA; pp. 395-410.
[4]   Stefik, M., Foster, G., Bobrow, D. G., Khan, K., Lanning, S. and Suchman, L. (1987). Beyond the Chalkboard: Computer Support for Collaboration and Problem Solving in Meetings. *Communications of the ACM* 30 (1), 32-47.
[5]   Buckingham Shum, S.J., Selvin, A.M., Sierhuis, M., Conklin, J., Haley, C.B. and Nuseibeh, B. (2006) Hypermedia Support for Argumentation-Based Rationale: 15 Years on from gIBIS and QOC. To appear in: *Rationale Management in Software Engineering,* (Eds.) Allen H. Dutoit, Raymond McCall, Ivan Mistrik, and Barbara Paech. Springer-Verlag.
[6]   Selvin, A. and Sierhuis, M. (1999). Argumentation in Different CSCA Project Types. In *Workshop on Computer-Supported Collaborative Argumentation*, CSCL Conf., Stanford, CA (12-15 Dec).
[7]   Conklin, J. (2005) *Dialogue Mapping.* Wiley, Chichester
[8]   Selvin, A. Supporting Collaborative Analysis and Design with Hypertext Functionality. *Jnl. of Digital Information*, 1, 4, 1999 [http://jodi.ecs.soton.ac.uk/Articles/v01/i04/Selvin/].
[9]   Rittel, H., and M. Webber. (1973). Dilemmas in a General Theory of Planning., *Policy Sciences*, Vol. 4, , pp 155-169. Elsevier Scientific Publishing Company, Inc., Amsterdam.
[10] Selvin, A. (2005) Aesthetic and Ethical Implications of Participatory Hypermedia Practice. *TR KMI-05-17, Knowledge Media Insitute, Open University*: http://kmi.open.ac.uk/publications/pdf/kmi-05-17.pdf
[11] Clancey, W.J., Sierhuis, M., Alena, R., Berrios, D., Dowding, J., Graham, J.S., Tyree, K.S., Hirsh, R.L., Garry, W.B., Semple, A., Buckingham Shum, S.J., Shadbolt, N. and Rupert, S. (2005). Automating CapCom Using Mobile Agents and Robotic Assistants. *1st AIAA Space Exploration Conference*, 31 Jan-1 Feb, 2005, Orlando, FL. AKT IRC ePrint 375: http://eprints.aktors.org/375
[12] Selvin, A M and Buckingham Shum, S J (2002) Rapid Knowledge Construction: A Case Study in Corporate Contingency Planning Using Collaborative Hypermedia. *Journal of Knowledge and Process Management* 9(2): pp. 119-128. http://eprints.aktors.org/48
[13] Vedro, S. (2003) Using World Modeling Interviews to Develop Lists of Shared Problems, Opportunities, Know-how and Assets Shared by Wisconsin Public Television and the U.W. System Learning Innovations Center. *Technical Report, Reforging the Links Project.* http://www.reforginglinks.uwex.edu/CIMIssues.html
[14] Buckingham Shum, S. and Okada, A. (2005) Modelling the Iraq Debate: Mapping Argumentation in a Document Corpus. *Proc. Compendium Institute Workshop*, 10-11 Nov, 2005, Washington DC http://www.kmi.open.ac.uk/projects/compendium/iraq/
[15] Schon, D. (1983) *The Reflective Practitioner.* New York: Basic Books.
[16] DeKoven, B. *Connected Executives.* The Institute for Better Meetings, 1990
[17] Buckingham Shum, S. and Hammond, N. Argumentation-Based Design Rationale: What Use at What Cost? *International Journal of Human-Computer Studies*, 40, 4, 1994, 603-652
[18] Selvin, A. and Buckingham Shum, S. (2005). Hypermedia as a Productivity Tool for Doctoral Research. *New Review of Hypermedia and Multimedia* (Special Issue on Scholarly Hypermedia), 11 (1), 91-101 PrePrint: http://kmi.open.ac.uk/publications/pdf/kmi-tr-05-8.pdf
[19] Garfinkel, H. (1967). *Studies in Ethnomethodology.* Englewood Cliffs, NJ: Prentice-Hall.
[20] Greenbaum, J. and Kyng, M. (Eds.) (1991). *Design at Work: Cooperative design of computer systems.* Hillsdale, NJ: Lawrence Erlbaum Associates.
[21] Trigg, R., Blomberg, J. and Suchman, L. Moving document collections online: The evolution of a shared repository. In *Proceedings of ECSCW'99* (Copenhagen Denmark, 1999) Dordrecht. Kluwer
[22] Hartswood, M., Procter, R., Rouchy, P., Rouncefield, M, Slack, R. and Voss, A. (2002). Co-realisation: Towards a Principled Synthesis of Ethnomethodology and Participatory Design. In M. Berg, D. Henriksen, J. Pors and B. Winthereik (Eds.), special issue on Challenging Practice: Reflections on the Appropriateness of Fieldwork as Research Method in Information Systems Research, *Scandinavian Journal of Information Systems*, 14(2), p. 9-30.
[23] Buscher, M., Hartswood, M., Mogensen, P., Procter, R, Shapiro, D., Slack, R. and Voss, A. (2002). Promises, Premises and Risks: Sharing Responsibilities, Working Up Trust and Sustaining Commitment in Participatory Design Projects. In T. Binder, J. Gregory, and I. Wagner, (Eds.) *Proceedings of the Participatory Design Conference*, Malmo, June 23rd-26th, p. 183-92.
[24] Pallotta V., Ghorbel H., Ballim A., Lisowska A., & Marchand-Maillet S. (2004) - Towards Meeting Information Systems: Meeting Knowledge Management. *Proceedings of ICEIS '04 (6th International Conference on Enterprise Information Systems)*, Porto, Portugal, April 14-17, p.464-469.

[25] Cutler, R., Rui, Y., Gupta, A., Cadiz, J.J., Tashev, I., He, L-W., Colburn, A., Zhang, Z., Liu, Z., Silverberg. S. (2002) Distributed Meetings: A Meeting Capture and Broadcasting System, *Proc. 10th ACM International Conference on Multimedia*, pp 503-512, Juan-les-Pins, France, 1-6 December

[26] Abowd, G., Chris G. Atkeson, Jason A. Brotherton, Tommy Enqvist, Paul Gulley, and Johan Lemon, Investigating the capture, integration and access problem of ubiquitous computing in an educational setting. In the *Proceedings of CHI '98*, pp. 440-447, May, 1998

[27] Moran, T., Palen, L., Harrison, S., Chiu, P., Kimber, D., Minneman, S., van Melle, W., Zellweger, W. (1997). "I'll get that off the audio": a case study of salvaging multimedia meeting records. *Proc. CHI Conference on Human Factors in Computing Systems*, Atlanta, 202 – 209.

Cooperative Systems Design
P. Hassanaly et al. (Eds.)
IOS Press, 2006

Cooperation and Ubiquitous Computing: an Architecture Towards their Integration

Federico CABITZA, Marco P. LOCATELLI and Carla SIMONE
University of Milano-Bicocca
{cabitza, locatelli, simone}@disco.unimib.it

Abstract. The paper discusses the relations between Ubiquitous Computing (UC) and cooperation pointing to two reference scenarios. UC technologies are still in a early stage: however, it is possible to envisage an evolution that makes smart objects pervasive in work settings. Under the hypothesis that these objects are likely to have very a specialized functionality, the smart environment has to possess distributed inferential capabilities to complement them toward an adaptive support to both individual and collaborative behaviors. CASMAS is a model informing an architecture to design collaborative UC environments: it combines inference capabilities with the management of contextual information that is modulated according to the structure of physical and logical spaces.

Keywords: Ubiquitous computing, cooperation, contextual information, agent based architectures

Introduction

Research on computer supported cooperative work recognized from the very beginning two main cooperation modalities - face-to-face and remote cooperation - and tried to understand their nature and to support them through effective applications. More recently, the concept of local mobility has been introduced as an in-between modality between face-to-face and remote cooperation, and as something that may cause the interruption of cooperative activities [1], but also as a property of most work situations [2]. Of course, this effects another fundamental aspect of cooperation, that is *continuity* both in the physical space (no matter if a person stays at her desktop or gets up and walks to another room, her work must be supported without discontinuity) and in the logical context of action (for example, if a person is working on a document with a coworker, they don't have to abandon their activity to find information related to the document).

In our view, the shift from the desktop computer metaphor to the ubiquitous computing one is promising in the aim to support cooperative work with a smooth form of coordination; in fact, people become able to act and interact, in a more natural and instinctive manner, within a computational environment that is aware of persons and activities and that is able to adapt the support it provides to the changing context. To reach this goal the integration of the themes of cooperation and the ubiquitous computing paradigm has to be strengthened, more than it is currently. In this view, we propose the notion of *community* (in the sense initially proposed, and denoted as Community of Practice, by Wenger [3] and further articulated by Andriessen [4], so the notion of community varies from "interest groups" up to "strategic communities") as a first class concept of this integration for its suitability in representing the plasticity of cooperation. In fact a community is spontaneously built and legitimates various degrees of participation of (new) people on the basis of its internal rules: this is usually called "legitimate peripheral participation". Beside this, a community autonomously organizes and builds its memory and interactions with other communities to enhance its capabilities as well as with the institutional context in which it operates.

The design of ubiquitous-computing environments to support cooperation requires a reference model able to take into account the above specifications and in particular the notions of community and flexible peripheral participation. To our knowledge such model has not yet been proposed, since the cooperation dimension is usually totally disregarded or left implicit and community is not a first class object. The aim of this paper is to give a contribution in this direction by defining an approach to conceive cooperative work that is inspired by the ubiquitous computing paradigm and by proposing a new model as a basic step toward an architecture able to adequately support the design of collaborative ubiquitous-computing environments.

The paper is organized as follows. The next sections discuss the relations between ubiquitous computing and cooperation: the latter are then illustrated trough a couple of scenarios. Then, the CASMAS (Community-Aware Situated Multi-Agent Systems) model and the related architecture are presented: the model integrates and enriches the main features of Santana, a framework for the management of distributed reactive behaviors [5] and of MMASS (Multi-layered Multi-Agents Situated Systems), a model to manage awareness information in cooperative applications [6]. How the model can manage the situations highlighted in the scenarios and the future steps in this research conclude the paper.

1. Ubiquitous Computing and Cooperation

Ubiquitous computing (UC) is still more an idea than a reality since embedding computation into real everyday objects is not a simple task from the technical point of view and it is usually achieved either in prototypes or quite expensive devices. However, the rapidity and unpredictability of the technological evolution suggest playing with this idea to be ready when it becomes feasible and be able to master the implications in application design. So, in the following we will consider some of the implications of UC without been too much constrained by the current technological achievements. We suppose that each object can have specialized computational capabilities making them reactive and proactive in relation to actors and/or other objects that are close of in their surroundings. This distributed computing power is connected through a wireless network that supports bi-directional information flows towards and from more traditional computational nodes (usually standard PCs).

Which is the role of UC in supporting cooperative work, both at the individual and collaborative dimension? Both of them are relevant since both have to be smoothly integrated in technologies that support cooperation. The UC literature is generally more focused on the individual dimension, and only recently it contained an explicit suggestion to consider cooperation in UC environments [7, 8]. A way to connect UC and cooperation is through the notion of context, since UC and context-aware computing share the same goal to make the environment "alive" and its context an important part of what determines the application's behavior [9]. More specifically, we like the idea to view context not as a representational problem but as an interactional problem, as proposed in [10]: context has to be seen as a relational property that holds between objects or activities; something may or may not be contextually relevant in relation to some particular activity; the scope of contextual features is defined dynamically; context is an occasioned property, relevant to particular settings, particular instances of action, and particular parties to that action; finally, context is not out there rather it arises from the activity. In fact, this view is more coherent with what we consider the main advantage of UC (once adequately developed): to bring back the notion of context as currently mediated and constrained by the desktop metaphor to its natural connotation, that of physical context, with all its affordances, possibly augmented by computing capabilities to become more significant. Actually, with UC each actor can live in her physical place [11] and act by using the computational capabilities of the place without the mediation of a virtual representation of what exceeds the limited space around the desktop computer: when the actor moves into a place or across places, her local context changes accordingly, and the new context becomes ready-at-hand in a natural and unmediated way. This has some immediate consequences on the technological support of work. First, what has been denoted as the discontinuity connected with the nature of desktop computing is drastically reduced by UC. Take the case of local mobility as identified by [1] as an underestimated phenomenon or described as a property of specific work settings in [2]. In both cases, UC can alleviate this problem since the augmented physical space becomes the locus where actions, the required resources and the associated computations are naturally connected by the application of well known, although sometimes unconsciously, practices that involve space and time: what has been called mobility work in [2], "that is the work that needs to be done in order to make the right configuration of people, places, resources and knowledge emerge". Notice that practices have been distorted and constrained by the interaction modalities imposed by desktop computers and can now come back to their previous nature, recovering their past effectiveness without loosing the advantages of computation. Second, in UC the context is naturally composed by a physical component and a logical component, as mediated by the computational capabilities associated to objects of various kinds, and moreover they are or can be smoothly integrated. This can happen in two ways: some computational information can be displayed on a physical device that has, by definition, a physical context; or the same object exists in the physical world together with its virtual counterpart - made available on a close display - that inhabits the logical contextual space. The next section illustrates these ideas through a scenario.

2. A Fanciful Scenario

My office has the typical furniture of a University room: cabinets, tables, a desktop computer, etc. The only difference is that they are all smart: books in cabinets carry a RFID-like tag that allows their localization and identification; the cabinets are able to maintain, in connection with my desktop computer and with a RFID detector, a database with all the information about the stored books. A special pen is able to read the main information about the book (meta-info) that is coded in the tag through a suitable tag reader. Beside my computer, on my desk there are some "sheets" of ee-paper (enhanced e-paper). Ee-paper (inspired from the prototype developed at MIT [12]) is a smart object with which one can interact by usual gestures (e.g., to turn over a page) and write with a pen. Moreover, it can interact with other smart devices (included another ee-paper) to load and exchange documents, and can be localized.

Today I am writing a paper for a conference: I like to write down the outline by hand so that I can use my graphical conventions in a flexible way. To this aim I am using the ee-paper so that when I am done I can move these notes on my computer and use them as a guide to the actual writing according the predefined style. When I write the section about the related work, I need to have access both to my bibliographical database and the books stored in the cabinets. To this aim, I move the text back on ee-paper. Clicking on references makes them recognizable by the computational capabilities of the cabinets when I approach them. This causes the cabinets to react in several ways. The cabinets show through some visual indicators where I can find the books I have used in the references set. This is useful because I am guided to look also to books that are related to the selected ones by physical location: for example to proceedings of the same series. In so doing, physical cues are very useful to remember events associated to these proceedings (e.g., a discussion with people attending the related conferences). Or the cabinet could show through another indicator where there are books related to the topics (meta-information) of the selected ones. In both cases I can quickly browse into the book and select some interesting references that, if they do not belong to my database, can be transferred by using the pen. The same reference can be loaded in the ee-paper in a specific section, for future use. Of course, books are not always where they are supposed to be: by interacting with the environment, the cabinets can locate the misplaced book on a side table or tell that the book is not in the room. In the first case, the physical position of the book, close to other sheets of ee-paper tells me that I am working on another document, a project proposal, where I can find a different set of related work from which I can be inspired and that I can incorporate in my current research paper as described above.

Suddenly I realize that at 10am I have to attend a working group meeting to finalize a project proposal. Some participants are late but the meeting must start because the deadline is close. The meeting room is smart: it is able through smart desks, tags, sensors, etc. to keep trace of the documents managed by each participant, to identify who is working on which of them or close to a smart-board (consider for example a setting similar to the one described in [13]). The missing people can be in different places. Someone is sick at home, others cannot leave their offices because they have some unexpected duties, and others are approaching from the building where they are teaching. They can play different roles in the project preparation and have different competencies to be used in different parts of the proposal. These pieces of information can be recognized by UC technologies able to identify and locate documents and people on the one hand, and by technologies managing the information constituting the logical space of collaboration (competencies, duties, roles, etc.) on the other hand. Irrespective of its current situation, each person has to behave so that the meeting is anyhow productive. Here, the technology has to support different degrees of participation of the community members to the cooperative process going on in the meeting. Moreover, the environment has to support the quiet development of the meeting itself. As for the last aspect, cellular phones have to be turned to the quiet state when participants enter the room apart from the case of the meeting coordinator that could be contacted by the missing members. Other functionalities can be available that are typical of smart environments: reduce the light when a projector is in use, activating the connectivity of each participants to her personal environment when she is approaching a computational device, etc.

People who are approaching on foot can be connected just by voice; who is in the car can in addition have the display of what is on the smart-board where the outline of the meeting and the assignments to people are listed. In this way they can start negotiating what involves them. When a participant enters the building where the meeting is held, she can take out of her briefcase an ee-paper sheet where the previous information is enriched (possibly on a different page) with a representation of the displacement of people, documents and other facilities within the meeting room. Functionalities like the ones provided by Babble [14] - but concerning here face-to-face conversations mediated by the involved documents - give an idea of what is cool in the meeting, who is involved and to which degree in the various discussions. The visualization of this information can be modulated by taking into account the degree of competency of each participant in the various topics as they are discussed in subgroups. This support helps the participant entering the room to take an active role avoiding the sense of confusion typical of these situations. At this point, the face-to-face meeting can be conducted by using the smart devices as described in the previous scenario. Let us consider now the other missing people. The sick person should be involved only when his participation is really necessary: this can be partially recognized by the work plan and assignments analysis. In this way, the person can be noticed that this will happen soon, can be informed of the current situation as described before (by automatically activate connections and data transfer) and finally can become fully active in the meeting, possibly in side discussions. Something similar happens with the busy person in her office: however, in this case participation is more continue, although with different intensity. Mutual awareness between the people inside and outside the meeting room is achieved through the representation of the displacement of pertinent smart objects in the room and on the desk of the external people, for example on smart-boards located in the meeting room, in the office and at home. Since the collaboration is almost asynchronous, suitable cues can indicate that some document or facility is actually in use in its physical space, so that it is possible to gain peripheral awareness of what is going on them and synchronize behaviors accordingly, by using the suitable media (e.g., voice) or even move to the meeting place if deemed necessary. During the coffee break, the discussion can go on: a colleague in the room shows some interest in the project and joins the discussion. She is a newcomer in the community: her peripheral participation can be made easier by loading on a smart-board the structure of the project, the points in which her contribution can be useful and finally, to let her recover the current status of the discussion so that when she joins the meeting her trajectory from periphery to the core of the community is made easier.

The department members not involved in the meeting could be interested in what is going on there but they do not want to explicitly interfere with the ongoing discussions: from the neutral information about who is currently inside, up to more sensitive information about the project. This information could be managed by a smart door serving as gateway between the inside and the outside (as e.g. in [15]). In fact, it could recognize the person approaching, and hence her role, and display the appropriate information; in the opposite direction, it could remember and appropriately transmit messages to people inside the room according to some policy (urgent, come to me later, etc.).

2.1. The Role of Ubiquitous-Computing Environments in Cooperation

The two above described scenarios illustrate some aspects that characterize our understanding on how UC environments can positively affect cooperation. Although we acknowledge the fact that UC as any technology must be properly re-appropriated within the cooperative practices, in the following we summarize the possible advantages UC can bring: UC can alleviate the discontinuity due to the local mobility characterizing almost all work situations, since the environment and the smart objects populating it extend the space "around" computation beyond the "desk". In fact, UC can allow actor using their physical spaces as flexible contexts for their work without requiring any explicit representation, and by recovering their usual work practices [16]; moreover, UC can support individual and cooperative activities in a seamless way by the use, exchange and access to computationally-enriched habitual-use objects: mobile computing could be another choice but, besides usability problems and technological limits (e.g., battery life), the main problem here is that it does not solve the problem of the separation between computation and environment, the latter being only able to guarantee computational access. Finally, UC can support the integration of physical and logical contexts of cooperation both in local mobility and remote situations, and consequently allows one to use her augmented environment as a coordination media. In fact, people can achieve coordination without communication by observing and modifying their shared environment: coordination emerges incidentally. UC environments add a new "dimension" to coordination without communication because the environment (and its remote representation) can change itself in an autonomous manner, by adapting to the changing situation in which cooperation occurs. A research on the influence of distance on cooperation [17] indicates that the perceived distance among people is relevant in cooperation and not the real one. UC changes the way people perceive the environment of the other persons during remote collaboration: this richer integration of physical and digital, spatial and logical, local and remote information can reduce the perceived distance (as cellular phones do with much less embodied, computational and visualization capabilities [18]).

3. CASMAS to Design Ubiquitous-Computing Collaborative Environments

An UC collaborative environment is composed of objects (we also include devices in this term) that show a variety of computational capabilities: from sensors to wall-boards, from documents to pieces of furniture, from desks to doors, and so on, up to traditional general purpose computers that can play the hidden role of servers or the visible role of terminals supporting individual work. A part from PCs, each object is dedicated to a specific functionality that can be provided by local computational power or by the interaction with a computational environment offering (mobile) connectivity. As alluded earlier, it is difficult to foresee the future technological development: however, the second case is more likely as long as the environment's reactive and proactive behaviors become more challenging. The smart behavior of these objects requires the availability of computational capabilities that are hidden and fully independent from the actors moving in the smart environment. The latter has to guarantee a service to objects acting as sensors and actuators, which is characterized by quality levels that can be achieved by purely architectural considerations: computation efficiency, reliability, robustness, and so on. On the other hand, the smart behavior of the individual objects and of the environment as a whole requires the availability of distributed inference capabilities able to transform elemental data into more complex information about people and the physical setting, up to the construction of knowledge on which to base smartness.

The collaborative dimension adds further requirements to recognize and support the communities acting in the UC environment. In fact, people freely move in the physical space carrying and approaching objects that altogether provide different forms of computational connectivity, as well as meet other people and establish with them various forms of cooperation. Moreover, considering the logical dimension, which is the dimension where information and coordination resources are managed to support these forms of cooperation, we can recognize a similar kind of dynamism: actors own, make available, approach and coordinate their access to these resources in a flexible way according to their needs, interests, duties or simply because they realize that an opportunity is offered to them or that the current state of affairs requires their coordinated intervention. The degree of participation of a person to a community is proportional to the person distance from the center of the community, i.e., from the locus where the (physical and/or logical) ties linking its members are stronger. The above mentioned distributed inference capability should also recognize and support modulated participation of actors in the different kinds of communities by enforcing the rules characterizing them and facilitating coordination without communication.

For the above mentioned reasons, CASMAS integrates and enriches the Santana framework, which offers distributed inferential capabilities together with knowledge sharing and mobility of reactive behaviors across computational sites, with the MMASS model in which the modulated diffusion of information on a topological space is a first-class concept.

3.1. A Brief Description of MMASS and Santana

MMASS (see Figure 1 for an example of instantiation) is a multi-agent model based on the perception-reaction paradigm. Agents are located on *sites* that constitute a topological space, represented as a graph, determining the agents mutual perception. In fact, agents can directly interact when they are located in close sites or can remotely interact when they are sensitive to the signals emitted by other agents. These signals within the MMASS model are called *fields* and their intensity is modulated by space according to a *diffusion function*, which takes into account the space topology. A *sensitivity function* characterizes each agent type and takes its current state as

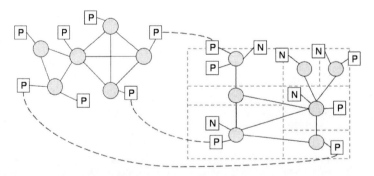

Figure 1. An instantiation of MMASS: an example with two layers and two types of agent.

argument. The perception of a field by an agent triggers a reaction that can cause a change of the perceiver's state or position or the emission of a field by the perceiving agent. A system can be composed of several topological spaces (multi-layers), each characterized by its agents and their behaviors; layers communicate by means of *exported-imported fields* through the *interfaces*. Applications can send information to the MMASS by means of imported fields and, in so doing, awareness information about those applications can be properly managed (more details on this architecture can be found in [6]).

Santana is a framework conceived for the development of distributed inference systems in the UC application domain: it is grounded on the interconnection metaphor in that any Santana environment is conceived as a web of computational sites offering services to objects of different computational and interactional capabilities. Interaction is realized through a common space (a sort of *blackboard*) where devices share contextual information (*facts*) as well as reactive behaviors (*rules*), which can be acquired by or moved across the computational sites. In this way, the pervasive environment can achieve an intelligent behavior as a result of *asynchronous inference activities* exhibited by distributed computational sites. Moreover, the blackboard approach makes the computational environment quite flexible towards dynamic situations: new devices, new actors leaving and joining the system, interaction patterns varying according to the context can be dynamically managed by means of suitable *meta-rules* that act as bridges between concepts (represented by declarative facts) and rules and that hence allow for the (de)activation of behaviors on an event-driven basis (i.e., the local, as well as the "global", control flow is not completely predetermined by the programmers of the objects involved in the same pervasive environment); in the following section two meta-rules added to CASMAS to enforce the concept of community are presented.

3.2. CASMAS Model

CASMAS blends the two models outlined above by borrowing from MMASS the notion of agent as entity able to perceive context and propagate information on that context, as well as the notion of modulated perception, to manage awareness information; and from Santana the capability to manage disparate and scattered objects, private and common information spaces and introducing here the notion of agent that is aware of context and endowed with behaviors that are adaptive and reactive to their context [19].

The rationale behind CASMAS is to model a cooperative UC environment as composed of two main parts. First, a set of common information spaces, called *fulcra* (see **Figure 2**), which manage both information and behaviors concerning communities or concerning individual actors. Each *fulcrum* is accessed by *C-agents*, one for each (human) actor involved in the community. Through the fulcrum, C-agents can share both declarative representations of context (facts) and reactive behaviors (rules) that characterize the community in terms of conventions, practices or shared knowledge. Accordingly, these behaviors are called *community rules* since by being shared and possibly followed by all the community members they literally make and demarcate the community.

All C-agents that stand proxy for a human actor (e.g., A) in some collaborative fulcra are also connected with the *private fulcrum* associated to A: this allows a smooth interaction between private and cooperative tasks and information repositories, thus

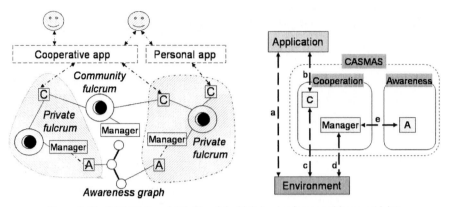

Figure 2. The CASMAS model (left) and the high-level software architecture (right).

fulfilling a well known requirement of cooperation; for example, the C-agent linked to the meeting fulcrum asserts the need to switch every "ringing device" in silent mode in the private fulcrum where devices through their C-agent are linked.

By being community-oriented, CASMAS owns two mechanisms to manage community rules that are implemented through suitable CASMAS meta-rules. The first one, called *community enforcing*, it is used to manage the enforcing of community rules, as well as their updating and overwriting once they have been fetched within each C-agent. By means of this mechanism, community rules can dynamically change to reflect a more context-aware alignment of the community members towards common and ever-changing cooperative goals. The second mechanism is called *community participating*. Through this mechanism is possible to set the degree of participation of a person to the community according to different factors that are recognized by the second part of the model (see below), e.g. her physical position and her coming appointments in the agenda. Furthermore, the two mechanisms enable a community to change dynamically its policies even according to the degree its members adopt the policies (in terms of number of rules activations [20]).

The second part of the CASMAS model encompasses a set of dynamic topological spaces that are "inhabited" by *A-agents* whose behavior is defined according to the MMASS model. Besides conveying contextual information, the role of A-agents is to pass to the *Manager* agent (a special purpose C-agent) the information (modeled in terms of exported fields) useful to compute the degree of participation of human actors in the communities that are built around the collaborative fulcra. What "shapes" the A-agents perception and computes how tight their mutual proximity is, and therefore establishes the degree of participation, is the interplay between sensitivity to fields and fields propagation on the topological graph, which depends on A-agents state and position.

The Manager is the bridge between MMASS and Santana, and allows them to be fully decoupled and autonomous in their use and implementation. The Manager is characterized by some *rendering rules*, that is rules that transform exported fields of the MMASS model into declarative representations (facts) by which the communication between the fulcrum and the A-agents populating the topological space(s) is managed.

3.3. CASMAS Software Architecture

The architecture is composed of a *Cooperation module*, which includes C-agents (C in **Figure 2**), a Manager, a private fulcrum for each actor or smart object, and the communities fulcra; and of an *Awareness module*, which includes A-agents (A in **Figure 2**), one for each actor or smart object, and one or more topological graphs. Although the previous sections did not explicitly refer to predefined (collaborative) applications, they can be one of the components of the smart environment since they are the tools that are possibly used by individuals and by communities to be supported in their work. Accordingly CASMAS must be open to interact with the environment and with software applications, in this way providing them with a "loose" integration and at the same time making them "community-aware" (more details can be found in [20]). Due to these requirements, the points of interaction between the high-level software architecture of CASMAS, the applications and the smart objects must be identified (see **Figure 2**). The interaction between the environment and CASMAS is delegated to C-agents in that they can interact both with the software applications and the environment (arrows b and c in **Figure 2**). Conversely, Managers can only interact with the environment (arrow d in **Figure 2**) and specifically with the localization devices in order to acquire physical locations. Of course software applications, which are entities outside the CASMAS architecture, can interact directly with the environment (arrow a in **Figure 2**).

The interaction between a C-agent (or the Manager) and the smart objects in the environment (see **Figure 3**) is bi-directional and mediated by the C-agent associated to the object. The former agent owns a "proxy fact" that represents the visible and modifiable state of the device and those rules that can be fired by the changes of the proxy fact; conversely, by modifying the proxy fact, this agent is able to modify the state of the corresponding device. In this way, the C-agent and the device are fully decoupled but the strict relationship between them is preserved by putting the rules only in the interested C-agent. Another important capability of the C-agent in charge of the device is that it can manage concurrent accesses to it, possibly allowing concurrent access to independent functions; for example, a display has the independent functions "show a message", which can be invoked by an application, and "augment brightness", which can be invoked by a light sensor in the room. Furthermore, this C-agent may be linked to different fulcra: in this way a smart object is available to different communities, e.g. devices in a public place like a wall-display are available to every community (and every people) that populates the place.

3.4. Modeling with CASMAS

In this section we present a way to model a small part of the scenario described in section 2 applying CASMAS and exploiting its main features: community reification and modulated propagation of awareness information; in so doing we provide a description of the interaction between entities of the model.

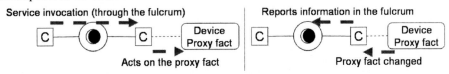

Service invocation (through the fulcrum) | Reports information in the fulcrum

Acts on the proxy fact | Proxy fact changed

Figure 3. Interaction with devices.

The scenario can be modeled in several different ways, according to the aim of the support given, the granularity of the localization areas and so on. We model the office considering that: a) the office identifies a community, even if it is assigned to only one person, and people that come to work in the office become members of this community; b) localization areas definition is based on the logical division of spaces in the office. We design the localization graph (**Figure 4**) providing one site for each area and linking every site with the site that represents an adjacent area. Awareness information is diffused on the localization graph, where A-agents, which represent objects and persons, are linked to the site that corresponds to their location; everyone that is linked to the graph emits at least a *presence field*, i.e. a field that tells others "I'm here", that is diffused on the localization graph and is perceived by other A-agents. Moreover, every object or person that could contribute to or take advantage from cooperation with other entities is linked to the office fulcrum (**Figure 4**) through the associated C-agent. As stated above, when someone comes to the office could become member of the office community; various criteria may be applied to determine when a person has to be added to the community. Here we propose a criterion based on two characteristics of the person, one physical and one logical: her location and her role. Only if a person is in the two localization areas between the L-desk and the top cabinet or in the square-desk area she could become member of the community. Anyway this is not enough because she must have a suitable role, for example a student that comes in the office does not become a member of the community even if he is in one of the areas mentioned before. In the same manner, if a coworker enters the office but stays at the door, for example because he comes to greet the person, he does not become a member of the community.

Many books are localized in the cabinets areas, some books and ee-paper sheets in the desks areas, and I am localized (here I is the person of the scenario) in the L-desk area. When I move in front of the (top) cabinet, the A-agent associated to the cabinet perceives my presence field with the highest intensity and switches its status to perceive the field emitted by the document that I loaded on the ee-paper; in this manner, the cabinet can be aware of the kind of information I am working on and analyze the fields that come from the *cabinet graph* (a graph that represents the distribution of books on the shelves); on the cabinet graph, books diffuse logical information to describe their content and shelf agents aggregate this information, allowing the emergence of knowledge related to the logical association among the book from their physical clustering done by the person. When I find a reference in a book (suggested to me by the cabinet), the book and the ee-paper, each one linked to the office fulcrum, cooperate to pass the reference from the book to the ee-paper so that it

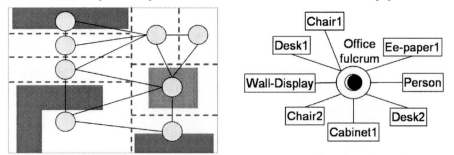

Figure 4. Localization graph (left); dashed lines identify localization areas, L shape and rectangle on the middle are desks, top and bottom rectangles are cabinets. Office fulcrum (right).

becomes available to me and I can use it in my article.

Now an overview of the configuration of the smart meeting room is presented, in particular to describe the provided support for the meeting. CASMAS allows the Smart Department to support remote cooperation, local mobility and opportunistic cooperation. People and devices are located on the localization graph (**Figure 5**). Everyone in the department is linked to the corresponding area, instead who is outside the department is linked to a site that identifies this special location. In this manner everyone that is involved in a community can be localized with respect to the main space occupied by the community, in this scenario this is the department, and can perceive the fields diffused on the graph, even if with a lower intensity due to her distance.

We identify a community for the meeting, by the definition of a *meeting fulcrum* (**Figure 6**); every device useful for the meeting activities and every person wherever she may be, such as PersonHome1 (the sick person that stay at home), PersonIn1 (the person in her office) and PersonIn2 (a person in the meeting room), are linked to the meeting fulcrum. On the left side of **Figure 6** (a part of) the configuration of the PersonHome1's CASMAS instantiation is depicted; PersonHome1 is able to participate to the meeting from her home thanks to the her C-agent that acts as a bridge between her private fulcrum, where the SmartBoard is linked, and the activities undertaken in the meeting fulcrum. On the right side of **Figure 6** there are the "SmartBoard CoffeeRoom" and the AnotherColleague C-agents; these agents are linked to the meeting fulcrum only during the coffee break, when people go to the coffee room and interact with the colleague that is interested to the meeting arguments and then decide to cooperate. The mechanism of adding a device or person to a fulcrum allows these entities to become aware of what happens in the community: the SmartBoard becomes an output device for the software applications used by the community and the person can acquire information related to the community activities and can coordinate and collaborate with the others. To support the modulated participation of persons to the meeting community, as described in the scenario, a logical graph is designed to describe the level of experience of every person in regard to the specific activity in which she is involved in the community. This graph is composed by a central site that represents the maximum possible level of experience for a specific activity and by a site for every person, which is linked to the central site through a weighted link: the weight of the link represents the distance of the person from the maximum level of

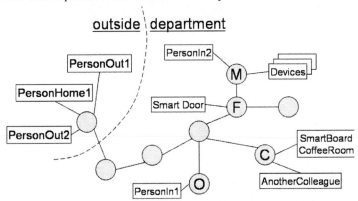

Figure 5. Localization graph for the Meeting. M is the meeting room, F is the area in front of the the the meeting room, C is the coffee room and O is the office of PersonIn1.

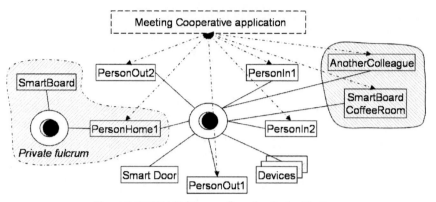

Figure 6. CASMAS' fulcra configuration for the Meeting.

experience achievable for the activity, and in regard to the field diffusion it determines how much the field intensity decrease.

4. Related Work

The well-known projects in the UC research area, such as the project Oxygen developed at MIT [21], the project Aura at Carnegie Mellon University [22], the project Gaia at University of Illinois at Urbana-Champaign [23] and the "Office of the Future" project at Georgia Tech [24], aim at creating technical platforms for UC but lack support for cooperation among people, which instead is our main goal; consequently, in our research we refer to these works mainly during the study of technological solutions for the development and deployment of CASMAS.

One of the innovative aspects of CASMAS is its ability to modulate the degree of members' participation to a community. Some systems disregard group creation and support people only once they have joined the group. For instance in [25] the proposed model allows the dynamic association of devices to people already belonging to a group. Other systems also support the process of group creation by using different criteria that can be explicit (typically data asked to people to match a possibly evolving stereotype) or implicit (features like interests and skills are inferred on the basis of users' interactions with the system). In the Group Adaptive System (GAS) [26], for instance, users belong to groups on the basis of common interests, which are determined through the analysis of the access to (web) resources and interactions among users. Grouping of people can also be based on simple features, like common preferences, e.g., the MusicFX system [27] uses explicit music preferences of people joining the fitness center for the first time, or combination of different characteristics of the users, as proposed by Orwant in [28]. Moreover, organizational structures to group people together are used: for example, in Agent Coordination Context [29] the access to information and services is regulated on the basis of users roles; in [30] the concept of "activity-based computing" is proposed to gather healthcare practitioners on the basis of the activities that they can perform. More in depth, in the activity based computing approach [8] activity is the main concept, instead within our model we want to identify community as a first class object and we use this concept to group people; of course activities are important inside a community and must be supported but we want to support coordination and collaboration even if there is not an explicit activity that represents collaboration among persons. Other approaches collect people according to their location (location-based systems): for instance, the GUIDE system [31] encourages the communication among visitors of a city located in the same place. In [32], users' location is proposed as a mean to build multi-user applications that encourage "serendipitous" meeting between colleagues. For example, the Social Net [33] uses the wireless capability of mobile devices to search for patterns of physical proximity, over time, in order to infer shared interests between users. Similarly, others authors [34] consider the possibility provided by ubiquitous environments to promote "opportunistic interactions" among users who are nearby and share the same interests.

Several research works related to UC, such as [35], provide direct interaction among entities as solution to the problem of coordination of entities in an UC environment; instead our approach provides coordination mechanism both mediated by and modulated on the agents' environment (represented as a graph) and direct coordination through the fulcrum. Furthermore, differently from [36] our approach doesn't provide agent mobility; instead it allows the exchange of rules that describe agents behavior (implementing agents by means of a rule engine).

As already noticed by Byun et al. in [37] there is an apparent correlation between context-aware computing and user modeling techniques although this is not widely explored: the former are used to define characteristics of the context which can be detected by sensors and the latter are used to define characteristics (and behaviors) of the users acquired through the interactions of the user with an application. Consider again the MusicFX application: the co-presence of people in a certain environment (the fitness center) and the acquisition of some characteristics of the users (the music preferences) can be combined together to propose services and information more suitably adapted to the group (to propose the music reflecting the overall taste of the people currently present in the fitness center).

CASMAS allows the definition of general criteria to establish the membership of people to a community through the notion of topological space and the metaphor of field diffusion that can represent both physical and logical aspects dynamically characterizing a user, as described in the previous scenarios. The approaches we have considered above do not take into account this aspect, at least in an explicit way. Some proposals, like the TOTA middleware [38], try to deal with this issue using the propagation of fields metaphor. However, here information associated to fields is modulated through the nodes of a graph reflecting exactly the topological structure of the underlying physical communication infrastructure. In CASMAS instead, the propagation mechanism is more general since it is possible to combine the mutual physical and logical location of users to define how the information can be modulated through the environment with a richer semantics.

5. Conclusion

The possibility to endow common use objects with computational capabilities is likely to have an impact on the way in which people interact with their environment and with actors they cooperate with. On the other hand, the dimension of cooperation, today almost disregarded by the classic research on UC, raises challenges to the solutions proposed by UC. This paper aims to contribute to this cross-fertilization by highlighting the main advantages UC brings to cooperation and by proposing a model and related architecture to design UC environments by taking into account the dimension of cooperation. The implementation of the architecture is ongoing: the integration of two preexisting components led to their re-implementation to improve their functionality. Since UC technologies are not yet available in a large scale we are constructing some emulators that will serve to test our approach. Specifically, we are mainly focusing on e-paper, smart-boards and e-pens in order to be able to deal, at least in their basic aspects, with the presented scenarios and, in a more realistic case, with the health care setting we are currently studying in order to understand how coordination and interoperability within and across hospital departments are achieved [39]. Irrespective of the actual availability of smart objects, the proposed model and architecture has its own value since the considered scenarios can take advantage from its two main features, distributed inference capability and flexible and adaptive management of contextual information, also in presence of more traditional computational devices. Incremental experimentation of these features, in combination with increasingly available smart objects, is part of our future work, in which we will continue to be care of well known concerns of UC such as privacy and comprehensibility of the behaviors of the system.

References

[1] Bellotti, V. and S. Bly, *Walking away from the desktop computer: distributed collaboration and mobility in a product design team* in *Proceedings of the 1996 ACM conference on Computer supported cooperative work* 1996 ACM Press: Boston, Massachusetts, United States p. 209-218

[2] Bardram, J.E. and C. Bossen. *Moving to get aHead: Local Mobility and Collaborative Work.* in *Ninth European Conference on Computer Supported Cooperative Work ECSCW'03.* 2003. Helsinki, FI: ACM Press.

[3] Lave, J. and E. Wenger, *Situated Learning: Legitimate Peripheral Participation.* 1991: Cambridge University Press.

[4] Andriessen, J.H.E. *Archetypes of Knowledge Communities.* in *Second Communities & Technologies Conference (C&T2005).* 2005. Milan, Italy: Springer.

[5] Cabitza, F., et al. *Being at One with Things: The Interconnection Metaphor for Intelligent Environments.* in *The IEE International Workshop on Intelligent Environments (IE05).* 2005. University of Essex, Colchester, UK.

[6] Simone, C. and S. Bandini, *Integrating Awareness in Cooperative Applications through the Reaction-Diffusion Metaphor.* Computer Supported Cooperative Work, The Journal of Collaborative Computing, 2002. **11**(3-4): p. 495-530.

[7] Campbell, R.H. *Beyond Global Communications: The Active World.* in *3rd IEEE International Conference on Pervasive Computing and Communications (PerCom 2005)- Keynote Speech.* 2005. Kauai Island, HI, USA: IEEE Computer Society.

[8] Bardram, J.E., *Supporting Mobility and Collaboration in Ubiquitous Computing.* 2003, Centre for Pervasive Computing: Aarhus, Denmark.

[9] Chen, G. and D. Kotz, *A Survey of Context-Aware Mobile Computing Research.* 2000: Dartmouth College.

[10] Dourish, P., *What we talk about when we talk about context.* Personal and Ubiquitous Computing, 2004. **8**(1): p. 19-30.

[11] Harrison, S. and P. Dourish, *Re-place-ing space: the roles of place and space in collaborative systems* in *Proceedings of the 1996 ACM conference on Computer supported cooperative work* 1996 ACM Press: Boston, Massachusetts, United States p. 67-76

[12] Jacobsen, J., Comiskey, B., et al., *The Last Book.* IBM Systems Journal, 1997. **36**(3).

[13] Arias, E., et al., *Transcending the individual human mind-creating shared understanding through collaborative design.* ACM Trans. Comput.-Hum. Interact., 2000. **7**(1): p. 84-113.

[14] J. C. Thomas, W.A.K., and T. Erickson, *The knowledge management puzzle: Human and social factors in knowledge management.* IBM SYSTEMS JOURNAL, 2001. **40**(4): p. 863-884.

[15] Barkhuus, L., *"Bring your own laptop unless you want to follow the lecture": alternative communication in the classroom* in *Proceedings of the 2005 international ACM SIGGROUP conference on Supporting group work* 2005 ACM Press: Sanibel Island, Florida, USA p. 140-143

[16] Lederman, R., Johnston, R.B. and Milton, S., *The Significance Of Routines For The Analysis And Design Of Information Systems: A Preliminary Study*. Proceedings of European Conference on Information Systems, 2003.

[17] Bradner, E. and G. Mark, *Why distance matters: effects on cooperation, persuasion and deception* in *Proceedings of the 2002 ACM conference on Computer supported cooperative work* 2002 ACM Press: New Orleans, Louisiana, USA p. 226-235

[18] Jacucci, G., et al., *Supporting the shared experience of spectators through mobile group media* in *Proceedings of the 2005 international ACM SIGGROUP conference on Supporting group work* 2005 ACM Press: Sanibel Island, Florida, USA p. 207-216

[19] Abowd, G.D. and A.K. Dey. *Towards a Better Understanding of Context and Context-Awareness*. in *Workshop on The What, Who, Where, When, and How of Context-Awareness - Conference on Human Factors in Computing Systems (CHI 2000)*. 2000. The Hague, The Netherlands: ACM Press.

[20] Cabitza, F., et al. *CASMAS: Supporting Cooperation in Ubiquitous Computing Environments*. in *PerCom (Accepted)*. 2006.

[21] Dertouzos, M.L., *The Future of Computing*. j-SCI-AMER, 1999. **281**(2): p. 52--??

[22] Pedro Sousa, D.G., *Aura: an Architectural Framework for User Mobility in Ubiquitous Computing Environments*. WICSA, 2002: p. 29-43.

[23] Roman, M., et al., *A middleware infrastructure for active spaces*. Pervasive Computing, IEEE, 2002. **1**(4): p. 74-83.

[24] MacIntyre, B., et al., *Support for multitasking and background awareness using interactive peripheral displays* in *Proceedings of the 14th annual ACM symposium on User interface software and technology* 2001 ACM Press: Orlando, Florida p. 41-50

[25] Wang, B., J. Bodily, and S.K.S. Gupta, *Supporting Persistent Social Groups in Ubiquitous Computing Environments Using Context-Aware Ephemeral Group Service* in *Proceedings of the Second IEEE International Conference on Pervasive Computing and Communications (PerCom'04)* 2004 IEEE Computer Society. p. 287

[26] Barra, M., et al., eds. *GAS: Group Adaptive System*. Lecture Notes in Computer Science. Vol. 2347. 2002, Springer-Verlag GmbH. 47.

[27] McCarthy, J.F. and T.D. Anagnost, *MusicFX: an arbiter of group preferences for computer supported collaborative workouts* in *Proceedings of the 1998 ACM conference on Computer supported cooperative work* 1998 ACM Press: Seattle, Washington, United States p. 363-372

[28] Orwant, J., *Heterogeneous learning in the Doppelganger User Modeling System*. User Modeling and User-Adapted Interaction, 1995. **4**(2): p. 107-130.

[29] Ricci, A., M. Viroli, and A. Omicini. *Agent coordination context: From theory to practice*. in *Cybernetics and Systems 2004, (EMCSR 2004)*. 2004. Vienna, Austria.

[30] Bardram, J.E. and H.B. Christensen, *Supporting Pervasive Collaboration in Healthcare - An Activity-Driven Computing Infrastructure*. 2004, Centre for Pervasive Computing: Arhus.

[31] Cheverst, K., et al. *Sharing (Location) Context to Facilitate Collaboration Between City Visitors*. in *IMC'00 Workshop on Interactive Applications of Mobile Computing*. 2000. Rostock, Germany.

[32] Ashbrook, D. and T. Starner, *Using GPS to learn significant locations and predict movement across multiple users* Personal Ubiquitous Comput. , 2003 **7** (5): p. 275-286

[33] Terry, M., et al. *Social net: using patterns of physical proximity over time to infer shared interests*. in *Conference Extended Abstracts on Human Factors in Computing Systems (CHI2002)*. 2002. Minneapolis, Minnesota, USA: ACM Press.

[34] Favela, J., et al. *Supporting Opportunistic Interactions with People, Resources and Agents in Ubiquitous Enviroments*. in *Mobile Ad-hoc Collaboration Workshop at CHI 2002*. 2002. Minneapolis, Minnesota, USA.

[35] Tafat-Bouzid, A.C., M; Hirsbrunner, B, *A coordination model for ubiquitous computing*. WSEAS Transactions on Computers, 2003. **2**(3): p. 819-823.

[36] O'Hare, G.M.P., et al., *Ambient Intelligence Through Agile Agents*. 3345 ed. Lecture Notes in Computer Science. 2005. 286-310.

[37] Byun, H.E. and K. Cheverst. *Exploiting User Models and Context-Awareness to Support Personal Daily Activities*. in *Workshop in UM2001 on User Modeling for Context-Aware Applications*. 2001.

[38] Mamei, M., F. Zambonelli, and L. Leonardi. *Tuples On The Air: A middleware for context-aware computing in dynamic networks*. in *23rd International Conference on Distributed Computing Systems (ICDCSW '03)*. 2003: IEEE Computer Society.

[39] Cabitza, F., et al., *When once is not enough: the role of redundancy in a hospital ward setting*, in *Proceedings of the 2005 international ACM SIGGROUP conference on Supporting group work*. 2005, ACM Press: Sanibel Island, Florida, USA. p. 158-167.

Cooperative Systems Design
P. Hassanaly et al. (Eds.)
IOS Press, 2006

Torres, a Conceptual Framework for Articulation Work across Boundaries

Federico CABITZA, Marcello SARINI, Carla SIMONE and Michele TELARO
University of Milano-Bicocca

Abstract. In this paper we present Torres, a conceptual framework that supports people belonging to different groups to articulate their activities. Our work is based on observations of how healthcare practitioners manage the interactions occurring when the patients' care crosses the borders of a healthcare facility. On the basis of previous works on reconciliation and of our observations, we aim to provide a framework to understand these interactions and to computationally support them so to convey the local knowledge needed both to guarantee the continuity of care and to promote the articulation of the related activities.

Keywords: Articulation work, Socio-technical Systems, Information Systems, Reconciliation, Health care, Distributed care

1. Outline of the paper

In this paper we present Torres, a conceptual framework that focuses on how people belonging to different groups (or communities, or operative units) articulate their activities to cooperate towards a common goal and on how to support this articulation work. We give first the background both to frame the phenomenon of articulation within the inter-group dimension (also called "global articulation work" in [1]) and to frame this interest within our wider research area of supporting health practitioners in their cooperative work (see Section 2).

Then we expose the main problems we observed occurring when traditional (often paper-based) forms fill the gaps in clinical practice and caring between different hospital facilities (see Section 3.1). Hence, basing on a qualitative analysis of these shortcomings, we expose the main assumptions, concepts and ideas that constitute the framework, which we think could be employed as a conceptual tool to more deeply consider how *socio-technical interfaces* (see Section 2) are deployed in real settings (see Section 3.2); then, we will propose some general indications to conceive comprehensive functionalities that could make *interface artifacts* (e.g., paper or web-based forms) more effective in their twofold function of information gateways and tools for articulation (see Section 3.4).

In Section 4, we relate the functionalities of these computationally augmented *interface artifacts* to their underpinning *local models*[1] and we will consider the role of

---

1 It is necessary to distinguish between the models that are produced within the Torres framework (local formal representations, LFRs) and those that are conceived and used in any field of work for any reason (we prefer calling these models *explicit representations*, ERs). LFRs are a kind of explicit representations but, more specifically, in Torres a *local formal representation* is any clear, explicit *and as*

modeling in the description (and characterization) of work settings as well as in the management of the related work practices. In considering modeling we widen the acceptation of the term "users" to include also those users that are hopefully included, as selected representatives, in those task forces and committees that are in charge of issuing regulations, protocols and artifacts by which cooperation is advocated either in a particular health-care setting (e.g., hospital) or in a wider scope (e.g., an administrative region).

2. Background and Motivations

The concept of articulation work was introduced by Anselm Strauss as a convenient way to refer to the specifics of "putting together tasks" and "aligning actions" [2], so that multiple and interdependent work trajectories ("courses of action [embracing] the interaction of multiple actors and contingencies that may be unanticipated") could be managed. Schmidt and Bannon [3] introduced this concept in the field of CSCW to indicate the work of alignment, both of actions, practices and meanings, that support "cooperative work" and that must be taken into account to understand the interwoven nature of mutually dependent actions of collaborating actors. As pointed out by Schmidt [4], people quite easily achieve articulation of their work trajectories when they can rely on co-located and synchronous communication and, accordingly, some studies (e.g., [5]) have confirmed that everyday social life (like talking, gesturing and even just standing somewhere at a specific time) can make people extremely good in handling the "contingencies that may be unanticipated and even and not entirely manageable" occurring in cooperative work.

We drew a similar conclusion in a previous work [6] of ours, when we studied the coordination phenomenon within a hospital ward, aiming at analyzing what has been called "local articulation work" [1]. With this term we propose speaking of *intra-system articulation work*, so to avoid the spatial connotation related to the notion of locality and to explicitly adopt the more general notion of socio-technical system [7], that is, a network encompassing technological parts (the hardware, the software, the control structures, the data and their structure), as well as the surrounding environment, the procedures, the operative processes, the laws and regulations, and obviously the users, i.e., who use the technology and interact with each other by shared practices, techniques and conventions. From now on, we use system as a shortcut of socio-technical system.

In that work, by focusing on how nurses coordinate with each other by means of formal and informal documents, paper and electronic forms and of the related practices that let information be extracted out of artifacts, we have seen that coordination heavily relies on a "good redundancy". This seems to turn the concept of efficiency related to digitalization into an open issue for hospital ward coordination, since redundancy or better yet the lack of redundancy can give us a key to understand in which context of cooperative work digitalization can be useful or even a necessary support. As a matter of fact, in our observations, we have seen that the phenomenon of "good redundancy" that characterizes coordinative practices within a single ward (i.e., within a local domain) seems to be lost in the case of the cooperation between wards and between

much as formal as possible representation of *what about a certain system* (in terms of work and practices) *has to be perceived from the outside world.*

wards and diagnostic laboratories, that is when we front what has been called "global articulation work" [1], i.e., articulation occurring in an *inter-system* domain. In this case, actors that interact across two (or more) systems' boundaries can not easily get an overview of the state of affairs of the other field of work and, informal communication is less effective due to the difficulties in achieving a common ground.

For these reasons, inter-system articulation work is so often mediated by some *socio-technical interface* that should be mutually recognized by actors of the systems involved in order to be able to bridge the gap of knowledge. By socio-technical interface we mean any means that "mediate" human interaction and "surrogate" face-to-face and co-located communication (e.g., phone calls, fax transmissions, e-mails, instant messaging, web and paper forms) as well as any protocol and convention that "regulate" the use of the (technological) interface and makes information exchange through them possible.

In this paper, we then focus on how to identify and characterize socio-technical interfaces so to be able to propose computational surrogates improving inter-system articulation work. In [8] the authors analyzed how the concept of interoperability is involved in supporting inter-system articulation work; they referred to a semantic interoperability rather than to a mere technological one that is mainly focused on the format of heterogeneous data. In fact, besides agreeing on the exchange format, actors must also find a compromise on the meaning of the exchanged data so that interdependent activities could be effectively articulated on the basis of these — even offhanded — agreements. This means that people have to find ways to interpret how who is collaborating with them organizes and accomplishes her work according to their own, so that interventions on the same work trajectory (e.g., the production of the same good, the provision of the same service, or the shared, "multidisciplinary" care on the same patient) are directed towards the same goal. One of the ways to get this mutual knowledge is called there *reconciliation*: this is the process by which members of different systems align the meanings related to their own worldviews in order to cooperate and act in mutually interdependent manner on the same work trajectory.

In order to align meanings to make inter-system articulation work possible, *explicit representations* play a relevant role since they are often the only way to make those meanings accessible. With the term *explicit representations* (ER), we refer to any outcome of the activity aimed to model and represent aspects of a certain work or domain according to different needs (e.g., in the hospital ward domain, to manage work shifts, to classify diet regimen): in this view, ER are something more general than either conceptual schema, classification schemes (as discussed in [9]) or ontologies. Explicit representations can be more or less formalized and more or less institutional: e.g., they can be provided either as references by some acknowledged authority (i.e., standards), or by local steering committees (e.g., the hospital management) to define and structure the field of work of their employees.

The previous implementations (e.g., [10]) of the Reconciler focused on explicit representations aimed at describing particular terminologies and jargons, so as to avoid misunderstandings and resolve in a semi-automatic manner terminological conflicts in written communication. Relying on the comprehension of the phenomenon of reconciliation provided by the deployment of the Reconciler, our current effort is directed towards the conception of a more comprehensive framework by which the communication-oriented functionalities devised in the former Reconciler are seen as part and parcels of a broader support to inter-system articulation work, that promotes a richer awareness about the part of protocols and practices that may influence the articulation of activities crossing the borders of a system.

3. Interfacing the chasm

In order to achieve a deep understanding of which practices are employed to cross the chasm between two different systems, we conducted some further observational sessions in the Internal Medicine ward studied in [6].

3.1. The grey area of articulation

During our informal talks with the head nurse of the ward in hand, one of the most urging concerns she manifested was that the *continuity of care* can be put at risk when a patient is referred to external services (e.g., specialistic referrals, visits, diagnostic imaging tests) as well as in any other case a patient trajectory unfolds across different systems. The head nurse suggestively defined the inter-wards articulation a "grey area" of care giving: in fact, nurses, when they interact with the outside world (e.g., to transfer the patient to another facility, like the Radiology or Cardiology wards), can not rely on the same background of shared knowledge that is the most important resource that makes acts meaningful and practices effective in any handoff [6].

These transfers and referrals are mediated by paper-based forms that encompass basic data to identify the inpatient as well as concise clinical data to "frame" her medical case; in fact, these forms are compiled by physicians to only convey a *minimum data set* of information necessary for the examination or the referral (i.e., which service is required and the reason why it is required). That notwithstanding, both forms and — most importantly — patients are "handled" and managed also by other practitioners (nurses, hospital assistants, clerks and lab technicians) on the basis of boundary conditions about caring and the overall status of the patient. Since, for the examination be accomplished, the involved inpatient has to be moved or has to follow a specific preparation, also the caring dimension is heavily affected by the service provision and vice-versa. The *interface artifacts* currently available do not provide nurses with specific and formal means to share the information needed to really maintain the illness trajectory [11] seamless with the practitioners of the external services taking in charge the patient. For this reason, referring a patient outside the ward can risk the quality of care that is enabled by the intimacy and sympathy that nurses reach with the inpatient on a daily basis.

3.2. All (information) flows

In Fig. 1.a we show the typical information flows that are involved in the interaction between two healthcare units (e.g, two wards), namely the Service Requester (SR) and the Service Provider (SP). To ask for a service, the *requesting* ward has to provide some clinical data to the *providing* unit: to this aim, the provider defines and publishes proper forms (mostly paper-based) that all the requesters are supposed to use to have access to its services. For obvious reasons, providers issue few general forms that must fit as many services and their requesters as possible. In the past, almost all requesters were from within the same hospital or, at least, the same catchment area; the same

a)   b)

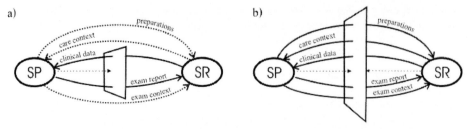

Figure 1. Information flows as they are exchanged through any socio-technical interface. (a) depicts the traditional situation in a hospital setting; (b) depicts the Torres interface to support inter-articulation work.

phenomena that we observed during our informal talks could arise more critical issues since, under the drive of more efficient resource management and relevant cost cuts, healthcare provision tends to be outsourced to a number of smaller and specialized units, which constitute a highly distributed and relatively loosely-coupled net of "competence systems" [12] active within a large territory[2] : these current trends in healthcare and the encouraging results for chronic diseases and long-term rehabilitation of the so called "Shared Care Systems" [13] make the number of potential requesters of a diagnostic, therapeutic or rehabilitative service virtually unknown. Also for this reason, providers can be what in [9] is defined a *classification schemes producer* in that the Service Provider often is the only party that unilaterally produces not only the information structure and the affordances of the forms, but also the explicit representations and conventions of use that are reified by the physical forms (this influence is represented by the rightward straight arrow in Fig. 1.a). Distributedness of care and unilaterality of scheme production make collaboration and articulation work across unit boundaries much more demanding than the local case: in fact there are some evidences that the longer *organizational distance* between the producer of schemes and their consumers, the stronger dependance on a high level of formalization of the articulation activities [14] as well as the bigger the risk of misunderstanding on the meanings that underpin the information exchange [9].

Forms cover different functions: on one hand, their completion and submission is the event that triggers all the processes underpinning the provision of a service. On the other hand they are the actual means by which clinical information about the required service are conveyed. Usually not all the flows depicted in Fig. 1.a are mediated by forms (or any other official and formal *interface artifact*): if this can only affect the efficiency of the interaction in small contexts where informal means (like phone calls or personal connections) can be employed, in other cases where the "organizational distance" is bigger effective interaction can be even completely precluded (this difficulty is represented by the dotted arrows in Fig. 1.a).

Let us now consider in more details the typical information streams flowing across different systems. If the patient must undertake any specific preparation in order to accomplish the service (e.g. for many endoscopic examinations the patient must fast) information about such preparation must be provided by SP. Preparation is the process aimed at fulfilling the service preconditions. There are different kinds of preparations, according to different services, that, if not fulfilled, can cause different consequences to all the involved actors (i.e. SR, SP and the patient). Preparations can represent a specific task for SR practitioners: e.g., if a patient must fast before a certain test,

---

2 This is especially true within the provincial context, where a large number of people live scattered in a wide regional area in which no city is much bigger — or more important — than the others.

specific actions have to be planned by SR nurses in order to coordinate a number of different actors (e.g., annotating the fast regimen on the patient documentation, communicating it to the kitchen, etc...). Preparations can also concern "getting information about the patient" and "inform the patient about the examination" (*informed consent*): e.g., some examinations can be dangerous according to the patient status and, if specific conditions are not checked, consequences can seriously impact on the patient health.

The caring contextual information, flowing from the SR unit to the SP unit, regards two different dimensions: activities guaranteeing continuity of care and activities guaranteeing coordination among practitioners. The former dimension comprises all the information regarding the inpatient that, although not strictly necessary for the specific service provision, the nurses feel necessary to convey according to the status of the inpatient, in order to assure the continuity of care. The latter dimension more specifically regards coordination. Although, once a service has been required, SP becomes accountable for it, service execution also affects processes occurring in the SR unit: e.g., activities between the SR and SP units must be accordingly coordinated both in case the patient must be transferred to SP to undertake an examination (in this case, either SR's practitioners have to bring the patient to SP or SP's practitioners come to take the patient) and in case the examination must occur at the patient bedside (as for electrocardiogram).

The arrow that in Fig. 1.a is labeled 'exam context' and that flows from SP to SR indicates the *effects* of the examination, that is everything SR nurses have to know about what happened during and immediately after the examination in order to assure the proper caring when the patient is back to the ward. All together with this information, the provider sends the requester a diagnosis report that constitute the essential and legal outcome of the service and that for its status the requester includes within the clinical documentation attesting the "illness trajectory" of the patient during her stay at hospital.

3.3. When Information flows break down

The analysis of different information flows among different wards shows that only few data are conveyed through formal official means (e.g. paper-based forms): only registry and clinical data are explicitly required to trigger any external service provision and referral (in figure 1.a they are denoted as 'clinical data' and 'exam report'). Accordingly, we can analyze breakdowns regarding the information flows depending on whether data are conveyed by means of an official channel or not. In the former case, breakdowns can occur whenever conveyed data are insufficient, ambiguous or misunderstood. As regards the latter case, in our case study, no formal and official channel is employed to convey information about the preparations, about the examination effects and about the actual caring and examination contexts. This lack of official means can result in two kinds of problems: a) loose coordination of care activities across different wards; and hence, b) possible seams in the continuity of care around the inpatient. In our case study, preparations as activities performed on the patient's body are not conveyed by means of a form: usually nurses know how to prepare a patient thanks to their professional background. Preparations as information requests are more often mediated by the request forms or some attachments, since they also imply legal consequences. For example, when a Magnetic Resonance Imaging (MRI) is prescribed, the Radiology ward provides a specific form to the SR unit so that, for example, nurses can check the patient does not have any steel object on. This form also contains a set of questions that the prescribing physician has to ask to the patient. On the other hand, when a woman has to undertake a pelvis RX, there is no form to help nurses (both SR and SP nurses) to be reminded to check whether the patient is not pregnant.

As regards the caring context flow, in order to guarantee the continuity of care dimension, nurses can feel necessary to convey patient's global conditions, even if examinations usually regard specific apparatus. For example, nurses could feel necessary to notice who takes in charge a patient for a cardiology examination that the patient suffers from dizzy spells, since they think that this is a case in which the patient deserves a special attention for her transfer. Lacking official means to convey this information, nurses can only recommend particular patient's needs to their willing colleagues when they bring them to the examination venue. Obviously, the efficiency of such an oral reminding depends on different situated factors (e.g. the level of acquaintance between two nurses, or their willingness to help). Moreover relying on all these situated factors or ad-hoc remedies can not always be feasible (e.g., nurses can even ignore who to call and how to relate to her) in a geographically distributed setting.

Also coordination can be affected by this lack of official channels: for example, if SP practitioners come to take the patient when she is already engaged in another activity, they have to come back again later; when SP practitioners ask to SR practitioners to bring them a patient, SP practitioners do not know if their colleagues have to interrupt an activity in order to accomplish the task. "Thinking locally" about coordination is simply not enough in cases like this and can have even more serious consequences since continuity of care and coordination are very often intertwined: e.g., if a cardiologist asks to SR nurses to take him four patients at the same time because he thinks that, in so doing, he can more conveniently manage the alternation of patients and hence save his time (and hence see more patients), two types of unintended repercussions can occur. This reasonable request can negatively affect internal coordination of the SR ward in that to transfer four patients all together could represent a significant interruption of the ward habitual activities. But this request can also affect continuity of care since transferred patients could remain out-of-ward for a longer time before undertaking the examination; moreover, if some critical conditions raise, patients would be assisted by practitioners that do not know their anamnesis and that could even be less competent for the specific pathology for which patients had been admitted in hospital.

As regards the exam context flow, the lack of official medium can risk the patient's health itself. For example, many endoscopic examinations (e.g. gastroscopy) require the patient take some sedative to facilitate the introduction of the probe. In this case, patients can be affected either in that they can not swallow anything for a while, or in that they can not even be able to move by themselves, according to the sedating modality. Obviously, SR nurses must be aware of these effects to prevent the patient being harmed when she comes back to the habitual ward activities. Like for the preparation procedures, nurses usually know this information but since some of these procedures can vary, and no every actual effect is beforehand known, the only way to be sure is an efficient information handoff between SP and SR nurses.

In the hospital in hand, information about preparations and standard exam effects are becoming progressively available on the LAN: the management has decided to publish this information to comply with international quality standards on a specific web site, namely the Q-Web, where each ward is supposed to put the detailed descriptions of all its internal procedures. That notwithstanding, the information that is available on line is much less significant (and hence used) than it could be if it were "connected" to the single patient cases, that is to the actual examination everyday undertaken at the hospital.

Also in the case of clinical data, i.e., in the case of data that are actually transmitted by means of a formal and official means, we detected some weaknesses that can lead to information breakdowns, by observing how paper-based forms are actually used by practitioners in their habitual practices. For example, in some forms (e.g, the Specialistic Consultancy Request Form) there are some fields whose labels either are not unambiguous or do not refer to something that applies to the requesting setting. This brings either to not filling in the corresponding field or to not properly filling them. The above mentioned form requires that both the ward name from which the inpatient is moved and the name of whom is filling the request form must be clearly indicated; for this reason, the form requires to fill in three fields, labeled respectively "operative unit", "section" and "director". Operative units is the way in which wards are named within the referred hospital setting but since this is not a standard way to call wards in Italian, misunderstanding can arise when the request comes from other hospitals that ignore that convention. Sections, within the referred setting, are different sectors of the same ward; but even in the same hospital there are wards that do not have any sector inside, this leading to an unintended blank in the submitted form. The director is the only person that, in the ward that published the request form, is in charge of requesting referrals; misunderstandings can then arise when a referral to that facility comes from settings (e.g., other wards or hospitals) where any physician is accountable for approving and signing the request form and not only the chief.

3.4. Shedding light on the grey divide

From our observations we can analyze and draw some non-functional requirements that interface artifacts must guarantee to be supportive for both the parties involved and to provide a base of mutual comprehension to make a sound alignment of meanings possible. Besides the quite obvious (but not that simple to get since quite opposing) requirements of *completeness* and *essentiality*, on one hand, and *accuracy* and *timeliness* from the other hand, we now consider those that in our opinion can more positively affect the hospital ward context: *comprehensibility*, *transparency* and *commitment*. The former regards the extent the requester is able to understand what she is supposed to fill in the form in order to use it and exploit it as a "representative" (or better yet, "proxy") of her needs and requirements. *Transparency*, rather than being related to disappearance (a common concept in human-computer interaction debate), refers to the capability of an interface artifact to conceal the excessive complexity of the interfaced reality (to which it represents a sort of gateway) as well as to make visible only selected portions of that reality, i.e., only what is meaningful in a particular context. To take an example from the observed forms, the legend at the bottom of a form explaining a certain term or some information need can be seen as a transparent glass on *which* and *how* work is carried out within the other system, in that it explains the rationale behind specific terms or form fields. With *commitment* we mean the ability to convey the need of a requesting actor to commit a colleague of another system about a particular patient, so that the latter practitioner can be considered bound (either emotionally or intellectually) to the care of that particular patient. As a result of more committed practitioners, the transfer to external facilities could be perceived by the patient herself as much as seamless and stressless as possible. Likewise, commitment refers to the need of the providers to get more accurate and complete requests by making the requester feel involved (and hence committed) in the provision process and part and parcel of it.

All these qualities must be fulfilled by any socio-technical interface, either based on paper or on any computational means. That notwithstanding, we think that the interface should be able to mediate — whenever necessary — all the information flows depicted in Fig. 1 (see the b case) so that information can be conveyed entangled with its context of production and its context of use.

It can be difficult or not at all feasible to conceive such an interface on a paper medium. As a matter of fact, in our previous work on hospital wards work [6], we draw conclusions that were in line with those of authors that think that an effective technological alternative to the paper-based forms in the hospital field of work [15] is quite difficult to conceive for the often underrated qualities of the paper medium. That notwithstanding the qualities that paper-based forms boast in a circumscribed local domain (e.g. non being disruptive in use and easily portable) simply do not apply in bridging the chasm of information and articulation between different systems. Instead, the fact that, in that context, paper-based forms require physical delivery, mediate only asynchronous and limited communication and, above all, can only be used for displaying static markings [16], brings us to consider how computer-based interface artifacts (like standard web forms) could be augmented in order to facilitate seamless care across borders.

In fact, if essentiality is usually achieved *a priori* by the definition of a proper minimum data set, it could be not easy to achieve the other qualities only by optimizing a paper-based form filling (i.e., its structure) and by merely optimizing forms exchange. Indeed, the driving reason for the adoption and acceptation of digital forms in stead of paper-based counterparts is to promote timeliness (and the correlated concept of efficiency) through the fast dispatch guaranteed by the electronic medium. Likewise, completeness and accuracy can be more easily obtained once requests are digitalized, e.g., by means of simple verification functions at client side, which match mandatory fields or allowable value lists with the submitted requests. What is still open to research is how to guarantee commitment, transparency and comprehensibility, however the interface is. As regards comprehensibility, and hence the need to reconcile involved parties on terms and their meanings, our framework propose to exploit the correspondences among local formal representations that are found by tools like the Reconciler [10], and to combine these correspondences with communication technologies (like chat) and with access to communication history on precise items of the form in order to build a context of interpretation that could facilitate the mutual comprehension.

As regards commitment, the same Radiodiagnostic Request form encompasses a specific section where who receives the forms is supposed to judge the request in terms of completeness and appropriateness (according to the DL187/2000 Italian law). Nevertheless, the efficacy of this section in creating a positive feedback mechanism is undermined in that the form is not returned to the requesting ward. For this reason, on the basis of our field studies, we think that commitment could be facilitated by conveying both caring and examination context through free-text areas and communication technologies (like instant messaging) and could be further facilitated by some feedback and mutual evaluation mechanism on the quality of the request and of the service provision.

In our framework, we think that to conceive suitable computer-based alternatives to existing paper forms and to be able to design them properly requires, first of all, a preliminary phase in which the information structure underpinning a specific form (i.e., what addresses specific information needs of the form provider) is extracted, both from the form's affordances and its habitual and effective use. In this way, parts of the worldviews of the practitioners using the interface artifacts (or better yet, the worldviews that are reified in specific forms) can be made explicit and the inner models that "inform" (i.e., shape) their information exchange be explicitly represented. As such, the explicit representations of the work carried out at the boundary of a system can finally be enriched properly so as to support articulation with the "external world". In fact, this "richer" information can be used for a twofold aim: on the one hand, to provide practitioners involved in designing or evaluating new forms with the necessary background knowledge to conceive and choose to adopt better traditional (e.g., paper-based) forms; and, on the other — and more ICT-oriented — hand, to provide computer-based system designers with the necessary models by which to implement computational artifacts that are really grounded in the practices that they aim to support but that they also inevitably end up by radically changing [17]. Torres is then proposed as a comprehensive framework aimed not only at detecting which dimensions of *inter-articulation* are critical in a given work setting, but also at facilitating the design of interface artifacts. To this aim Torres provides designers (or anyone is accountable for tuning the "interface" over time) with some tools by which to model their domain consistently with the above mentioned requirements.

4. Models as a part of CSCW design

As reported in the previous section as a result of our observations on the field, the artifacts (i.e., the request forms), which are used at the interface to mediate "formal" and "official" communications between members of different systems, often are not "rich" enough to convey all the needed information according to the context. We think that such interface artifacts must be made much richer than are actually, in that they must be able to "inform" their users on both sides, i.e., to shape the thought and the action of who receives the information and to make more aware who sends data of their meanings and their consequences. Enriching the information structure behind any interface artifacts requires — at some extent – a modeling process.

As a matter of fact, it was already recognized in the literature (e.g., [18]) the positive value for practitioners (or at least for their acknowledged representatives) of being involved in the design of the artifacts they will end by using; this process in fact requires people to reconsider carefully their own work and this often cause them to become more aware of it and of its (often hidden and implicit) mechanisms. During our interviews at the hospital it was pretty clear that organizing committees of motivated representatives of the involved users and having them design new kinds of forms at support of their everyday practice was a key factor within the more general improvement process of the internal procedures of the hospital. That notwithstanding we were told that modeling their work practices and the related documental artifacts was a quite tough task, especially for the worker categories that were most useful in the modeling process: who was not accustomed to doing that (e.g., nurses, physicians).

What we propose in this paper, Torres, is a conceptual framework by which to conceive, design and build supportive interface artifacts on which members of different systems can base their interaction and articulate their activities around some common cooperative work trajectory (e.g., the healing treatments on a patient). In our proposal, we focus on modeling and more specifically on modeling a local domain with the aim to characterize articulation work occurring across the domain's boundaries. In order to facilitate modeling and hence the participation of final users in the design process, we propose a simple two-phase process.

Artifacts can be seen as the tools that enable — as well as constrain — any collaborative activity since they embody a whole history of social practices in their design and physical shape [19]. As a consequence of this, the first phase assumes the central role of artifacts in mediating interactions across inter-system borders. Accordingly, in this phase, we propose the designer to adopt a loose semantics formalism (e.g., the Entity-Relationship model, Semantic Networks) so that also unskilled people could use it and describe in an approximate but yet simple way their work domain. This phase also aims to make explicit the information structure of artifacts and, in so doing, to also make visible the practices that are inscribed in them, since these two aspects are often intertwined [17]. From our point of view, considering also practices is an added value to the framework, even if often it could not be easy for people to make their usual (*ready-at-hand*) work practices emerge and become explicit within any formal representation of them.

If we consider the scenario depicted in the previous section — the service request and provision — we see that users from the requesting facility will consider the form that mediates the provision of the service from their peculiar point of view. In order to support alignment of the meanings the form refers to, we propose that users from both the providing facility and the requesting facility trace a formal representation of the form: we call this representation an Artifact Formal Representation (AFR), which encompasses all the concepts encompassed in the form that do locally have a meaning (whatever it is). After that the AFRs have been drawn, we propose both teams to identify all other relevant concept that in their local domain has something to do with the AFRs concepts. In this phase users can use any relationship to relate concepts together and hence make Local Formal Representations (LFRs) as peculiar and specific as they like. Our intent is not to have people represent their work practices thoroughly and in fine-grainedly: we rather think that is important to motivate people in identifying the (linguistic) elements which could be problematic in the considered practices and give them way to reach a mutual understanding in discussing them. Starting from concrete items of the actual forms that is used to mediate the request of a service, using a simplified formalism and modeling one's own domain with the specific aim to characterize it "at the terminal", all these indications should provide the next phase with some explicit representation to work with, no matter how complete or rigorous it is.

In the second phase – after that a LFR of the local domains, whose users need to interact and coordinate with respect to some common goal, has been conceived – the framework proposes the modelers (e.g., domain experts and users' representatives) to enrich the semantics of these explicit representations by relating them to a simplified model of the articulation work occurring in their work settings. To do that, Torres provides the modelers with two tools: the AW model and a meta-model, i.e., a set of framework-specific relationships by which to relate the elements of the LFR to the categories of the AW model (see next section for details). The result of this second phase is then called an Enriched Local Formal Representation

(ELFR), i.e., a domain dependent representation of a work setting that is derived from artifacts that are used to articulate across borders.

The ELFRs facilitate a semi-automatic task of detecting *correspondences*[3] between concepts of different LFRs on which to base the deployment of a richer set of functionalities in the computational interfaces that support inter-system coordination. In fact, on the one hand, users are facilitated in being aware of possible correspondences among elements of different ELFRs by the automatic search for all possible relevant concept-chains that share some previously aligned meaning. On the other hand, the correspondences that are proposed by the computational system (see next section), once they are validated (i.e., either confirmed or rejected) by users, can be used to facilitate the comprehension of part of the internal processes that are related to the provision of the service so to promote comprehensibility by means of transparency and even mutual commitment.

Our artifact-centered and bottom-up approach is then in contrast with top-down approaches where the users are provided with an upper and widely agreed ontology of the domain in hand; in fact, as reported in the literature [20], for the users it could be difficult to comply with an ontology (if any) whose elements do not tightly fit their usual work practices, which is common for the obvious need of generality implied in high-level standard ontologies. Instead, our two phase approach aims at conducting progressively the users to define in more and more details a representation of their work domain which reflects their work practices. The additional effort requested to users for their modeling activity should then be rewarded by the opportunity of using more effectively interface artifacts that could fulfill the requirements mentioned in Sec. 3.4 and, moreover, achieve sufficient *flexibility* and the ability to promote reconciliation between different or even incommensurable perspectives about the same concepts or goals.

5. The Torres AW model and meta-model

Since our main aim is to support people in modeling how interdependent activities are articulated across boundaries, we propose to enrich the semantics of the local formal representations by identifying and making explicit the relationships occurring between them and an Articulation Work (AW) model[4] . The basic AW model proposed in Torres is based on Ariadne, a notation that was proposed to support people in the design of (local) coordination mechanisms [21] by which interdependent activities of human actors are articulated. To this aim, Ariadne provides some basic and empirically-based constructs called "Categories of Articulation Work" (CAW). CAWs are the basic constructs by which the main concepts involved in the phenomenon of articulation work are represented. Since we conjecture that, in order to represent articulation work "at the terminals", some of the inner details of the articulation work in the whole work setting in hand can be left unexpressed, the Torres AW model

---

[3] Correspondences is the name we give the "relationships" crossing the "chasm" between different LFRs.
[4] We have realized a lightweight Java application, named Reconciler v.2, by which to easily draw LFRs and correspondences among them. We are augmenting this application by including some algorithms by which "meaningful" correspondences will be suggested to users and put forward for their consideration and further consolidation. Its documentation, as well as an RDF representation of the AW model will be progressively updated at the following URL: http://www.mac.disco.unimib.it/torres/ .

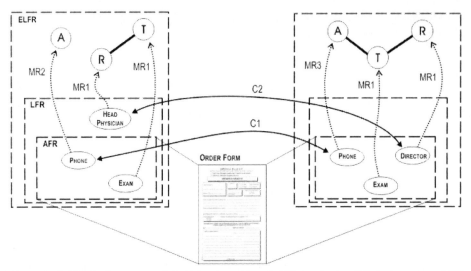

Figure 2. ELFRs for the requester (left side) and provider of a RX examination. Thin broken arrows (MR1, MR2, MR3) describe Torres meta-model relationships between formal representations (i.e., the specialized AW model in the upper half, the LFRs in the lower half). Correspondences (thick black arrows, C1, C2) between different LFRs are identified through the semi-automatic approach of the Reconciler tool.

borrows from Ariadne a limited set of categories and related attributes and relationships, namely the CAWs of Role, Actor, Resource, Task and Activity[5] and a few relationships between them. For example, between the CAWs Role and Task there is a relationship *is-responsible-for*, by which it is expressed the fact that, once a human actor assuming a particular Role is assigned to a Task (the CAW expressing a unit of work), she is responsible for the accomplishment of the specified task.

The Torres meta-model is a set of relationships by which designers can relate any concept of a LFR to a specialized category of the AW model that can enrich and better specify its semantics (see broken arrows in Fig. 2). The main relationship of this kind is *refers-to-caw* (see relationship MR1 in Fig. 2, e.g., the relationship that specifies that the Head Physician is a Role). In addition, concepts involved in some process in a LFR can be linked to Activities of the AW model by means of specific relationships that are inspired by a process-oriented paradigm (like IOPE [22]). More specifically, the *is-Input* relationship relates concepts that represent information elements fed into and processed in a certain activity to the activity itself; *is-Output* connects information elements that come as a result of the activity accomplishment (see relationship MR2 in Fig. 2); *involved-in-Preconditions* connects concepts that must be involved as conditions necessary for an activity to start with the activity itself (see relationship MR3 in Fig. 2); *involved-in-Effects* connects concepts that are subject to some change after and because of the activity's completion; *is-Resource-involved* connects concepts that are either tools or objects of an activity.

By relying on these relationships, different families of correspondences can be detected: in the example provided in Fig. 2, C1 represents an Homonymy

---

5 In particular, in Torres we adopt the concept of Activity as "simple process" [22], i.e., as something not further articulated, a black box: accordingly the Ariadne CAW Activity in the AW model subsumes all the correlated concepts (e.g., those of process and action).

correspondence between concepts which have the same label (Phone) but different meanings since they refer to different activities for the requesters and the providers of the service. In this case the system would notify the user with a warning about the Phone concept which could be related to different practices and hence has different meanings for the provider and requester of a service. The C2 correspondence instead represents a Synonymy correspondence between the Head Physician concept of the requester and the Director concept of the provider, since both of them are detected as entities that can be responsible of an Exam. In this case the system would suggest the users that the two entities are synonymous and then let them validate or reject the proposed correspondence.

5.1. Supporting alignment of meanings with Torres

Let us now briefly consider how the local formal representations can be used to facilitate the alignment of meanings to solve some of the typologies of problems we identified in Section 3.3 as a result of our observations at the ward.

As a first example, let us consider how to convey comprehensibility by means of the transparency of an interface that make visible the underpinning LFRs. In particular let us see how this can be used to have requesters compile more complete requests. In the Radiodiagnostic Request Form the field "phone number" is often left blank since the practitioner filling the form (the requester of the service) does not perceive the relevance of providing either her pager's or ward's phone number to the Radiology facility (the provider). Sometimes she can be right, it is just a perfunctory request that can be disregarded; other times, instead, she would better fill it in since it can come up with being really important. Consequently, the filling practitioner should be warned of the mandatory value of the "phone number" field on the request form in all those cases that the exam can not be scheduled at a precise time (according to the type of examination and on the current work-load) but inpatient has to be summoned in turn. In this particular case, the phone number is then necessary to make coordination possible. The awareness of this context-dependent relevance of supplying the phone number can be promoted by the service provider who includes the Phone number concept (described in the corresponding AFR) as a precondition on performing the activity of scheduling the examination (see in Fig. 2 the relationship 'involved-in-Precondition' between the Phone-number data concept and the A" activity — the exam scheduling). Since in this case the system is able to detect that the same Phone concept in the two AFRs is related to different activities by means of different meta-relationships according to the considered requester or provider points of view, the system can notify some warning about possible misunderstandings related to the use of the phone field by different parties. Hence, the requesting practitioners are supported by the system in the process of aligning the meaning they give to the "phone number" field of the order form with the meaning intended by who created the form, and hence in understanding when that information matters according to the requested examination.

Another issue related to comprehensibility is about the presence in the form of some items (fields) about which who is supposed to fill in them would need further clarifications; an even worse case can be that the filler would misunderstand what is requested and hence the request be submitted partially or completely nullified. All these are examples of when comprehensibility affects activities at the requester's side. For instance, let us consider the Specialist Consultancy Request Form defined by the provider of the service: it encompasses a "director" field where it is apparently requested the signature of a director. Consequently, from the provider's point of view, the AFR encompasses the Director concept. Not all the hospital facilities do have a director; moreover, even in the case they have one, to involve her explicit approval for each referral request could be unfeasible. In our case study, the AFR of the requester's domain does not encompass the concept of director and consequently also the LFR does not, while the latter contains a Head Physician concept since it is in direct relationship with some concepts referred by the form (e.g., the exam text-field). One could wonder whether for the service to be provided the director signature is really (i.e., legally) necessary (e.g., for the reimbursement of the service). By opening a contextual window in the web form, users at the requester's side could then validate the correspondence of synonymy between the local Head Physician concept and the Director concept as detected by the system (see C2 in Fig. 2). As illustrated in Fig. 2 this correspondence is proposed by the system since *refers-to-caw* relationships (MR1 arrows) connect the Head Physician and Director concepts with an instance of the Role CAW (R), each in its own local representation; and since these roles are responsible for tasks that refer to concepts related to the same form item (i.e., the exam concept). In this way, the requester, whenever has to validate or reject this correspondence suggested by the system, is facilitated in deducing that the field Director in the form requires just the name of someone officially playing the role of "who is accountable for the prescription of a diagnostic procedure", i.e., a mere synonymous for "Head Physician": in the case in hand, just the physician on duty. In this case, when the suggested correspondence is validated, the meaning of the "director" field for the requesters is aligned with the acceptation of the form's providers.

6. Future Works

In this paper we presented Torres, a conceptual framework focusing on how to support people involved in inter-system collaboration. Our claim is that by means of Torres it is easier to consider how socio-technical interfaces are deployed in real settings and how to make them more effective in their twofold function of information gateways and tools for articulation. In order to reach this aim, Torres provides the designers with a generic model of articulation work as well as a set of relationships by which to relate their specific artifact-centered models to that.

Since there is a growing tendency in distributing — or better yet, sharing – care so to achieve high quality of care while optimizing resource management, we decided to apply and adapt our conceptual framework to the healthcare domain first. We observed that there is a strong need for supporting the reconciliation of care for patients that are in the charge of different facilities with complementary competencies and that the lessons learned from participatory modeling can not be neglected to achieve full semantic interoperability.

From the implementation's point of view, our future work is intended to focus on how to properly get the requirements defined within the framework by means of computational means. This implies to consider also how to properly present information besides having properly modeled, i.e., making real computational interface artifacts usable. Our implementations will be deployed in a prototypical case and our hypothesis will be evaluated with the participation of the involved nurses. Final evaluations will be reported in a future work.

Acknowledgements

We acknowledge the tight and profitable collaboration with the management and personnel of the "Alessandro Manzoni" Hospital in Lecco (Italy). In particular, we would like to thank Ms Rossana Pezzotta and all the Internal Medicine nurses for their courtesy and helpfulness. Special thanks are also due to Gianluigi Viscusi for sharing his time and knowledge in defining the conceptual grounding of the framework.

References

[1]   P. Carstensen, L. Færgemann and T. Schilder-Knudsen.   The duality of articulation work in large heterogenous settings - a study in health care. In *Proc. of ECSCW'05*, pp. 163–184.

[2]   A. Strauss.   The articulation of project work: An organizational process.   *The Sociological Quarterly*, 29(2):163–178, 1988.

[3]   K. Schmidt and L. Bannon. Taking CSCW Seriously: supporting Articulation Work.   *Journal of Computer Supported Cooperative Work*, 1(1):7–40, 1992.

[4]   K. Schmidt.   Modes and mechanisms of interaction in cooperative work.   Technical report, Risø National Laboratory, 1994.

[5]   R. H. R. Harper and J. A. Hughes. What a f-ing system! Send 'em all to the same place and then expect us to stop 'em hitting. Managing technology work in air traffic control.   In G. Button (ed.) *Technology in Working Order. Studies of work, interaction, and technology*, pp. 127–144. London: Routledge, 1993.

[6]   F. Cabitza, M. Sarini, C. Simone, and M. Telaro.   When once is not enough: The role of redundancy in a hospital ward setting. In Proc. of *Group'05*, pp. 158–167.

[7]   E. Trist and H. Murray.   *The Social engagement of social science: a Tavistock anthology*, vol. 2. Philadelphia: University of Pennsylvania Press, 1993.

[8]   C. Simone, G. Mark, and D. Giubbilei.   Interoperability as a means of articulation work.   In *Proc. of WACC'99*, pp. 39–48.

[9]   C. Simone and M. Sarini. Adaptability of Classification schemes in Cooperation: what does it mean? In *Proc. of ECSCW'01*, pp. 19–38.

[10] M. Sarini and C. Simone. Recursive articulation work in ariadne: The alignment of meanings. In *Proc. of COOP'02*, pp. 191–206.

[11] A. Strauss, S. Fagerhaugh, B. Suczek, and C. Wiener.   *The Social Organization of Medical Work*. Chicago: University of Chicago Press, 1985.

[12] O. J. Kvamme, F. Olesen, and M. Samuelsson.   Improving the interface between primary and secondary care: a statement from the European Working Party on Quality in Family Practice (EQuiP). *Quality in Health Care*, 10:33–39, 2001.

[13] P. Pritchard and J. Hughes. *Shared Care. The Future Imperative*. London: Royal Society of Medicine Press, 1995.

[14] P. H. Carstensen. Computer Supported Coordination. Technical report, Department of Computer Science, Roskilde University, 1996.

[15] R. H. R. Harper, K. P. A. O'Hara, A. J. Sellen, and D. J. R. Duthie. Toward the paperless hospital? A case study of document use by anaesthetists. *British Journal of Anaesthesia*, 78:762–767, 1997.

[16] A. J. Sellen and R. H. R. Harper. *The Myth of the Paperless Office*. Cambridge MA: MIT Press, 2003.

[17] M. Berg. Accumulating and Coordinating: Occasions for Information Technologies in Medical Work. *Journal of Computer Supported Cooperative Work*, 8(4):373–401, 1999.

[18] F. Kensing and J. Blomberg.   Participatory design: Issues and concerns.   Journal of Computer Supported Cooperative Work, 7(3–4):167–185, September 1998.

[19] W. J. Orlikowski. Action and artifact: the structuring of technologies-in-use. Technical report, Sloan School of Management, Massachusetts Institute of Technology.

[20] H. T. Randall, J. Blomberg, and L. Suchman. Moving document collections online: the evolution of a shared repository. In *Proc. of ECSCW'99*, pp. 331–350.

[21] K. Schmidt and C. Simone. Coordination Mechanisms: Towards a conceptual foundation for CSCW systems design. *Journal of Computer Supported Cooperative Work*, 5(2-3):155–200, 1996.

[22] S. A. McIlraith and D. L. Martin.   Bringing semantics to web services.   *IEEE Intelligent Systems*, 18(1):90–93, 2003.

Cooperative Systems Design
P. Hassanaly et al. (Eds.)
IOS Press, 2006

Multimodality and parallelism in design interaction: co-designers' alignment and coalitions

Françoise DETIENNE[a,1] and Willemien VISSER[a]

[a] EIFFEL2 (Cognition & Cooperation in Design) - INRIA (National Institute for Research in Computer Science and Control), France

Abstract. This paper presents an analysis of various forms of articulation between graphico-gestural and verbal modalities in parallel interactions between designers in a collaborative design situation. Based on our methodological framework, we illustrate several forms of multimodal articulations, that is, integrated and non-integrated, through extracts from a corpus on an architectural design meeting. These modes reveal alignment or disalignment between designers, with respect to the focus of their activities. They also show different forms of coalition.

Keywords: Design, multimodality, collaboration, graphical representation, gesture

Introduction

Collaborative design takes place through interaction between designers. We will see that this apparently unequivocal statement, which may even seem tautological, conveys characteristics of design thinking that are essential, in our view. During co-design sessions, individual design plays of course —also— an important role [see e.g., 1, 2]. Yet, an essential part of collaborative design thus takes place —that is progresses— through interaction. This interaction takes different forms and refers to various representation-construction activities [see 3]. The different forms that interaction may take in collaborative design —verbal, graphical, gestural, postural— are, in our view, not the simple expression and transmission of ideas previously developed in an internal medium, developed in a kind of *mentalese* (such as Fodor's "language of thought"). They are more, and of a different nature, than the trace of a so-called "genuine" design activity, which would be individual and occur internally, and which verbal and other forms of interaction would allow to share with colleagues, once it has been developed.

In this paper, we present an analysis of various forms of articulation between graphico-gestural and verbal modalities in interactions between designers in a collaborative design situation. After a brief introduction of the theoretical framework that we adopt for design interactions, we present our methodological framework and illustrate several forms of multimodal articulations, that is, integrated and non-integrated, through extracts from a corpus on an architectural design meeting. This

---

[1] Corresponding author: Françoise Détienne, EIFFEL2, INRIA, bât. 23, Rocquencourt B.P. 105, 78153 Le Chesnay Cedex, France

corpus was collected in the context of the MOSAIC project conducted in the COGNITIQUE program "Cognitions, interactions sociales, modélisations" [4]. The meeting, which took place in a preliminary phase of a renovation project, involved three architectural designers, Charles, Louis, and Marie.

1. From individual to collaborative design

Since the early days of research on design activities [e.g., 5], many, if not most, empirical design studies, especially the cognitive ones, use simultaneous verbalization [6, 7]. Asking people to "verbalize their thoughts" or to "think aloud" is, however, only necessary for data collection on individually conducted activities. People working together do "naturally" express their thoughts —or, at least, part of them. The analysis of the two families of corresponding corpora requires different specific methods.

Our position is that going from individual to collaborative design merits emphasis on two new foci: *multimodality*, referring to the importance of the graphico-gestural dimensions in relation to the verbal dimension of interaction, and *parallelism*, referring to the importance of activities that one or several co-designers conduct in parallel (simultaneously, or with more or less overlapping) in addition to those they conduct in sequence.

"Multimodality" refers to the use of various semiotic systems (verbal, graphical, gestural, postural).

Our use of the term "parallelism" covers both strictly simultaneous actions, and actions with more or less overlapping between them.

1.1. From merely verbal to multimodal interactions

Many previous studies of design, for example on software design, have analysed collaborative activities that take place in face-to-face meetings, such as idea-generation and technical review activities [8-11]. In these studies, researchers have identified various types of collaborative design activities based on verbal interactions between co-designers.

One set of collaborative activities is related to *activities on the objects of design*, the artefacts. These activities concern the evolution of the design problem and solution, for example, elaboration of the problem, generation of a solution and identification or enhancement of alternative solutions. Are also of this kind evaluative activities —for example, the evaluations of solutions or alternative solutions based on argumentation.

A second type of activity concerns the *construction, by a group of co-designers, of "common reference", or "common ground"* [what Visser prefers to qualify as "inter-designer compatible representations", 3]. For example, clarification or cognitive synchronization activities take place when a group negotiates or constructs such common representations of the current state of the solution.

Group management activities are a third kind of design activity. These activities are frequently related to issues of process. Project-management activities that concern the coordination of people and resources —the allocation and planning of tasks— are of this kind. Meeting-management activities —the ordering and postponing of discussion topics— are another example.

All these activities, which characterize collaborative design, do not only occur in a verbal mode, but also in graphical and gestural modes. The importance of graphical representations, as intermediate or intermediary representations, has been underlined in the literature on design. However, there have been only few attempts to systematize the analysis of these various modes of interaction in design, especially their construction rather than their use [3]. This is the line of research adopted in this paper.

1.2. From sequential to parallel interactions

Based on the analysis of verbal interactions, a body of work has focused on the types of activities occurring in design meetings and their sequential organization [9, 11-13], such as sequences of "moves" or "turns" in the argumentation process. Accounting for designers' spontaneous sequential organization of activities is of particular interest with respect to design methods that specify steps in design.

D'Astous, Détienne, Visser and Robillard [9], for example, analysed the argumentative moves in software technical review meetings. One of their results was that the elaboration of a solution tends to be followed by either its evaluation or the development of an alternative solution. In the second case, there is an implicit negative evaluation of the previously proposed solution.

In another study, Détienne, Martin and Lavigne [12] examined the negotiation patterns leading participants to converge in multidisciplinary meetings in aeronautical design. They found a typical temporal negotiation pattern composed of three steps: (1) analytical assessment of the current solution, that is, systematic assessment according to constraints; (2) if step 1 did not lead to a consensus, comparative or/and analogical assessment; (3) if step 2 did not lead to a consensus, use of one or several argument(s) from authority.

With regard to our particular interest in multimodal interaction, we shift our focus from a view that analyses sequences of actions, to a view that analyses how strictly simultaneous or more or less overlapping actions are articulated. Focus is then no longer on the sequential organization of activities (which is still quite relevant), but rather on the articulation of activities that one or more designers implement in parallel (that is, in strict simultaneity or with more or less overlapping between the activities).

Accounting for parallel activities is particularly relevant for analysing the alignments and oppositions between designers during their collaborative activity. It is also of special interest for the development of computer tools to support collaborative design, such as augmented-reality environments that enable synchronous collaboration without imposing a master/slave mode.

2. Taking into account graphics and gestures in collaborative design

Intermediate representations are the representations that clearly occupy the greatest part of the design activity during a project. Graphical and gestural interactions play a role that is, at least, as important in the construction of these representations as purely verbal expressions.

2.1. Intermediate and intermediary representations

The representations produced and used in early and later intermediate design phases are generally not of the same type as the final representations, which specify the implementation of the artefact. They allow designers to focus on different aspects of their design [14], which may or may not be maintained until the final design stages.

In addition to being intermediate between the requirements at the start of a design project and the specifications at its other extremity, representations have also an intermediary function. Two types of intermediary representations are to be distinguished: they can be intermediary between designers and their artefact, and between several designers. In their first role, they function as tools and are often qualified as "cognitive artefacts", by reference to Norman [15]. With respect to their second role, Boujut and Laureillard [16] or Schmidt and Wagner [17] propose the concepts of "cooperative features", "coordinative artefacts" and "intermediary objects" to characterize the particular role that these intermediary representations play in collaborative processes. They may have functions such as construction of common ground concerning design principles, or tasks; reminders of such principles, and open problems; traces of activities; and representations of design decisions. In this way, they may support co-design, argumentation, explanation, and simulation, or be an external memory of design rationale [17].

2.2. Graphico-gestural representations

In semiotics, ethology, and more recently pragmatic linguistics and psycholinguistics, analysis of gestural interaction represents already a considerable body of research work [18-21]. Often referring to "workplace studies", ethnography or ethnomethodology for their theoretical and methodological position [24, 25], many authors nowadays mainly present their data and results in narrative, anecdotal terms, providing rather detailed descriptions of "cases", but without much generalisation (or generalisability) in their results and conclusions. For instance, Brassac and Le Ber [22, see also 23] present detailed descriptions of co-present agronomists and computer scientists collectively designing a knowledge-based system, using "cognitive, corporal, documentary and material" resources. The authors describe verbal (oral), gestural, and graphical (both writing and drawing) activities, showing several examples of interaction between verbal and graphical activities.

In the cognitive ergonomics of design, research on graphico-gestural interaction is at its beginnings [26, 27]. An important difference with more narratively oriented approaches is our aim to reach generalisable results concerning design and to be able to compare different design situations with respect to explicit dimensions. Up to date, cognitive ergonomics has examined graphical and other types of external representations, but mostly the representational structures, not their elaboration [3].

In an empirical study on collaborative design in a technology-mediated situation, Détienne, Hohmann and Boujut [28] showed that graphical representations of the design artefact played a central role. In the synchronous mode, whiteboard and shared CAD applications were used to co-produce solutions and to support argumentation and explanation. Supporting online co-production activity was the most frequent use of technical devices. Computer graphics and sketches on the Netmeeting whiteboard supported this activity.

It is not only in distant interaction, however, that other than verbal representations play an important role. In their analysis of small group conceptual design sessions in co-presence, Tang [29] and Tang and Leifer [30] have identified the importance of gesture, in addition to graphical representations. They have proposed a framework for the analysis of workspace activity that establishes relationships between actions that occur in the workspace and their functions. The "conventional view" of workspace activity considers this space as "primarily a medium for storing information and conveying ideas through listing text and drawing graphics". The authors aim to extend this conventional view, adding three other aspects to workspace activity: "gestural expression", "developing ideas", and "mediating interaction" [30, p. 247]. Besides drawing or sketching, already identified in previous research to occur often in collective-design meetings, gesture was found to take place frequently. The main function of gesture was to mediate interaction between the different design participants: more than half of the gestures fulfilled this function through participants engaging or asking for attention.

On the website page that presents the research on gesture in her STAR team (Space, Time, and Action Research, retrieved November 24, 2005, from http://www-psych.stanford.edu/~bt/gesture/), Tversky notices that "although it is typically thought that gestures accompany speech, gestures often accompany listening (Heiser, Tversky, MacLeod, Carletta, and Lee, in preparation) and non-communicative thinking (Kessell, 2004). In both cases, they seem to serve to augment spatial working memory, much as sketching a diagram would." Tversky also refers to research in which the combined use of graphics and gesture, rather than verbal expression, was identified. "In collaboration with diagrams, dyads save speech by pointing and tracing on the diagram. Partners look at the diagrams and their hands, not at each other (Heiser, Tversky, and Silverman, 2004). Having a shared diagram to gesture on facilitates establishing common ground and finding a solution. It also augments solution accuracy."

3. Our method: articulating modalities

In order to analyse the articulation between modalities in a collaborative design setting, we have adopted a functional perspective based on local design goals that interlocutors may share or not, at a particular moment in their interaction. Our distinction between local goals is based on the pursuit of the functional design activities identified previously in our COMET method [31].

3.1. The COMET method

With our colleagues of the CNAM [see e.g., 32], we have developed COMET for the analysis of collaborative design processes [31], integrating protocol analysis as developed for the analysis of individually conducted activities, and pragmatic linguistics' verbal-interaction analysis [33][2].

Underlying our development and use of this method, is our aim to formulate a generic model of the socio-cognitive aspects of collaborative designing. The descriptors (categories) distinguished in COMET are design actions and objects that numerous empirical cognitive design studies have shown to be characteristic of designing.

According to COMET, verbal turns are cut up into one or more individual Units according to a coding scheme developed on a Predicate(Argument(s)) basis. Each

---

[2] In COMET, we did not introduce, however, the means to   analyse linguistic phenomena such as modalisation procedures, for example expressions of addressing or of politeness [Araújo Carreira, 2005 #2626] Neither did we introduce the means to describe graphical and gestural interaction.

predicate only admits a number of possible arguments. Predicates (ACT) correspond to actions implemented by participants; arguments (OBJ) correspond to objects concerned by the action (the actor, the object of the action, tools and other elements involved; see the examples presented hereafter). According to the form of the predicate (Assertion or Request), each unit is modulated (MOD). The default value of a unit is assertive: modulation is coded explicitly only if its predicate is a request. Thus, each Unit is coded as MOD[ACT/OBJ], where MOD may be absent —in which case it is assertive (see Table 1).

Table 1.   Basic coding scheme, presenting the elements of each category [from 31]

Modulation (MOD)	Predicate (ACT)	Argument (OBJ)
Assertion	Generate (GEN) Proposing a new element into the dialogue (a solution, a goal, an inferred data, etc.)	Problem data (DAT)
Request (REQ)	Evaluate (EVAL) Judging the value of a subject. This evaluation can be negative, positive, or neutral.	Solution elements (SOL)
	Inform (INFO) Handing out new knowledge with respect to the nature of a subject	Domain objects (OBJ)
	Interpret (INT) Expressing a personal representation of a subject. This representation is made by expressions such as "I believe that…", "I think …" or "…maybe…".	Domain rules or procedures (PROC)
		Goal (GOAL)
		Task (TASK)

In this paper, we introduce a modification in the SOL category in order to distinguish between solutions, depending on their reference to a problem. We consider that solutions are associated with problems (which constitute a kind of superordinate category with respect to the other arguments). Two solutions SOL1_PBp and SOL2_PBp to the problem PBp belong to the same category, whereas two solutions to different problems, SOL3_PBq and SOL4_PBr, belong *per se* to different object categories.

Using these predicate and argument categories, we establish two distinctions between activities, one depending on their type of predicate, and the other depending on their argument. The first distinction differentiates elaborative (Generate), evaluative (Evaluate) and clarification activities (Inform and Interpret). The second distinction tells apart three groups of activities: activities in the group space (Task or Goal), the problem/solution space (Problem data and Solution elements attached to a same problem), and the domain space (Domain objects, Domain rules or procedures).

3.2. Description of graphico-gestural activities

The endeavour in which we are engaged at present consists in extending the analysis of verbal interactional data to that of other semiotic systems, that is, to analyse design interaction's multimodality. Up to now, we have developed a description language for the graphico-gestural activities [26, 27], and we are examining the articulation between graphico-gestural and verbal dimensions in collaborative design interaction. This has been applied to our corpus of architectural design and specifically to the analysis of the overhead view (top right view in Figure 1).

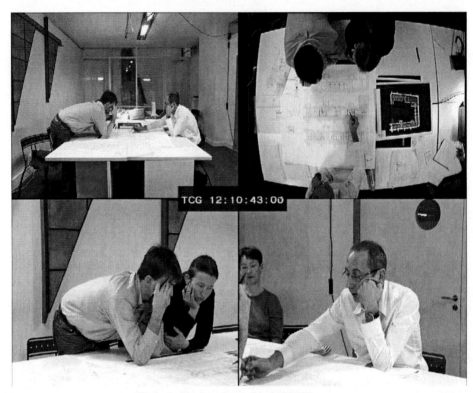

Figure 1. The four views of the MOSAIC corpus

Our graphico-gestural description language accounts for movements performed, by hand with or without a tool (pen, pencil, ruler or other), on external representations, in particular, plans and draft papers. It uses the same predicate structure as COMET, i.e., Predicate(Argument(s)), which corresponds to Action(Object(s)) units, completed by their duration and localisation. Each graphico-gestural unit is the description of one action performed by a designer, from time t0 to time t1, on an object (plan, draft paper, or other document), in a particular area of the table, by hand only or with a tool. The graphico-gestural actions are: Point (pointing), Delimit_2D (delimitation in two dimensions), Delimit_3D, Graph_trac (graphical tracing or drawing), Text_trac (textual tracing or writing), Moving (e.g. moving a plan from a peripheral to a central area), Rotating (e.g. rotating a plan in someone's direction), and Overlaying (e.g. overlaying a plan with a draft paper).

3.3. Integration between activities

Based on the COMET frame, enlarged in order to account for multimodal interaction, designers are considered to pursue the same local goal if their objects are in the same category (at a more or less global level), even though the modalities adopted to pursue them are different. In this case, we consider that their *activities* are *integrated* [27].

Different designers working in an integrated mode may thus perform each one the same type of action on what constitutes, at a more or less global level, the same object (e.g., generate together a solution to a particular problem, or generate alternative solutions to this problem), or perform different types of actions on the same object (e.g., one generates, the other evaluates a solution). In both cases, there is an *alignment between the designers* with respect to their sharing a same focus of work, and, more generally, a same local goal. The actions may be conducted through identical or different modalities, which may be redundant or complementary [35, 36]. In this text, we focus on examples of activities that are performed through different modalities.

For example, two designers working on the same object (e.g., the same alternative solution or two alternative solutions to a particular problem) may conduct the same action (generation) through two modalities, verbal and graphical: one designer verbally formulates the solution, while a colleague draws or details it in a sketch (i.e., works on the same global solution, even if she develops a different elementary solution). Two designers working on the same object may also conduct different actions on it through distinct modalities. One designer generates a solution in a verbal mode, while the other evaluates the solution by simulating it through gestures.

Designers are considered to pursue different local goals if the objects on which they are working come from different categories (e.g. solutions to distinct problems or a solution vs. a task). In this case, we consider that their *activities* are *non-integrated*. This indicates *disalignment* between designers, in particular, a shift between activities such as transitions from one focus to another type of focus: (1) from one focus to another in the problem/solution space (i.e., shift of problem concerned by the activities), or (2) from a focus in one space to a focus in another space (problem/solution space, group space, domain space). In this case, there is, by definition, neither redundancy nor complementarity between modalities.

4. Exploiting different modalities for alignment and disalignment

Collaboration between partners in a design meeting can take many different forms. This section presents examples of different ways in which design partners may articulate their activities, exploiting the possibilities provided by different modalities that are available for interaction, i.e. verbal, graphical and gestural, in our current analysis.

4.1. Integrated activities

Integrated activities have been identified both in individually and in collectively performed actions. Indeed a designer talking, and drawing or gesturing at the same moment, has been observed frequently during the meeting analysed. In example 1 (see Table 2), Louis is simultaneously generating a solution [GEN/SOLa_PB1] and indicating, with his hand, a two-dimensional zone on the drawing, in order to reinforce his proposal.

Table 2. Example of an integrated multimodal design activity (between 12 :08 :27 and 12 :08 :28): one designer (Example 1)

Line identif	Actor Verb	Actor Gr-Ge	Verbal action (transcription)	Gr-Ge action	Attr1 (obj1)	Attr3 (tool)
1	L	L	We reverse the problem and, finally, we do u:h	Delimit_2d	C16+P1	hand

Integrated activities have also been observed in collectively performed actions. An example of designers collaborating through integrated activities, using complementary action modalities, concerns the co-elaboration of a solution to a same problem: a same type of activity on the same object (the same problem), implemented through graphical, gestural and verbal actions (see Example 2 in Table 3).

Table 3. Example of an integrated multimodal design activity (between 12:08:28 and 12:08:38): two designers co-elaborating a solution, through graphical, gestural, and verbal actions (Example 2)

Line identif	Actor Verb	Actor Gr-Ge	Verbal action (transcription)	Gr-Ge action	Attr1 (obj1)	Attr2 (obj2)	Attr3 (tool)
1		L		Graph_trac	C16	C16_over_P1	pencil
2		L		Delimit_2d	C16+P1		hand
3	C		on both sides here reducing (.) but there there what is a pity is that one has a beautiful vaulted hall				
4		C		Graph_trac	C16	C16_over_P1	

Louis who, previously, has formulated a solution proposal starts to sketch it (line 1), underlining his proposal by a hand gesture (line 2); Charles continues, detailing the solution, consecutively in a verbal (line 3) and a graphical (line 4) mode. Louis' gestural underlining of his proposal is redundant with his graphical elaboration. Charles' detailing of the proposal is complementary with Louis' elaboration. All these segments are coded as solution-generation activities [GEN/SOLa_PB1]. One may notice that they are expressed through various modalities.

4.2. Non-Integrated activities

Our last example is more complex. It shows both integrated (INT) and non-integrated (Non-INT) activities. It is composed of three parts (INT, Non-INT and INT), whose global structure is INT—Non-INT//INT, that is, (1) an integrated activity is (2) interrupted and followed by a non-integrated activity, following which (3) an integrated and a non-integrated activity continue in parallel (see Example 3 in Table 4).

All three designers are involved. An integrated activity by two designers (Marie and Charles, line 1 to 4) is interrupted by the third one (Louis, line 5) who attacks another non-integrated activity, which he pursues in parallel with his two design colleagues who continue, now in coalition, their joint solution elaboration (line 6 to 14).

Marie's verbal formulation and evaluation of a solution proposal for the bar in the little lounge ([GEN/SOLa_PB1] and [EVAL+/SOLa_PB1], lines 1 and 3), overlaps with a positive evaluation that Charles formulates concerning her proposal ([EVAL+/SOLa_PB1], line 2). Marie's overlapping turn is a collaborative one and she simply continues her proposal, gesturally "drawing" the proposal with her pencil. Then Louis interrupts the bar-elaboration activity by the verbal proposal of a solution for

Table 4. Example of a composite [integrated – non-integrated // integrated] multimodal design activity (between 12:07:51 and 12:08:38): a coalition of two designers (M and C) co-elaborating a solution for one problem, and a third one (L) elaborating a solution for another problem (Example 3)

Line identif	Actor Verb	Actor Gr-Ge	Verbal action (transcription)	Gr-Ge action	Attr1 (obj1)	Attr2 (obj2)	Attr3 (tool)
1	M		that that would have been a space				
2	C		yes better=				
3	M		=ideal for the bar and there yes when one is there one feels that: the- there something is taking place that will be:=				
4		M		Movem_2d	C16+P1		pencil
5	L		=or indeed if one decides to [di- to dig				
6	M		[xxx little sounds or: while there there it is it is still \ and it is too far from there to go and sit there to wait				
7		M		Point	C16+P1		pencil
8	C		yes				
9			(..)				
10	M	M	it:is (:) in fact one is waiting over here	Point	C16+P1		hand
11			(…)				
12	C		yes (..) that's true				
13	L		no indeed if one decides to to dig one coul[::d				
14	M	L	[or otherwise one may wait in the bar	Position	C_Virgin	C16	hand

another problem (the lift) ([GEN/SOLb_PB2], line 5). Within less than a second, Marie continues her elaboration of the bar ([GEN/SOLa_PB1], line 6), so that Louis and she, during a split second, come to work in parallel. Marie carries on, while Louis breaks of —at least, the explicit expression of his activity. Marie continues to elaborate the bar solution ([GEN/SOLa_PB1], lines 7 and 10). This continuation of the bar elaboration is both an individually integrated activity (Marie elaborating her solution idea verbally and graphically) and a collectively integrated activity (Marie's solution elaboration being supported by Charles, lines 8 and 12). However, Louis comes back, and the parallel non-integrated activity on the bar (PB1: M and C) and the lift (PB2: L), which had started at line 5, continues during another eight turns.

5. Discussion

We have analysed and illustrated two modes of articulation between modalities in parallel interactions, which reflect either alignment or disalignment between co-designers. In the integrated mode, co-designers share their concern with a particular category of object, each designer performing the same or a different action on it, through identical (e.g. verbal) or different (e.g. verbal and graphical) modalities. This reflects an alignment between designers with respect to the sharing of a same focus of work [37]. Furthermore, there is a semantic redundancy or complementarity between the different semiotic modalities (Ex. 1 and 2). In the non-integrated mode, co-designers work on different objects (pertaining to different categories) and pursue different local goals. This translates a gap between the designers' focus, resulting for example, from a shift from one design problem to another one (Ex 3). At a more general level, this also indicates shifts between spaces of representation (problem/solution space, group space, domain space).

It is worth to discuss the present analysis and results with respect to the coalition concept. Indeed, our analysis, based on a triadic design situation, illustrates a coalition process: alignment of two co-designers with respect to a problem, combined with opposition towards a third co-designer focused on another problem. This coalition is of another nature than the ones analysed in pragmatic-linguistics analyses of trilogs based on verbal corpora [38]. These linguistics studies show that relationships between participants in a meeting between three people sharing the same global focus can be of various natures, particularly convergence versus divergence with respect to theses or proposals in an argumentation process. As soon as three people are together, coalitions between two of them against the third one may appear. Caplow [1971, quoted in 39, p. 54] even defends that it is one of the essential characteristics of triadic conversations. Zamouri [39] concludes, based on the analysis of a verbal corpus, that coalitions always emerge from a conflict, which may be initiated, for example, by a counter-proposal.

Such a kind of coalition linked to the argumentation process could be involved in our integrated mode, were co-designers are aligned with respect to the same problem-focus and develop alternative solutions concerning which they may agree or not. For example, there could be a coalition of two designers —one generating verbally a solution, while the second draws it— against a third designer generating an alternative solution, be it verbally or graphically.

An original contribution of our study is to show that coalitions may also occur at another level, with respect to gaps in the focus of people's work. Our third example illustrates this kind of coalition: two designers working on one problem while the third one works on another problem. One could also have coalitions between designers working in different categories of spaces (problem/solution space, group space, domain space).

Another original contribution of the present study is to show that coalitions may be expressed not only in a verbal mode, but also through particular articulations of different semiotic systems ("modalities").

An important issue will be to understand whether coalitions and disalignments with respect to categories of spaces may be disturbing or on the contrary may help designers to advance in their work. Still another issue is whether these kinds of coalition reflect disagreements between designers. Although further work is necessary to handle these questions, we can already advance some reflections based on different cases of disalignments.

- Disalignments between problem space and group space: One or two designers deal with a problem/solution in the problem space while one or two others start setting up another goal or another task in the group space.
  - o This case may reflect an implicit disagreement on the completeness of the solution at hand. Some of the designers (but not all) consider the solution is complete and try to skip to another task.
  - o This case may also indicate that some of the designers (but not all) evaluate that the problem at hand has some relationships with another task, which then can be interesting to deal with at this point.
- Disalignments between problem space and domain space: One or two designers deal with a problem/solution in the problem space, while one or two others switch to exchanges on domain objects, domain rules or procedures.
  - o Again, this case may reflect an implicit disagreement on the solution at hand. However, the disagreement is not on the completeness but rather on the adequacy of the solution. Some of the designers (but not all) consider the solution is inadequate and refer to domain knowledge that is relevant for an argumentation move.
  - o This case may also reflect a thematic drift, triggered by the problem/solution at hand. Whereas this drift does not provide knowledge required for evaluating the solution at hand, it is useful in a cognitive synchronization process.

Further work could examine these different cases based on protocol data and could search for other cases of disalignment. To this end, we believe that the methodological framework that we have developed can offer great potentialities to systematise the identification and statistical analysis of various types of coalitions and disalignments: search for patterns of co-occurrence of both graphico-gestural and verbal activities with respect to different spaces; search for combinations of these co-occurrences with sequential patterns. In this objective, we believe that the methodological cost of both developing our coding scheme and applying it to a corpus is compensated by the possibilities of treatments they offer, in contrast with a more narrative approach.

With respect to the development of computer tools, accounting for parallel activities is of particular interest for the support of synchronous collaborative design. Our results show that simultaneous activities may occur "naturally" through various modalities and that the forms of articulation between modalities are meaningful with respect to people's alignment regarding their work. Coming to understand the way in which people are aligned or not concerning their focus of work is very important for such kind of devices. Our work is preliminary regarding this issue.

Further work could examine the way in which alignments and disalignments are expressed through particular shifts between modalities. We did not analyse the role of attention in this text. Different forms of articulation require more or less attention on behalf of the partners who are interacting. Two partners in alignment may exploit the same modality at the same moment, but, if cooperative design elaboration is aimed, such a form of articulation will generally lead to problems of attention. Using different modalities can thus offer ways to progress together without disturbing attention. In disalignment situations, special attention from others might be required. Using the same modality (as in Example 3) can be a way to engage others to shift focus.

Acknowledgements

This research was funded by the COGNITIQUE program "Cognitions, interactions sociales, modélisations" (MOSAIC project).

References

[1]   W. Visser, "Collective design: A cognitive analysis of cooperation in practice," in *Proceedings of ICED 93, 9th International Conference on Engineering Design*, vol. 1, N. F. M. Roozenburg, Ed. Zürich, Switzerland: HEURISTA, 1993, pp. 385-392.
[2]   W. Visser, "Conception individuelle et collective. Approche de l'ergonomie cognitive [Individual and collective design. The cognitive-ergonomics approach]," in *Cognition et création. Explorations cognitives des processus de conception (ch. 14) [Cognition and creation. Cognitive explorations of design processes]*, M. Borillo and J.-P. Goulette, Eds. Bruxelles, Belgium: Mardaga, 2002, pp. 311-327.
[3]   W. Visser, "Designing as construction of representations: A dynamic viewpoint in cognitive design research," *Human-Computer Interaction*, in press.
[4]   F. Détienne and V. Traverso, "Présentation des objectifs et du corpus analysé," in *Actes des Deuxièmes Journées d'Etude en Psychologie ergonomique - EPIQUE 2003 (Boulogne-Billancourt, France, 2-3 octobre)*, J. M. C. Bastien, Ed. Rocquencourt, France: Institut National de Recherche en Informatique et en Automatique, 2003, pp. 217-221.
[5]   C. Eastman, "On the analysis of intuitive design processes," in *Emerging Methods in Environmental Design and Planning. Proceedings of the First International Design Methods Conference*, G. T. Moore, Ed. Cambridge, MA: The MIT Press, 1970, pp. 21-37.
[6]   J. S. Gero and T. McNeill, "An approach to the analysis of design protocols," *Design Studies*, vol. 19, pp. 21-61, 1998.
[7]   N. Cross, H. Christiaans, and K. Dorst, Eds., *Analysing design activity*. Chichester, United Kingdom: Wiley, 1996.
[8]   P. D'Astous, P. N. Robillard, F. Détienne, and W. Visser, "Quantitative measurements of the influence of participant roles during peer review meetings," *Empirical Software Engineering*, vol. 6, pp. 143-159, 2001.
[9]   P. D'Astous, F. Détienne, W. Visser, and P. N. Robillard, "Changing our view on design evaluation meetings methodology: A study of software technical review meetings," *Design Studies*, vol. 25, pp. 625-655, 2004.
[10] J. D. Herbsleb, H. Klein, G. M. Olson, H. Brunner, J. S. Olson, and J. Harding, "Object-oriented analysis and design in software project teams," *Human-Computer Interaction*, vol. 10, pp. 249-292, 1995.
[11] G. M. Olson, J. S. Olson, M. R. Carter, and M. Storrosten, "Small group design meetings: An analysis of collaboration," *Human-Computer Interaction*, vol. 7, pp. 347-374, 1992.
[12] F. Détienne, G. Martin, and E. Lavigne, "Viewpoints in co-design: A field study in concurrent engineering," *Design Studies*, vol. 26, pp. 215-241, 2005.
[13] J. Stempfle and P. Badke-Schaub, "Thinking in design teams. An analysis of team communication," *Design Studies*, vol. 23, pp. 473–496, 2002.
[14] M. W. Newman and J. A. Landay, "Sitemaps, storyboards, and specifications: A sketch of web site design practice," in *Proceedings of the conference on Designing interactive systems: processes, practices, methods, and techniques (DIS'00)*, D. Boyarski and W. A. Kellogg, Eds. New York: ACM Press, 2000, pp. 263-274.
[15] D. A. Norman, "Cognitive artifacts," in *Designing interaction: Psychology of the human-computer interface*, J. M. Carroll, Ed. New York: Cambridge University Press, 1991, pp. 17-38.
[16] J.-F. Boujut and P. Laureillard, "A co-operation framework for product-process integration in engineering design," *Design Studies*, vol. 23, pp. 497-513, 2002.
[17] K. Schmidt and I. Wagner, "Coordinative artifacts in architectural practice," in *Cooperative systems design: A challenge of the mobility age (Proceedings of the Fifth International Conference on the Design of Cooperative Systems, COOP 2002)*, M. Blay-Fornarino, A. M. Pinna-Dery, K. Schmidt, and P. Zaraté, Eds. Amsterdam: IOS Press, 2002, pp. 257-274.
[18] J. Cosnier, "Communication et langages gestuels," in *Les voies du langage. Communications verbales, gestuelles et animales*, J. Cosnier, J. Coulon, A. Berrendonner, and C. Kerbrat-Orecchioni, Eds. Paris: Dunod, 1982, pp. 255-304.

[19] *Proceedings of the 2nd Conference of the International Society for Gesture Studies (ISGS), Interacting bodies - Corps en interaction.* École Normale Supérieure Lettres et Sciences humaines, Lyon, France, 2005.

[20] F. Quek, D. Mcneill, R. Bryll, S. Duncan, X.-F. Ma, C. Kirbas, and R. Ansari, "Multimodal human discourse: Gesture and speech," *ACM Transactions on Computer-Human Interaction,* vol. 9, pp. 171-193, 2002.

[21] A. Kendon, "An agenda for gesture studies," *Semiotic Review of Books,* vol. 7, pp. 7-12, 1996 (also available at http://www.univie.ac.at/Wissenschaftstheorie/srb/srb/gesture.html Retrieved January 23, 2006).

[22] C. Brassac and F. Le Ber, "Inscription spatiale d'une activité cognitive collective de représentation de l'espace," *Intellectica,* vol. 41, 2006 (sous press).

[23] C. Brassac, "Action située et distribuée et analyse du discours : Quelques interrogations," *Cahiers de Linguistique Française,* vol. 26, pp. 251-268, 2004.

[24] P. Luff, J. Hindmarsh, and C. C. Heath, *Workplace studies: Recovering work practice and informing system design.* Cambridge, United Kingdom: Cambridge University Press, 2000.

[25] M. Nilsson, "Workplace studies revisited," in *28th Information systems Research seminar In Scandinavia (IRIS 28).* 2005.

[26] F. Détienne, W. Visser, and R. Tabary, "Articulation des dimensions graphico-gestuelle et verbale dans l'analyse de la conception collaborative [Articulating the graphico-gestural and verbal dimensions in the analysis of collaborative design]," *Psychologie de l'Interaction,* à paraître.

[27] W. Visser and F. Détienne, "Articulation entre composantes verbale et graphico-gestuelle de l'interaction dans des réunions de conception architecturale [Articulating the verbal and graphico-gestural components of the interaction in architectural design meetings]," in *Actes de SCAN'05, Séminaire de conception architecturale numérique : "Le rôle de l'esquisse architecturale dans le monde numérique".* Charenton-le-Pont, France, 2005.

[28] F. Détienne, J.-F. Boujut, and B. Hohmann, "Characterization of collaborative design and interaction management activities in a distant engineering design situation," in *Cooperative systems design,* F. Darses, R. Dieng, C. Simone, and M. Zacklad, Eds. Amsterdam: IOS Press, 2004, pp. 83-98.

[29] J. C. Tang, "Findings from observational studies of collaborative work," *International Journal of Man-Machine Studies,* vol. 34, pp. 143-160, 1991.

[30] J. C. Tang and L. J. Leifer, "A framework for understanding the workspace activity of design teams," in *Proceedings of CSCW 88: 2nd Conference on Computer Supported Cooperative Work.* Portland, OR: ACM, 1988, pp. 244-249.

[31] F. Darses, F. Détienne, P. Falzon, and W. Visser, "COMET: A method for analysing collective design processes," Institut National de Recherche en Informatique et en Automatique. Rocquencourt, France, Research report INRIA 4258, 2001, Accessible at http://www.inria.fr/rrrt/rr-4258.html.

[32] F. Détienne and P. Falzon, "Cognition and Cooperation in Design: The Eiffel research group," in *Human-Computer Interaction - Interact 2001,* M. Hirose, Ed. Amsterdam: IOS Press, 2001, pp. 879-880.

[33] C. Kerbrat-Orecchioni, *Les interactions verbales,* vol. I, II, III. Paris: Armand Colin, 1990, 1992, 1994.

[34] M. H. Araújo Carreira, "Politeness in Portugal: How to address others," in *Politeness in Europe,* L. Hickey and M. Stewart, Eds. Clevedon, United Kingdom: Multilingual Matters, 2005, pp. 306-316.

[35] M. L. Knapp, *Nonverbal communication in human interaction.* Belmont, CA: Wadsworth (Thomson Learning), 2002.

[36] J. C. Martin, S. Grimard, and K. Alexandri, "On the annotation of the multimodal behavior and computation of cooperation between modalities," in *Proceedings of "Representing, annotating, and evaluating non-verbal and communicative acts to achieve contextual embodied agents",* workshop organized in conjunction with the Fifth International Conference on Autonomous Agents. Montreal, Canada, 2001, pp. 1-7.

[37] R. E. Grinter, "Recomposition: Putting it all back together again," in *Proceedings of the ACM Conference on Computer Supported Cooperative Work (CSCW1998).* Seattle, 1998, pp. 393-403.

[38] C. Kerbrat-Orecchioni and C. Plantin, Eds., *Le trilogue.* Lyon: Presses Universitaires de Lyon, 1995.

[39] S. Zamouri, "La formation de coalitions dans les conversations triadiques," in *Le trilogue,* C. Kerbrat-Orecchioni and C. Plantin, Eds. Lyon: Presses Universitaires de Lyon, 1995, pp. 54-79.

Cooperative Systems Design
P. Hassanaly et al. (Eds.)
IOS Press, 2006

Editable Chat Logs: A Concept for Seamless Integration of Chat Conversations and Documents in Shared Workspaces

Anja HAAKE

FernUniversität in Hagen, Computer Science Department
Universitätsstraße 1, 58084 Hagen, Germany

Abstract. This paper introduces the concept of editable chat logs for shared workspace systems. In shared workspaces offering a chat for synchronous communication, editable chat logs allow to keep and archive transcripts of chat conversations as documents in the group memory. As any other document in the shared workspace, the transcript can be subject to future conversations. Moreover, the transcript can be edited to create new documents or to reuse (parts of) the conversation within other documents. In this way, editable chat logs provide for a seamless integration of chat conversations and documents.

Keywords: Shared workspace systems, room-based groupware, synchronous and asynchronous communication, formal and informal communication, volatile and perennial communication, wikis, CSCW, CSCL

Introduction

Shared workspace systems, or shared workspaces for short, enable document-based cooperation by providing a common space where all documents related to the task at hand can be stored and thus accessed by the team members. Some systems also support the joint viewing and even the manipulation of (some kinds of) documents within the group in a shared workspace. To better support team communication, shared workspaces allow to integrate asynchronous or synchronous communication tools directly into a teams' workspace that contains the teams' documents. To enable discussions with respect to (parts of) documents, some systems allow conversations to reference (parts of) the documents.

A prerequisite for asynchronous communication is to persistently keep the communication expressions such as annotations, news contributions, or email-messages within the teams' workspace. Some systems also keep the transcript of the synchronous chat sessions to enable both, synchronous and asynchronous communication through the chat tool. Such a persistent chat log supports late-comers or team members that could not attend a synchronous session. In general, keeping a persistent transcript of the chat sessions enriches the group memory.

During the last two years, we used the chat tool of the CURE web-based shared workspace system in various CSCW and CSCL tasks. The CSCW tasks comprised project work, such as software developments or working groups in the context of university organisation. Examples for CSCL tasks are cooperative exercises, with or without tutor guidance, seminars or lab courses. Our experiences indicate the need for a better integration of chat conversations and documents in shared workspace systems. CURE offers shared workspaces for groups. Each workspace (called room) contains documents, represented either as editable wiki documents or as external documents that have been uploaded into the room. Group communication and coordination is supported by configurable presence and activity awareness indicators, change notifications, and up to two communication channels, a threaded mail forum that keeps asynchronous email exchange persistently for the group and a persistent chat tool. In both communication tools, chat expressions and emails, the wiki syntax also used for wiki documents can be used. The persistent chat keeps all chat messages in the time-order for the whole lifetime of a room, similar to other shared workspace systems [1].

In our applications, synchronous group chats were used for both informal and formal conversations in teams. On the one hand, team members met accidentally in the shared workspace and engaged in a synchronous discussion, which often led to a (partial) solution to a problem to solve. On the other hand, team members met virtually at scheduled points in time to synchronously discuss a topic or an open problem. In both cases, all participants found it very helpful to have the ability to refer to the documents in the workspace while discussing. In addition, all participants liked the expressive power of the wiki syntax while chatting, in particular groups working with formulas such as tutor-guided cooperative exercises in math. The discussants appreciated that the chat transcript is persistent and accessible for other group members who could not participate in the actual chat session and that no extra work is required to inform others, e.g. writing an email, because all conversations can be looked up in the persistent chat transcript.

However, the users felt the need to keep and archive transcripts of individual chat sessions for later look-up in the group memory. Moreover, while looking up chat transcripts of former chat sessions, three different use cases arose:

Firstly, the users demanded the pure look up of information.

Secondly, users demanded functionality to discuss parts of the former discussion while looking up the persistent chat transcript jointly. Examples include joint reviews of tutored math exercises by students while preparing for an exam, or joint look up of former chat sessions by software development team members to review former discussions and decisions makings. Things that have been said, either in the actual or a former conversation, should be available in the communication context. This requirement is consistent with findings in communication theory [2] and approaches pursued in systems like KOLUMBUS [3], offering annotations for documents that may be annotated themselves.

Thirdly, users wanted to use the chat transcript as the starting point for the creation or enhancement of documents. Detailed requirements ranged from compiling chat sessions into condensed minutes up to reusing parts of the conversation directly in new or existing documents. Examples include condensed, result-oriented minutes of virtual meetings of software development teams or SIGs, tutors who wanted to reuse (parts of) the chat transcript to enhance their learning material, or students who liked to reuse parts of discussions of exercises to prepare their own material for learning and exam preparation.

All these requirements can be characterized as needs to better integrate chat conversations and documents:

- Archiving: Transcripts of synchronous conversations should be kept persistently as documents in the group memory.

- Discussion: As any other document, the transcript should be subject to future conversations.
- Reuse: As any other document, (parts of) a conversation transcript should be editable to create new documents or be reusable within other documents.

This paper introduces the concept of editable chat logs to cope with these requirements. Section 1 summarizes the state-of-the-art on how to integrate chat conversations and documents in groupware. Section 2 introduces the concept of editable chat logs and Section 3 illustrates its implementation in a new release of the CURE shared workspace system. Section 4 reports on first experiences gained in two use cases. Section 5 discusses the concept of editable chat logs with respect to related work, and Section 6 concludes with a summary and an outlook on future work.

1. State-of-the-Art

Chats have been introduced to support light-weight, synchronous communication for distributed groups. They allow distributed users to exchange text messages synchronously. Two general kinds of chat systems can be distinguished: While instant messaging (IM) systems [4, 5] can be used by an individual user to contact another user(s) to initiate a chat session, text chat systems [6, 7, 8] aim to provide a central service or place where individuals can meet to exchange messages. Text chats are offered as pure chat services [6] or are integrated into groupware platforms [1]. Some aim to support large, distributed ad-hoc-groups [9] whereas others are mainly targeted to support smaller groups, in particular at the workplace [8]. Shared workspace systems deal with smaller groups at the workplace. Therefore we will focus on the application of these kinds of chats.

One of the first text chat systems, IRC, Internet Relay Chat [10], and most IM tools aim to support transient or volatile communication needs: When a user enters a chat session that is already running for a certain amount of time, he can participate in the discussion but has no access to previously exchanged chat messages of that session. When the last user leaves a chat session, the transcript of chat messages exchanged is lost. Persistent chat tools aim to support both, ephemeral and perennial conversation needs by keeping transcripts of chat messages across chat sessions. Adding persistence allows for asynchronous communication and makes text chat systems more useful for formal communication [11]. Persistence accommodates late comers and keeps group members up to date who could not participate in a synchronous chat session. In general, as recent studies show, having the dialogue history helped collaborators to communicate efficiently and led to faster and better task performance; and it help to establish common ground in small groups engaged in tightly coupled collaborative tasks [12]; persistence facilitates social awareness and knowledge sharing [13]. In particular at the workplace, chat was used overwhelmingly for discussions related to work [8].

In the sequel of this section we will analyse related work with respect to the aspects of archiving, discussion and reuse of persistent chat transcripts.

1.1. Archiving of chat conversations

During the last two years of using the CURE persistent chat, our users asked for means to archive chat transcripts for later use. Similar requirements have been published by [1] who conducted a long-term study of using a persistent chat system whose aim is to support collaboration within corporate workgroups: The authors report on needs for simpler archiving mechanisms that permit "past episodes to be packaged, indexed (so they may be searched if needed [...]), and archived. This would make them available and useful, but 'out of the way'."

Functionality to archive chat transcript in documents has been developed in the context of Instant Messaging (IM) tools. IM tools have to be installed by every individual user. They provide a user-constructed list of frequent IM partners, the ability to exchange text chats (and data) with those partners and awareness indicators of which of those partners are currently online [5]. Users may contact each other to instantiate a chat session. More users may be invited. The IM tool ICQ has a history feature, storing chat/IM transcripts per contact person. These personal histories are useful to look up conversations and information exchanged such as URLs. Moreover, these transcripts are so useful that additional software tools have been developed to convert ICQ histories into plain text, HTML or XML documents that can be further exchanged and manipulated [14]. However, all this functionality is not embedded in a shared workspace: There is no common document repository or group memory. All documents exchanged and transcripts stored have to be managed by the individuals on their own. Also Halverson et al. report: "While the IM client can be used to save conversations, this was not sufficient for the group's needs, as it only produced a record for an individual." (cf. p.182 in [1]).

1.2. Discussing chat conversations

The issue of discussing conversations is twofold: discussion of previous chat messages while chatting, and discussion of chat sessions that have been archived in a document in a subsequent chat. These two kinds of discussing previous discussions are backed by communication theory, stating that conversational expressions are completed by their context, comprising what has already been said and referenced material [2].

Referencing previous chat messages while chatting is a serious issue in all chat tools: Chats are usually characterized as tools for synchronous communication although their nature is truly quasi-synchronous: Although the posted messages are available synchronously to all participants, the production of those messages is not available to all participants, only to the individual typists [15] (as in contrast, to conversations in face-to-face situations or in software tools like UNIX talk). This quasi-synchronous nature and the persistence of chat messages supporting references to what has already been said in a chat conversation, lead to multiple parallel discussions threads in a single chat causing an incoherent discussion [15]. As a remedy, chat users use devices such as naming, use of similar utterances and repetition to direct a comment to a specific previous chat messages. Recently, so called threaded chats [17, 18, 31] allow to explicitly reference to a previous chat message by a link and offer views on single threads in a chat conversation.

With respect to the issue of discussing conversations archived in a document, research on annotating documents has to be considered. Annotations to documents have been proposed as simple text based annotations of single authors to whole documents (CoNote [19] and CaMILE [20]), to hierarchical subsections of a document (KOLUMBUS [3]), to an arbitrary part of a web page (WebAnn [21]) or even as whole chats that may be anchored into a document [29]. Whereas in [29] anchored chats can not be annotated or discussed themselves by another anchored conversation, text based, single author annotations in KOLUMBUS may be annotated themselves. As Kienle and Herrmann [3] report, this functionality is in particular useful for document review. Using annotations that can be annotated themselves may lead to discussion threads. The concept "offers the users two different perspectives on the items of content that are stored and displayed by the system: an item can be considered as context (e.g. the material that helps to solve the task) or as communicative expression (e.g. the description of the task or questions about it). An item which is contributed as a communication act [...] can become part of the context later."

The approaches of KOLUMBUS and WebAnn allow to link annotations directly to a smaller part of a document and anchored chats allow linking a conversation into a document [29]. Anchored chats and the annotation concept of KOLUMBUS make it difficult to find conversational contributions, in particular in large documents or document bases. To cope with this problem, KOLUMBUS introduced a central annotation view similar to a mail box [22], similar as WebAnn does for the discussion of a document [21]. However, annotations are no means of synchronous communication.

1.3. Reusing the content generated in chat conversations

To our knowledge there is no work reported on the issue of reusing content generated during chat discussions in shared workspace systems. The authors of [1] report, how during the use of Lotus Notes a new idea may start with an email thread, but as it develops it will get moved into a document stored in a document database. Similar mechanisms for mail are also provided by wikis, e.g. the CURE threaded mail forum stores all exchanged mail for a group as editable wiki pages and qwikWeb [30] provides a similar service. As we learned from our users, such a kind of morphing conversational units into documents is also required for chats, not only for e-mail. As pointed out in Section 1.1, some archiving of chat transcripts in documents is provided by IM systems, however, this is not sufficient for a group's needs, as it only produces a record for an individual [1].

In the sequel we will introduce the concept of editable chat logs that fulfils all three requirements discussed here for groups.

2. The Concept of Editable Chat Logs

2.1. A conceptual chat model

For defining the key properties of editable chat logs we first define a simple model of a chat tool. A *chat tool* allows distributed users to exchange chat messages synchronously. To implement this functionality, we may conceptually define a chat tool as consisting of a central server and a set of clients to this server, one for each user.

The *client* user interface offers the user a window to compose their message text and an operation to send the composed message text to the server. Another window of the client, the *chat transcript view*, visualizes the list of all messages sent from all user clients to the central server. The client receives the actual list of these messages from the server.

Actually, the central data structure of a chat *server* is the *chat transcript*, a list of all messages sent from all user clients to the server. Whenever the server receives a chat message from a client, the server appends the chat message consisting of the message text, the author, and the arrival time to the chat transcript. Thus, the arrival of chat messages at the server determines the global total order of chat messages, resulting in a unique sequence of chat messages. By propagating changes to the chat transcript, the chat transcript view in the clients is kept up to date. Chat messages that have been sent to the server are immutable. They can only be displayed in the chat transcript view of the clients.

This simple model does not detail any implementation issues, such as when to update the clients with exactly which information or if a single server is used or a set of networked servers etc. It is general enough to leave room for these and other issues but precise enough reflecting the quasi-synchronous nature of today's most commonly used chat tools and to cover aspects of chat persistency and thus also asynchronous use of chats. Transient chat tools loose their chat transcript when a chat session ends and the last user shuts down her client. Persistent chat tools keep the chat transcript across chat sessions, even when no client is currently running.

2.2. Editable chat-logs

Based on the conceptual chat model, a *chat log* is defined as a (sub) sequence of chat messages of the chat transcript. The basic idea to make this sequence of messages accessible to archiving, discussion and reuse is to transform such a sequence of chat messages into a document that can be stored, read and edited as any other document in the shared workspace system.

The properties and operations of documents in shared workspace system can be defined as follows: A shared workspace systems is able to store and retrieve all types of supported documents. The shared workspace system provides a document identifier/name and/or some meta data for every kind of document. All this information can be used by the users for searching and identifying documents. We summarize these aspects of all types of supported documents in shared workspaces in the notion of *archivable documents*. Archivable documents can be specialized in two different classes of documents: editable and external documents. In addition to the properties and operations a shared workspace system offers for archivable documents, the content of *editable documents* can be displayed for reading and editing by the group in the shared workspace. However, not all shared workspace systems offer reading and editing representations for all types of supported documents. Some shared workspace systems just allow uploading files that have to be downloaded by each individual user for reading and editing, i.e. the workspace primarily is a tool for communication, coordination and document exchange, as for example BSCW [23]. The actual work on the documents has to be performed outside the shared system. We call these types of documents *external documents*.

For editable chat logs, we focus on shared workspace systems offering at least one type of editable document. An *editable chat log* is an editable document containing a (sub) sequence of the chat transcript as its content. As an editable document of the shared workspace system, an editable chat log can be archived, read and edited as any other document:

- The general archiving functionality of documents in a shared workspace system applies to editable chat logs. Thus, transcripts of synchronous conversations can be kept persistently as any other document in the group memory (Archiving).
- The ability to read the editable chat log in the shared workspace system is the prerequisite for future conversations about the transcript in the group (Discussion).
- The editing representation of an editable chat log allows the reuse of (parts of) the content of the chat transcript in new or in existing documents (Reuse). To allow for the maximum benefit from the reuse of content of archived transcripts, the editing features for chat messages should be consistent with the editing features for documents in the shared workspace system.

Furthermore, we require that the initial version of an editable chat log has to be immutable. Allowing changes to the initial content of an editable chat log would corrupt the requirements on archiving and discussion. Keeping the original chat log is important for general archiving, documentation [1] and review. As recent studies have shown, original chat logs can also be a valuable source for re-learning [16]. Therefore, the editing of the initial version of an editable chat log should offer reuse of content but must not change its content.

To support editable chat logs, a shared workspace system needs an operation (1) to define a sub sequence of chat messages of the chat transcript of its chat tool and an operation (2) to transform this sequence of chat messages into an editable document for which the immutability of the initial version is guaranteed.

The definition of an editable chat log is based on abstractions from the conceptual chat model and the model of editable documents. For a given shared workspace system, the design of editable chat logs depends on the chat and document model supported by the shared workspace system and its intended applications. The definition of an editable chat log in this paper is general enough to leave room for these design decisions, such as which chat messages should go into an editable chat log, which search, referencing, and editing mechanisms should be provided for editable chat logs, or how a version of the initial chat log should be kept. These issues will be discussed in Section 5 taking into account experiences gained (cf. Section 4) with a first implementation of editable chat logs in the shared workspace system CURE (cf. Section 3) and related work.

3. An Implementation of Editable Chat-logs

We implemented the concept of editable chat logs in the CURE shared workspace system. CURE has been used since autumn 2003 as a CSCW and CSCL environment at the FernUniversität in Hagen. The actual user basis comprises more then 1800 people. In this paper, we will only describe those features of CURE that are relevant to illustrate the concept of editable chat logs. Detailed descriptions of CURE have been published elsewhere ([25] for groupware tailoring and wiki pages in groupware, [26] for the application of CURE in CSCL, and [27] for access rights management for groupware). This is the first publication dealing with the chat tool of CURE and its role in the overall communication and cooperation features of a shared workspace system.

Before discussing the implementation of editable chat logs, the CURE system without editable chat logs is introduced.

3.1. The CURE Shared Workspace System

Shared workspaces in CURE are called rooms. A room in CURE contains documents, called pages, and tools for group coordination and communication. CUREs types of pages include editable wiki pages and file pages, the latter representing external documents that have been uploaded into the workspace. Whereas file pages support document exchange, wiki pages can be read and manipulated within the shared workspace system. The wiki syntax of CURE in particular supports various types of links (e.g. links to other wiki pages, to file pages, to other rooms or to external sources) and next to standard wiki mark-ups a syntax to input formulas. As common in wikis, all changes to wiki pages are kept automatically in separate versions.

To build up whole CSCW/L environments, a room may be connected to adjacent rooms, resulting in a tree structure of rooms. Rooms may be further interlinked to cope with additional organizational structures. All registered users possessing appropriate access rights for a specific room may enter the room and use the material stored on pages and the tools available for coordination and communication [27]. Since wiki pages may be contained in every room, CURE can be considered as shared workspace system offering a wiki for every room. Or putting it the other way round, CURE can be considered as a wiki engine with group communication, coordination and group formation features for the individual wikis.

Among other awareness and communication tools, a room may offer a persistent chat tool. While composing chat messages, the users may use the full wiki language, including the linking and formula features. At the user interface, a room with a chat provides two window panes (You may refer to Figure 1, since the general lay out of the user interface is still the same in the new CURE release shown in Figure 1.): The upper window pane is dedicated to visualize all content related information of rooms, comprising the display of the content of the current page, but also lists of folders and pages, version histories of pages, search forms and other navigational tools. The lower window pane is dedicated to the chat tool. If users configure a room with no chat [25], this pane will not be available in the room. While chatting in the lower pane, a wiki or file page may be displayed in the upper window pane.

While the chat is a synchronous communication tool showing the same sequence of chat messages to all of the room users, the presentation of pages in the upper pane is independent, i.e. users may look at different documents while chatting. The chat pane may be expanded to get a more comprehensive view of the chat transcript, thus seeing more of what has already been said.

CUREs chat tool is a simple chat. It offers no threads, i.e. there are no explicit references from chat messages to previous chat messages. Teams in CURE rely on social protocols to keep the discussions coherent (e.g., addressing discussants by name, use of similar utterances and repetition to direct a comment to a specific previous chat message, cf. [15]). Moreover, references to documents are always references to the whole document. They are primarily used to direct discussants to a page to discuss.

CUREs chat has been used for formal and informal communication. Presence indicators for users support spontaneous synchronous communication. To support conversation contexts and also asynchronous communication, the chat is persistent for the whole lifetime of a room, i.e. all chat messages are kept in the chat transcript at the server side. However, to cope with performance issues and providing an efficient implementation, the server sends only the most recent 40 messages to the clients. Thus, the chat transcript view at the client side visualizes the last 40 messages only. To make older messages accessible to the user, the chat transcript view provides an HTML-link to look up so called chat records. (This link is no link in terms of the wiki syntax, i.e. the chat transcript view does not visualize a CURE document as HTML in a standard web browser; it is rather a visualization of the chat transcript in HTML!) Following this link, the upper window pane shows a list of the chat records recorded so far: Older chat messages are packaged in portions of 40 messages and are entitled with the range of chat messages they archive, i.e. starting from 1-39, 40 – 79 etc. Chat records may be looked up individually. The list of chat records and an individual chat record are shown in the upper window pane and may be read while the user is chatting.

With this functionality, CURE already supports simple archiving and discussion – however, the archiving concept of chat records was primarily designed to solve the problem of how to offer a complete chat history to the user. Chat records are no documents. They can not be identified by their name or any other identification mechanisms. Users can not define links to them. They are maintained by the chat tool and can only be accessed by looking up the list of chat records in the chat tool.

3.2. Editable Chat Logs in CURE

As described in the previous section, the initial chat archiving mechanisms of CUREs chat tool were not consistent with other information look up mechanisms. In particular, the packaging into 40 messages distorted the structure of the discussions: messages of a single chat session may be distributed over several portions. In addition, the portions of archived messages can not be identified by a name and thus not be referenced by the users, particularly not in discussions. There is no editing view on chat messages that have been sent to the server. To reuse content of previous conversations, users have to rely on the copy/paste functions of their browser. Depending on the browser, layout and linking information is lost. In all browsers, reusing images is difficult. In particular for formulas, which are gif-images computed from latex input, the latex input string is completely lost for reuse. We solved all these problems by introducing editable chat logs into CUREs chat tool.

To implement editable chat logs in CURE, we first had to implement an operator that defines which sequences of chat messages of the chat transcript should be transformed into an editable document. To require as little effort as necessary from our users with respect to archiving of conversations, we decided to implement an automatic recognition mechanism for chat sessions. The messages of a single chat session should be recorded in an editable document. Chat sessions are separated by a time span of chat inactivity. As a starting point, we chose 20 minutes of chat inactivity to define the end of a chat session. All chat messages starting with the most recent chat message up to the last message before the next 20 minutes break were considered as one chat session and are transformed into an editable wiki page.

Since chat messages are composed using the wiki syntax, the transformation of the sequence of chat messages into a wiki page was straight forward: The chat tool had to store the chat message strings in the chat transcript instead of HTML representations of chat messages. Starting with the first chat message in the sequence, the arrival time of the message and a link to the author of the message followed by the chat message string were added to the content of the wiki page. The wiki mark-up for a horizontal line was added to separate the chat messages from each other. Finally, the wiki page is entitled with the date and time information of the beginning and end of the chat session.

Because wiki pages are versioned documents, their initial version is immutable by definition. Therefore, a wiki page generated in the way described above from a sequence of chat messages is an editable chat log. It can be stored, displayed and edited as any other document. Its initial version is immutable. It offers maximum benefit in reuse, since the composition of chat messaged in the chat tool and the editing capabilities for document content are identical.

3.3. The Users View on Editable Chat Logs in CURE

The introduction of editable chat logs changed the behaviour of the chat tool in the following way: To provide conversation context and to support asynchronous work, all messages of a chat session will still go to the chat transcript view while the users are chatting. Even when the chat session ends, i.e. no user is entering messages any more for the duration of the session separation time span, the messages will stay in the transcript view to support asynchronous communication: Users entering after the session will immediately see the results of the most recent chat session. However, when a new chat message is entered by a user after the defined time of chat inactivity, all previous chat messages will automatically be compiled into an editable chat log and stored in the chat log repository. The chat log repository can be accessed via a "CHAT-LOG"-link shown at the top of the chat transcript view (cf. Figure 1. The figure shows a re-enacted example chat in German based on real data.).

Figure 1. An example of a chat with editable chat logs in the new release of the CURE shared workspace system

The chat log repository displays the chat logs as a list of documents. Initially, the chat log of a chat session is entitled with the date and time information of the beginning and end of the chat session. Clicking on its title, the chat log will be shown in a display representation in the document pane (cf. Figure 2). While reading the chat log, the rooms' chat can still be used, i.e. users can discuss previous discussions.

Clicking the button showing the pen in Figure 2 will open an edit view on the editable chat log (cf. parts of the editable content in the black box in Figure 2). The editing of editable chat logs conforms to the editing of wiki documents in CURE. All mark-up that has been input by the users while composing their chat messages, including link and formula definitions (underlined on the screen dump), is now available in the editable chat log. The content of an editable chat log may also be copied to other wiki documents preserving all mark-up.

In edit mode, the editable chat log can be renamed, thus giving the log a more meaningful name. This name may then be used to identify the chat log like any other document in the system, i.e. chat logs may be referenced from other documents, mails and chat messages. They can particularly be referenced in discussions.

Since the editable chat log is a wiki document itself, the built-in automatic versioning also preserves the initial version of the chat log. Inspecting the version history of a document, the chat tool may be used also, i.e. team members may jointly discuss the history of a document, in particular the history of an editable chat log.

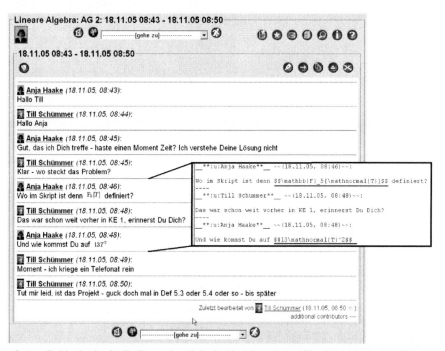

Figure 2. An editable chat log in display mode and (in the black box) three of its chat messages in edit mode

4. Experiences

The new release of CURE comprising editable chat logs was put in operation for general use in December 2005. Since August 2005, we used editable chat logs extensively while compiling the CURE User's Manual and we did some extensive tests with various user groups. Our findings are based on interviews.

Having transcripts of conversations as identifiable documents was appreciated by all chat users. All users welcomed the ability to refer to editable chat logs as documents. They used it to refer to chat sessions from documents and to discuss previous discussions by chat and also by mail. However, the users would like to have a more fine-grained referencing mechanism. The design of a general mechanism to reference to parts of wiki pages is subject to future work. In addition, while appreciating the full text search functionality on chat logs, users demanded additional search functionality, e.g. to search for chat logs where a certain person has uttered something on a certain key word.

The reuse of content of previous chat sessions was very well received. All users appreciated that the original mark-up is preserved and that it can be reused. In particular, groups using formulas appreciated the new functionality, since latex input strings of chat messages are preserved and can be edited.

The automatic detection of chat sessions was received differently. All users agreed that the packaging of chat messages now is much better and meaningful than before (cf. Section 3.2). On the one hand, users wanting to work on a summary of a chat session immediately after the end of the session requested an operation to trigger the generation of the editable chat log - having to wait 20 minutes makes no sense from their perspective. On the other hand, users who already missed discussions more often warned to not empty the chat transcript completely and/or too soon: An empty chat transcript raises the impression that no recent conversation took place. As Halverson et al. put it, the archive "is out of the way" [1]. But being out of the way reduces activity awareness for asynchronous communication: Looking up the chat archive is a step of indirection users may not be willing to perform and group communication as a whole may suffer.

The critique suggests separating the aspect of visibility of chat messages in the actual chat transcript from archiving of conversations in documents, i.e. it may be useful to copy and transform some chat messages into an editable chat log for reading and editing while still having them visible in the chat transcript view of the chat tool. A subsequent question, at least for threaded chats having an explicit notion of references among chat messages, then would be, if the referencing of a chat message that already has been archived in a chat log but still is available in the chat transcript should have any consequences for the chat log: Should the chat log be updated with respect to the new chat message? Should someone, and if, who, get a notification on the new chat message referencing the archived chat message?

Another aspect with respect to asynchronous communication via the chat tool was raised user groups using the persistent chat as a kind of bulletin board. For example, a team member published a (part of a) solution to an exercise in the chat. The next team member added her comment/contribution to the solution, sometimes some hours or even a day later. Some users were negatively surprised that their comment to a persistent chat message more than 20 minutes later emptied the chat transcript: Their conversation spreading over a longer period of time was disrupted and could not be perceived as a single conversation in the chat transcript view. Obviously, a remedy in the archive could be to copy the disrupted chat logs into a single chat log that may also be named appropriately. However, the comments of the users suggest designing more sophisticated means for determining when and which parts of a conversation should go into a chat log.

5. Discussion and Comparison to Related Work

The central idea of editable chat logs is to provide an archive of a chat transcript in the form of a document that can be used, i.e. stored, archived, searched, displayed, referenced and manipulated, as any other document by a group of users in a shared workspace system.

Considering the *issue of archiving*, editable chat logs are different from histories of IM systems stored in documents [14] since they are available in the group context. As our experiences show (cf. Section 4), taking into account the aspect of a group of users raises new research questions that are not prompted by histories of chat transcripts of ephemeral IM tools.

The exact operations for identifying and searching editable chat logs depend on the underlying model for editable documents. Therefore, our model does do not define detailed search mechanisms. As a starting point, the general search mechanisms on documents provided by the shared workspace system (often search on title, authors, and a full-text search on the documents' content) are applicable to searching chat logs. More sophisticated search mechanisms taking into account structures of the chat logs' content may be useful. Which search and indexing mechanisms are required exactly and would best foster collaboration is an open issue.

Considering the *issue of discussion* of conversations, editable chat logs serve as reference material. In threaded chats [17, 18, 31] previous chat messages can be referenced in the conversation context. The concept of editable chat logs (Not its actual implementation in CURE!) allows the users to package chat messages as desired. Applied to threaded chats, a chat log may also be defined taking into account the reference structure of the chat messages. In this way, for example single threads may be extracted into an editable chat log.

In KOLUMBUS [3], an annotation which is contributed as a communication act can become part of the reference material. Editable chat logs are a concept to morph chat transcripts into reference material. But annotations are no synchronous communication means. Although an overall view on annotations is available [22], there is no sequential view or a notion of conversation session. However, original transcripts of chat sessions are needed in group work for several purposes, such as documentation [1] or re-learning [16].

The concept of editable chat logs makes no assumptions on the granularity of references to the referenced material, except that a single document must be referable. WebAnn [21] offers the most flexible means to define the scope of a conversational comment and could be applied to make fine-grained references to editable chat logs, in particular to the immutable initial version.

Having a more detailed look on the *issue of reuse*, the model makes no assumption on how an initial version of an editable chat log should be kept, or if editing of a chat log should result in a new version or in the derivation of a new document. More sophisticated version support mechanisms on electronic documents [24] could offer additional useful functionality on editable chat logs. For the seamless integration of chat conversations and documents in a shared workspace it is important that the original chat log is preserved and its content can be reused. Moreover, allowing for full reuse of the content, the editing capabilities of chat messages should be consistent with (at least) a sub set of the editing capabilities of editable documents in the shared workspace system.

6. Conclusion and Future Work

The central idea of editable chat logs is to provide an archive of a chat transcript in the form of a document that can be used as any other document by a group of users in the shared workspace system. The concept of editable chat logs enables a conversation to morph into a document and thus is a step towards the seamless integration of conversations and artefacts, and towards a greater degree of seamless interplay between conversation and documentation in shared workspace systems. An editable chat log can serve as a source of knowledge, can be interlinked with other documents and be used as context for further conversations, either by chat or mail or any other conversational means that is able to refer to this document!

The means for all functions available on archived conversations should be the same as for any other document. We pursued this approach in a first implementation of editable chat logs in a groupware system with wiki pages. As a consequence, the implementation was very simple and users were immediately able to make use of the archived conversations: they could reuse results achieved during synchronous conversations, return to previous conversation for re-learning or do a joint analysis of former decision makings by chatting about a previously archived conversation. The implementation for another shared workspace system should take into account the notion of editable documents in this system.

Our experiences with the first implementation of editable chat logs suggest further work: The discussion of conversations would definitely benefit from more fine-grained referencing mechanisms to parts of the conversations' content [21]. Future work is required on special indexing for chat logs. Semantic mark-up of chat messages as e.g. questions, answers or foundation (cf. [22]) may be useful for such mechanisms. Another research issue is how to determine the content of a chat log depending on the kind of chat and its modes of use by its different user communities. Furthermore, there are open topics on keeping archived chat messages in the chat transcript: How much history should stay in the chat transcript? If a chat message already archived in a chat log is referenced in the chat transcript, should the chat log be updated or should users be informed? All these research questions are related to integrating chats in shared workspace systems and focus on a better integration of conversations and documents.

Acknowledgements

Thanks are due to Till Schümmer for pushing the development of CURE and to Jörg Haake for fruitful discussions about this paper.

References

[1]   C.A. Halverson, T. Erickson, J. Sussmann. What Counts as Success? Punctuated Patterns of Use in a Persistent Chat Environment. Proc. of Group'03, pp. 180-189.

[2]   T. Herrmann. Kommunikation und Kooperation. In: G. Schwabe, N. Streitz, R. Unland (Eds.). CSCW-Kompendium: Lehr- und Handbuch zum computerunterstützten kooperativen Arbeiten. Springer Verlag, Heidelberg, 2001, pp. 15-25.

[3]   A. Kienle, T. Herrmann. Integration of Communication, Coordination, and Learning Material – a Guide for the Functionality of Collaborative Learning Environments. Proc. of the 36th Hawaii International Conference on System Sciences, 2003, electronic version

[4]   B.A. Nardi, s. Whittaker, E. Bradner. Interaction and outeraction: Instant messaging in action. Proc. of CSCW 2000, pp. 80-88.

[5]   M.J. Muller, M.E. Raven, S. Krogan, D.R. Millen, K.Carey. Introducing Chat into Business Organizations: Toward an Instant Messaging maturity Model. Proc. of Group'03, pp. 50-57.

[6]   E. Bradner, W.A. Kellog, T. Erickson, T. The adoption and use of babble: A field study of chat in the workplace. Proc. of ECSCW 1999, pp. 139-158.

[7]   E. Churchill, S. Bly, S. It's all in the words: supporting work activities with lightweight tools. Proc. of Group ' 99, pp. 40-49.

[8]   M. Handel, J. Herbsleb, IM everywhere: What is chat doing in the workplace? Proc. of CSCW'02, pp. 1-10.

[9]   J.P. Birnholtz, T.A. Finholt, D.B. Horn, D.B S.J. Bae. Grounding Needs. Achieving Common Ground via Lightweight chat in large, distributed, ad-hoc Groups. Proc. of CHI 2005, pp. 21-30.

[10] Oikarinen, J. and Reed, D, Internet Relay Chat. Request for Comments 1459, IEFT, Mai 1993

[11] M. Jacovi, V. Soroka, S. Ur. Why Do We ReachOut? Functions pf a Semi-persistent Peer Support Tool. Proc. of Group'03, pp. 161-169.

[12] D. Gergle. D.R. Millen, R. Kraut, S.R. Fussell. Persistence Matters: Making the most of Chat in Tightly-Coupled work. Proc. of the ACM Conf. on Human Factors in Computing Systems 2004, pp. 413-438.

[13] T. Erickson, D.M. Smith, W.A. Kellog, M. Laff, J.T. Richards, E. Bradner. Socially translucent systems: Social proxies, persistent conversations, and the design of „babble". Proc. of the ACM Conf. on Human Factors in Computing Systems 1999, pp. 72-76.

[14] Belkasoft ICQ History Extractor. http://www.belkasoft.com/bihe/en/home.asp; last access: 7.11.2005

[15] J. O'Neill, D. Martin. Text Chat in Action. Proc. of Group'03, pp. 40-49.

[16] H.-R. Pfister, W. Müller, T. Holmer. Learning and Re-learning from net- based cooperative learning discourses. Proc. of ED-MEDIA 2004 World Conference on Educational Multimedia, Hypermedia & Telecommunications, pp. 2720-2724.

[17] T. Holmer, M. Wessner. Gestaltung von Chat-Werkzeugen zur Verringerung der Inkohärenz. In: M. Beißwenger, A. Storrer (Eds.). Chat- Kommunikation in Beruf, Bildung und Medien. Stuttgart: ibidem, pp. 181-199, 2005.

[18] W. Geyer, A.J. Witt, E. Wilcox, M. Muller, B. Kerr, B. Brownholtz, D.R. Millen. Chat Spaces. Proc. of DIS 2004, pp. 333-336.

[19] J. Davis, D. Huttenlocher. Shared Annotation for Cooperative Learning. Proc. of CSCL'95, pp 84-88.

[20] M. Guzdial, J. Turns, J. (2000), Effective Discussion through a computer-mediated anchored forum. Journal of the Learning Sciences, Vol. 9, No. 4, pp. 437-470.

[21] A.J. Bernheim Brush, D. Bargeron, J. Grudin, A. Borning, A. Gupta. Supporting Interactions Outside of Class: Anchored Discussions vs. Discussion Boards. Proc. of CSCL 2002, pp. 425-434.

[22] A. Kienle, T. Herrmann. Konzepte für die Lerngruppe. In: J. Haake, G. Schwabe, M. Wessner (Eds.). CSCL-Kompendium: Lehr- und Handbuch zum computerunterstützten kooperativen Lernen. Oldenbourg Verlag, München, 2004, pp. 171-183.

[23] BSCW Handbuch Version 4.1. OrbiTeam Software GmbH: Bonn. February 2003.

[24] A. Haake. CoVer: A Contextual Version Server for Hypertext Applications. Proc. of ECHT'92, pp. 43-52.

[25] J.M. Haake, T. Schümmer, A. Haake, M. Bourimi, B. Landgraf. Two-level tailoring support for CSCL. Proc. of CRIWG'03, LNCS, Springer: Heidelberg, 2003, pp. 74-82.

[26] J.M. Haake, T. Schümmer, A. Haake, M. Bourimi, B. Landgraf. Supporting flexible collaborative distance learning in the CURE platform. Proc. of the 37th Hawaiian International Conference on System Sciences, 2004, electronic version.

[27] J.M. Haake, A. Haake, T. Schümmer, M. Bourimi, B. Landgraf. End-User Controlled Group Formation and Access Rights Management in a Shared Workspace System. Proc. of CSCW'04, pp. 554-563.

[28] A. Haake, S. Lukosch, T. Schümmer. Wiki-Templates: Adding Structure Support to Wikis On Demand. Proc. of WikiSym 2005, The 2005 International Symposium on Wikis, ACM Press, pp. 41-51.

[29] E.F. Churchil, J. Trevor, S. Bly, L. Nelson, D. Cubranic. Anchored conversations: Chatting in the context of a document. Proc. of CHI 2000, pp. 454 -461.

[30] K. Eto, S. Takabayashi, T. Masui. qwikWeb: integrating mailing list and WikiWikiWeb for group communication. Proc. Of WikiSym 2005, The 2005 International Symposium on Wikis, ACM Press, pp. 17-23.

[31] M. Mühlpfordt, Martin, M. Wessner. Explicit Referencing In Chat Supports Collaborative Learning. Proc. of the CSCL 2005, May 30 - June 4, 2005, Taipei, Taiwan, 2005

Cooperative Systems Design
P. Hassanaly et al. (Eds.)
IOS Press, 2006

Mediated Communication Behavior in Distributed Networks of Practice

Eli HUSTAD

Agder University College, Department of Information Systems, Kristiansand, Norway

Abstract. This study examines mediated communication behavior in distributed networks of practice (DNoPs) in a multinational enterprise working in the marine insurance industry. The study describes and compares mediated communication behavior in five different distributed networks of practice as a combination of the knowledge activities that take place during communicative action, the media used to support communication, the networks' perceptions of different media, and the contextual factors that influence both communication and media selection. The networks experienced several challenges in the communication process such as technological instabilities that excluded participation, complex and highly equivocal messages, physical and social-psychological distance between participants, and media limitations. Different theoretical perspectives for mediated communication provide a framework for discussion and integration of the empirical findings in this study.

Keywords: Networks of practice, communication, knowledge, media choice, social influence

Introduction

In recent decades, the stream of knowledge management (KM) literature has paid increasing attention to informal organizational groups like communities of practice (CoPs) and networks of practice (NoPs) and their significance for knowledge creation and transfer, learning and innovation [1], [2], [3]. Since communities of practice are characterized as emergent and self-organizing, representing a kind of "invisible" network existing *beside* the formal organizational structure, they create veins for knowledge flows and a "tighter" organization stimulating the integration of subsidiaries and headquarters in a multinational [4].

In multinationals, the geographical distance prevents the communities' members located in different business offices from meeting face-to-face on a regular basis. Thus, they are dependent on computer-mediated communication (CMC) to perform knowledge activities and to sustain relationships [5]. There are several studies that focus on dispersed teams and the use of communication technology to enable group processes in the context of virtual organizations [6], [7] and virtual teamwork [8], [9], [10]. However, only a few empirical studies focus on communication media use in distributed networks of practice (DNoPs) [11], [12]. With this research gap in mind, the main purpose of this study is to illuminate how distributed intra-organizational networks of practice communicate to perform their knowledge activities across geographical locations by using different communication media tools. Through an interpretive case study in five different locations of a multinational company, this investigation examines a selection of different distributed networks of practice in respect of their *mediated communication behavior*. The study describes and compares mediated communication behavior in these networks as a combination of 1) the knowledge activities that take place during communicative action 2) the media used to support communication in different knowledge activities 3) the networks' perceptions of different media, and 4) contextual factors that influence both communication and media selection. Findings indicate that mediated communication behavior in these networks is a multifaceted phenomenon, which is socially constructed and strongly context-dependent.

Different theoretical perspectives of mediated communication provide a frame for discussion and integration of the empirical findings in this study. Both rational models and alternative social and contextual-considering perspectives constitute distinct opportunities for explaining the empirical findings.

The paper is organized as follows. Section one introduces theoretical concepts, followed by a review of different communication theories that explain mediated communication. Section three describes the research methodology and provides a description of the research site. Section four reports the findings from the empirical study while section five provides a discussion of the results. Finally, section six presents conclusions and implications from this research for theory and practice as well as suggestions for future research.

1. Concepts related to distributed networks of practice and their knowledge activities

A community of practice consists of a tightly knit group of members engaged in a shared practice who know each other and work together, typically meet face-to-face, and continually negotiate, communicate, and coordinate with each other directly. In contrast to co-located communities, distributed networks of practice consist of a larger, loosely knit, geographically dispersed group of participants engaged in a shared practice or common topic of interest [1], [2]. Due to the physically distributed nature of networks of practice, the ties linking the members together are generally weaker in terms of lower degree of involvement, lower emotional intensity, intimacy, and reciprocity. In addition is knowledge less redundant in a distributed network since new insights and perspectives from different environments might stimulate the diffusion of new creative ideas [13]. It is important to distinguish DNoPs discussed in this study from electronic NoPs, or online communities, which consist of a large number of "strangers" who are weakly linked together through asynchronous computer-mediated communication technologies such as threaded discussion boards and email distribution lists [14], [15]. DNoPs are also different from project teams. DNoPs like CoPs evolve over time and interact on a continuous basis rather than being project or deadline driven [16]. In communities, participation is often voluntary, and the shape of a community, its objectives and memberships are fluid and emerge through participation. In contrast, project teams carry out specific tasks, where each team member has a specific role and job description [17].

Members of DNoPs perform different types of knowledge activities, such as knowledge sharing, creation and transfer. Knowledge sharing is defined here as the *sharing of critical business knowledge* related to daily work practices and problem solving in terms of both procedural (know-what) and declarative knowledge (know-how) [4]. Knowledge creation refers to the creation of strategic knowledge in terms of improving business processes and development of innovative products giving long-term competitive advantages and organizational capabilities [18].

To communicate across time and distance, members of intra-organizational DNoPs are highly reliant on computer-mediated communication channels. Contemporary organizations often have a variety of different channels through which employees can transmit and receive information. Examples are synchronous communication technologies such as video and telephone conferences, desktop videoconferences, instant messaging/chat, and asynchronous communication technologies like e-mail, fax, SMS, and document management systems. A company's intranet is often the common organizational junction and entrance to these technologies as they facilitate communication and knowledge activities between network members across geographical sites. Several former studies have focused on the context of distributed meetings, technology support and its challenges in respect of synchronous communication like videoconferencing [19], desktop videoconferencing [20], data conferencing [21] and electronic meeting systems [22].

2. Communication theories and media perceptions

Several theoretical perspectives have been developed and extended to explain choice and use of communication media in specific situations. Most of these theories are comparative, addressing how and why mediated communication is different from face-to-face communication. This paper discusses some of the most known and applied perspectives that constitute potential explanation models for the empirical findings in this study. The different perspectives constitute two contradictions of explanatory models in terms of rational choice models and alternative perspectives, which emphasize contextual factors.

2.1. Rational choice models

The best-known rational choice models of media use are media richness theory [23] and social presence theory [24]. In social presence theory, the conceptualizing of communication media is along a single continuum of 'social presence', a degree of a medium to facilitate awareness of the person and the interpersonal relationships during interaction. Communication is efficient when the medium selected has a social presence degree that matches the level of interpersonal involvement required for the task.

In media richness theory the assumptions are that communication media vary in their level of richness, or the ability of a medium to facilitate shared meaning or convey information and to reduce equivocality [23], i.e., the existence of multiple and conflicting interpretations [25]. According to media richness, the classification of communication media is along a continuum of richness, where richness is the ability of a medium to carry nonverbal cues (e.g., facial expression, tone, natural language, body language) and provide rapid feedback, to facilitate personal focus and to use natural language. Face-to-face communication is the richest channel followed in decreasing order by videoconference, telephone, e-mail, written personal, written formal and numeric formal media. The media richness hypothesis has generally been verified when tested on 'traditional media' like face-to-face communication, telephone, letters and memos [23], [26], but when tested on 'newer media', like e-mail, voicemail and videoconference, more inconsistent empirical findings raise doubt about the generality of media richness [27]. In contrast, findings from other studies support media richness theory by providing evidence that those media mentioned above are less suitable for negotiation and personal interactions compared to face-to-face communication [24]. Additionally, email and computer conferencing did negatively affect group cohesiveness [28], [29]. These conflicting results have motivated a reconsideration of the descriptive and predictive validity of media richness theory, and a broader set of predictor variables has been added to research models attempting to explain both media selection behavior and media perceptions. In studies by Trevino, Lengel and Daft [30], the discussion is on how situational determinants such as geographical distance and time pressure influence media choice. One conclusion was that message content plays a less important role for media choice when situational constraints are high.

To summarize, several empirical studies emphasize that rational models cannot *fully* explain communication media use [28], [31], [32], and in some cases a combination of rational and social theories are proposed as complementary explanations to media choice [33]. In next section, I review a selection of additional or alternative theories to rational choice models.

2.2. Alternative theories to explain mediated communication behavior

The media richness theory pays no attention to the social context of individuals making media choices since it assumes that media have fixed properties (or that individuals have the same perceptions of media richness), individuals make choices independently of the people around them, and choice making is purely cognitive [31]. Because of these limitations, a broad range of alternative explanations has developed. In this paper, I draw attention to the social influence model [28], [31], the channel expansion theory [34] the emergent network perspective [35], and the adaptive structuration theory (AST) [36] as alternative theoretical perspectives to rational models for explanation of communication media behavior in distributed networks of practice. While these theories all take a somewhat different perspective, they do share the same underlying assumption that communication richness is not an intrinsic, objective property of the communication medium alone. Rather, the same medium could support rich communication among some users in some organizational contexts, while only supporting lean communication among other users in other contexts. Along these lines, the best medium for communication is not the decision of a single person since it emerges from the organizational context and from the interactions among people in the context using the medium over time [28].

Fulk, Schmitz and Steinfield [31] have developed the *social influence theory of technology use* to explain media choices. According to this, social determinants as work group norms, co-workers and supervisors attitudes and behaviors will influence media choice. The theory has the same basic assumption as rational choice models in that individuals cognitively process stimuli, but differs in the explanations of how cognitions develop and change. If a manager's attitude and behavior is positive towards one medium or a set of different media, then he or she might influence other individuals' media attitudes. In addition, the objectivity of the media richness is considered as a perception that can vary influenced by social factors, so that participants will construct the meaning and use of specific media. For instance, in work environments where everyone use e-mail to communicate, organizational members will find e-mail more efficient than telephone or a face-to-face approach in accomplishing specific tasks despite that e-mail is considered as a leaner medium [28].

The *channel expansion theory* tries to explain inconsistencies in both media richness and social influence [34]. The theory focuses on different experiences as important in shaping how an individual develops richness perceptions for a given channel such as skills and knowledge related to media, message and organizational context.

In the *emergent network perspective* [35], the basic underlying assumption is that adoption and use of communication media are social and contextual. By emphasizing the interplay between the duality of social environment and application of communication technologies, the perspective constitutes a recursive model and draws on a combination of structuration theory, structural action and recursive characters, the emergent perspective on action in organizations and network theory. The argument is that perception and use of media are the outcome of interplay among actors, context and technology, which consists of recursive processes such as "effects of networks on media attitudes and usage" and "effects of media usage on networks". This interplay is an adaptive process that allows for widely divergent outcomes in different settings. According to the emergent perspective, the uses and consequences of information technology emerge unpredictably from complex social interactions, and unexpected applications of a medium will occur over time [37]. The perspective is in strong contradiction to the media characteristics approach, and argues that organizational communication is much more complex since both multiple goals and strategies enact in a single communication situation. The emergent network perspective touches on individual, dyadic and group parameters of the network.

The main principle in *adaptive structuration theory* (AST) is that implementation and use of a communication technology adapt to local situations, and that unintended user patterns might emerge when a new technology appropriates into its social setting [36]. The theory, which shares similarities with the emergent network perspective, builds upon social structuration theories, literary studies and communication theories. In AST, the contextual variables are "constructed" into social processes of technology use. When a group applies a medium over time, new ideas and emerging ways of using the medium lead to the emergence of new social structures. Appropriation happens when a group accepts a medium and it becomes a part of their social structure. Through reciprocal interaction between the medium and its users, the group adapts to the medium and visa versa.

3. Research site and qualitative methods

To examine computer-mediated communication in distributed networks of practice, an interpretive case study was performed. I chose a case study because of the importance of studying computer-mediated communication in networks of practice in their real-life context [38]. Insure (pseudonym) is a multinational company in the marine insurance industry that provides marine liability insurance for regional sailing ships. Today Insure has three different product divisions: Protection & Indemnity, Marine, and Energy, and business areas comprising claims handling and underwriting activities. Insure has approximately 350 employees working in ten different locations worldwide.

Collection of empirical evidence took place in five organizational sites of the company (three offices in Norway, one office in England and one office in Finland) comprising approximately thirty in-depth, open-ended and semi-structured interviews, observation of internal organizational videoconferences and open-ended email-discussions in different distributed networks of practice. Secondary material was collected from the company's intranet consisting of internal reports, presentation materials, workshop reports, meeting agendas, minutes, and documents. The process of data collection and analysis proceeded iteratively, allowing themes to emerge from the empirical material for categorizing, and then to be examined more deeply as relevant.

4. Findings

Through the investigation, interviewees provided information about different networks of practice in which they participated, giving the possibility to identify and confirm consistence of several DNoPs 'spun' throughout the organization. The identification criteria for these networks relate to the definitions of networks of practice and communities of practice, i.e. as self-organizing and emergent, self-selecting and not defined by the organization's hierarchical structure, consisting of members inside and across departments and divisions, responsible for establishing their own agendas and leadership [2], [16]. Approximately twenty different DNoPs were identified during the investigation. The networks were further classified into three main categories in respect of their primary knowledge activities such as 1) knowledge sharing and learning 2) knowledge creation and incremental innovation and 3) knowledge creation and radical innovation [39]. The networks varied in terms of composition and characteristics, knowledge activities, primary communication channels, types of interactions and meetings.

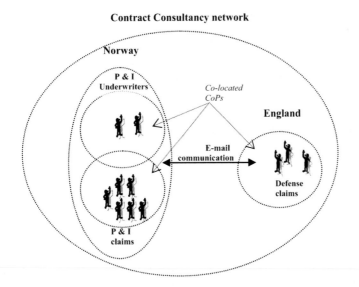

Figure 1. An example of a distributed network of practice, the contract consultancy network

Figure 1 illustrates one example of a DNoP (the contract consultancy network, table 1) consisting of members who participate from two different locations; Norway and England. The members do also belong to local CoPs in respect of three different business functions such as P&I claims (six participants, Norway), P&I underwriters (two participants, Norway) and P&I defense (three participants, England).

Some networks were mandated and held structured meetings with agendas, while others were more informal and ad-hoc. Both heterogeneous and homogenous networks were identified; some crossed boundaries of business divisions, departments, business areas and knowledge disciplines, while others had members belonging to the same functional area. Since the study focuses on distributed networks of practice, all networks were crossing boundaries of locations. In this paper, the focus is on mediated communication behavior in a selection of different DNoPs representing the three main categories mentioned above.

4.1. Comparison of networks

Table 1 compares the DNoPs in Insure. In the P & I contract consultancy network (network 1) the main purpose is to build expertise through problem solving of complex contract questions. While the P & I working group (network 2) is concerned with product development in respect of market demanding innovation, claims managers (network 3) and finance underwriting (network 4) focus on process improvements and business integration. The marine underwriting (network 5) is a typical occupational community consisting of senior and junior underwriters who exchange information about world market rumors and clients' accounts. The networks do also vary in respect of meeting forms and primary communication channel choice. In addition, they vary in terms of complexity in message content during the communication process and different contextual factors that influence the overall communication behavior.

While network 1 and 2 prefer asynchronous communication media such as email, the other networks prefer synchronous communication and carry out their meetings through telephone or video conferences. Due to complex message content in network 1 and 2, media supporting textual richness seem to be preferred. However, in some occasions, email does not meet the distributed participants' needs and directly interaction would have been the most appropriate. Nevertheless, contextual factors in terms of geographical distance, organizational time-pressure and efficiency demands prevent members from meeting face-to-face. Network 3 and 4 experienced coordination and meeting administration challenges due to many different locations involved and different time zones. However, some participants regarded telephone as the most efficient medium for members with extensive traveling activities. In network 5, contextual factors such as technological instabilities and coordination problems did to some extent exclude participation from some of offices.

Analysis of interviews, email discussions, meeting minutes, and observations of video meetings formed the basis for the interpretation of the degree of equivocality in the networks' message content. The content of messages relates to the problems and topics of each network's daily knowledge activities and practice. To classify the message content in respect of level of equivocality [40] or uncertainty it was necessary to analyze the characteristics of the activities and communication processes performed in the networks. The following scenario describes a discussion process in the contract consultancy network (network 1, table 1) in terms of five sense-making strategies as introduced by Weick to interpret the network's activities and message content [40].

Table 1. Mediated communication in distributed networks of practice in Insure

Network of practice	Primary media choice	Purpose and knowledge activities	Contextual influence on communication behaviour
Network 1 P & I Contract consultancy 10 core members *2 locations* (Norway, England)	e-mail	***Problem-solving building expertise learning*** Discussion of complex contract questions from clients, requests from underwriters to legal expert group, problem solving, discussion, training and learning	Complex messages, knowledge-intensive, high equivocality, conflicting, multiple interpretations of contract questions Time pressure to solve the problem quickly ***Asynchronous*** communication Email gives textual "richness" – advantage due to complex content. Situational constraints – distance and efficiency demands prevent occasionally desired face-to-face meetings
Network 2 P & I Working group 8 core members *2 locations* (Norway, England)	e-mail	***Market-demanding radical innovation*** Development of new products, refinements and further development of existing products	Complex messages, knowledge-intensive, high equivocality, conflicting, multiple interpretations of new product ideas, innovative discussions ***Asynchronous*** communication Email limits participation from experts situated in branch offices. Dominance of co-located head office members. Situational constraints and social-psychological distance
Network 3 Claims managers 14 core members *7 locations* (Norway 3 locations, England, Finland, Sweden, Hong Kong)	**Telephone conference**	***Process improvements building expertise incremental innovation*** Plans for new business establishments, discussion of complex and new claims, loss prevention, cover- and underwriting issues, and exchange of legal experiences and expertise with the goal of creating improvements	Medium high equivocality in messages during discussions Low equivocality in messages for information exchange ***Synchronous*** communication, efficient and flexible medium for traveling members Coordination challenges - several locations involved. Different time-zones
Network 4 Finance-underwriting 5 core members *4 locations* (Norway 3 locations, England)	**Telephone conference**	***Process improvements building expertise incremental innovation*** Brainstorming and discussion about improving underwriting control systems, decision management methods, integration across business divisions, strategic discussions, management styles and philosophies.	Medium high equivocality in messages during brainstorming and discussions Low equivocality in messages for information exchange ***Synchronous*** communication, efficient and flexible medium for traveling members
Network 5 Marine underwriting 23 core members *6 locations* (Norway 3 locations, England, Finland, Sweden)	**Video conference**	***Market info exchange learning*** Info about clients' accounts, underwriting guidelines, world market rumors	Low equivocality in messages, information and marketing information ***Synchronous*** communication Technological infrastructure instabilities, coordination challenges, difficult to connect several locations at same time, exclusion of offices

In respect of *action*, the first step in solving a complex contract question in the contract consultancy network starts by initiation of the communication process from a claims handler. Then the participants share different opinions, ask questions, and propose solutions through an email discussion.

As some requests may raise legal dilemmas, multiple and conflicting interpretations may arise from participants in the networks. Through *deliberation* participants search for possible internal or external information with some similarities to this particular question. In *contextualization*, participants might search for documents created in former events. During *triangulation*, different opinions summarize into a set of alternative legal solutions. During *convergence*, the network mutually agrees on a final solution, which becomes the reply and feedback to the customer.

In this scenario, which builds upon the analysis of interviews and message content in emails, the activities and the message content in the communication process have high complexity and equivocality.

Regarding the working group (network 2, table 1) it is possible to apply similar reasoning as above. The members are performing idea generations related to innovation. Networks 3 and 4 (table 1) both have goals for improving and changing business processes, which are creative activities where individual experiences are important to reduce equivocality. However, the topics and problems do not have the same level of complexity as indication of findings from network 1 and 2. In the marine underwriting network (network 5), the uncertainty of an activity may be high. However, the equivocality is lower since a framework already exists for where and how the underwriters can collect information. Well-known sources consist of market information, and the underwriting guidelines and quality management system on the company's intranet give directions to optimal solutions.

Compared to the other networks the marine underwriters still have to convey information, deliberate, and converge on a shared set of goals, but the volume and the degree of complexity will be less. Considering these arguments, the equivocality is low in respect of activities and message content in this network.

All of the networks use email to a very high degree for daily, informal interactions. However, the networks vary in terms of the primary means of synchronous interaction. The networks with highest equivocality in message content use email as their primary communication channel, while the networks with medium high equivocality use telephone conference. The marine underwriting network with low equivocality in message content was the only network using videoconference frequently.

The networks have different types of challenges in the communication process, both technical problems and contextual impediments such as geographical distance, time pressure, time differences and motivation connected to participation that all together influenced the communication behavior and the outcome of the process.

5. Discussion

By comparing and contrasting the networks in this study (table 1), findings indicate both differences and similarities in mediated communication behavior. In the following, I discuss the empirical substantiation in relation to the different theoretical perspectives of mediated communication introduced earlier.

5.1. Message content, level of equivocality and media use in the networks

With regard to media richness and social presence theory, the findings indicate a reverse relationship for networks 1, 2 and 5, since richness of media decreases as the equivocality of messages increases in these networks. Networks 1 and 2 with high equivocality in activities and messages use the lean medium email as their primary communication channel, while network 5 with low equivocal activities and messages uses videoconference as its primary communication channel. Networks 3 and 4 with medium high equivocality in activities and messages use telephone conference as their primary communication channel. Since members in all the networks are geographically distributed, they do not have the opportunity to meet face-to-face on a frequent basis. Videoconference is the richest medium used in these networks. However, with regard to media richness and social presence, one would at least expect that they would choose the richest medium available in the organization for high equivocal activities when face-to-face is not possible. Thus, the relevance of rational models for explaining these findings is low. Media richness to some extent explains media behavior in Networks 3 and 4, since the members use a synchronous medium (telephone conference) for medium high equivocal activities. Figure 2 illustrates media preferences in DNoPs in Insure as compared to media richness and social presence theory.

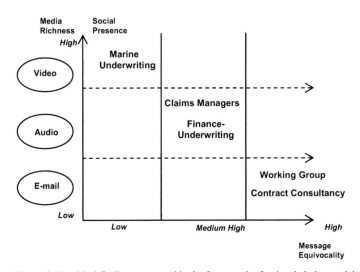

Figure 2. Empirical findings presented in the framework of rational choice models

5.2. Contextual impediments and technical challenges in the networks

With respect to the distributed character of these networks, situational constraints like geographical distance and time pressure can to some extent explain why the rational models provide limited explanatory power for the empirical findings. In some occasions, members of the networks would prefer direct face-to-face interaction when possible, to enable a communication process such as a roundtable discussion with natural language, multiple nonverbal cues, in addition to obtaining rapid feedback and contributions.

...people in London are very certain of being included on the e-mail list and participating in working groups and that sort of thing...but the experience is that, because they are getting information by e-mails as opposed to discussing around the table, the participation is not nearly the same [ ] I do know that the people in London often feel a little isolated. They feel the head office is making the decisions, and they are a little bit out of the game. Being very proactive gives an opportunity to participate in something, but you have to make sure that you *do* participate...But they think that *we* should be kind of proactive, finding the feeling that *they* are satellite kind of...I mean we get good quality response from them, it is just the problem... they are removed...   (1)

The physical distance is challenging, and the peripheral members also have a feeling of isolation. The "satellite" metaphor indicates a kind of social-psychological effect of geographical distance, which influences the motivation to participate. This effect raises doubt about the media's ability to bridge the social distances associated with geography [41]. During the workshop, physical proximity seems to put an end to the social-psychological distance among core and peripheral members in the network since the communication process gives better outcome than mediated communication through email.

In respect of the working group network (network 2) one of the interviewees had experienced that it was much easier to get contribution and input from the peripheral members during face-to-face workshops compared to email. A reason for that could be the complex nature of the communication process, which has characteristics as innovative and ambiguous, and where the requirements for common grounding and communication costs are high. Use of email in the same situation could cause high understanding costs since the context is lacking [42].

This week, I will be in London to do some workshops on our additional covers. Last time I did that was probably two years ago, and that's something we have been criticized for, we don't do that often enough...go over and do a round with the colleagues there, and go through, not just the marketing stuff and general stuff on the website, they are much more sophisticated in competence than that...what was happening last time, it was really good input, and because some of our best claim people are there, they came up with all these examples and problems. We realized we had overlooked things, they had really good input. It was actually a very good process both ways...   (2)

In the contract consultancy network they use email for efficiency reasons, since they often have a high time pressure to solve these contract questions on a short time schedule. Coordination and integration of common tasks across distance and time zones are critical in organizations with geographically dispersed offices. Face-to-face communication becomes difficult in respect of traveling time and expenses. In addition, organizational resources, accessibility to media and time pressures constitute other examples of facilitators and/or impediments of media choice. Highly competitive markets might increase the time-pressure for many employees and managers. As discussed in Trevino, Lengel and Daft [30] situational constraints such as time-pressure and geographical distance may influence media choice since employees prefer telephone conference or emails to communicate despite the equivocality of the task situation. Situational constraints such as time pressure in the claims managers' network and the finance-underwriting network may explain why telephone conference is the primary communication channel for these networks. The members of these networks are mostly managers operating in a hectic international business market.

Email, which is a lean medium from a media richness perspective, is in the contract consultancy network regarded as 'rich'. In their context, social norms and rules have influenced communication behavior, and they find email more efficient than telephone and videoconferences to accomplish complex contract questions. With email, individuals may spend more time to understand the meanings attached by others to situations since they may reflect and reread messages. However, equivocality arises not only due to the nature of the task, but also because people attach meanings to situations, and these meanings are not objective and singular, but are rather subjective, socially constructed, and multiple [40]. In addition, networks of practice reduce equivocality through a series of iterative cycles in which members communicate around a problem and improve their communal understanding through new iterations [43].

However, media choice is not consistent across the networks with high equivocality of messages, since the claims managers' network and the finance-underwriting network prefer telephone conferences as the primary channel, as opposed to contract consultancy and the working group who prefer email. The social influence model may explain this inconsistency, since social determinants such as the networks' norms and the members' behavior will influence media choice differently. In addition, a member's behavior and positive attitude towards one medium may influence other members in the network to adopt the same positive or negative attitude.

With respect to equivocality, one would expect both the claims managers' network and the finance-underwriting network to choose video over telephone. Nevertheless, the coordinators in these networks could not see any particular extra value in favor of video; the case was rather the opposite as illustrated in the following quotation:

I don't really see the big value-added with videoconferencing…you're more dependent on having a meeting room in each office that has the necessary video equipment so you have to have that room booked. There usually is a little bit of technology "clutter", you usually lose 15 minutes in the beginning each time…And there are also so many of us who travel a lot. So, for example if I book a video meeting in two weeks, then I have to be there right at that time. But if I have a telephone meeting, then I could just as well be here, at home, at an airport, anywhere. Also, a lot of the underwriters travel a lot, so if you need to use the videoconference, does that mean that you can't participate? In the groups that I work with, the culture is that if you are out traveling then this is not an excuse for not to participate. You participate no matter where one is. (3)

In the marine underwriting network, members have different individual perceptions of media, which is in harmony with social influence theory where media perception and media choice are subjective and socially constructed. These findings are in contradiction to media richness theory, which considers media perception as an objective variable. However, videoconference is the primary channel in this network despite different opinions among the members. Different theoretical perspectives can explain this observation. One possible explanation may be that the use and experience of videoconference have developed over time, and have become an established norm and routine in the organization for these types of knowledge activities. Second, dominating members in the network may have strong social influence on media choice decisions. Third, according to AST, the video technology has structural features, which represent the resources and capabilities offered by this media. These features influence on the social structures in these networks and both enable and constrain the interaction. It supports coordination among the members, but does also provide strictly procedures for accomplishing interpersonal exchange. In addition, it has occasionally instabilities that exclude participations for some of the members in certain locations. Fourth, members have learned to use this channel and have developed experiences with the media, the message topics and their communication colleagues. Thus they prefer the channel that has become "richest" to them as explained in channel expansion theory [34]. This is to some extent concurrent with AST where the members' knowledge and skills of a media influence the appropriation of structure [36], as illustrated in the following quotation:

...we have learned a way of working, but it must be under control and agenda so everybody knows how the
system (video) is working, and when it is your turn to make comments, otherwise it will be useless...   (4)

To explain findings from this case study which focuses on groups and not
individuals, it is likely to believe that theoretical perspectives focusing on
communication media perception and use in groups will be most appropriate. For
instance in media richness theory, the focus is on individual media choice and in
particular on managers' choice and perceptions. In addition, the rational models have
several weaknesses. These theories take for granted that communication tasks have
single purposes, and that each medium has objective, fixed properties. It assumes that
the transmitter and the receiver in the communication process have different status; the
transmitter is active, while the receiver is passive. However, an audience or a single
receiver will actively reconstruct meanings of messages during interactions in groups
or through dialogues [44]. Since rational models presume that media choice is
objective, it pays no attention to the social context surrounding individuals making the
choice. In DNoPs, collective behavior may influence communication media use and
decisions, and it is not possible to make a choice independently of others. Each
geographical site involved in the communication process will have different
surroundings and distinctive contextual factors that influence the communication
process locally. With respect to adaptive structuration theory, the contextual variables
at each location are constructed into the social process of technology use for the co-
located users participating in a distributed network. However, the appropriation and
adaptation of a medium in terms of emerging and new ways of using may be more
comprehensive and complex since different locations will influence the creation of
appropriation differently. Especially during videoconferences, local conditions and
technical instabilities influenced the communication process differently in each
location. In such cases, the branch offices were most vulnerable since the technological
impediments made participation challenging and sometimes impossible.

The communication process in DNoPs has a complex character, and the
technological complications are examples of duality and interplay where the media
create impediments that influence and limit the members' participation.

Each co-located community, as well as each individual member may have its own
strategies and goals to communicate. The complicated communicative mechanism that
occurs is not a stand-alone process but is the interplay between communication media,
participants and their local context. Each location has concrete activities of people in
specific settings and situational determinants influence individual action as a response
to the environment and to the improvisational nature of human activities, which is a
central issue in situated action theory [45]. In this sense, distributed interaction across
locations is dependent of situated action at each location. The latter includes different
social, psychological and cultural factors in each geographical location, as well as
multiple goals and strategies commonly enacted simultaneously in a single
communication situation [44].

6. Conclusion and implications

This study has analyzed mediated communication behavior in intra-organizational
DNoPs in a multinational company. Findings indicate that mediated communication
behavior is a multifaceted phenomenon, which has to consider not only task and media
characteristics, but also individual perceptions of media, multiple goals, contextual

issues, and unintended appropriation and adaptation of communication media related to each network and location.

The networks vary in respect of boundaries crossed, knowledge activities performed, primary communication channels used, and challenges in the communication process. Both rational and social perspectives of mediated communication constitute potential explanation models for the empirical findings. However, the relevance of the rational choice models has limited value in this study. While media richness and social presence theories constitute individual-level rational choice explanations of media behavior [27], the emergent network perspective [35], the social influence model [31] and AST [36] focus on media use and media perceptions for both groups and individuals. In addition, these theories pay attention to the whole context of mediated communication. However, none of the theoretical perspectives introduced in this paper, can individual explain all the aspects of communication media behavior in the distributed networks under observation. Findings indicate that a combination of different perspectives is better to give an all-encompassing explanation of the phenomenon rather than individual theories as stand-alones.

Because of new organizational forms such as project oriented organizations, extensive use of virtual teams, and emerging communities, it has become important to change the level of analysis from individuals to groups to get an increased and extended contextual understanding of organizational communication in respect of mediated communication behavior in networks. Findings in this study indicate that distributed communication in networks of practice requires design of working environments that limit both technological and organizational impediments. Examples of suitable working environments for networks are open office landscapes and office sharing in each location, in addition to appropriation and adaptation of communication media to support distributed interactions in the networks. For example in a case study at the Boeing Company, findings indicated several benefits from using data conferencing in distributed teams to support their regularly scheduled meetings [46]. Data conferencing technology augments distributed meetings with application sharing. Drawing upon experiences from this case study, data conferencing might support DNoPs better than pure videoconferencing meetings for sharing presentation material and documents. For example, a coordinator may run a presentation for a collocated audience and make it available on whiteboards or at individual personal computers at multiple sites. It might make the coordination and adaptation easier and decrease the feeling of distance when several locations are involved.

Since this study focuses only on a limited number of DNoPs in one company, an extension to focus on several organizations as well as inter-organizational networks could increase the knowledge about mediated communication further. By applying ethnographic research methods like in-depth observation of local CoPs at each geographical location, it might be possible to increase the understanding of contextual factors and technical impediments that are formative for communication patterns and integration of different local communities in a distributed network.

Acknowledgements

I thank the management and employees at Insure who showed great interest in this study and made it possible. I specially thank Bjørn Erik Munkvold and Robin Teigland for helpful comments and suggestions on various drafts of this manuscript. Finally, I thank the anonymous reviewers for valuable comments.

References

[1]   J. S. Brown. & P. Duguid, Organizational learning and communities of practice, *Organization Science*, **2** (1991), 40-57.

[2]   J. S. Brown. & P. Duguid, *The social life of information,* Harvard Business School Press, Boston, 2000.

[3]   E. Wenger, *Communities of Practice: Learning, Meaning, and Identity*, Cambridge University Press, Cambridge, 1998.

[4]   M. Hansen, *Knowledge Integration in Organizations*, Ph.D. Dissertation, Graduate School of Business, Stanford University, 1996.

[5]   E. Vaast, The use of intranets: The missing link between communities of practice and networks of practice? In P. Hildreth & C. Kimble (eds.), *Knowledge Networks: Innovation through Communities of Practice*, Idea Group Publishing, Hershey, 216-228, 2004.

[6]   M. K. Ahuja & K. M. Carley, Network structure in virtual organizations, *Organization Science*, **10** (1999), 741-757.

[7]   G. DeSanctis & P. Monge, Introduction to special issue: Communication processes for virtual organizations, *Organization Science*, **11** (2000), 693-703.

[8]   L. Chidambaram & B. Jones, Impact of communication medium and computer support on group perceptions and performance: A comparison of face-to-face and dispersed meetings, *MIS Quarterly*, **17** (1993), 465-516.

[9]   A. Majchrzak, R.E. Rice, A. Malhotra, N. King & S. Ba, Technology adaptation: The case of a computer-supported inter-organizational virtual team. *MIS Quarterly*, **24** (2000), 569-600.

[10] D. Sole & A. Edmondson, Situated knowledge and learning in dispersed teams, *British Journal of Management*, **13** (2002),17-34.

[11] P. Hildreth, C. Kimble & P. Wright, Communities of practice in the distributed international environment, *Journal of Knowledge Management,* **4** (2000), 27-38.

[12] E. Wenger, R. McDermott & W. M. Snyder   *Cultivating Communities of Practice,* Harvard Business School Press, Boston, 2002.

[13] M. S. Granovetter, The strength of weak ties: A network theory revisited. *Sociological Theory*, **1** (1983), 201-233.

[14] R. Teigland, *Knowledge Networking: Structure and Performance in Networks of Practice.* Published Doctoral Dissertation, Stockholm School of Economics, Stockholm, 2003.

[15] M. M. Wasko & S. Faraj, Why should I share? Examining social capital and knowledge contribution in electronic networks of practice, *MIS Quarterly*, **29** (2005), 35-57.

[16] E. Wenger & W. M. Snyder, Communities of Practice: The Organizational Frontier, *Harvard Business Review*, January-February, (2000), 139-145.

[17] E. Hustad, & B. E. Munkvold, Communities of Practice and other Organizational Groups, in E. Coakes & S. Clarke (eds.), *Encyclopedia of Communities of Practice in Information and Knowledge Management*, Idea Group Reference, USA, 60-62, 2005.

[18] R. M. Grant, Toward a knowledge-based theory of the firm, *Strategic Management Journal*, **17** (1996), 109-122.

[19] R. S. Fish, R. E. Kraut, R. W. Root & R. E. Rice, Evaluating video as a technology for informal communication, *Proceedings of the SIGCHI conference on Human factors in computing systems*, Monterey, California, 37-48, 1992.

[20] J. Webster, Desktop videoconferencing: Experiences of complete users, wary users and non-users, *MIS Quarterly*, **22** (1998), 257-286.

[21] G, Mark, J. Grudin & S. E. Poltrock, Meeting at the desktop: An emirical study of virtually collocated teams, *Proceedings of the 6th European conference on Computer Supported Cooperative Work (ECSCW'99)*, Copenhagen Denmark, 159-178, 1999.

[22] R. Anson & B. E. Munkvold, Beyond face-to-face: a field study of electronic meetings in different time and place modes, *Journal of Organizational Computing and Electronic Commerce*, **14**,127-152, 2004.

[23] R. L. Daft, R. H. Lengel & L. K. Trevino, Message equivocality, media selection, and manager performance: Implication for information systems. *MIS Quarterly*, **11** (1987), 354-366.

[24] R. E. Rice, Media appropriateness: Using Social Presence Theory to compare traditional and new organizational media, *Human communication research*, **19** (1993), 451-484.

[25] K. E. Weick, Cosmos vs. chaos: Sense and nonsense in electronic contexts, *Organizational Dynamics*, **14** (1985), 51-64.

[26] G. S. Russ, R. L. Daft & R. H. Lengel, Media selection and managerial characteristics in organizational communication, *Management Communication Quarterly*, **4** (1990), 151-175.

[27] M. L. Markus, Electronic mail as the medium of managerial choice, *Organization Science*, **5** (1994), 502-527.

[28] A. S. Lee, Electronic mail as a medium for rich communication: An empirical investigation using hermeneutic interpretation, *MIS Quarterly*, **18** (1994), 143-157.

[29] M. L. Markus, Finding a happy medium: Explaining the negative effects of electronic communication on social life at work, *ACM Transactions of Information Systems*, **12** (1994), 119-149.

[30] L. K. Treviño, R. H. Lengel & R. L. Daft, Media symbolism, media richness, and media choice in organizations: A symbolic Interactionist Perspective, *Communication Research*, **14** (1987), 553-574.

[31] J. Fulk, J. Schmitz & C.W. Steinfield, A social influence model of technology use, in J. Fulk and C.W. Steinfield (eds.), *Organizations and Communication Technology*, Sage, London, 117-140, 1990.

[32] D. Te'eni, Review: A Cognitive-Affective Model of Organizational Communication for Designing IT, *MIS Quarterly*, **25** (2001), 251-312.

[33] L. K. Treviño, Webster, J. & Stein, E. W. Making Connections: Complementary influences on communication media choices, attitudes and use, *Organization Science*, **11** (2000), 163-182.

[34] J. R. Carlson & R. W. Zmud, Channel expansion theory and the experiential nature of media richness perceptions, *Academy of Management Journal*, **42** (1999), 280-284.

[35] N. S. Contractor & E. M. Eisenberg, Communication networks and new media in organizations. In J. Fulk & C. Steinfield (eds.), *Organizations and Communication Technology*. Sage, London, 143-172, 1990.

[36] G. DeSanctis & M. S. Poole (1994). Capturing complexity in advanced technology use: Adaptive structuration theory, *Organization Sicence*, 5 (1994), 121-147.

[37] M. L. Markus & D. Robey, Information technology and organizational change: Causal structure in theory and research, *Management Science*, **34** (1988), 583-598.

[38] R. K. Yin, *Case Study Research: Design and Methods*, Sage Publications, London, 1989.

[39] E. Hustad & R. Teigland. Taking a differentiated view on intra-organizational distributed networks of practice: A case study exploring knowledge activities, diversity and communication media use. In P. Van Den Besselaar, G. De Michelis, J. Preece & C- Simone (eds.), *Communities and Technologies 2005*, Springer, Netherland, 239-261, 2005.

[40] K. Weick, *The Social Psychology of Organizing*, MA. Addison-Wesley, Reading, 1979.

[41] E. Bradner & G. Mark, Why distance matters: Effects on cooperation, persuasion and deception, *Proceedings of the CSCW'02*, New Orleans, USA, 226-235, 2002.

[42] H. H. Clark & W. E. Brennan, Grounding in communication, in L. B. Resnick, J. M. Levine & S. D. Teasley (eds.), *Perspectives on Socially Shared Cognition*, American Physiological Association, Washington, 127-149, 1991.

[43] A. Schenkel, *Communities of Practice or Communities of Discipline: Managing Deviations at the Öresund Bridge*. Published Ph.D. dissertation, Stockholm School of Economics, Stockholm, 2002.

[44] N. S. Contractor & P. R. Monge, Managing knowledge networks, *Management of Communication Quarterly*, **16** (2002), 249-258.

[45] L. A. Suchman, *Plans and situated actions: The problem of human machine communication*, Cambridge University Press, Cambridge, 1987.

[46] S. E. Poltrock & G. Mark, Implementation of data conferencing in the Boeing Company, in B. E. Munkvold (ed.), *Implementing collaboration technologies in industry: Case examples and lessons learned*, Springer Verlag, London, 129-158, 2003.

Cooperative Systems Design
P. Hassanaly et al. (Eds.)
IOS Press, 2006

Intelligent Automation in Collaborative Systems

Joshua INTRONE and Richard ALTERMAN
Volen Center for Complex Systems
Brandeis University
Waltham, MA 02454
[jintrone, alterman]@cs.brandeis.edu

Abstract. Intelligent automation has been a source of research and debate within the design community for several decades. When adding intelligent automation to single-user systems, two critical issues must be addressed. First, sufficient knowledge must be acquired about the user and her context to make high-level inferences at runtime. Second, the automation must be useful and delivered in a manner that does not impair the user's domain activity. These issues are equally relevant for collaborative systems. However, collaborative systems offer a potential solution to these problems by virtue of their privileged position as mediating artifacts within a collaborative process. Because coordination information must be exchanged through the system, there is an opportunity for the system to gain insights into user activities and context. Because mediating artifacts add structure to the information that passes through them to improve coordination, this information is made more accessible to standard AI algorithms. Thus, within a design solution for coordination problems in groupware, a solution to some of the issues with intelligent automation can also be found. Empirical evidence from a testbed domain is presented that validates this approach, along with a discussion of how the approach can be generalized to other collaborative systems.

Keywords: Coordinating Representation, Intelligent Interfaces, Awareness, Bayesian Networks, Plan Recognition

Introduction

Computer systems often function as artifacts that mediate people's activities or communication [1][2]. As mediating artifacts, the design of computer systems is intended to improve users' work by modifying the nature of the task. A computer might provide structure that serves as a resource for activity [3], or it may introduce a layer of abstraction that transforms work in a complex domain [4].

A difficulty in designing systems that do this effectively is that the facilities they provide must be designed prior to their actual use, and hence are limited to providing the kind of support that the designer can envision at design time. Early on, this resulted in systems that were only appropriate for narrow groups of end-users in constrained settings [5]. This problem has been a driving force for the design community, and many techniques have been developed to grapple with the problem. One large subfield of research in user interface design has sought to better understand the nature of activity and tool use in order to improve the work at design-time. Another large subfield has focused on ways to defer design decisions by anticipating many eventualities to be detected at runtime. Both subfields have encountered their share of difficulties, and very often, the methods employed by the two approaches are seen as incompatible [6].

In this article, a technique for the harmonious integration of recently developed design techniques and intelligent automation in collaborative systems is presented. This approach rests on the observation that structure in a mediating artifact can both simplify work and at the same time render a portion of the users' runtime context interpretable for the computer. The solutions offered are drawn from the rich bodies of work on situated activity and distributed cognition.

In the early sections of this article, an ethnographic analysis technique that guides the development of mediating artifacts that improve collaboration is described. The primary focus of this article will be to show how the coordination work that people do via these mediating artifacts can be used by standard AI algorithms to introduce automation that improves the users' performance in a domain task. The article concludes with a discussion about how intelligent automation might generally be incorporated into collaborative systems to improve awareness, based on recent research and our experiences.

Difficulties with Design

The field of HCI has gone through many stages in its ongoing evolution [5]. At the outset, the design of interfaces was based upon measurements of cognitive variables in carefully controlled laboratory environments. These methods proved to be difficult to translate into real-world applications, as they were only applicable to prototypical users in rarified contexts. Subsequent developments in the field have led to insights that human activity is inherently situation dependant [7], and that the social, organizational, and political context often has as much to do with the acceptance of a piece of software as design itself [5].

The importance of runtime context and situation-dependence raises many design issues. How is it possible to design artifacts for a context that is not known at design time? If the only constant is the dynamicity of situation, how can static software representations be satisfactory? Identifying the kind of structure might be usefully incorporated in mediating artifacts that support work activity (e.g., [3][8][9][10]) has been a central research focus in CSCW since Suchman's observations about situated activity [7].

Difficulties with Automation

One way to deal with some of the above problems is to try to build interfaces that are sensitive to the user's runtime needs [11][12]. These systems try to infer the user's goals, context or characteristics in order to tune their behavior to use at runtime.

In some treatments, these systems are conceived of as a collaborative partner with the user [13]. In order to be a good collaborator, the system must have sufficient access to the context and user information that will allow it to make useful and timely inferences about the user's needs. Unfortunately, the computer is handicapped in this regard, as it can only "see" the user's activity and context through the narrow aperture of the user interface. In order to overcome this problem, a user knowledge acquisition strategy must be designed to provide the system with access to the information needed to make good inferences [14].

A fundamental problem is how to design a knowledge acquisition strategy that does not introduce too much work for the user or otherwise impair the usability of the system. Natural language interfaces might be a way to do this, but natural language understanding is not yet at a point where solutions are feasible for real-world systems. Another approach is to add a structured language to the interface so the user can express higher level intentions in a form the computer can understand, but this requires the user to manage two tasks instead of one. As the developers of one human-computer collaborative system noted, "it is often more efficient and natural to convey intentions by performing actions" ([15], page 23).

Another approach to knowledge acquisition is to add interface structure as part of the task that is mediated by the system. For example, the Epsilon collaborative learning environment [16] requires collaborators to use sentence openers (chosen from a list) for every line entered into chat. This allows the system to monitor the chat and help out with ineffective conversations. It important, however, to balance interface structure for knowledge acquisition with usability concerns. Outside of work discussed in the next section, the authors are not aware of any rigorous methodological approach for adding interface structure that both supports powerful machine inferences but does not impair natural use of the system.

In addition to the knowledge acquisition problem in designing intelligent automation, the functionality provided by the automation should be useful, and it must not interrupt the user or hinder domain activity. Mixed-initiative approaches, such as that proposed by Horvitz [17], provide some guidelines in this regard. Horvitz advocates balancing the cost of the interruption against the expected utility of the automation itself. This entails recognizing where in a task a user is, and what the information requirements for that task are. However, mapping interface activity to a task structure is essentially a keyhole plan recognition problem, which has proven difficult to do in the general case.

Rather than grapple with the problems of identifying task boundaries in user interface activities, we seek to identify a more reliable and generally applicable approach for collaborative systems. To this end, the problem of awareness in collaborative activity is examined at the end of this article.

Mediating Artifacts that Support Coordination

The study of mediating artifacts in everyday and work activities has become widespread in HCI and CSCW. Suchman & Trigg [18] described the role of structured tools (e.g., the "complex sheet") in coordinating the distributed activities of the staff in an airport. Hutchins [2] explained how artifacts allow portions of a task to be "precomputed," effectively mediating communication between the designer and the user. Norman [1] has focused on the role an artifact plays in mediating the user's interaction with a domain, transforming the domain task into a form that makes it more cognitively accessible to the user. Schmidt & Simone [10] describe how artifacts serve to support the articulation of coordinated work activity, and introduce a notation (Ariadne) for the description of adaptable mechanisms that coordinate workflow. Activity theorists (e.g., [19]; also see [20]) highlight the role of mediating structures – which may be material artifacts, but might also be policies, conventions, etc. – in activity systems, which encompass a much larger range of factors than traditional HCI treatments.

Each of these approaches is representative of a rich and evolving line of research, but none provide concrete, design-level guidance that can indicate what kind of structure should be incorporated into a mediating artifact, or predict which artifacts will be used and which introduce too much work. Ethnographic methodologies informed by activity theory and distributed cognition do provide guidance about how we might conceptualize activity and the role of mediating artifacts, and draw the analyst's attention to the need for mediation, but such theories stop short of explicit design recommendations for the artifacts themselves.

Recently, Feinman & Alterman [21] have provided just such a design level approach. It draws together insights from the ethnomethodological approach of Suchman & Trigg [18] and the analytical techniques introduced by Hutchins[2]. It provides a methodology for moving from the analysis of practice to concrete recommendations for structure that will be useful in a particular collaborative system. This structure is instantiated in shared mediating artifacts that can be incorporated in an existing platform. Following Suchman & Trigg, these artifacts are referred to as *coordinating representations* (CRs).

The methodology for designing and introducing coordinating representations is one solution to the design problems described above. The structure introduced to the interface by coordinating representations is also a solution to the knowledge acquisition problem. In the following, validating evidence is provided for these two claims. Finally, the shared information that accumulates in a coordinating representation may be well suited to providing awareness that is generally useful in collaborative systems.

1. Experimental Platform

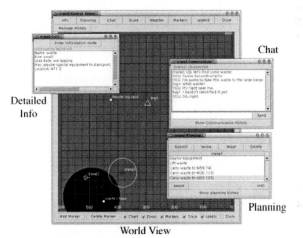

Figure 1: The VesselWorld System

To study the above problems, an experimental platform called VesselWorld (shown in Figure 1) was developed. VesselWorld has many features relevant to the study of groupware systems in general. The domain task entails varying degrees and types of coordination, collaborators have different roles and responsibilities, and awareness must be explicitly maintained. VesselWorld proved to be very challenging for its users; in studies, each user group was trained for two hours before data was collected, and performance usually didn't stabilize until after another five hours of use.

VesselWorld presents a relaxed WYSIWIS environment, in which three participants play the role of ship's captains, and their joint goal is to remove toxic waste barrels from a harbor without spillage. The main interface is a shared map. Each ship has a geographically limited view of the harbor within this map, so each user has different directly observable domain information. The progression of a VesselWorld session is turn-based, such that every user must submit a step to the server before the server can evaluate the steps and update the world on each client screen. Users may plan any number of steps in advance, although each step can only involve objects that are currently visible, and only one step can be submitted to the server at a time. Users' actions are not visible to one another during the planning phase of each step, so awareness must be explicitly maintained. Communication may occur at any point, but all communication occurs through a text-based chat window that is part of the system.

Each ship has different capabilities. Two of them have cranes that can be used to lift toxic waste barrels from the harbor and load them onto a large barge (which has a fixed position). The third user is a tugboat that can be used to drag small barges from one place to another. For notational convenience, we adopt the convention of referring to the crane operators as "cranes" and the tugboat operator as the "tug." The cranes can load multiple wastes onto the small barge, and at least one of them must also be present to unload the barrels and place them on the large barge.

Toxic waste barrels are of different types and require different coordination strategies. A single crane may lift a small or medium barrel, but two cranes must join together to lift and carry a large barrel, and an extra large barrel may be jointly lifted but can only be carried on a small barge by the tug. Toxic waste barrels may require specialized equipment to be moved, and the cranes carry different types of equipment. The tug is the only actor who can determine the type of equipment a toxic waste barrel requires.

The users are scored by a function that takes into account the number of steps it takes to remove all of the waste barrels, the number of barrels cleared, the number of errors (dropped waste barrels) made, and the difficulty of the problem. In all user studies, the users were instructed to try to maximize their score.

To support analysis, VesselWorld logs complete interaction data that can be used to replay user activity. This is an important component of the methodology described in Alterman, et al. [22]. More details upon this portion of the methodology can be found in Landsman & Alterman [23].

2. Intelligent Automation in VesselWorld

Planning in VesselWorld is laborious and error prone. Errors often occur due to forgotten plan steps or joint plans that have become unsynchronized. Errors also occur because of forgotten or misunderstood commitments. In early versions of the system, a shared component was added to address these problems [22]. The CR allowed users to manually specify their goals and sequence their activities; however it was never used by users. In exit interviews, the users explained that the component introduced too much work, and was too hard to use. Hence, we sought to add intelligent automation to VesselWorld to provide this functionality. As envisioned, a semi-automated component would infer each user's goals, and make them visible to all users. Additionally, once these goals were identified, the system could automatically generate synchronized plans for users.

In order to infer user goals, the system needs to know about the state of the domain (where the toxic waste barrels are and associated information). Unfortunately, it is assumed that the simulated world is "outside" of the system itself, so the system has no direct access to the domain at runtime. Furthermore, without this information, the system cannot automatically generate plans. Thus, as discussed above, a major hurdle in providing the envisioned automation was in acquiring the information necessary to infer user intent.

2.1. Obtaining State Information

At runtime, the system has access to user locations and recently executed plan steps, but the only source of information about toxic waste barrels is exchanged by the users via chat. This information is very hard for the system to interpret.

An excerpt from chat during a typical planning session shown in Figure 2 demonstrates this. In the dialogue, users frequently refer to wastes by their latitude and longitude coordinates on the shared map. In the first line of the example, Crane2 announces a waste at "120, 420." In lines 2-4, Crane1 asks for clarification about the specifics of the waste. In lines 5-6, the Tug replies (having apparently already investigated that toxic waste barrel) with the corrected coordinates "105, 420" and specific information about the barrel. In line 8, Crane2 thanks the Tug for the clarification, and the Tug closes the conversational turn in line 9.

1.	Crane2: I found a waste at 120 420
2.	Crane1: ok
3.	Crane1: what type of waste?
4.	Crane1: large,small?
5.	Tug1: 105 420 needs a dredge, i think that is where you are
6.	Tug1: small
7.	Crane1: ok
8.	Crane2: Thanks for checking
9.	Tug1: no problem

Figure 2: Excerpt from chat during VesselWorld session

Automatically extracting information about toxic waste barrels from chat logs would be very difficult; the sample dialogue illustrates some of these problems. There are three active participants, and conversational turns that might be used to narrow the reference resolution scope are hard to identify. Also problematic is that referring expressions can change from utterance to utterance even within the same conversational turn. For example, line 1 refers to the waste as "120 420" and line 5 refers to the same waste as "105 420." People can sometimes handle such ambiguities, but this is problematic for natural language processing algorithms.

Rather than developing specialized algorithms to deal with the nuances of three-way, live chat in the VesselWorld domain, it would vastly simplify our task if users were to enter all the information the system needs in a structured form. Although this might seem to unnecessarily burden the user, the next section explains why it is reasonable for this domain, and describes empirical evidence supporting this claim.

2.2. Coordinating Representations

Coordinating representations (CRs) can be introduced to collaborative systems to enhance people's ability to coordinate their activities in a joint task. Feinman &

Alterman [21] describe an approach to developing CRs by examining collected usage data from an existing collaborative system for evidence of recurrent coordination problems, explicit talk about coordination, and emergent structure. They also detail a technique for analyzing the co-referencing activity of users who are engaged in a collaborative task. The results of this methodology are a set of recommendations for structure to be incorporated into the platform. This methodology was employed to develop coordinating representations for VesselWorld.

One of the difficulties observed in the analysis of VesselWorld usage data was with users' ability to manage information about domain objects. Some of the groups handled these difficulties by developing mnemonic expressions. However, users did not always agree on consistent expressions, and coordination errors in the maintenance of this information were frequent. Thus, a CR called the Object List (Figure 3) was designed to support the organization and naming of objects in the world, and was added to the VesselWorld system.

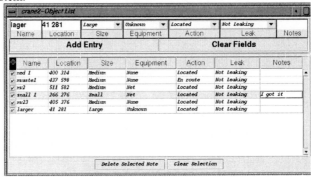

Figure 3: The Object List CR.

The Object List is a tabular WYSIWIS component that helps users to manage and coordinate reference and state information. Users enter and maintain all of the data in the Object List. Each row of data contains several fields of information about a specific object. The "Name" field is a free-text field, assigned by the user. The "Location" field may be filled in by clicking on the field and then on an object that is shown in the primary map (and hence has fixed structure). The "Size", "Equipment", "Action", and "Leak" fields are filled in using drop-down menus. The "Notes" field is also a free-text field, and is provided so that any other relevant information about the toxic waste barrel may be communicated. Entries in the Object List can be displayed on the primary map interface as icons that are annotated with the name that is in the "Name" field at the coordinates in the "Location" field.

In studies it was found that the Object List, and one other CR, were used and significantly improved user performance [22]. Groups that used the CRs had fewer errors, spent less time chatting, and on average took half the amount of time to solve problems. These findings demonstrate that it is possible, using the methodology described, to develop CRs that do not compromise the usability of the system. Rather, they become part of the domain activity of the users, while introducing structure that helps them coordinate. In using a CR, collaborators also create a structured stream of data about their shared context that the system can use to infer user needs.

2.3. Information Provided by the Object List

Use of the Object List generates two types of information that might be used for intent inference. One type is structured information about shared domain objects (toxic waste barrels). This information is not perfect – it is only entered into the Object List as users discover and examine wastes, and it is subject to errors, omissions, and duplication – but it is well-structured and can be readily used by the system.

Another, unanticipated type of information provided is the set of names assigned by users to toxic waste barrels in the Object List. VesselWorld collaborators used these names regularly in chat to refer to objects they were planning to deal with (lift, move, or otherwise). Thus, these names can be used to mine chat for clues about user intentions. A frequency analysis of references preceding actual lifts was performed to establish the utility of this information.

Table 1: Probability a reference precedes a lift at time *t* (in minutes)

	t-5 to *t*		*t-10* to *t-5*		*t-15* to *t-10*	
	Joint	Single	Joint	Single	Joint	Single
Lift	.62	.42	.27	.15	.25	.08
~Lift	.15	.11	.10	.07	.08	.04

It was found that the occurrence of references to toxic waste barrels in chat were predictive of lift actions for roughly a fifteen-minute window of time preceding a lift. Table 1 depicts the likelihood that a reference for an object will appear in chat for the three consecutive five minute windows preceding the lift of an object at time *t*. In the table, "Joint" and "Single" refer to whether or not a waste barrel requires both or just one crane to lift. In the ~*Lift* conditions, values reflect the likelihood some barrel is referred to prior to the lift of some other barrel.

There is about a sixty percent chance that a toxic waste barrel will be referred to in chat in the five minutes preceding the lift if that barrel requires assistance, and about a forty percent chance if that barrel can be lifted singly. Prior to fifteen minutes before the lift, references were not a very good predictor of lift actions.

2.4. An Intent Inference Procedure

An intent inference procedure was developed to predict user goals, using information about toxic waste barrels and references to them in chat. Two Bayesian Networks (BNs) were developed to assess likelihoods for crane and tug goals. The analysis presented here is restricted to the portion of the crane network that predicts the cranes' lift intentions. This BN is shown in Figure 4; it models the likelihood that an actor has the intention to lift (or jointly lift with the other crane) a specific toxic waste barrel based on information about the state of the world, including:

- The type of equipment required for the waste barrel.
- The size of the waste barrel (which determines whether a single crane can lift the barrel, or if it needs help from the other crane).
- Whether the cranes are close to or heading towards the barrel.
- If the crane is currently holding a barrel.

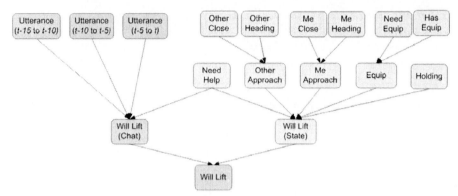

Figure 4: Schematic of BN used to infer crane lift intentions

The network also uses reference information from chat. According the results of the frequency analysis above, three five minute windows of chat history, with one node for each five minute window, are included in the network.

A primary aim of this article is to quantify the utility of the information provided by collaborators for predicting user intentions during normal use of the Object List. To do this, the performance of the above intent inference process was compared across four information conditions; with complete domain information (with or without chat), and with information from the Object List alone (with or without chat).

2.4.1. Evaluating Intent Inference

Table 2: Population summary for evaluations

Group	Sessions	Avg. # of wastes per problem	Total Hours
Group 1	10	11.7	9.9
Group 2	6	11	8.4
Group 3	9	14.3	9.1
Group 4	16	14.5	8.7
All	41	13.5	34.3

The intent inference procedure was evaluated using a dataset spanning roughly 34 hours, which contained usage data from groups that used a version of VesselWorld with the Object List. This data is summarized in Table 2. The usage data contains information about all domain actions, chat, and use of the Object List. It does not however, contain complete and accurate information about the initial state of the domain (where each waste barrel is, what kind of equipment it requires, etc.). For the sake of the following evaluation, complete domain information was derived from the domain definition files that were used to initialize each session of use.

The four information conditions compared were:

- Complete Info – All information about toxic waste barrels (size, location, equipment) is known at the outset, and is correct.
- Object List – Information about toxic waste barrels is taken from the Object List as it becomes available, which is subject to user errors.
- Complete Info + Chat – The Complete Info condition, plus the occurrence of references in chat. This condition uses the names associated with objects in the Object List, but uses complete domain information in the inference process.

- Object List + Chat – The Object List condition, plus chat reference occurrences.

In the non-"Chat" conditions, the belief network shown in Figure 4 was used without the nodes specific to chat (a darker shade in the figure).

For each information condition the network was trained (using the $EM(\eta)$ algorithm [24]) on the complete dataset in Table 2, and then tested against the same data. Training and testing on the same data set is not typically appropriate for validating a particular machine-learning technique. However, the aim here is to establish the relative utility of various information sources rather than to validate the generality of the technique.

Two performance metrics were calculated in each condition; the proportion of correctly guessed goals, or correct goal rate (CGR); and the proportion of guesses that were false, or the false positive rate (FPR). A guess is made whenever a relevant state variable changes. Any uninterrupted sequence of correct guesses leading up to the execution of the predicted goal is counted as a single correct goal. The total number of goals is the number of wastes lifted. Thus,

$$CGR = correct\ goals\ /\ total\ goals$$
$$FPR = incorrect\ guesses\ /\ total\ guesses$$

The results of the evaluation are presented in Table 3. A single factor ANOVA demonstrated that differences between groups were highly significant for CGR ($F(131,3)=10.84, p<.0001$), and significant for FPR ($F(131,3)=3.98, p<.01$).

Table 3: Intent inference results for different info sources

Condition	CGR (StdDev)	FPR (StdDev)
Complete Info	.83 (.14)	.53 (.13)
Object List	.70 (.17)	.60 (.16)
Complete Info + Chat	.87 (.12)	.51 (.11)
Object List + Chat	.77 (.15)	.58 (.15)

The "Complete Info" case, in the top row of the table, provides a baseline against which results for the other conditions may be compared. It is a rough indicator of the best the intent inference procedure can do, given complete and accurate information about the state of the world. Across the four user groups in the dataset, the CGR for the "Complete Info" case ranged from .77 to .91, and there was a weak correlation between problem size (number of toxic wastes) and performance ($r=.23$), reflecting the fact that it is more difficult to make good guesses when there are more options to choose from. In general, these metrics indicate that the inference procedure is effective.

As expected, the intent inference procedure does not perform as well with information from the Object List alone. However, results from the "Object List" condition were still good, and demonstrate that use of the Object List was reliable enough to be useful for intent inference.

The "Complete Info + Chat" condition demonstrates that references add significant information that cannot be derived from knowledge about the state of the domain. Thus, regardless of access to state information (for instance, if there were intelligent sensors placed in the world) the Object List adds information that still improves intent inference.

The combination of reference information from chat and domain information from the Object List (the "Object List + Chat" condition) improves the performance of the procedure to a point where it is nearly as good as with complete information alone. This result provides validation of the claim that, for VesselWorld, the addition of the Object List provides a rich source of structured information that can be used to infer users' intentions. The introduction of a semi-automated component that uses this information, described in the next section, provides validation that this level of intent inference is good enough to improve the users' domain performance.

3. A Semi-Automated Component

The intent inference procedure above was developed to drive a component that would improve users' awareness of each other's goals, and fix some of the difficulties they had in creating and coordinating plans. The component that was developed for this purpose is shown in (Figure 5). The top portion of the component (everything above the "Get Plan" button) contains the same information for each user. It displays the five most plausible goals calculated by the intent inference procedure for each user at any point in time. When a user selects from among these goals, the goal is copied into the top row of the component, making it apparent to others, and the user is given the option to retrieve an automatically generated plan.

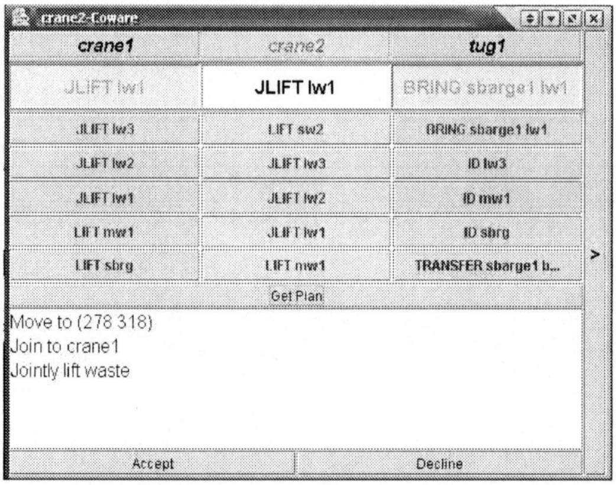

Figure 5: The adaptive component

The specific function of the component is as follows:

1. After each update to state information, (e.g., plan execution, information added to the Object List, a reference to an object mentioned in chat, etc.) the system updates the lists of plausible goals for each user.

2. When a user selects a goal, it is copied to the top row so that all users can tell what was selected. The user that selected the goal is then given the option to request an automatically generated plan by clicking the "Get Plan" button.

3. The system generates a plan that the user can inspect. If the goal involves other users, they are invited to join the plan. If all invited users accept the invitation, a plan is generated; if they do not, the requesting user is so informed and a plan is not generated.

4. The user may then accept the plan, in which case it is copied into the user's planning window for execution. If the plan is generated from correct state information (i.e. the Object List reflects correct state information), and no user modifies the state in such a way that conflicts with the generated plan, the plan will succeed.

The component does not interrupt users. Rather, it is a resource that collaborators can use to monitor one another's goals, and to generate accurate plans. We expected to find that the component would be heavily used, that use would result in fewer planning errors, and users would use it, instead of chat, to maintain awareness of each other's activities.

3.1. Evaluation

To evaluate the component, a single 40-hour study with four teams of three people was performed. The players were a mix of students and local-area professionals, with varying degrees of computer proficiency. Each team was trained together for two hours in the use of the system, and then solved randomly chosen VesselWorld problems for approximately ten hours. To alleviate fatigue concerns, the experiment was split into four three-hour sessions.

The participants were divided into two populations of two teams each, one that had the automated component, and one which did not. For the teams with the component, the inference procedure used information from the Object List and chat to infer user goals. The following results report on the last 5 hours of play time for each group, by which point user performance had stabilized.

Use of the automated component was analyzed, and several metrics were compared across the two groups, including: time taken per waste barrel, number of mouse clicks; amount of communication; and the number of joint and single errors. Additionally, exit interviews were provided to determine if the component was well received, and if it was in fact used to stay aware of other users' activity. All interview questions were answered on a seven point scale.

The component was used. All groups used the component to generate plans within the system. Users confirmed a goal every 1.5 minutes (SD=46 seconds), requested a plan for each confirmed goal, accepted 71% of plans requested (SD=19%), and completed the execution of 83% (SD=6.75%) of these plans. Overall, this indicates that roughly 59% of confirmed goals resulted in a plan that was executed to completion.

In answer to the question, "What did you think of the component?" the average survey response was 5.4 (SD=.8) (1= "Hated it", 7= "Loved it"). To the question "How did the component influence the difficulty of the problems," the average response was 5.6 (SD=.8) (1="Harder", 7= "Easier").

For each problem solving session, one quarter of all plan steps submitted to the server were generated by the component (SD=8%). Finally, the component generated plans for 43% (SD=15%) of the domain goals it could have predicted for the cranes. It was not possible to obtain a similar statistic for the tug because it is difficult to recognize goals in the collected log files (goals for the tug are not bracketed by easy to detect plan steps like "LIFT" and "LOAD").

Joint errors were reduced. Although there was no significant change in the number of individual errors by groups that had the adaptive component, these groups did have 45% fewer joint errors (failures during joint actions) per minute (p=.069). This difference is not significant at the .05 level, because of the small sample size and overall low proportion of joint errors. However this finding corroborates prior analysis of use of the VesselWorld system [22], which indicated that joint errors were usually the result of plan submissions becoming unsynchronized. Because the component generates coordinated plans in advance, users may simply submit each step and be assured that actions will be coordinated.

Cognitive load was reduced. The average time per waste decreased slightly for users with the plan-generation component, but this difference was not at all significant. With closer investigation though, it was found that the amount of clock time taken by users between steps of automatically generated plans was 57% less than in groups without the component (p<.01). Time taken between the submission of automatically generated plan steps was also less than time taken between manually generated plan steps within groups that had the component (52% reduction, p<.01). Furthermore, there was no significant difference in the number of mouse clicks per waste. Because the reduction in clock time for groups with the component cannot be explained by a reduction in the amount of interface work, we conclude that the component reduced the cognitive load of the collaborators.

The component was NOT used to maintain awareness. The overall amount of chat was not reduced in groups that had the component. By itself, this finding does not necessarily indicate that the component did not improve awareness; however none of the survey respondents indicated that the component was used to monitor other users' goals.

In general, these results demonstrate that intent inference using information provided by the users as part of their coordination work was good enough to support useful automation. Furthermore, the automation resulted in improved domain performance and reduced cognitive load, and in this respect it was successful. However the component did not appear to improve users' awareness of one another's activities. The following discussion examines this result more carefully.

4. Discussion

This paper has presented validation for an approach to adding useful intelligent automation to collaborative systems. To a large degree, this approach can be readily applied to other collaborative systems. The analytical process that led to the development of the Object List in VesselWorld is a repeatable design technique that has been documented in detail and shown to work with other systems [22][21]. CRs introduce work that people are willing to do and improves their performance in a domain task. They also add structure to coordinating information. Others have discussed the potential of structured collaborative information in supporting user-sensitive runtime support (e.g., [9], also see [25] for a theoretical treatment). The work that was reported upon here provides a concrete example of how this information can be used to produce powerful runtime inferences, which in turn support the integration of useful automation.

The automation added to VesselWorld addressed users' planning needs. However, these needs are fairly specific to the VesselWorld domain; moreover, users did not use the automated component to maintain awareness, which is a more persistent problem in groupware environments. We examine this result more closely against the backdrop of existing awareness research.

Awareness is a multi-faceted issue that is central to groupware development ([26][27]). One difficulty with supporting awareness in collaborative settings stems from asymmetries in information production and consumption [28][29]. Individuals who are responsible for generating awareness information do not always reap its benefits, and consumers of awareness information cannot guide its production. An approach to this problem is to passively collect information about user activity, and then to make it available as background information that collaborators may use as necessary.

This was the approach taken with VesselWorld. The Object List structured a portion of the coordinating information that was generated, enabling automated inferences about activity. These inferences were published as background for the shared activity. However, our empirical studies indicated that while this background information did not interfere with activity, it was not useful. Clearly, some design guidance for providing the right *kind* of awareness information is necessary.

CRs may collect information that is well suited for supporting *activity awareness*, which is awareness of how work is embedded within the context of the overall activity [30]. Activity awareness is distinct from "social awareness" (awareness of who is around) and "action awareness" (awareness of what is happening). The term "activity" is used to point to an activity theoretical framework, and as such this concept of awareness is more richly textured than can be effectively summarized here.

The role of activity awareness in collaborative settings becomes clearer if the role of context in activity is considered. In ordinary work environments, tasks cannot be neatly organized into preplanned episodes of behavior. New tasks appear dynamically, and existing tasks may bifurcate or be de-prioritized. Each time a new task is engaged, the relevant external information must be brought into focus and cognitive resources realigned accordingly in order to proceed. Upon returning to an earlier task, that task's state must be recovered so that activity may proceed. Context shifts increase cognitive load, and each such shift is a potential loss of prior context [31][32].

Collaborative work is characterized by rapid shifts between individual and carefully coordinated activity [28][27]. These shifts are partially informed by pre-defined workflows, but they are just as often unpredictable and opportunistic. Support for activity awareness in collaborative environments is one way to ameliorate some of the problems inherent in the continual context switching that characterizes collaborative activity. For example, as collaborators in a virtual environment move from a shared super-task to individual sub-tasks, helping them to maintain awareness of the super-task should help eliminate errors like forgotten commitments. The use of shared timelines in a collaborative learning environment as described by Carroll, et al. [30] is such an approach.

The forgotten or misunderstood commitments observed in VesselWorld may be attributed to a lack of activity awareness. As more toxic waste barrels are found in a VesselWorld session, more complicated plans are formed which involve multiple segments - for instance, "Get the wastes in <region>" or, "Get the two Extra Large wastes," which involves several sub-plans and all three users. In executing these more complex plans, individual users must move through several layers of context, which are not explicitly available in any external representation. A loss of high-level context will result in forgotten or mis-remembered commitments, and lack of an external representation of high-level context makes it difficult to catch misunderstandings early on.

The automated component may not have been used to maintain awareness in VesselWorld because it provided information about the immediate individual goals (a form of action awareness) rather than the encompassing shared goal. For any given user, a reminder about their own current (low-level) goal is not very helpful, especially since the plan-generation component automatically generates plans for low-level goals. A reminder about other users' low-level goals may not be useful without seeing how they fit into the encompassing shared task context. A more useful automation would provide this kind of information.

In general, providing a background collaborative context based on passively gathered information can overcome asymmetries in the production and consumption of awareness information. One type of awareness that may be supported is about shared, high-level context and its relationship to individual activity. This type of awareness is especially important as collaborators move through various phases of coupling, because there is substantial opportunity to lose track of encompassing, shared context.

Coordinating representations are useful for generating the information required to provide this kind of awareness because they capture and structure information that constitutes the users' shared context. The computer, as a mediating artifact with significant abilities to summarize, sort, and synthesize structured data is in a good position to automatically combine and provide this information in the background. We conclude that while the specific automation provided in VesselWorld may not be easily generalized to other domains, CRs may be generally useful for supporting automated activity awareness.

5. Summary

This article has presented an approach that combines ethnographic design with intelligent automation in order to improve collaborative activity, and this approach has been validated with an example. Specific attention has been given to the utility of information that is generated by users in the course of their collaborative work, and it has been shown that, in VesselWorld, this information is nearly as good as complete knowledge of the state of the domain. It was shown how this information can be used to support useful run-time automation, in the form of planning support.

The presented approach is built on the observation that mediating artifacts can structure communication to improve coordination. In adding structure to coordinating information, it is made accessible to autonomous algorithms. The approach may be generalized to other collaborative domains. With regards to the design of coordinating representations and the knowledge acquisition problem, there is a strong case for the generality of the approach to be found in existing and prior research. With regards to automation, existing research that guides the development of generally useful awareness support has been highlighted. The approach we've presented allows the system to passively monitor coordinating information that may be very useful for generating activity awareness. In future work, this hypothesis will be investigated more directly.

References

[1]   Norman, D. A.:1991, "Cognitive artifacts." In J. M. Carroll, editor, *Designing interaction: psychology at the human-computer interface*, Cambridge University Press. 17-38.
[2]   Hutchins, E.:1995, "Cognition in the Wild." Cambridge, MA. MIT Press.
[3]   Schmidt, K.:1997, "Of Maps and Scripts," *Proceedings of Group'97*. Phoenix, AZ. ACM Press, NY: 138-147.
[4]   Hutchins, E., Hollan, J., Norman, D.:1985, "Direct Manipulation Interfaces." *Human-Computer Interaction.* 1, 311-338.
[5]   Carroll, J.:1997, "Human-computer interaction: psychology as a science of design." *Int. J. Human-Computer Studies* 46, 501-522.

[6] Maes, P., and Shneiderman, B.:1997, "Direct Manipulation vs. Interface Agents: A Debate," *Interactions*, 4(6), ACM Press.

[7] Suchman, L.:1987, "Plans and Situated Actions. The Problem of Human Machine Communication." Cambridge University Press.

[8] Kaplan, S., Tolone, W., Bogia, D., Bignoli, C.:1992, "Flexible, Active Support for Collaborative Work with Conversation Builder," in *Proceedings of CSCW '92*. Toronto, Canada, 378-385.

[9] Malone, T., Lai, K., Grant, K.:1997, "Two Design Principles for Collaboration Technology: Examples of Semiformal Systems and Radical Tailorability." In J. Brandshaw (Ed.), *Software Agents*, AAAI Press/The MIT Press, 109-143.

[10] Schmidt, K., and Simone, C.:1996, "Coordination mechanisms: Towards a conceptual foundation of CSCW Systems Design," *Computer Supported Cooperative Work. The Journal of Collaborative Computing*, 5(2-3), 155-200.

[11] Hefley, W.E. and Murray D.:1993, "Intelligent User Interfaces." In *Proceedings of IUI'93*, Orlando, Florida. ACM Press, NY, 3-10.

[12] Benyon, D.:1993, "Adaptive Systems: A Solution to Usability Problems." User Modeling and User Adapted Interaction, 3, 65-87.

[13] Rich., C. and Sidner, C. L.:1998, "COLLAGEN: A Collaboration Manager for Software Interface Agents." *User Modeling and User-Adapted Interaction*. 8(3-4):315-250.

[14] Jameson, A.:2002. "Adaptive interfaces and agents." In J. A. Jacko & A. Sears (Eds.), *Human computer interaction handbook*. Mahwah, NJ: Erlbaum.

[15] Lesh, N, Rich, C., and Sidner, C.L.:1999, "Using plan recognition in human-computer collaboration," In *Proc. 7th Int. Conf. on User Modeling*, pp. 23—32.

[16] Soller, A.:2004, "Computational modeling and analysis of knowledge sharing in collaborative distance learning," *User Modeling and User-Adapted Interaction*. 14: 351-381

[17] Horvitz, E.:1999, "Principles of Mixed-Initiative User Interfaces." In *Proceedings of CHI' 99*. Pittsburgh, PA. ACM Press, NY, 159-166.

[18] Suchman, L. and Trigg, R.:1991, "Understanding Practice: Video as a Medium for Reflection and Design." In Joan Greenbaum & Morten Kyng (eds.), *Design at Work: Cooperative Design of Computer Systems*, Lawrence Erlbaum Associates, Hillsdale, New Jersey.

[19] Engeström, Y.:1987. "Learning by Expanding: An Activity-Theoretical Approach to Developmental Research." (Helsinki: Orieta-Konsultit).

[20] Nardi, B.:1996, "Context and Consciousness: Activity Theory and Human-Computer Interaction." Cambirdge, MA. The MIT Press.

[21] Feinman, A., and Alterman, R.: 2003, "Discourse Analysis Techniques for Modeling Group Interaction." In Brusilovsky, P., Corbett, A., and de Rosis, F, editors, *Proceedings of the Ninth International Conference on User Modeling*, 228-237.

[22] Alterman, R., Feinman, A., and Introne, J.: 2001, "Coordinating Representations in Computer-Mediated Joint Activities." *Proceedings of the 23rd Annual Conference of the Cognitive Science Society*, Boston, MA, 43-48.

[23] Landsman, S., and Alterman, R.:2005, "Using Transcription and Replay in Analysis of Groupware Applications". *Brandeis University Technical Report CS-05-259*.

[24] Bauer, E., Koller, D., & Singer, Y.: 1997, "Update rules for parameter estimation in Bayesian networks." In *Proceedings 13th Annual Conference on Uncertainty in Artificial Intelligence (UAI)*, 3–13.

[25] Alterman, R.: 2000, "Rethinking Autonomy." *Minds and Machines*, 10:1 15-30.

[26] Tatar, D., Foster, G., Bobrow, D.: 1991, "Design for Conversation: Lessons from Cognoter." *Int. J. of Man-Machine Studies*. 34(2), 185-209.

[27] Gutwin, C., Greenberg, S.: 2002, "A Descriptive Framework of Workspace Awareness for Real-Time Groupware." *Journal of Computer Supported Cooperative Work*. 11:411-446.

[28] Dourish, P. and Bellotti, V.:1992, "Awareness and Coordination in Shared Workspaces." *Proceedings of CSCW*, Toronto, 107–114.

[29] Grudin, J.:1988, "Why CSCW Applications Fail: Problems in the Design and Evaluation of Organisational Interfaces." In *Proceedings of CSCW '88*, Portland, Oregon. 83-95. 30.Carroll, J., Neale, D., Isenhour, P., Rosson, M.B., McCrickard, D.S.:2003, "Notification and Awareness: Synchronizing Task-Oriented Collaborative Activity." *Int J. Human-Computer Studies*, 58, 605-632.

[30] Carroll, J., Neale, D., Isenhour, P., Rosson, M.B., McCrickard, D.S.:2003, "Notification and Awareness: Synchronizing Task-Oriented Collaborative Activity." *Int J. Human-Computer Studies*, 58, 605-632.

[31] Kirsh, D.:2001, "The Context of Work," *Human-Computer Interaction*. 16, 305-322.

[32] Kirsh, D.:2000, "A few thoughts on cognitive overload," *Intellectica, CNRS*, 30, 19–51.

Cooperative Systems Design
P. Hassanaly et al. (Eds.)
IOS Press, 2006

The integration of asynchronous and synchronous communication support in cooperative systems

Andrea KIENLE
Fraunhofer Integrated Publication and Information Systems Institute (IPSI)
Dolivostraße 15, 64293 Darmstadt, Germany;
e-mail: andrea.kienle@ipsi.fraunhofer.de

Abstract. This paper presents the design and a first evaluation of the cooperative system KOLUMBUS 2 that integrates synchronous and asynchronous communication support and the joint work on material. The design is theory driven and bases on context-oriented communication theory and media synchronicity theory. The evaluation revealed mixed acceptance. While the design of KOLUMBUS chat with references, clipboard and list of topics was widely accepted problems occurred with the integration. Based on these results ideas for further improvements are shown.

Keywords: synchronous communication, asynchronous communication, integration of different communication media, system design, evaluation

Introduction

In the past various communications support was developed to enable cooperation in groups. Own evaluation and results from theories of media use showed the necessity to integrate asynchronous and synchronous communication support within one system in order to support different parts of communication processes. An integration of different communication modes was also required in earlier publications (see e.g. [1]), but has not widely been realized yet. This paper presents the design and a first evaluation of the cooperative system KOLUMBUS 2 that integrates different communication modes and the joint work on material. It bases on a former work that integrates cooperative work on material and asynchronous communication in a system called KOLUMBUS [2], [3].

Section 1 presents the theoretical background that consists of the theory of context-oriented communication and theories of media use. From these theories I extract requirements for the integration of synchronous communication support in KOLUMBUS 2 (section 2). In section 3 related work concerning chat systems is presented with the aim to check whether an already existing system or a new development is necessary to meet the requirements. Section 4 describes the design of KOLUMBUS 2, especially the synchronous communication support and its integration in the existing support of work on material and asynchronous communication. Section 5 presents first findings of an evaluation of this system; the evaluation took place in a seminar at the University of Dortmund (Germany), Education Institute, during the winter term 2004/2005. The paper ends with a conclusion and an outlook on further research.

1. Theoretical background

1.1. Context-oriented communication theory

The context-oriented communication theory [3] bases on a model that focuses on the question of how mutual understanding can increased in dialogues. This model emphasizes the relevance of context: communication can only succeed if the communicators' expressions are completed by the context that can be perceived by themselves and the recipients [4]. The term "situative context" can partially be referred to Ducrot's and Todorov's definition of the speech situation [5]. The situative context of the communicators is represented by what they perceive during communication and by what they have perceived prior to the communication act. Since context can refer to the past, an expression of the moment can become part of another expression's context in the future. The starting point or the boundaries of the context of a communication act cannot be defined deterministically. It is the task of the communicators to delineate the scope of context that can support their communication.

By referring to the available context two essential advantages are achieved: on the one hand, the explicitness of the conveyed content does not need to be maximal, because only these pieces of information have to be given that are required to complete the context in such a way that the message can be reconstructed and understood by the recipient. For example *"Where is the car?"* can be answered with *"behind the yellow house"* if there is only one yellow house which is part of the perceptible context. The communicator has to anticipate the scope of context that is available for the addressee. This anticipation can be supported by knowledge about the communication partner.

Eventually, the need for explicit communication can be reduced, for example in the case of common context of the communication partners (*"where is the car?"* – *"same place as yesterday"*). On the other hand, the available context assists in finding out whether the communication partners understand each other: depending on how a situation evolves there are either indicators for the success of a communication task or an identifiable necessity to recheck the comprehension of the message or simply to improve the communication (*"could you close the window, please"* – ….. *"why are you not closing the window – don't you understand me?"*).

The theory of context-oriented communication theory led to a sophisticated concept of annotations where annotations serve as communicative contributions and (segmented) material is used as context. This concept is realized in the cooperative system KOLUMBUS which was evaluated in different settings [2], [3].

Figure 1 gives an example of a content tree that consists of annotations (communicative contributions) and text and picture items (material). More information about KOLUMBUS can be found in section 4. The evaluation of KOLUMBUS was the starting point for the work on theories of media use and the integration of synchronous communication support.

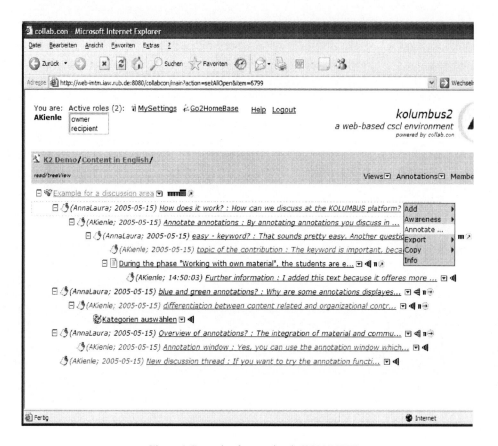

Figure 1. Example of a tree view in KOLUMBUS

1.2. Theories of Media Use

A widely referenced theory of media use is the media richness theory (MRT) [6]. Media richness theory proposes that task performance can be improved when the task needs corresponded to a medium´s ability to convey information. Media richness is defined as the ability to enable users to communicate and improve understanding. Richer media were those with a greater language variety (e.g. the ability to convey natural language rather than numeric information), a greater amount of channels (e.g. verbal and non-verbal elements), a greater personalisation (of the communicative contribution) and a more rapid feedback.

The media richness theory argues that certain media are better able to transmit information depending upon whether the information is used in situations of uncertainty of equivocality. Uncertainty exists when a framework for interpreting a message exists, but information is missed to interpret the message. Equivocality exists when there are different, possibly conflicting interpretations for the information. While uncertain tasks require more information equivocal tasks require negotiation among members to converge to consensus. Daft and Lengel [6] argue that media capable of sending "*rich*" information are better suited to equivocal tasks, while the "lean" are best suited to tasks of uncertainty.

Most evaluations of the effects of media richness did not support its assumptions. Rice [7] for example showed that the degree of media richness is relatively unimportant for reducing uncertainty. Various studies (see e.g. [8], [9]) run counter to the assumptions of MRT.

Based on these studies media synchronicity theory (MST) [10] was developed. The authors describe media by five characteristics: Immediacy of feedback (extent to which users are able to give rapid feedback), parallelism (number of simultaneous communications), symbol variety ("*height*" of medium, in MRT language variety + amount of channels), rehearsability (extent to which participants can elaborate their message before sending) and reprocessability (extent to which a message can be processed again).

Media synchronicity is defined as the "*extent to which individuals work together on the same activity at the same time*" ([10], p. 5). High media synchronicity means a high level of feedback immediacy and a low level of parallelism, whereas low media synchronicity means a low level of feedback immediacy and a high level of parallelism.

While in the MRT tasks has been the key element, the key element of MST is the division of tasks in two different communication processes:

- **Conveyance**: conveyance is the exchange of information, followed by deliberation of meaning. This communication process can be divergent – not all participants need to focus on the same information at the same time and they need not agree on its meaning.
- **Convergence**: convergence is the development of shared meaning for information and it is convergent – as the name already implies. Participants aim at agreeing on the meaning of information. This means that participants must understand each other's view.

Following the media synchronicity theory low media synchronicity is preferred for conveyance and high media synchronicity is preferred for convergence. Dennis & Valacich conclude that for each task different communication media is necessary due to the different communication processes: „*We believe that the key to effective use of media is to match media capabilities to the fundamental communication process required to perform the task. Because most tasks require individuals to both convey information and converge on shared meanings, and media that excel at information conveyance are often not those that excel at convergence. Thus choosing one single medium for any task may prove less effective than choosing a medium or a set of media which the group uses at different times performing the task, depending on the current communication process (convey or converge). Media switching may be most appropriate.*" ([10], p. 9).

To conclude: the work on different theories of media use mined that we cannot define the right communication support for all needs. In fact different communication support is necessary. The newest theory with the largest basis on evaluation is the media synchronicity theory. If we would follow the proposal of Dennis and Valacich we would offer different communication media for the support of cooperative work. However, this runs counter to our work on context-oriented communication theory that requires a tight integration of communication and context that especially includes former or other communications. Therefore I propose different communication modes within one system. This system should not only support different communication modes with different levels of synchronicity but also the handling of context.

2. Requirements for an Integration

To realize the findings of the media synchronicity theory KOLUMBUS 2 should support different communication modes with

- **High synchronicity** (high immediacy of feedback and low parallelism). It can be supported by a moderated chat.
- **Middle synchronicity** (high immediacy of feedback and high parallelism). It is proposed as a non-moderated chat.
- **Low synchronicity** (this means low immediacy of feedback and high parallelism). This is already supported by asynchronous communication in form of annotations.

KOLUMBUS 2 should also support
- **Rehearsability**: Annotations already can be edited before sending. This should also be supported for chat contributions.
- **Reprocessability**: Annotations can already be edited, readdressed, copied etc. This should also be supported for chat contributions.

KOLUMBUS in its first version was developed following the theory of context-oriented communication. This should also be true for an extended system in order to keep the advantages of this design. Therefore KOLUMBUS 2 should additionally support

- **Integration of the different communication modes**: Following the topics below it means an integration of chat contributions and annotations.
- **References to other communicative contributions**: This is already given for the asynchronous communication support by annotating annotations and should also be supported for the synchronous mode.
- **Integration of communicative contributions and material**: This is already given for asynchronous communication and should also be supported for the contributions developed during synchronous communication processes.

In conclusion it can be stated that the existing system KOLUMBUS supports only a part of the media mix that is required from the media synchronicity theory. Therefore a synchronous support in form of a combination of a moderated and non-moderated chat has to be realized. This support has to fulfill the demanded characteristics of media and a tight integration in the existing system in order to meet the requirements from context-oriented communication theory.

3. State of the art chat tools

The search for suitable chat tools that meet all requirements mentioned above was not successful. In order to give a state of the art some tools that meet at least one of the requirements are presented here. These chat tools concern especially the possibility to reference between chat contributions or between chat contributions and material and the persistence of chats.

References to other communicative contributions are for example realized in the chat tool Threaded Chat [11]. Here contributions can be referred to one other as a "reply-to". The contributions are presented as a tree. This presentation leads to problems, e.g. as new contributions are added to different, potentially distant branches of the tree. To deal with that problem, Academic Talk [12] provides two views in the same window: one presents the contributions in chronological order, the other in logical (tree) order as defined by reply-to relations.

The relations between chat and material can be for example found in the Anchored Conversations tool [13] that allows chats to be connected to a specific point in a document. This tool does not support references from one contribution to another or to different parts of the material to the same point of time. Threaded discussions and web pages are linked in Kukakuka [14]. Again references to parts of the material are not possible.

The GraffiDis tool [15] supports relations of chat contributions to texts and graphics and offeres a kind of persistence. Users enter contributions (which can also consist of graphics and other material) at any places of the chat area. After a time the contributions are faded out to the background colour. With a "history slider" a user can navigate through the chat in chronological order. Relations between contributions are indicated by nearby positions in the chat area. References to contributions are not possible after a certain distance in time as the previous contribution already faded out.

So far, none of these approaches supports references to contributions, references to shared material and a persistent storage of the content. This is realized in ConcertChat [16]. Concert Chat supports single and multiple references and the relation of chat contributions even to parts of material which can be text, a web page or a joint whiteboard. The combination of chat and whiteboard especially supports communication and the joint work on material at the whiteboard. ConcertChat stores all chat contributions and the development of the material on the whiteboard. They can be later processed by calling the related number of past chat contributions or using a scrollbar for the whiteboard content. However, ConcertChat does not support sophisticated storage of material and its integration in asynchronous communication.

To conclude, some chat tools support parts of the requirements elaborated above. They especially do not offer possibilities for the segmentation of material and are therefore not suitable to be integrated in the concept of KOLUMBUS. Therefore an own development of synchronous communication support is necessary.

4. The integration of different communication modes in KOLUMBUS 2

KOLUMBUS 2 was developed by the University of Dortmund, Informatics & Society and the Ruhr University of Bochum, Information and Technology Management. A former version, KOLUMBUS, was built to support the integration of asynchronous communication (in form of annotations) and joint work on material (e.g. text or pictures). Basic concepts of that work are still part of the actual development and area shown at a glance in the first subsection; for further information see [2], [3]. The other two subsections deal with the design of KOLUMBUS Chat and its integration in the already existing system. These two subsections will show a valuable integration of synchronous and asynchronous communication support that follows the media synchronicity theory as well as the context-oriented communication theory.

4.1. Basics of KOLUMBUS 2

The central feature of KOLUMBUS 2 is the segmentation of content into small units (called items), enabling the members to use and annotate the stored content in a very flexible manner. While communicative contributions have the form of annotations content is represented by text, pictures, binaries, links or annotations. The content can be presented as a hierarchical structure of items viewable in a web-browser. Items of material can be inserted at the same hierarchical level of another item or on the next lower level. In this way users can build a hierarchy of their contributions. All existing functions (e.g. annotate, add, copy, and change) can be applied to every item. Annotations can be inserted on every hierarchical level. The higher they are placed in the hierarchy, the more general their intention is. Discussions occur by annotating annotations.

KOLUMBUS 2 provides two different views of content. In the tree view (see figure 1 some pages before), each item is represented as a node in a hierarchical tree-structure. To support searching and to focus on relevant content, parts of the tree or the whole tree can be expanded or minimized. Figure 1 also shows the menu that can be activated at every single item (by using the triangle behind the items). It allows users e.g. to add communicative contributions (in form of annotations) or material.

By contrast to the tree view, the paper view shows content in a visually more attractive and readable way. Here, different types of presentations are combined to form a single document. Within the paper view, KOLUMBUS supports perception of meaningful structures. In the paper view it is also possible to expand or reduce the scope of displayed items, and to use the menu.

Both, the tree view and the paper view, can be used to work with individual's own material, as well as that of others. To differentiate between annotations and material, the tree view uses different icons, while the paper view employs different colours. In the paper view, the communicative character of annotations is increased by prefixing the annotation with the author's name, similar to the convention with newsgroups.

4.2. The design of KOLUMBUS Chat

Based on the system described above the KOLUMBUS Chat was developed [17]. KOLUMBUS Chat bases on the generic NFC chat that offers usual chat functionalities [18]. Following the concept of KOLUMBUS, a chat is represented as an item and can be added at every position in the content structure. In order to achieve different degrees

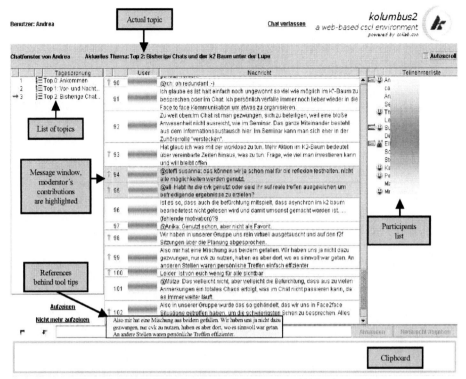

Figure 2. KOLUMBUS chat (moderated), names are hidden due to privacy reasons

of media synchronicity a moderated and a non-moderated chat are offered. When starting the chat item in the integrated (tree- or paper-)view a chat window opens (see figure 2 for an example of a moderated chat that was part of the evaluated seminar). In the following I concentrate on the description of the moderated chat since it is more complex than the non-moderated chat and offers more functionality.

In the middle of a chat window you can see the message window (in figure 2 names are hidden for privacy reasons). Moderator´s contributions are highlighted by a background colour (magenta, in figure 2 shown as grey), directing attention of the participants to the moderator's inputs. As in most chat systems a list of participants (here at the right side) is available. Different icons indicate the status of the members (typing, has the floor etc.). The message window as well as the list of participants is also part of the non-moderated chat.

List of topics: The list of topics supports the integration of material and synchronous communication as well as the later integration of the chat contributions into the integrated KOLUMBUS 2 content structure. Topics can be text (realized) and (in a conceptual status) links to other material sections. The topics are not only part of the content structure of KOLUMBUS 2 but also used during the chatting step to structure the discussion process.

The list of topics is defined by the initiator of the chat in order to prepare and pre-structure the chat. During the chat the moderator is able to choose a topic (by clicking on it) that is then placed in the headline of the chat. When changing the topic a contribution in the message window is generated by the system in order to direct attention on it. The list of topics has also relevance for the storage of chat contributions in the item tree (see next subsection).

Clipboard: In the moderated chat participants have to request the floor and the moderator is able to give the floor to one or more participants. Each user has – independent of the floor – the possibility to type up to three messages and store it in the clipboard at the bottom of the chat window. This was stimulated by the required characteristic of rehearsability. Before sending to the audience a user takes a prepared message from the clipboard to the input box, can edit it if necessary and sends it to the others.

References: Participants can explicit refer to an existing contribution by clicking on the accordant message and compose the own message in the input box. References are indicated by an arrow in front of the message. The arrow is a tool tip that shows the referenced message when moving the cursor on it (see the example at the bottom of figure 2). The explicit reference also has an effect on the later permanent storage of the chat contributions (see next subsection). Clipboard and references are also available in a non-moderated chat.

4.3. The Integration of Chat in asynchronous Communication and Material

The previous subsection deals with the communication support during synchronous steps. This subsection describes the integration of the chat contributions in the KOLUMBUS 2 content structure that presents all types of items (material, synchronous and asynchronous communication) in an integrated view. This integration bases upon two arguments: one is the demanded characteristic of reprocessability of media (derived from the media synchronicity theory), the other is the requirement for the integration of communicative contributions in the context (derived from the context-oriented communication theory).

When a chat is finished the chat contributions are inserted in the integrated content structure of KOLUMBUS 2. This step takes the topics and the explicit references between chat contributions into account: all chat contributions are inserted as children of the topic item to which they are posted and references are inserted as discussion threads. The presentation of the chat contribution is similar to annotations (asynchronous communication) since the name and date are placed in front of the message.

To describe the integration by an example figure 3 shows at the top a chat discussion between Andrea and Marcus. After the chat this discussion is integrated in the KOLUMBUS 2 content structure (see figure 3 at the bottom). Because the references are taken into account the contributions are placed in a different manner than in the chat window: contributions that were related by the referencing functionality are shown as discussion threads. In our example two discussion threads occurred.

These threads can be handled in the same manner as other items in the KOLUMBUS 2 content structure, e.g. can be expanded or minimized. Furthermore they can be seen as a starting point for further work. At each chat contribution the whole menu (see figure 1) is available behind the triangle button so that the users can either add material or further discuss the topic by annotating. In the bottom part of figure 3 both discussion threads are further discussed (after finishing the chat session) by using annotations. This shows the tight integration of synchronous and asynchronous communication support.

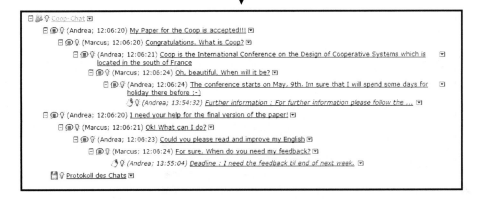

1	Andrea	My Paper for the Coop is accepted!!!
2	Marcus	Congratulations. What is Coop?
3	Andrea	I need your help for the final version of the paper!
4	Andrea	Coop is the International Conference on the Design of Cooperative Systems which is located in the south of France
5	Marcus	Ok! What can I do?
6	Andrea	Could you please read and improve my English
7	Marcus	Oh, beautiful. When will it be?
8	Marcus	For sure. When do you need my feedback?
9	Andrea	The conference starts on May, 9th. Im sure that I will spend some days for holiday there before :-)

Figure 3. Chat contributions in the integrated KOLUMBUS 2 content structure
(names are hidden due to privacy reasons)

Additionally to the adding in the KOLUMBUS content structure a protocol of the chat is stored as a binary (see last line in the bottom part of figure 3). The protocol presents the contributions in chronological order, it can be downloaded and read outside the system. The combination of a presentation in threads (in the KOLUMBUS 2 content structure) and in chronological order (protocol) seems to be necessary because re-learning demands different presentations for different learners [19].

5. Experiences

First experiences with KOLUMBUS 2 that supports the integration of synchronous communication, asynchronous communication and the work on material was used during a seminar at the University of Dortmund (Germany), Education Institute, during the winter term 2004/2005. In the following the setting, the methods of collecting and analyzing data and first results are presented.

5.1. Setting

In order to gather experience with the integration of the cooperative work on material, synchronous and asynchronous communication it seems to be necessary that all these functionalities are needed to fulfill the given tasks. Therefore the seminar was carefully prepared as a blended learning seminar that combined asynchronous elaboration and discussion of group results in subgroups as well as moderated seminar chats and face-to-face meetings of the whole group. The overall topic of the seminar was the potential of e-learning for the support of learning at universities and at the workplace.

Fourteen students which formed four subgroups of three to four students participated in the seminar. Each subgroup had to work on a preparation of a moderated seminar chat and talk that had to be given in one of the face-to-face meetings. Both (seminar chat and talk) dealt with a specific topic of e-learning that was on a non-detailed level given by the tutor and had potential for own research questions and solution ideas of the students.

In more detail the students had the following tasks:

- **Individual work**: work on the task of the subgroup by using the KOLUMBUS 2 content structure and annotations. This individual work could be seen as a preparation step for the work in each subgroups. Following the media synchronicity theory this step was the conveyance part of the overall task.

- **Work in subgroups**: Joint preparation of a moderated seminar chat and a talk for one of the face-to-face meetings concerning the given topic. For this step the groups were expected to use the content structure and annotations for the elaboration of the presentation and the preparation of chat and non-moderated chats to support the finishing of their artifacts. Following the media synchronicity theory the step combined a conveyance and a convergence part.

- **Moderated chats and face-to-face meetings in the whole seminar group**: The whole group met in a rhythm of two weeks rotational in moderated chats and face-to-face meetings. The chats prepared by a subgroup dealt with the chosen topic of the concerning subgroup and should give a feeling for the problem to the whole group. Furthermore the moderated chat was before the presentation of the subgroup so that the content of the chat had to be reflected for the concluding talk. In both, the moderated seminar chats and the face-to-face meetings, a common sense for problems and solutions should be found. Following the media synchronicity theory this step served for the convergence in the whole group.

5.2. Collection and Analysis of Data

For the collection and analysis of data a mix of quantitative and qualitative methods was used. The quantitative part based on log files: they were recorded concerning different events in KOLUMBUS 2 (e.g. add or download material or annotations, participation in chats for each member). The evaluation of the log files was conducted using the KOLUMBUS analytical tool [17] that is a prototypical KOLUMBUS module that supports the analysis of logged events in the related KOLUMBUS content area. Authorized users select persons from a list of participants, actions from an action list (e.g. annotate, add text or documents, download) and times periods. Results are shown as tables and graphs.

The qualitative part of the study mainly based on group interviews of the student group after each face-to-face meeting and a closing interview at the end of the seminar. The regular interviews were on the work with the different functionalities of

KOLUMBUS 2 and its appropriateness to support the tasks. The closing interview concerned the overall rating of the setting (blended learning, theme, KOLUMBUS 2) and further improvements of the seminar concept and of KOLUMBUS 2. Furthermore an additional interview with the tutor was conducted at the end of the seminar. The interviews are recorded, typed and analyzed in order to add reasons to the quantitative findings and evaluate the concepts of KOLUMBUS 2 and the seminar.

5.3. Results

The overall results revealed that the concept of the seminar was suitable to foster different tasks of conveyance and convergence. The functionalities were used as expected: for the work on material the students used the content structure; for the work in subgroups they used a mix of content structure, annotations and chat, all planed seminar chat occurred as moderated chats. The findings concerning the content structure and the use annotations were similar to those of former evaluations (see [2], [3] for details). Therefore I concentrate in the following on results concerning the functionalities of (moderated) chat and its integration in other parts of the system.

5.3.1. Results concerning the chat functionalities

List of topics: For all moderated seminar chats a list of topics was prepared; they consisted of two to four topics for the chats of 45 minutes. The students were asked for the relevance of these topic lists and the answers were twofold. On the one hand it was confirmed by all subgroups that the discussion of the topics was a good preparation for the moderated chat because the subgroup has to agree on a topic list for their chat. This argument also shows that the given task of preparing a list of topics was a good vehicle to foster a convergent process in the subgroups. On the other hand it was reported that the topics have a lower relevance during the chat itself. Most students argued that they concentrated on the message window and often did not remember the actual topic. Only when the topic changed and the automatically generated contribution appeared in the message window the students became aware of the topic list. However, for the following persistent integration of the chat contributions in the KOLUMBUS content structure the topics had a great relevance because they divide the complex content with a high amount of chat contributions in smaller groups.

   Clipboard: The statements of the students concerning the usage of the clipboard are again different. Most of the students confirmed that they often used the clipboard during the moderated seminar chats but nearly never in non-moderated chats of the subgroups. Reasons for the usage in moderated chats were mainly seen in the long period of time before the floor was given to the student. To bridge this time the students prepared their own statements. This usage increased on the one hand the speed of the moderated chat because the participants had not to wait the typing phase of a member which already has the floor. On the other hand the participants had less concentration on the actual development of the chat when they typed own messages into the clipboard. In unmoderated chats the participants did not see the need to bridge waiting time because everybody can type at every time.

   References: The students often used the referencing functionality during the moderated seminar chat. Table 1 gives an overview of the amount of overall contributions; contributions that explicit refer to the other chat contributions and the quotient of both concerning for each of the five moderated seminar chats.

Table 1. Contributions of moderated seminar chats; names of chats are anonymized

Moderated chats	overall contributions	referencing contributions	referencing/overall
chat 1	217	93	42,8 %
chat 2	140	58	41,4 %
chat 3	171	87	50,9 %
chat 4	127	47	37,0 %
chat 5	146	60	41,1 %
Sum	**801**	**345**	**43,0 %**

The threads that emerged by referring to other chat contributions consisted of a different number of contributions and depths: the depth varied between 2 and 8, the number of contributions between 1 and 12. Students mentioned that they used the referencing function mainly because of the long period of time that passed between reading of messages and having the floor. Therefore the students wanted to emphasize the relation between the own contribution and a former contribution of another member. In the non-moderated chats of the subgroups students did not or not often use references. In the interviews they argued that all reasons for using the references as mentioned before were not given in a non-moderated chat of three to four students.

5.3.2. Results concerning the integration of chat

The results concerning the integration of chat were mostly disappointing. The content of the moderated seminar chats were input for the closing talk of the subgroups in the face-to-face meetings. Therefore it was expected that at least the members of the corresponding subgroup would use the imported chat contributions as a starting point for their asynchronous discussion by using annotations. In fact no asynchronous discussion was integrated in the stored chat contributions although the tutor motivated this step more than one time.

The missing integration of synchronous and asynchronous discussions was discussed in the closing group interview. Students confirmed that they took the content of the seminar chats into account during the preparation of their talk. One subgroup tried to integrate an asynchronous discussion in the stored chat but did not find a suitable position in the content structure *"Where should I add an annotation? It seemed to be inappropriate to further discuss in the bla bla of the chat. For a further discussion a conclusion of the chat which was also stored in the content structure would be necessary."* (student 13, translation by author). Other groups rated an asynchronous follow up discussion of the chat as unnecessary. These students emphasized that they remembered the important parts and statements because all of them participated as discussant or moderator and the preparation of the talk had to be done directly after their seminar chat. These arguments show some limitations of the seminar concept.

Another possible usage of the stored chats can be seen in reading it after its end. However, this usage was only confirmed by the tutor which wanted to reconstruct a chat some weeks after it occurred. Students again emphasized that they had no reason to perceive the chat again.

5.4. Discussion

In general the assumptions of the media synchronicity theory were confirmed by the study: for conveyant tasks media of lower synchronicity (asynchronous work on material and communication in form of annotations) was used, for convergent tasks media of higher synchronicity ((moderated) chat) was used. The integration of the different media in one system was offered but not used. Therefore it could be concluded that the system is as appropriate as a mix of different systems that support either synchronous or asynchronous communication or the storage of material. In fact the already proven concept of the integration of asynchronous communication and the support of work on material in KOLUMBUS (concerning positive results in this study as well as in former studies are not presented in this paper) give proper reasons to further follow the integrated concept and work on the scenario of usage as well as on a more suitable integration support.

Concerning the scenario it can be stated that an integration of chat contributions in the content tree for a later elaboration or discussion is only necessary in some settings: Either the chat content is needed in later steps or group members which did not participate in the chat relied on the chat content. Both were not given during the study presented here.

Concerning the integration an intermediate step seems to be necessary. During this intermediate step a conclusion of the chat (or of the discussion concerning a topic from the topic list) has to be added to the stored chat contributions. Here different approaches are possible: an automatically conclusion based on keywords in the contributions or a conclusion elaborated by a moderator. In another study we worked on the group support by moderation [20]. In that study conclusions revealed as one important task of a moderator and were helpful for the progress of the group process.

The study presented here also mined some important hints on the design of the KOLUMBUS Chat. References and the clipboard were widely accepted and used functionality in the study – at least for the moderated chats in the whole seminar group. From this study it is unclear whether the group size or the moderation modus or its combination caused the usage.

6. Conclusion and further Research

This paper presented the design and a first evaluation of the cooperative system KOLUMBUS 2 that integrates synchronous and asynchronous communication support and the joint work on material. The design is theory driven and bases on context-oriented communication theory and media synchronicity theory; the evaluation revealed mixed acceptance. Actually I am working on a deeper analysis of the chats in order to find reasons for the changing number of contributions and references. This content analysis of the chat contributions could also reveal hints about the role of the list of topics in the moderated chats.

Further research deals on the one hand with the design of the chat tool itself and conditions for using the functionalities. Studies are necessary to gather valid results of the correlation between group size, moderated modus and the use of references and clipboards. On the other hand a revised design of the integration of synchronous communication in the other parts of the system is requested. The design should include an intermediate step which especially contains conclusions (e.g. by the moderator) of the synchronous communication.

Acknowledgements

I thank the KOLUMBUS 2-Team at the Ruhr University of Bochum, Germany for the development of KOLUMBUS 2 and the student group PG 454 for the development of KOLUMBUS Chat and the analytical tools. Many thanks also to Marcus Reinecke who carefully prepared and organized the seminar, all the participants of the seminar for their willingness to prove KOLUMBUS 2 and Martin Wessner for his helpful hints on earlier versions of this paper.

References

[1]   G. DeMichelis; E. Dubis; M. Jarke; F. Matthes; J. Mylopoulos; K. Pohl; J. Schmidt; C. Woo; E. Yu: Cooperative Information Systems: A Manifesto. In: M. Papazoglou; G. Schlageter (Eds.) : Cooperative Information Systems: Trends & Developments, 1997.

[2]   A. Kienle; T. Herrmann: Integration of communication, coordination and learning material – a guide for the functionality of collaborative learning environments. In: Proceedings of the 36 th Hawaii International Conference on System Sciences, 2003, 33.

[3]   A. Kienle: Integration of Knowledge Management and Collaborative Learning by technical supported Communication Processes. Accepted for the International Journal of Education and Information Technologies , Kluwer Academic Publishers, Netherlands, 2006.

[4]   G. Ungeheuer: Vor-Urteile über Sprechen, Mitteilen, Verstehen. In Kommunikationstheoretische Schriften 1, Ungeheuer (ed.), Rader, Aachen, 1987, 229-338.

[5]   O. Ducrot; T. Todorov: Encyclopedic Dictionary of the Sciences of Language. Baltimore: Johns Hopkins University Press, 1987.

[6]   R. L. Daft; R. H. Lengel: Organizational Information Requirements, Media Richness and Structural Design. In: Management Science, Vol. 32, No. 5 (1986), 554-571.

[7]   R. E. Rice: Task analyzability, use of new media, and effectiveness: a multi- site exploration of media richness. In: Organization Science, Vol. 3, No. 4 (1992), 475- 500.

[8]   A. R. Dennis; S. T. Kinney: Testing Media Richness Theory in the New Media: The Effects of Cues, Feedback, and Task Equivocality. In: Information Systems Research, Vol. 9, No. 3 (1998), 256-274.

[9]   J. S. Valacich; B. E. Mennecke; R. Wachter; B. C. Wheeler: Extensions of media richness theory: a test of the task-media fit hypothesis. In: Proceedings of the 27th Hawaii International Conference on System Sciences, 1994, IV, 11-20.

[10]   A. R. Dennis; J. S. Valacich: Rethinking Media Richness: Towards a Theory of Media Synchronicity. In: Proceedings of the 32nd Hawaii International Conference on System Sciences, 1999.

[11]   M. Smith; J. J. Cadiz; B. Burkhalter: Conversation Trees and Threaded Chats. In: Proceedings of the Conference on Computer Supported Cooperative Work, 2000. New York: ACM, 97-105.

[12]   S. McAlister; A. Ravenscroft; E. Scanlon: Combining interaction and context design to support collaborative argumentation using a tool for synchronous CMC. Journal of Computer Assisted Learning: Special Issue: Developing dialogue for learning, Vol. 20, No 3 (2004), 194-204.

[13]   E. F. Churchill; J. Trevor; S. Bly; L. Nelson; D. Cubranic: Anchored Conversations: Chatting in the Context of a Document. Proceedings of the SIGCHI Conference on Human Factors in Computing Systems, 2000, 454-461.

[14]   D. Suthers; J. Xu: Kükäkükä: An Online Environment for Artifact-Centered Discourse. Proc. of WWW   2002,   Honolulu,   472-480.   available   online: http://www2002.org/CDROM/alternate/252/index.html

[15]   J. Leponiemi: Visualizing Discussion History. International Journal of Human-Computer Interaction, Vol. 15, No. 1 (2003), 121-134.

[16]   M. Mühlpfordt; M. Wessner: Explicit Referencing In Chat Supports Collaborative Learning. Proceedings of the CSCL 2005, Taipei, Taiwan.

[17] Projektgruppe 454: Endbericht der Projektgruppe 454 – Interaktions- und Kommunikationsanalyse in dem CSCL-System KOLUMBUS 2 (Final report of project group 454 – Analysis of interaction and communication in the CSCL-System KOLUMBUS 2), University of Dortmund, 2005.

[18] T. Lyristis: NFC Chat, 2005. Available online: http://nfcchat.sourceforge.net

[19] H.-R. Pfister; W. Müller; T. Holmer: Learning and Re-learning from netbased cooperative learning discourses. In L. Cantoni & C. McLoughlin (Eds.), Proceedings of ED-MEDIA 2004 World Conference on Educational Multimedia, Hypermedia & Telecommunications. Norfolk, VA: Association for the Advancement of Computing in Education (AACE), 2004, 2720-2724.

[20] A. Kienle; C. Ritterkamp: Facilitating asynchronous discussions in learning communities - The impact of moderation strategies. Accepted for The International Journal on Behaviour & Information Technology, 2006.

Cooperative Systems Design
P. Hassanaly et al. (Eds.)
IOS Press, 2006

Five Levels of Collaboration – Five Levels of ICT Support?

Heini KORPILAHTI and Toni KOSKINEN

Software Business and Engineering Institute, Helsinki University of Technology,
Finland

Abstract. The research work presented in this paper employs the awareness evaluation model developed by Neale, Carrol, and Rosson [1]. The model presents five collaboration levels based on how closely the tasks of different persons are coupled together. These levels are light-weight interaction, information sharing, coordination, collaboration, and cooperation. We applied the model in distributed process industry environment. Our goal was to identify the existing collaboration situations and place them to different categories of the model. In addition, we viewed these different collaboration levels from the standpoint ICT-mediated collaboration support. This meant that we identified both the requirements for ICT-mediated collaboration support and applications capable of fulfilling the requirements set by the interaction situations. As a result we noticed that one of the characteristics of interaction situations classified into these categories is a constant switching of collaboration levels. By this we mean that during interaction situations people are seamlessly shifting from one level to another. When reflecting this finding in ICT support, it seems to indicate that in the same way the support for higher collaboration levels should make possible seamless transitions from one level to another. More detailed results are presented in the paper.

Keywords: Awareness Evaluation model, work coupling, ICT support

Introduction

Computer-based support for distributed work has been discussed in the areas of CSCW research and groupware for many years. The topic has remained in focus because of the complexity of the phenomenon. Distributed collaboration between people can take various forms and it can be classified into many different categories according to time, location, the purpose of the collaboration, the organisational position, and so on. Nowadays, applications supporting distributed interaction and collaboration are appearing everywhere. People are interacting through computer-mediated communication channels both in work and leisure-time contexts. At the same time, applications meant to support work contexts are adapting some of the features that were originally designed for leisure-time contexts and vice versa.

The research work presented in this paper employs the awareness evaluation model developed by Neale, Carrol, and Rosson [1]. The awareness evaluation model presents five levels of collaboration based on how tightly the tasks of different people are coupled together. We are utilising the model in analyses of a distributed process control environment, particularly in analysing interaction situations and the possibilities of providing ICT-based support to them at the different levels presented in the model. Regarding ICT-based support, Poltrock and Grudin [2] have identified three categories of groupware: communication support, information-sharing, and coordination. These categories match Neale at al's categories of different collaboration levels quite closely. Communication support includes technologies such as email, videoconferencing, instant messaging, and VoIP. Applications utilising these technologies are increasing rapidly as new ways of utilising communication support are introduced. Information-sharing has been around for a while. It covers tools such as document management and sharing systems, which are the best-known applications in this category. Support for coordination aims to capture and coordinate the work flows of distributed groups. The most traditional applications in this category are work flow management systems. However, in many cases the work processes are not completely formal and therefore support for ad hoc coordination is also required. In these situations instant messaging tools have assumed a significant role in fulfilling coordination needs.

The goals of the study were, first of all, to analyse the applicability of the awareness evaluation model in classifying the interaction situations of the process control environment into the different work coupling levels of the model. In order to do this we identified the existing interaction situations and placed them into the different levels of work coupling of the awareness evaluation model.

Second, and perhaps as a main research goal, our aim was to include the ICT support viewpoint in the analysis of identified interaction situations. This meant that we identified both the requirements for ICT-mediated collaboration support and applications capable of fulfilling the requirements set by the interaction situations. Since this interaction happens mainly in distributed settings, the role of ICT as a mediator of information is emphasised. By choosing suitable tools for different interaction situations, the efficiency of co-located work is improved. Although our analysis was carried out within process industries, at least some of the results can be applied to other industrial domains as well.

While the work was being carried out we found out that there were some complementary factors that could be taken into account when utilising the awareness evaluation model in the way it has been applied in our study. Although this was not our actual research goal, in the final chapters we will present these findings as well.

As mentioned earlier, the research environment of the study is process control (see Figure 1). During the later paragraphs of the paper we will present a detailed description of the interaction situations in this environment. In order to improve understanding of those situations, we will present the environment briefly in the following chapters.

The process control environment is demanding in many ways. As a result of the complex work environment, a single person cannot create a complete overview of the situations at hand. Therefore work requires constant collaboration between different, often geographically distributed stakeholders. Decisions are based on distributed knowledge sources, such as one's own experience and information provided by systems and other persons. The importance of knowledge and expertise in process control is obvious, for various reasons: production processes are not fully predictable; a great proportion of the decisions needs to be made in real time; the distances between control rooms are long, and uninterrupted production is carried out in shifts.

Figure 1. A modern control room environment and a view of a distant expert centre. The expert centre can take on some of the responsibilities related to process monitoring or problem-solving.

Traditionally, process control and maintenance have been conducted locally as on-site operations, but currently the responsibilities and corresponding tasks are being re-organised. As a result of the outsourcing of some parts of the process control work, maintenance and expert services can now be bought from companies specialising in these areas. As before, process control and maintenance work still requires successful collaboration between different heterogeneous user groups such as operators, maintenance personnel, remote experts, supervisors, and shift foremen. However, as a consequence of recent changes these groups are not necessarily from the same organisation and may not even work in the same geographical location. In this new kind of trans-organisational and networked environment, the role of the supporting information and communication technology infrastructure is emphasised, since it plays a crucial role as a mediator of information between different stakeholders. ICT should make possible versatile, efficient, and natural interaction between distant partners and even be capable of (semi)-automatically mediating some parts of the contextual information so that decision-makers are aware of the situations at hand. Since the evolution towards network-managed production and maintenance is currently ongoing, the role and implementation of different ICT services and technologies is constantly developing. A more detailed view of the role of different stakeholders can be found in the later paragraphs of the study.

1. Awareness Evaluation Model

In recent years the concept of awareness has increased its influence on both social and technical research in CSCW. The concept of awareness originated from several workplace studies. The results of these studies indicated that collaborative work in distributed settings requires individuals to remain conscious of each other's contributions and activities. Many concepts of awareness have been introduced in the field of CSCW research. Social awareness means awareness of the social situation of the members: what they are doing, whether they are talking to someone, whether they can be disturbed, and so on. According to Tollmar et al, social awareness is a key element in our everyday work [3]. On the basis of their results, they concluded that social awareness is an essential prerequisite for good collaboration. Action awareness concerns the ability to know what other collaborators are doing. For instance, if documents are stored in a shared repository, it might be important to know whether someone is currently editing certain documents. The concept of action awareness is closely related to workspace awareness as defined by Gutwin and Greenberg [4].

The awareness evaluation model [1] utilised in this study considers awareness mainly as project work that supports group performance during complex tasks. Activities are seen as long-term endeavours directed towards major goals. To reach these goals a group needs to assign roles, negotiate, coordinate, make decisions, and so on. The above-mentioned activities fall within the concept of activity awareness [5], which is adopted from activity theory. The role of activity awareness can be seen as complementary and related to social and action awareness [6]. Activity awareness requires a person to be aware of other people's goals, situations, constraints, etc. In order to coordinate group collaboration efficiently, individuals need to manage deadlines, resources, work practices, social roles, and so on.

Neale et al presented the awareness evaluation model in their paper "Evaluating Computer-Supported Cooperative Work: Models and Frameworks" [1]. The model was developed for the purpose of evaluating distributed CSCW systems supporting both asynchronous and synchronous interaction. The awareness evaluation model presents five levels of collaboration that are defined on the basis of the level of work coupling. These levels are light-weight interaction, information sharing, coordination, collaboration, and cooperation. As the work coupling or the interdependencies between tasks rises, the work supposedly also requires more information sharing and communication and so the level of collaboration changes. Communication and collaboration require the people involved to have a shared understanding of the situation and the work to be done. In the awareness evaluation model this requirement is presented through the concepts of context, awareness, and common ground. As work gets more tightly coupled and we move to higher levels of collaboration, the need for awareness of the doings of the other actors also becomes more important. This awareness and shared understanding forms the common ground needed.

Neale et al [1] describe the different levels of work coupling as follows: activities at the light-weight interaction level are only loosely tied to the work objectives. During light-weight interaction useful work-related issues are shared as a part of a more versatile everyday flow of information that can include details, for example, about people's lives and current work situations. This information helps people both to understand other's behaviour as group and work community members and to support them when they need to find information sources and follow approved work methods.

Information sharing can be unidirectional or occur in inform-acknowledge pairs. As shared information clearly has a sender and receiver, this implies that there also exists a reason why the information is being shared and that the people participating know the reason. This reason probably has a connection to the task at hand, which separates information sharing from light-weight interaction. During information sharing important work-related background issues are shared and they help people to understand the relationships between their tasks and the tasks of the others.

At the coordination level work tasks start to have clear interdependencies and so it is necessary to coordinate them in order to keep the group functional and complete other shared activities. Distributed work requires members to coordinate activities, the content of work, and related work processes. The amount of coordination depends on how aware people are about the discussions, tasks, processes, and other work-related details.

The collaboration level of work coupling involves group members who are working towards a common goal. Although the work is carried out independently, the tasks have a high degree of interdependence. At the collaboration level people need to share goals and tasks and actively share knowledge.

At the cooperation level people have shared goals, common plans, and shared tasks. Many of the tasks are carried out concurrently as shared activities. Tightly coupled tasks are usually ill-structured, requiring constant reassessment of priorities and goals, which results in a high demand for face-to-face interaction and regular personal contacts related to how to proceed.

In order to perform work coupling at different levels, people need to manage contextual factors that underlie collaborative activities. A context enables people to understand and organise their work as a part of the group's effort to reach its goals. It has been stated that sharing information about one another's current work context is a core mechanism for initiating a proper conversation between cooperating partners [7]. In face-to-face situations people can manage contexts quite easily, as they can reach conclusions on the basis of a rich set of available information sources. However, contexts have proven to be difficult to manage in distributed settings, since the information is often fragmented or not even available.

2. ICT-mediated Collaboration Support in Process Control

Production and maintenance staff use process control systems as tools to automate process functions and gather and present information to be used in decision-making. Nowadays, the role of these systems is to automate, inform, store, and network [8]. Process control systems have often acted as internal communication media within organisations. However, the outsourcing of functions and tasks has led to situations where there is a need to cooperate in trans-organisational settings. Therefore tools for exchanging expertise and knowledge across organisational boundaries are becoming more common. Recent theories of organisational memory are increasingly pointing out that not all knowledge can be made explicit or stored in a system [9]. Therefore the role of information technology is to make recorded knowledge retrievable or, in distributed settings, make individuals with knowledge increasingly accessible [10]. In process control this means that part of the knowledge accumulates in the different activities of a control system and therefore is available for decision support purposes [11]. However, a significant part of this expertise cannot easily be stored in an explicit form and therefore real-time co-operation and the exchange of thoughts between people is required. In the following paragraph we will briefly present some everyday collaboration tools found in the process control environment.

Since control rooms are nowadays silent office-like facilities they are also equipped with the usual office communication tools, such as email, internet, phones, and so on. These tools are also utilised for communication purposes. However, modern networking technology has opened up new possibilities for transferring and displaying process-related information in distributed settings. The most widely-used tools supporting the exchange of information and knowledge are electronic diaries and remote support connections. Electronic diaries are used as discussion and information exchange tools mainly within organisations. They enable people to inform other shifts and stakeholders about the main incidents related to operations and maintenance. In addition, they can be used for decision support purposes in order to solve similar situations at a later date. Remote support connections are usually provided by suppliers of process equipment and automation or, in some cases, they can be provided as internal corporate-level ICT services. Through these networks, the local sites are connected to remote expert centres or other plants and all the participants have the same information available, a different situation than in the case of local control rooms. These connections are nowadays utilised for monitoring and problem-solving purposes.

In many ways the collaborative aspects of process control systems are just beginning to emerge. As the working environment requires a great amount of skills and knowledge from the humans that are carrying out the process control, interaction between the human actors in the context increases in importance. The interaction between people happens more often through the supporting and integrated information and communication technology (ICT) that provides the necessary communication channels [8]. The collaboration network can include closely or loosely connected external participants in the process control community interacting with the socio-technical system. A major part of this interaction is conducted in a formal and pre-determined way, but, as the requirements for dealing with more dynamic and abstract issues are constantly increasing, support for non-formal modes of interaction and collaboration between people is needed.

3. Research Methods and Environment of the Study

This study is part of an ongoing research project called TechMedia (Technology Mediated Knowledge Services for Industry), which aims at discovering new possibilities for knowledge-based services in the process control environment. [12] These services are produced in a network of cooperating organisations and information sharing between remote parties is one of the basic elements for any intended development. This has naturally defined the target environment and perspective of our work.

3.1. Data and Methods

The empirical part of the paper is based on interview and observation materials gathered from the Finnish process industry and affiliated service providers. Data were gathered from two different types of environments, namely from specialist organisations (expert centres) that sell knowledge services to their customers and from customer side process plants, including pulp mills and power plants. The interviews were carried out by using semi-formal ethnographic interviews [13] that were partially steered by using a predefined list of topics. These topics included the current working environment, communication, tools, artifacts, decision-making, problem-solving, and collaboration-related issues.

Target groups at plant sites included process plant supervisors (N=3), control personnel (N=18) and maintenance personnel (N=14). At the expert centres, service managers (N=5) and specialists (N=11) were interviewed. Interviewees from both process plants and expert organisations were chosen on the basis of the fact that they had worked together and a client-service provider relationship existed. With the exception of the interviews with the management, the interviews were held in real working environments. This made it possible to observe the work in its context and see what kinds of tools and artifacts were used. Whenever necessary we also asked interviewees to demonstrate the use of the tools and artifacts in order to improve our understanding of practical aspects of how they were utilised.

Data analysis included three phases. All the data were first analysed qualitatively according to the predefined interview topics and an affinity diagram was created in order to form an overview of the environment studied. This overview was then further elaborated by analysing the structure of the collaborative network in question. We decided to use interaction flow models [14] to visualise the network-related findings such as stakeholder groups, tasks, and communication. Flow models suited our purposes well as they concentrate on the structure and functioning of collaborative networks of people. They also bring out needs and problems in the interaction which indicate potential for further improvements. Flow models were first created separately for all the persons interviewed and then combined, first to represent different groups and then to represent the whole network. The last phase of the analysis concentrated on the ICT support. To be able to identify support-related factors, we needed to analyse the collaboration in a more structured and detailed manner. For this purpose we used Neale et al's model, which helped us to find different aspects of the collaboration. On the basis of the different levels of the model, we looked for different kinds of interaction situations, the requirements that these situations posed for tool support, and finally tools that matched the requirements.

For more information about the data-gathering and how we have used interaction diagrams in our research see the previous papers [15] and [16].

3.2. Target Environment

The main collaborating groups in our target environment are the experts at expert centres and employees responsible for process control in the client production plant (see Figure 2). Remote collaboration also exists inside the main groups as experts can be located in different offices and production plants, besides being distributed work environments internally, can also collaborate with other plants.

At the production plant there are usually 3-5 workers on one shift working in the control room(s). These operators are led by a shift foreman and together they monitor the production process using several screens and make any necessary adjustments to process steering values and production material feeds. Operators also make minor repairs to the systems and participate in larger repairs and revisions that are the responsibility of the maintenance crew.

Groups working at production plants focus on short-term process control situations. Therefore local personnel do not always have time to consider different improvement possibilities on a longer time scale. This type of analysis, which often also falls outside the core competencies of production plant employees, is nowadays being offered by remote expert centres. They analyse the operation of the plant from a broader perspective and additionally are able to include the latest knowledge obtained from different production sites that they work with.

In our case these expert organisations are part of larger corporations whose primary products are process control and information systems and automation delivery. Expert services are based on this know-how accumulated during the development of primary products and are seen as one possible way for these organisations to continuously broaden their product range. The services they offer include e.g. remote support for process monitoring, process optimisation, problem-solving, maintenance, training, and process planning. Furthermore, these remote experts can form dynamic expertise networks that can be gathered and utilised in problem-solving situations.

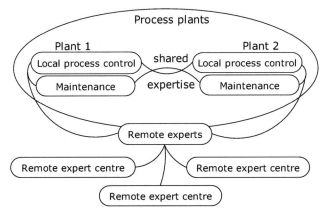

Figure 2. Collaborating groups

The whole concept of remote experts and expert centres is relatively new and therefore the services are constantly evolving. Nowadays, the functions of process expert centres and automation suppliers are based on service agreements between production sites and expert centres. Agreements are often expressed in the form of target values for different process values or production levels and the profit for the service provider is partly tied to the extent to which the objectives are reached. Commonly, the agreed approach for collaboration with the client plant includes periodic reporting of the plant's performance, process optimisation based on this reporting, and helping local production personnel with problematic situations [12, 15 and 16]. Process optimisation-related suggestions can result in further development activities or projects. When this additional work requires more resources than are included in service agreements, these activities are agreed via separate contracts.

When asked about the cooperation with their clients, the expert centre workers stressed the importance of the long-time customer relationship that is needed to build trust between the cooperating parties. The experts felt that it was required of them to prove their competence and know-how before all the client employees involved were ready to fully participate. To be able to offer credible solutions to their clients, experts need as much contextual information from the factory as possible. Some of this information is transferred automatically to expert centres through remote connections to the client's automation system and analysis tools, but an equally large portion of information about what is happening, what decisions are made, what actions are carried out, and what the underlying reasons for changes are is still missing. At the moment experts have to solve these challenges mainly by themselves and their activeness and social skills play a crucial role in getting information, creating cooperation relationships, and maintaining these relationships.

Challenges for information-sharing and storing also appeared elsewhere in the network, both within organisations and between them. Both experts and plant personnel felt that some problems were likely to be solved again and again as the solutions were not communicated in a form accessible to everybody. On the plant side of the network this was also partly due to the work culture. People have been doing the same job for such a long time that there is a great deal of know-how that is only stored in the minds of the workers. Problems, when they arise, are traditionally discussed and solved without the information getting stored or shared inside the factory, let alone with the remote experts.

4. Support for Distributed Work According to Categories Presented in the Awareness Evaluation Model

4.1. Light-Weight Interaction

Light-weight interaction is an important part of the framework in which collaboration occurs. When people are working together in the same place light-weight interaction is a natural part of the social processes that occur. People effortlessly manage the non-structured information that they gather from several sources and combine it in a way that is useful to them and increases their awareness of the surrounding situation. Remote collaboration changes the situation and the support for interaction inevitably creates a certain unnaturalness when compared to face-to-face interaction.

The challenge for supporting light-weight interaction is that the most suitable form of information and interaction procedures is difficult to define when the tool is supposed to offer support for social processes. One possible approach is to offer solutions where the form and content of the shared information is as flexible as possible. If presented with a wide range of different kinds of information, users are encouraged to browse the information and pick whatever seems interesting or useful to them. The same requirement for flexibility also applies to support for communication. Users should have the chance to throw out comments and questions to the whole group or work community without pointing out exactly who should provide the answers. This is important since, when interacting at this level, people do not necessarily know who has the information they need, who is going to use the information they are sharing, or how it is going to be used.

The implementation of support can take an informal approach and be based on, for example, bulletin boards, intranets, portals, or email lists. A more formal approach would be to build on project databases or information storage. In both cases support for light-weight interaction should be integrated with other tools and work practices. In this way it can be integrated into the main tasks of the users and offer a quick overview of the situation without requiring too many user resources.

Informal information channels support the exchange of experiences and perceptions related to the work and offer the possibility of making the work community more visible. A more passive approach is to concentrate on efficiently sharing the existing information that, from the technological perspective, can easily be shared. For example, distributing existing documents to a wider audience through a project database would improve the activity awareness of people and also support learning and problem-solving based on the material gathered. This approach can be further improved through facilitating information searching, informing people about new and potentially useful documents, and attaching some less formal information to documents.

In the process control environment, support for sharing work community-related information through communication networks is missing and, as a result, light-weight interaction between the organisations is limited and occurs randomly. This lack of contextual information is noticed especially by expert centre workers who need to understand the situation at the client's site in order to be able to make accurate interpretations during problem-solving situations and process improvement efforts.

At the production sites the process control work requires shifts working together to have a clearly shared view of the state of their work and, as a result, verbal communication has assumed a central role in the work culture. Problems arise when not all the information is communicated between shifts or between control and maintenance personnel. The need for more extensive support for communication has been noticed by local personnel, as well as automation system manufacturers, and nowadays features such as experience repositories and ways of commenting on stored information entries are being added to the systems as they are increasingly developed towards being all-inclusive information and communication solutions.

4.2. Information Sharing

Information sharing in a distributed work environment is more closely task-related than light-weight interaction. This means that interaction occurs more directly between people and that they have a clearer idea about how the information is going to be used, which may affect the way that shared artifacts are created. According to Neale et al's definition, information sharing can be unidirectional or occur in inform-acknowledge pairs. Examples of generic interaction situations of this kind include reporting and informing activities concerning work-related issues. The characteristics of information sharing imply that the required support should include tools to discuss the format of artifacts and an information channel for the transfer of these artifacts. Tools that offer the required interaction channel can, to a great extent, be the same tools that support light-weight interaction, e.g. email, bulletin boards, and document storage. Additionally, when interaction happens in real-time distributed work environments inform-acknowledge activity can occur within a tighter time frame than any interaction at the light-weight level. In these kinds of situations the tools should also inform recipients when the information becomes available – preferably automatically. In practice this can be mediated through phone conversations, instant messages, and, in mobile settings, by short text messages.

In process control remote cooperation most often happens at the information-sharing level of the awareness evaluation model. Expert centre workers use the data from a client's automation system and trend tools to analyse plants' processes. The results of analysis and recommendations are then delivered to clients in the form of reports. Feedback from the documents delivered is valuable to the experts and sometimes meetings are organised to discuss the reports together with the clients. Feedback enables experts to estimate how accurate their conclusions about the situations have been and thus develop their services further. However, a more common approach is that the clients go through the report and, on the basis of its content, decide which modifications are needed. As a result experts do not always get to know about all the changes that may affect their future analysis.

For the control room personnel the most important tool for information sharing is the process diary. This diary is regularly filled with specific information about what has happened in the process and what kinds of actions have been taken. This information forms a process history that has a central role in information sharing among different groups at the plant, mediating discussion about process-related topics and offering one kind of organisational memory that can be used when solving recurring problems.

4.3. Coordination

Work at coordination level consists of tasks that can be done independently as long as different resources and work products are coordinated efficiently. Interaction situations at coordination level include communication about division of the tasks and responsibilities, following the progress and status of work and delivering the work products to others. Requests for further modifications on delivered work products can result in repetition of these stages. Based on an article by Malone and Crowston [17] coordination can be carried out based on goal-relevant interdependencies between activities. Interdependences are analyzed in terms of common objects that are shared and as a result need coordination. The reason for coordination can be that some objects are needed as a prerequisite to the next activity or that the objects or resources are needed for several activities possibly even at the same time. This kind of ordering, synchronizing activities or allocating resources can be done with calendars and workflow tools. As the work is done independently it is important that participants have a shared vision about what is expected as an outcome. Videoconferencing tools can be used for this purpose when new work phases are launched.

Support for coordination gets more complicated if the situation requires also understanding and awareness of the work of others. This can be the case when the shared object (e.g. document) by itself can not mediate all the needed information or the shared object can not be used to mediate the information at all and a substitute object is needed. In this type of situation support should include visualisation of work status and possibility to mediate the information missing from the actual work product.

In previous studies [18] it has been noticed that through increasing awareness in distributed teams the need for organized coordination activities reduces. So instead of just supporting coordination activities with the traditional groupware tools like group calendars and workflow tools one should address the awareness in distributed settings as well – particularly the activity awareness concept. Nowadays, perhaps the most powerful tools for increasing awareness in distributed work environments are instant messaging tools. They have capabilities to mediate status information (location and situation-related status), deliver instant messages, have phone conversations (VoIP), share documents, and organize teleconferences and group chats. This kind of realtime support may also be useful when coordination needs to be carried on shorter time perspective than pre-defined long term coordination. For example in some problem solving situations the workers need to quickly form an understanding on how the needed activities are divided among them. In many cases work coupling in these situations gets tighter and work is done on collaboration or even cooperation level.

Coordination in our target environment is built in the work practices. The general framework for coordination is pre-defined in the contracts between the process plant and the expert services provider. These contracts define how often experts report their findings and what are the most important production process variables that the collaboration aims to improve. After this the expert centre tries to support the work at the plant and find the possible improvements needed for attaining the goals. Planning and realizing the improvements becomes the task that requires most of the coordination. Things like when the improvements are realised, in which order and by whom the work is done needs to be decided and communicated. Usually some of the changes require the plant to be run down before the work can be done. This means that repairs are scheduled according the plant's maintenance plan.

4.4. Collaboration

In collaboration level the distributed team members work towards shared goals. In these situations the role of instant messaging tools is emphasized. They provide various ways to reach other team members whether they are available or not. Instant messaging tools are also scalable, so they can be used through mobile terminals as well. According to recent studies [19] instant messaging tools provide more reliable reachability of persons than for instance phone. This is due to the fact that instant messengers do not require you to answer to the contact requests instantly. Although you receive the notification of contact request as it occurs, you can respond to the request when it suits to your work situation.

In our target environment many of the collaboration level activities are carried out at the client site where most of the needed information and people are located. Example of collaboration level activity is analysis work performed when the client orders a more detailed report on a specific subject. Since expert services are quite new concept for the companies in this branch of industry, there exist no specific tools to support the work at collaboration level. Some videoconferencing applications have been introduced among the expert centres but as they were found out to be too unreliable and difficult to use they have not gained wider popularity as a collaboration tool with the client sites.

When considering the collaboration level support one should take into account that the work of experts as well as local personnel is not just distributed but mobile in nature as well. Therefore the videoconferencing tools are not the ideal solution considering the collaboration on daily basis. Our suggestion would be to utilize instant messaging tools that are relatively simple and scalable to mobile devices as well. For instance, in acute problem solving situations instant messaging tools would enable quick creation of ad-hoc virtual teams that could be utilized in solving the problem.

4.5. Cooperation

Cooperation level includes the highest level of work coupling. Shared tasks require significant amount of discussion among the participants in order to proceed with the work and many of the activities are carried out concurrently. Tasks that require cooperation are mostly carried out face to face since usually they require or at least benefit from the multimodal interaction between different team members. Creators of the awareness evaluation model state that the cooperation level activities are poorly supported by current technologies and to support cooperation in distributed settings is even more challenging. This is a consequence of the fact that the activities meant to be supported are in most cases quite ill structured and the work situation is constantly assessed and redirected.

From technological perspective shared desktops combined with advanced videoconferencing tools can provide support for cooperation. However this technology is not easily scalable and it requires expensive investments on equipment in each team member location. In addition, even with the latest videoconferencing technology, the interaction is not nearly as naturalistic as in face to face situations. Nowadays, cooperation in distributed settings on a regular basis is rare, due to the technological limitations and the fact that often it is not the most efficient way to organize cooperation level activities. This is true also in our case environment where cooperation occurs mostly in local settings. An example of this kind of local cooperation is the customisation of new process software that is an important part of automation deliveries and requires close interaction between the experts and the local personnel.

5. Conclusions and Discussion

On the basis of our experiences, it can be stated that the awareness evaluation model seems to offer an interesting way to study the collaboration characteristics of the work environment. It seems that the work coupling levels presented in the awareness evaluation model provide rather accurate predefined categories to model the interaction situations of process industries. As described in Section 4, the different collaboration levels or characteristics of the levels can be identified from the target environment as well. This indicates that the awareness evaluation model can bring structure to the modelling of complex distributed work environments. Our assumption is that the importance of the collaboration and cooperation levels of work coupling would have been greater if we had focused more on work coupling within the process plant instead of mainly focusing on the collaboration between expert centres and the production plant.

During the identification of interaction situations and while classifying them into different collaboration levels, we noticed some differences regarding the role of each level. At least in the process control environment, it seems that the two lowest levels of collaboration have an active role in most interaction situations. They provide a basis for collaboration taking place in interaction situations classified under the categories of coordination, collaboration, and cooperation. We also noticed that one of the characteristics of interaction situations classified into the previously-mentioned categories is a constant switching of collaboration levels. By this we mean that during interaction situations people are seamlessly shifting from one level to another. When reflecting this finding in ICT support, it seems to indicate that in the same way the support for higher collaboration levels should make possible seamless transitions from one level to another.

We consider that the awareness evaluation model can support the analysis and design of ICT support. Regarding ICT support, we noticed that a certain tool cannot be placed on a specific level of work coupling. Different tools, depending on their purpose of use, can provide support for work coupling on several levels. If a tool provides an interactive communication channel between different stakeholders it is likely to support collaboration on multiple levels as well. Tools that are designed for a specific purpose are not as flexible in terms of level-switching. Tools providing a collaboration channel can be used in very different ways. For instance, the most recent instant messaging tools can provide support for all five levels of work coupling. The nature of the tasks, combined with the technical features of the ICT support, are the most decisive factors when considering how the ICT tools could be placed on different levels of work coupling. When considering the ICT support for distributed collaboration one should also notice that ICT support sometimes actually reduces the frequency of collaboration. Lack of support may result in people being required to interact frequently on issues that should belong under the light-weight interaction or information-sharing categories. With improved ICT support these interaction situations could be reduced or even replaced with, for instance, electronic notice and bulletin boards. In some cases this may improve the allocation of work resources, but it should be noticed that regular and interactive collaboration situations are irreplaceable, since they are essential when building trust, a feeling of community, and awareness among distributed stakeholders.

When applying this model in the way described in this paper it could be useful to pay attention to the fact that, depending on the case, the importance of the different work coupling levels varies. It is likely that some levels of the awareness evaluation model will be more important than others, depending on the work environment, goals, group size, etc. These issues should be taken into account when designing or considering ICT support for distributed work environments. Another issue that could be taken into account when applying this model is the heterogeneity of the group. What are the individual differences within a group in terms of education, work experience, and skills? Additionally, it is important to know whether the goals of the group are similarly important to all group members. In our case study the goals of both the process plant personnel and experts were similar: to keep the production process up and running and improve the quality of the production. However, the process plant personnel used 100% of their working time to fulfil this goal, compared with the experts' 10%. Our assumption is that by taking into account these complementary factors the usefulness and the accuracy of the model increases.

Acknowledgements

The study presented in this paper is a part of the Technology Mediated Knowledge Services for Distributed Work Environments research project (TechMedia). The project is funded by the National Technology Development Centre of Finland (TEKES) and the industrial partners in the project (Metso Corporation, Metso Automation, Metso Paper, Fortum Service, Jyväskylä Science Park, and RecIT Solutions). We would like to thank all members of the research project for participating in discussions related to the topics presented in this paper.

References

[1]   Neale, D.C., Carroll, J.M., and Rosson, M.B. (2004). Evaluating Computer-Supported Cooperative Work: Models and Frameworks. In Proceedings of the CSCW'04, Chicago,Illinois,USA, November 6-10, 2004.
[2]   Poltrock S.E., and Grudin, J. (1999). CSCW, Groupware and Workflow: Experiences, State of Art, and Future Trends. ACM CHI'99 Tutorial, ISBN: 1-58113-158-5, 120-121.
[3]   Tollmar, K., Sandor O., and Schömer A. (1996). Supporting Social Awareness @ Work Design and Experience, Proceedings of the 1996 ACM conference on Computer supported cooperative work, p.298-307, November 16-20, 1996, Boston, Massachusetts, United States.
[4]   Gutwin, C., and Greenberg, S. (1996). Workspace awareness for groupware. In: Proceedings of the ACM CHI '96 Conference on Human Factors in Computing Systems (Companion). Association for Computing Machinery, NewYork, pp. 208–209.

[5]   Carroll, J.M., Neale, D.C., Isenhour, P.L., Rosson, M.B. and McCrickard, D.S. (2003). Notification and Awareness: Synchronizing task-oriented collaborative activity. International Journal of Human-Computer Studies, 58 (5), 605-632. Elsevier, 2003.

[6]   Ganoe, C. H., Somervell, J. P., Neale, D. C., Isenhour, P. L., Carroll, J. M., Rosson, M. B., and McCrickard, D. S. (2003). Classroom BRIDGE: Using collaborative public and desktop timelines to support activity awareness. In Proceedings of the ACM '03 Symposium on User Interface Software and Technology (UIST) (pp. 21-30). New York: Association for Computing Machinery.

[7]   Bardram, J., and Hansen, T. (2004). The AWARE architecture: supporting context-mediated social awareness in mobile cooperation. In Proceedings of the 2004 ACM conference on Computer supported cooperative work table of contents, Chicago, Illinois, USA, p. 192 – 201, 2004.

[8]   Paunonen, H., Oksanen, J., Nieminen, M., Koskinen, T., and Kovalainen, M. Collaborative Interaction in Process Control. In P. Karwowski (Ed.), 2nd Edition of the International Encyclopedia of Ergonomics and Human Factors, Taylor & Francis, (in Press).

[9]   Ackerman, M., Pipek, V., and Wulf, V. (Ed.) (2003). Sharing expertise: beyond knowledge management. Cambridge, MA: MIT Press, 2003., 418.

[10] Ackerman, M. (1998). Augmenting Organizational Memory: A Field Study of Answer Garden. In ACM Transactions on Information Systems (TOIS), 16 (3), 1998, p. 203-224.

[11] Paunonen, H., and Oksanen, J. (1998) Informating Process Control Systems – Knowledge-Based operation Support. In 7th IFAC/IFIP/IFORS/IEA Symposium on analysis, design and evaluation of man-machine systems. September 16-18., Kyoto, Japan, 1998.

[12] Koskinen, T., Korpilahti, H., Paunonen, H., Oksanen, J. and Kovalainen, M. (2004). Contextual Inquiry into On-line Remote Expert Services in Process Control. In: Proceedings of the IFAC/IFIP/IFORS/IEA Symposium; Analysis, Design and Evaluation of Human-Machine Systems. September 7-9, 2004, Atlanta, USA.

[13] Anschuetz, L., and Rosenbaum S. (2003). Ethnographic interviews guide design of ford vehicles website. In: CHI '03 extended abstracts on Human factors in computer systems, Ft. Lauderdale, Florida, USA, April 05-10, 2003.

[14] Beyer, H. and K. Holtzblatt (1998). Contextual Design: Defining Customer-Centered Systems. Morgan Kaufmann Publishers, San Francisco.

[15] Koskinen, T., Jormanainen, E., Korpilahti, H., and Nieminen, M. (2004). Grounding Design Work on Scenarios: User-Centred Design Framework in the Finnish Process Industry. In Proceedings of the HAAMAHA'04, Galway,Ireland, August 25-27, 2004.

[16] Nieminen, M., Koskinen, T., Korpilahti, H., and Jormanainen, E. (2004). Context Validation with Interaction Diagrams – Early Design Support for Collaborative Process Control Applications. In Proceedings of the HAAMAHA'04, Galway,Ireland, August 25-27, 2004.

[17] Malone, T.W. and Crowston, K. (1990). What is Coordination Theory and how Can It Help Design Cooperative Work Systems? In Proceeding of the CSCW 90.

[18] Dourish, P., and Bellotti, V. (1992). Awareness and coordination in shared workspaces. In Proceedings of the ACM CSCW '92 Conference on Computer Supported Cooperative Work (pp. 107-113). New York: Association for Computing Machinery.

[19] Isaacs, E. (2003). A closer look at the our common wisdom, ACM QUEUE, November 2003.

Cooperative Systems Design
P. Hassanaly et al. (Eds.)
IOS Press, 2006

A thin mobile client for a groupware application

Kiran MADALA, Ivan TOMEK, Elhadi SHAKSHUKI, Rick GILES
kiran.madala@acadiau.ca, ivan.tomek@acadiau.ca,
elhadi.shakshuki@acadiau.ca, rick.giles@acadiau.ca
Jodrey School of Computer Science
Acadia University, Wolfville, Nova Scotia, Canada

Abstract. Until recently, desktop clients were sufficient platforms for running groupware. The dramatic increase in the use of mobile devices, user mobility and the growth of sophistication of device resources now requires the exploration of alternative clients running on devices such as PDAs and mobile phones. This paper describes our exploration of a BlackBerry thin client for an open source groupware application called the Collaborative Virtual Workspace (CVW). It outlines our development process and implementation and the challenges that we encountered, and outlines our plans for future work.

Keywords: Mobile groupware client, Collaboration, CVW

Introduction

Collaborative software traditionally focuses on client-server applications with desktop clients. In the last few years, however, several developments have created pressure to develop clients on mobile devices such as laptops, PDAs (Personal Digital Assistants), and mobile phones. These stimuli include increasing globalization and mobility of workforce, explosive growth in the use of mobile devices, and their increasing sophistication. Increasing connectivity, higher resolution and better displays, built-in Web browsers, faster CPUs, and larger memories are all helping to make mobile devices more competitive in a variety of uses and acceptable as work platforms.

Although interest in mobile computing is growing dramatically and represents an area with enormous research and commercial potential, relatively little information is available about development techniques, design issues, constraints, portability, architectural models, relative advantages and disadvantages of different technical approaches, user satisfaction, and other aspects of their deployment. Our work on a mobile client for CVW [1], a major open source groupware application, was motivated by all of these considerations.

Mobile clients can be divided into two categories – thin and rich clients. According to [2], a *thin client* is one in which the mobile application uses a Web browser built into the mobile device as its link to the server. Most of the work is also performed by a server that generates messages written in a markup language, and processes HTTP requests from the mobile client. A *rich client*, on the other hand, is one where the mobile device runs a client application using its processor, memory, operating system, and other software to implement operations otherwise performed by an application running on a desktop client. To explore the main development avenues, we developed both types of mobile clients for CVW - a thin client for a BlackBerry and a rich client for a PDA. (For the purpose of this work, we do not consider laptops as mobile clients because their software and hardware resources are essentially equivalent to those of desktop machines.) In the following, we focus on our thin client.

The rest of this paper is organized as follows: Section 1 places our work in the context of work on groupware applications and selected reported uses of mobile computing. Section 2 outlines the functionality of CVW and its architecture. Section 3 is dedicated to our thin client. It describes our development process and illustrates the differences between desktop and thin clients. Section 4 summarizes our experience to date, describes our present work, and outlines our plans for future. An appendix summarizes the major technologies we used and justifies the choices we made.

1. Related work

Work most relevant to this paper can be divided into four categories: general studies of mobility and collaboration, articles on development processes and design guidelines for mobile applications, groupware applications that are conceptually similar to our project, and various uses of mobile devices to support collaboration. There are many publications related to these areas and the following is only a sampling that provides a justification for the work reported here, and a bibliography for those who wish to explore these issues in more detail.

General studies of mobility and collaboration include, among others, work by Luff [3, 4], Roth [5, 6], Krebs [7], and Stanton [8]. Although this research is very useful, it is of general nature and thus marginally related to the main subject of our paper, which is an example implementation of a mobile client for groupware.

Publications related to design of mobile applications include Danesh [9], Grundy [10], Marsic [11], Jones [12], Sun [13], and Roth [14]. As noted below, we used guidelines from Shadish [15] to help us decide general window layouts, flow of control, and other essentials, but otherwise followed our own development process, largely because few related publications existed at the start of our project. Familiarity with publications of this kind is a necessary complement to the work reported here.

Among environments that are similar to CVW we include those that integrate multiple collaborative features, such as communication, shared access to documents, whiteboards, and other objects, awareness support, and possibly (but rarely) end-user extendibility. Some of the best known among these include TeamRoom [16, 17], wOrlds [18], Orbit [19], Habanero [20], BSCW [21], CURE [22], Marratech [23], Sideshow [24], Isabel [25], and Community Bar [26]. None of these applications has so far extended user support with a mobile client as far as we know. As a consequence, they don't provide a gauge for comparison and the work reported in this paper is thus pioneering in this respect.

Although we have not seen use of mobile thin clients in CVW-like applications, there have been numerous experiments with them in other areas of collaboration, mainly in education and e-business. Examples include Mandryk [27], Zurita [28], Jipping [29], Chan [30], and Bellotti [31]. The work reported in these and related publications should be studied when designing groupware clients, but does not relate directly to the project reported in this paper.

2. CVW functionality and architecture

As stated earlier, the focus of the work described here has been to prototype a thin mobile client for CVW, a major groupware application. To set background for the rest of the paper, this section describes the functionality of CVW.

CVW stands for Collaborative Virtual Workspace and is an open source application developed by MITRE Inc. It is based on the MOO [32] model, and presents the user with a virtual environment that emulates those aspects of the physical world that are most important for collaboration. The concept was proven to be well suited for collaboration of geographically dispersed teams as well as other uses such as social communication and collaboration [33].

To get an insight into CVW principles, consider the user's experience. When users log in, they are placed in their virtual home room in a virtual building. The virtual building is divided into floors with a fixed layout of rooms whose purpose and uses are similar to those of their physical counterparts: They can be used as offices of individual team members, libraries holding collections of documents, meeting rooms, help-desk rooms, and so on[1]. Once logged in, users can use the main window (Figure 1) to perform the most common functions, and specialized windows for other functions such as moving from one room to another (if they have appropriate room access rights). They can also access CVW objects deposited in these rooms, such as documents and whiteboards, move them from one room to another, and manipulate them, again on the condition that they have permission to do that.

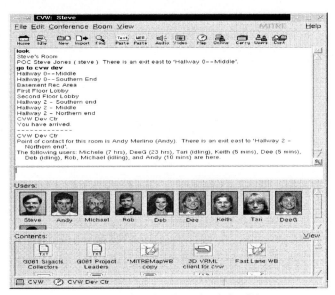

Figure 1. CVW: The main window [1]

Within the confines of a room (and to some extent across these confines), CVW offers chat-like text-based communication and provides access to documents created

---

[1] We will mostly dispense with the adjective 'virtual' from now on because all objects in CVW are virtual.

within CVW or imported from the user's platform. It also offers tools such as shared whiteboards for real-time collaboration, video and audio conferencing, acoustic phone, an event and chat recorder, and other facilities resembling physical world amenities. There is support for user groups that can be used, for example, to allocate access rights to rooms and documents, to simplify communication with multiple users, and so on. A unique feature of CVW is that users can extend it at runtime in two ways:

- Authorized users can define new types of objects and new functionality via the embedded LambdaMOO object-oriented programming language operating within the MUD Client Protocol (MCP) [34, 35]. Both LambdaMOO and MCP are parts of the environment and are directly accessible to authorized users through the client user interface.
- With some restrictions, any user can instantiate existing object templates, making it possible to create new building floors, rooms, whiteboards, documents, and other objects.

To understand the rest of the paper, it is necessary to understand the principle of *CVW architecture* (Figure 2). As already mentioned, CVW is largely a client-server application. Its clients are stand-alone applications with custom windows running on desktop computers. They interpret MCP messages from the server, and construct MCP messages from user actions and send them to the server. The server consists of a MOO server and a document server. The *MOO server* includes an interpreter of MCP commands and their LambdaMOO code definitions, and a database containing LambdaMOO object definitions and the current state of the building 'universe'. The *document server* stores 'foreign' objects such as Word or PDF documents whose types are specified in an administrator-defined registry, and serves them to clients. Clients display these documents by invoking appropriate applications. Some features, such as conferencing, operate outside this model.

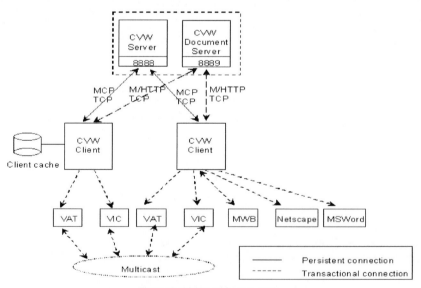

Figure 2. CVW architecture [36]

Closer examination of CVW reveals certain limitations. These include the lack of support for mobile clients, a user interface that many users don't find appealing [37], an unnaturally limited conceptual metaphor (a single 'building'), limited scalability (MITRE's documentation reports a limit of 300 simultaneously active users), unsatisfactory support for LambdaMOO programming, and no explicit support for software agents, a feature that could greatly enhance CVW's functionality. In this paper, we focus on the mobile client.

3. CVW thin client

Our development of the thin client was driven by consideration of the differences between the resources provided by desktop computers and browser-based small mobile devices. These include limited screen size, constraining input facilities, smaller memory size, slower CPU speed, and the necessity to rely on the built-in browser. After choosing the BlackBerry as our platform, we started by evaluating the importance of individual CVW functions, and the feasibility of their implementation on a thin mobile client. We also considered the fact that the project is a feasibility study and that learning about this type of device, the associated development technology, and functionality limitations are more important than building a definitive client with a complete set of CVW features. In view of these factors, we decided to start by implementing the following subset of CVW functions:

- Login.
- Floor map (navigation).
- Room contents (users and objects).
- Detailed user information.
- Object information.
- Pop up communication.
- Same room chat.
- Logout.

Certain desktop CVW functions have not been implemented either because they cannot be satisfactorily implemented with the limited resources of a mobile phones (such as display of Word documents or Excel spreadsheets) or because our focus was on exploring development, implementation, and functionality issues rather than completeness (thus we have not implemented, for example, user group support, and conferencing and 'phone' functions of CVW although phone is a natural part of a complete BlackBerry client).

After determining the functionality of our prototype, our next step was specification of the behavior of the user interface. We started by developing a state diagram showing transitions between specialized windows implementing the selected functionality (Figure 3). The diagram's states correspond to windows that implement the functions listed above.

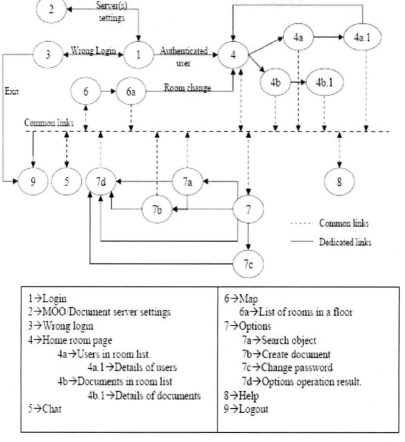

1→Login
2→MOO/Document server settings
3→Wrong login
4→Home room page
    4a→Users in room list.
        4a.1→Details of users
    4b→Documents in room list
        4b.1→Details of documents
5→Chat

6→Map
    6a→List of rooms in a floor
7→Options
    7a→Search object
    7b→Create document
    7c→Change password
    7d→Options operation result.
8→Help
9→Logout

Figure 3. Partial state diagram showing transitions among thin-client UI functions/windows

After defining the behavior, we developed sketches of individual windows following several basic principles [38, 15] including the following: compact representation in the limited display space, attention to navigation which is much more awkward on mobile devices than on desktops, look-and-feel uniformity across windows (for example, consistency of bottom-of-window command line across windows), minimization of scrolling, and the use of lists instead of graphics where necessary. This stage of development took several iterations as we consulted the subsequent proposals with other members of our development team working on related projects.

The next step was a choice of the overall architecture (Figure 4). We decided to leave the MOO and document servers unchanged and implement the thin client by creating an Application Server - an intermediate layer between the MOO Server and the thin client. To the CVW server, the Application Server appears to be a standard desktop client with which it communicates using the same HTTP and MCP protocols and commands as with desktop clients.

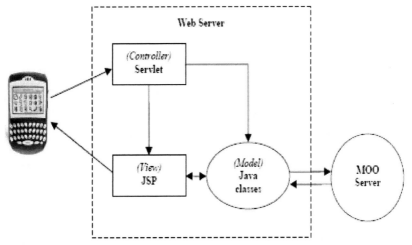

Figure 4. Thin client architecture

We then proceeded to implementation using a 7290 BlackBerry simulator [39]. Just as its physical counterpart, the simulator includes a browser that supports XHTML Basic [40, 41, 42] and our first implementation consisted of a set of an inter-linked 'hard-coded' XHTML files implementing the windows listed above, served by an Apache Tomcat HTTP server [43]. (XHTML, Apache Tomcat server, and other technologies used in the project are briefly discussed and evaluated in the Appendix.) To illustrate the nature of XHTML files, the following is an XHTML definition of the simplest CVW window, the login window:

```
<?xml version="1.0" encoding="UTF-8"?>
<!DOCTYPE html PUBLIC "-//W3C//DTD XHTML Basic 1.0//EN"
"http://www.w3.org/TR/xhtml-basic/xhtml-basic10.dtd">
<%@page pageEncoding="UTF-8" errorPage="errorpage.jsp" session="false"
isThreadSafe="true"%>
<html xmlns="http://www.w3.org/1999/xhtml" xml:lang="en">
  <head>
    <title>CVW Login</title>
    <link href="style.css" rel="stylesheet" type="text/css" />
  </head>
  <body>
   <form action="LoginHandler" method="post" onsubmit="return
ValidateForm (this)">
      <p><label> Login ID</label> <br />
      <input type="text" name="Username" size="10" /><br /></p>
      <p><label>Password</label> <br />
      <input type="password" name="Password" size="10" /></p>
      <p><input type="submit" value="Submit" class="textfont" /></p>
   </form>
    <p class = "textfont"><a href= "settings.jsp">Settings</a></p>
</body>
</html>
```

The next step after testing the hard-coded windows was full implementation of the Application Server. Its architecture is inspired by the JSP Model 2 architecture [44] and separates presentation and implementation using the Model-View-Controller pattern. The Model serves dynamic content by combining servlet and JSP technologies. JSP is used to display content, and the servlet acts as the controller and processes requests from the client. It creates beans and objects required by JSP, and decide which JSP page to forward to the client.

The principle of operation of the depicted architecture is as follows: When the user initiates an operation by clicking a button displayed by the BlackBerry browser, the BlackBerry sends the request to the Application Server, which extracts its MCP part and sends it to the MOO server. The MOO server performs the required processing, and returns one or more MCP messages to the Application Server, exactly as if it were a desktop client. For each received MCP command, the Application Server decides on an appropriate response in a manner very similar to a desktop CVW client, and generates JSP pages for the thin client if required. It then sends the generated JSP code to the BlackBerry whose browser displays the result to the user. The sequence diagram in Figure 5 gives an example of a sequence of exchanges between a thin client and the servers.

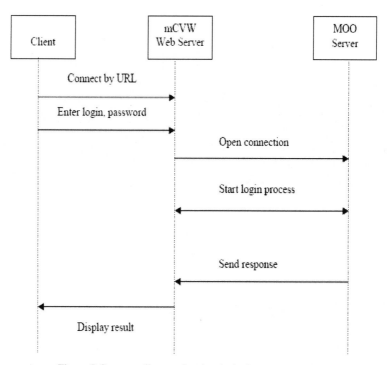

Figure 5. Sequence diagram showing the login sequence

As already mentioned, a major part of the project has been the design and implementation of the user interface. The design was dictated by several factors, including the desired functionality, the limited screen size, existing CVW client's functionality, results of our earlier semi-formal evaluation of the existing user interface, general UI design principles, and similarity to the rich client that was being designed at the same time but was subject to different constraints. To illustrate the differences between BlackBerry and desktop displays, several desktop client windows and their BlackBerry counterparts are discussed next.

Figure 6 shows the desktop map window used for navigation and its BlackBerry equivalent. Where the desktop provides two alternative displays (tree-based and graphics-based) our BlackBerry interface provides only one. Both, however, could be provided at the cost of complicating the user settings window. Figure 7a shows the BlackBerry chat window. On the desktop, the same facility is only a part of the main window (Figure 1) making navigation easier. This is a typical penalty paid for the small display area – multi-function windows on desktop clients often have to be split into more specialized windows on a mobile device, adding steps to user navigation. The 'Contents of the room' frame in the main window is another interface that had to be converted into a specialized window. In fact, to provide the same information as the desktop client two separate windows are needed in the mobile client as shown in Figures 7b and 7c. It should be noted that our user studies showed that a large proportion of users preferred specialized windows to multi-function ones and so this may not be as large a problem as it appears.

Figure 6. Building map: Desktop window (left) and BlackBerry view (right)

Figure 7. Sample BlackBerry windows: chat (a), objects in a room (b, c)

4. Conclusions, current and future work

The main points of this paper are that current technology and usage requires complementing desktop-based groupware clients with mobile clients, and that the development process, the technologies, and user experiences are not as well understood as for desktop clients. To illustrate this, we presented experiences from the development of a prototype of one such client.

Mobile clients present several challenges. Connectivity is subject to intermittent connections, problems of connection handover, and others; we have not addressed these issues. User interfaces ported from desktops to mobile phones and PDAs require complete redesign because display areas are very small and manipulation of the user interface is quite different and more difficult. Software functionality, such as available markup language constructs in the case of thin clients, is more limited than on desktops. Hardware and software resources are much more constrained and small display size is the most important obstacle. Moreover, different mobile devices provide different hardware and software resources (for example, implementing different browsers and supporting different markup language standards) and manipulation styles, and solutions implemented on one device may not be optimal on another device, or may not work on it at all. There is also a shortage of guidelines and published experience to help in the development of new mobile clients, and insufficient usability data to support them.

Judging by our experience with CVW, groupware servers are not currently designed to accommodate a variety of client devices. As a consequence, they must either be somewhat awkwardly patched, which is a quick solution but not a scalable one, or used unchanged, or redesigned. Although we chose to use the existing server unchanged for reasons of expediency, redesign is often desirable because older servers usually have other design shortcomings, such as restrictive assumptions about auxiliary databases, network communication protocols, internal intermediate languages and their interpreters, limited extendibility and modifiability, and outdated implementation principles, such as use of implementation languages that do not support functions such as garbage collection. In a project that was a complementary part of the work reported here, we found that redesign may require starting from scratch. We re-validated the importance of certain software principles that should make further work with our server easier, in particular that good layered, modularized, pluggable design pays off.

The work described above has now been completed and the implementation tested on the BlackBerry simulator. We are presently fine tuning details of the user interface, to be followed by testing its operation on a physical BlackBerry and evaluation of its usability with several users. When this is done, we will perform a detailed comparison of rich and thin clients and formulate guidelines to help designers determine which of the two approaches is better under given device constraints for specific uses. We will then implement a more complete thin client for our new server that extends CVW functionality and modifies several of its design and implementation principles.

5. Appendix: Technologies used in the BlackBerry client

5.1. XHTML Basic

XHTML stands for eXtensible HyperText Markup language. It was introduced to replace HTML because of its cleaner and more rigorous definition than HTML.

XHTML is a w3c recommendation for Web development [45] and 'XHTML Basic' is a subset of XHTML that includes a subset of XHTML modules [46]. It is designed for browsers of low power machines such as PDAs, cell phones, and other handhelds, and does not include some XHTML features such a frames and inline style attribute [47].

XHTML is not the only markup language used on mobile devices; others include [2] HDML (Handheld Device Markup Language), WML (Wireless markup language), and C-HTML (Compact HTML). The main reasons why we chose XHTML Basic are that XHTML Basic is the basis for the specifications for both WAP2 and enhanced i-mode in the future, that leading mobile micro-browser vendors will include support for XHTML Basic in their future versions, and that XHTML Basic will be the common mobile markup language, unifying the WAP and i-mode camps.

5.2. JSP - Java Server Pages

JSP is a server-side scripting language developed for producing dynamic Web content [48]. It takes advantage of Java technology by inheriting its security and scalability. JSP applications are thus independent of cross platform constrains since they can run on any machine running a Java virtual machine. Compared to other Java Web development technologies such as applets, a JSP application doesn't need to be tested on different types of clients because it is processed on the server side. JSP is extensible in that it allows developers to define their own tags through tab libraries. This is an advantage over servlets, another Java technology for developing dynamic Web content [49].

Other available server-side languages include PHP (Personal Home Page, or PHP: Hypertext Preprocessor), ASP (Active Server pages), and CGI / Pearl. Our reasons for choosing JSP are that JSP applications are independent of cross platform constrains since they can run on any machine running a Java virtual machine and that JSP is extensible in allowing developers to define their own tags through tab libraries.

5.3. Web server - Jakarta Tomcat

Jakarta Tomcat is a free open source servlet container developed by Apache software foundation [50]. It provides an environment to run Java code on a Web server. Since it also includes a HTTP server it can function as an independent Web server [51]. Tomcat is developed using Java hence it has the advantage of running on any platform that has a Java virtual machine.

Other available Web servers include Zeus Web Server, Internet Information Services, Web sphere, and JBoss. We chose Tomcat because it is platform independent (developed in Java), provides a Java container to process Java code, provides good learning resources, and can be extended for other server-side programming languages such as PHP.

5.4. BlackBerry Simulator

The BlackBerry 7290 device Simulator 4.0 simulates a screen of 240 x 160 pixels with two types of memory (32 MB flash memory and 4 MB SRAM) [52]. The browser offers support to web scripting languages such as XHTML Mobile Profile, WML [2], Compact HTML [2], JavaScript (version 1.3 and subsets of 1.4 and 1.5), WMLScript(1.2.1) and limited support for Style Sheets [53].

References

[1]   The MITRE Corporation, "CVW Overview," [Online document], (2000 October), Available http://cvw.sourceforge.net/cvw/info/CVWOverview.php3.

[2]   Martyn Mallick, Mobile and Wireless Design Essentials, Indiana: John Wiley, 2003.

[3]   Paul Luf, Christian Heath, Mobility in Collaboration, CSCW'98, Seattle, 1998.

[4]   Paul Luff, Christian Heath, Mobility in Collaboration , Proceedings of 1996 ACM conference on Computer supportive cooperative work, pp. 354 - 363 , Boston, Massachusetts, United States, 1996.

[5]   Jörg Roth, The Resource Framework for Mobile Applications: Enabling Collaboration Between Mobile Users. International Conference on Enterprise Information Systems (ICEIS), 2003.

[6]   Jorg Roth, Seven Challenges for Developers of Mobile Groupware, CHI 2002.

[7]   Allan Meng Krebs, Ivan Marsic, Adaptive Applications for Ubiquitous Collaboration in Mobile Environments, Proceedings of the 37th Annual Hawaii International Conference on System Sciences (HICSS'04), Track 1-vol. 1, pp.100031.3, January 2004, IEEE Computer society, 2004.

[8]   Danae Stanton, Helen Neal, Designing Mobile technologies to Support Collaboration, Personal and Ubiquitous computing, vol. 7, Issue 6 (December 2003), pp.365-367, Springer-Verlag, 2003.

[9]   Arman Danesh, et al.., Geney: Designing a Collaborative Activity for the Palm Handheld Computer, CHI 2001.

[10]   John Grundy, et al., Building Multi-Device, Component-Based Thin-Client Groupware: Issues and Experiences, AUIC 2002, Melbourne, Australia.

[11]   Ivan Marsic, An Architecture for Heterogeneous Groupware Applications, ICSE 2001, Toronto, Canada.

[12]   Matt Jones, Norliza Mohd-Nazir, Kevin Boone, George Buchanan, Improving Web Interaction on Small Devices, The International Journal of Computer and Telecommunications Networking, vol. 31 , Issue 11-16 (May 1999), pp. 1129-1137, Elsevier North-Holland, Inc, 1999.

[13]   Sun Microsystems, "Applications for Mobile Information Devices," [Online document], Available HTTP: http://java.sun.com/products/midp/midpwp.pdf

[14]   Jorg Roth, The Resource Framework for Mobile Applications, ICEIS 2003, 5th International Conference on Enterprise Information Systems, April 23-26, Angers, France, vol. 4, 87-94, 2003.

[15]   Bill Shadish, "Ten commands for pocket PC user interface (Do's & Don'ts)," [Online document], (2004 November), Available http://www.pocketpcmag.com/_archives/nov04/Commandements.aspx.

[16]   M. Roseman, S. Greenberg, TeamRooms. Network places for collaboration. Proceedings of CSCW'96, 1996.

[17]   Mark Roseman, Saul Greenberg, "TeamRooms: Groupware for Shared Electronic Spaces," [Online document], Technical Report, University of Calgary, Available HTTP: http://www.markroseman.com/pubs/trchi.pdf.

[18]   William J. Tolone, Simon M. Kaplan and Geraldine Fitzpatrick, Specifying Dynamic Support for Collaborative Work within wOrlds. In Proceedings of the 1995 ACM Conference on Organizational Computing Systems (COOCS '95), pp. 55-65, Milpitas, CA, August 1995.

[19]   Tim Mansfield, Simon M. Kaplan, Geraldine Fitzpatrick, Ted Phelps, Mark Fitzpatrick, Richard Taylor, Toward locales: Supporting collaboration with Orbit. Information & Software Technology 41(6), pp.367-382, 1999.

[20]   Annie Chabert, et al., Java object-sharing in Habanero, CACM, vol. 41, no. 6, June 1998.

[21]   William Appelt, WWW Based Collaboration with the BSCW System, in Proceedings of SOFSEM'99, Springer Lecture Notes in Computer Science 1725, pp.66-78, November 26 - December 4, Milovy (Czech Republic)

[22]   Haake Haake, et al., Supporting Flexible Collaborative Distance Learning in the CURE Platform, HICSS'04, 2004.

[23]   Marratech, "Collaborating in the virtual office, or sleeping on the job?,"[Online document], Available HTTP: http://www.marratech.com/virtual.html.

[24]   Microsoft Research, "Collaborative and Multimedia Systems," [Online document], (2001 fall), Available HTTP: http://research.microsoft.com/coet/.

[25]   Juan Quemada et al., Isabel, A CSCW Application for the Distribution of Events, COST 237 Workshop.

[26]   Gregor McEwan, Saul Greenberg, Supporting Social Worlds with the Community Bar, Group 2005, Sanibel Island

[27]   Regan L. Mandryk, et al., "Supporting Children's Collaboration Across Handheld Computers," [Online document], [CHI 2001], Available HTTP: http://www.edgelab.ca/geney/chi2001_handheld.pdf.

[28]   Gustavo Zurita, Miguel Nussbaum, Computer Supported Collaborative Learning Using Wirelessly Interconnected Handheld Computers, Computers & Education, vol. 42 , Issue 3 (April 2004), pp.289-314, Elsevier Science Ltd., 2004.

[29]   Michael J Jipping, et al., Using Handheld Computers in the Classroom: Laboratories and Collaboration on Handheld machines, SIGCSE BULL. pp. 169-173, 2001.

[30] S. Chan, X. Fang., Brzezinski, Jack., Y. Zhou, S. Xu, and J. Lam, Usability For MobileCommerce Across Multiple Form Factors, Journal of Electronic Commerce Research, 3(3), 2002.
[31] V. Bellotti, S. Bly, Walking away from the desktop computer distributed collaboration and mobility in a product design team. Proceedings of the ACM 1996 Conference on Computer Supported Cooperative Work(CSCW `96), Boston, MA, pp. 209—218, 1996.
[32] C. Haynes, J.R. Holmevik, High Wired: On the Design, Use, and Theory of Educational MOOs. University of Michigan Press, 1998.
[33] E. Churchill, S. Bly, Virtual environments at work: Ongoing use of MUDs in the workplace, Proceedings of WACC'99.
[34] "LambdaMOO Programmer's Manual," [Online document], (1993 August), Available HTTP: http://www.ccs.neu.edu/home/ivan/moo/lm_toc.html.
[35] "The MUD Client Protocol (MCP)," [Online document], Available HTTP: http://www.moo.mud.org/mcp/.
[36] The MITRE Corporation, "CVW Architecture Overview," [Online document], Available HTTP: http://cvw.sourceforge.net/cvw/info/docs40/ArchOverview.php3.
[37] Two unreported usability studies with students and faculty interviews at Acadia University.
[38] Reza B'Far et al., "Designing effective user interfaces for wireless devices," [Online document], Available HTTP: http://archive.devx.com/wireless/articles/rb0501/rb0501-1.asp.
[39] Research In Motion Limited, "BlackBerry Simulator User guide," [Online document], (2003 April), Available HTTP: www.blackberry.com.
[40] Openwave Systems Inc., "XHTML Mobile Profile reference version 1.0," [Online document], (2001 October), Available HTTP: http://developer.openwave.com/docs/51/xhtml-mp-ref.pdf.
[41] Chuck Musciano & Bill Kennedy, HTML & XHTML the definitive guide, O'Reilly, 2000.
[42] Laura Lemay, Teach Yourself Web publishing with HTML and XHTML in 21 days, Indiana: Sams, 2003.
[43] The Apache Software Foundation, "The Apache HTTP Server Project," [Online document], Available HTTP: http://httpd.apache.org/.
[44] Govind Seshadri, "Understanding JavaServer pages Model 2 Architecture: Exploring the MVC design pattern," [Online document], (1999 December), Available HTTP: http://www.javaworld.com/javaworld/jw-12-1999/jw-12-ssj-jspmvc.html.
[45] W3C HTML Working Group, "XHTML 1.0 The Extensible HyperText Markup Language (Second Edition)," [Online document], 2002 August 1 (Rev), [Cited 2000 January 26], Available HTTP: http://www.w3.org/TR/xhtml1/.
[46] W3C HTML Working Group, "XHTML Basic," [Online document], (2002 December), Available HTTP: http://www.w3.org/TR/xhtml-basic/.
[47] Paul Wallace, Andrea Hoffman, Daniel Skuka, Zev Blunt, Kyle Barrow, I-Mode Developer's Guide, Addison Wisley, 2002.
[48] Damon Hougland, Aaron Tavistock, Core JSP, NJ: Prentice Hall, 2001.
[49] Jason Hunter, Java Servlet & JSP Cookbook, O'Reilly, 2003.
[50] The Apache Software Foundation, "Apache Tomcat," [Online document], Available HTTP: http://tomcat.apache.org/.
[51] Wikipedia, "Apache Tomcat," [Online document], Available HTTP: http://en.wikipedia.org/wiki/Apache_Tomcat.
[52] Research In Motion Limited, "BlackBerry 7290 Wireless Handheld," [Online document], Available HTTP: http://www.blackberry.com/products/blackberry7200/blackberry7290.shtml.
[53] Research In Motion Limited, "BlackBerry Handheld wireless browser version 4.0 Content Development Guide," [Online document], (2004 October), Available HTTP: http://www.blackberry.com/developers/resources/index.shtml.

Cooperative Systems Design
P. Hassanaly et al. (Eds.)
IOS Press, 2006

The Underwhelming Effects of Location-Awareness of Others on Collaboration in a Pervasive Game

Nicolas NOVA[a,1], Fabien GIRARDIN[b], Gaëlle MOLINARI[a] and Pierre
DILLENBOURG[a]
[a]*CRAFT, School of Computer Sciences and Communication, Ecole Polytechnique
Fédérale de Lausanne (EPFL), Lausanne, Switzerland*
[b]*Interactive Technology Group, Dept of Technologies,
University of Pompeu Fabra, Spain*

Abstract. In this paper we seek to empirically study the use of location-awareness
of others in the context of mobile collaboration. We report on a field experiment
carried out using a pervasive game we developed called CatchBob!. Using both
quantitative and qualitative data, we show the underwhelming effects of
automating location-awareness. Our results indeed shows that automating this
process does not necessarily improve the task performance and that it can be
detrimental to socio-cognitive processes involved in collaboration such as
communication or the modeling of partners' intents. The paper concludes with
some potential impacts for location-based application practitioners.

Keywords: location-awareness, socio-cognitive processes, pervasive game, cscw,
field experiment.

Introduction

One of the most promising domains of Computer Supported Cooperative Work lately
has been the emergence of a new class of mobile applications called 'location-based
services' (LBS in the remainder of this document). These LBS take advantage of
people's physical location to provide users with various services. The actual utility of
such applications in mobile systems has been demonstrated in a wide range of
application examples, in obvious domains such as fieldwork [1] and tourism [2], as
well as mobile gaming [3]. Among all of those services, one of the most obvious
features behind LBS is positioning and tracking of individual. Such systems allow
users to find and track a person, a group or an artefact. They offer both synchronous
and asynchronous information about the location of people or objects in the physical
environment. Consequently, these services raise important issues in terms of
cooperation; our research helps to clarify this issue by looking at how it impacts group
interactions.

---

[1]Corresponding Author: CRAFT/EPFL Station 1 Ch-1015 Lausanne, Switzerland; E-mail:
nicolas.nova@epfl.ch

LBS raise interesting problems already approached by the CSCW community: the awareness issue and how it influences collaboration. Dourish and Belloti have given one of the best-known definitions for this very concept: *"awareness is an understanding of the activities of others, which provides a context for your own activity"* [4]. Drawing on this definition, location awareness would be "the understanding of the others' position" in the spatial environment. Moreover, Gutwin and Greenberg insisted on the knowledge dimension of awareness [5]. They indeed stated that it is knowledge about a state of the work environment in a limited portion of time and space. Since there is a lack of awareness information in computer supported environments, designers hence provided users with tools to support this functionality. Those tools are supposed to facilitate team collaboration by showing information about presence (is anyone in the workspace?), their identity (who is that?), their location (where is an individual?), their action (what is somebody doing?), and so forth. In this context, making others' position available on a mobile device is a way to gather and broadcast some specific kind of information on the 'where' category: location awareness. From the user's point of view, we could define it as *the appraisal and the understanding of information about the spatial positions of the partner(s) in the environment.* Some studies in virtual environment tackled this issue by showing that people pay attention and benefit from knowing their partners' spatial location when carrying out a joint activity. In a study about virtual textual reality better known as MOO, it has been shown that location awareness supported implicit coordination and division of labour among the group [6]. A previous project we had conducted about 3D virtual games [7] also revealed that providing players with spatial information enabled a better performance to the game task and improved the construction of the representation an individual build of his/her partner's strategies and intents. Those studies revealed to what extent knowing the partners' whereabouts can positively affect collaborative processes involved during group collaboration: processes which support the performance of a joint activity by a group of people [8]; that is to say all the socio-cognitive interactions such as the division of labour among the partners, the establishment of a shared understanding, communication, coordination strategies or mutual modeling (i.e. inferences made by each of the individual about their team-mates' intents, beliefs, and goals) [7].

Surprisingly, there seems to be little research so far about the very topic of collaborative processes in a context of location-based applications usage. The existing studies about it put more emphasis on the design aspects than on the empirical investigation of how users' behaviour is influenced by knowing where the partners or the competitors are located. With regard to this lack, our focus in this paper is to present a study which aimed at investigating the impact of location-awareness on group processes in mobile settings. It addresses the way it might influence collaboration processes such as mutual modeling and communication.

This paper first describes the existing projects that addressed how those aforementioned socio-cognitive processes are impacted by mobile technologies and LBS. The second section presents our research scope as well as the platform we designed to fulfill our needs. After a presentation of the main results, the final section discusses the potential outcome and their consequences for practitioners.

1. Related work

Although most of the literature about LBS is technology-driven, it is a rapidly moving field and there is now some established research projects geared towards the understanding of location-awareness usage. Scholars recently focused on the use of location information in a mobile context in cell phone conversations. One of the most common features of those conversations is the giving of a geographical formulation as part of an opening of a phone call; to answer to the famous "Where are you?" question. In a study of cell phones users [9], Arminen found that strict geographical location is relevant only on few instances, such as instructing somebody on how to find place X. Weilenmann also revealed in her analysis of recorded mobile phone conversations, that location was relevant only to plan a future meeting [10]. Then, it seems that in terms of problem solving, giving one's location is useful for group coordination to meet each other. The location is relevant for the parties involved in the conversation as formulated by Arminen. Besides, drawing on ethnographic studies of mobile workers Laurier pointed out that these "locational formulations" allow dispersed cell phone users to mutually establish and share a spatio-temporal context [11]. An Australian study also looked at the usability of SMS used in a group rendezvousing and wayfinding activity [12]. Given that users had to figure out the approximate location of their partners as well as developing a representation of the area being explored, they sometimes misattributed delays and formed inaccurate models of behavior/location. Recently, Intel designers developed a system that would support both manual and automatic location disclosure on cell phones [13]. They found that automating this process, while at times valuable, suffered because the explicit communication act by the sender and its accompanying knowledge of intended context for interpretation was lost.

However, it is certainly in the field of mobile computing that location-awareness usage has recently been more investigated. Obviously most of studies focused on location-based services usage and how location-awareness impact individual or collaborative behavior has been conducted using games [14] [15] [16] [17] [18] in which the task is often about wayfinding, finding and collecting objects or rendezvousing. At the sociological level, [18] studied a location-based game deployed in Japan called Mogi Mogi[2] in which players have to collect virtual and localized artefacts in Tokyo. The authors noticed that knowing the others' positions on the screen of the cell phone created an affordance for social encounters and then led to specific forms of conversational openness. Investigations at smaller group levels also shed some light on this phenomenon. An experiment of a location-awareness tool in museum settings showed that location was a powerful resource for collaboration [19], since it eased referential communication, by allowing people to better understand what their partners were looking at. Moreover, experimenters found that location-awareness allowed participants to quickly find what their friends were looking at and hence find them too look at the same thing. Another study examined how location-aware technology impacts social behaviour within the context of rendezvousing (meeting at an agreed upon time and location) [20]. Three different technology conditions were investigated: mobile phones, PDA displaying location information of others and both mobile phones. All of the groups were able to complete the rendezvous tasks without much difficulty but participants exhibited very different behaviours depending on the

---

[2] http://www.mogimogi.com/

technology used. The location-awareness feature was very good at gathering contextual information, such as location, in a very unobtrusive manner but it provided little assistance to users in interpreting the associated state of the person.

Among the issues related to location-awareness usage, different studies explored the notion of uncertainties due to technological pitfalls [21][3][22]. These investigations bring forward the fact that ubiquitous computing is still a maturing field in which lots of problems may arise like unreliable network, latency, bandwidth, security, unstable topology, or network homogeneity. Consequently, users learn or set strategies to adapt or to rectify the aforementioned systems failures. One of the solutions to overcome problems due to location awareness discrepancies is to let users manually reveal their positions as reported by Benford et al. [14], which happened to be quickly learned, by users. In this study, authors found that rather than reporting themselves to be at a different place, the users were in fact reporting themselves to be at a different time. The result also showed that self-revealing a position is an act of communication (not only x and y coordinates or a place name) that can reveal past or future intentions. However, the limitations of those self-reported positioning are that the mobile player had to know where they were and/or where they were heading, which is not always the case. Finally, a Wizard-of-Oz study revealed that giving information about the proximity of a searched object can reduce the searchers' walking distance to the object but also that it may increase the search time [23] if the system demands too much of the user's attention.

Other research, which deploy game to understand location-based services usage, do not directly put the emphasis on how location-awareness modifies collaboration. They instead focus on tactics developed in a mobile setting [16] or on the difficulty to represent group formation on the display [15].

2. Research scope

In the previously mentioned studies, the effects of location-awareness of others are often addressed only as a side investigation of the research project. Our focus is to tackle this issue more deeply, dealing with their potential effects on collaboration processes we defined in the introduction: the socio-cognitive interactions involved when people collaborate. This study aims at investigating whether location cues influence collaboration processes such as the task performance, mutual modeling, and communication. Our point here is to deepen the results described in the previous section, expanding these issues through the use of a different methodology. We indeed rely here on a field experiment based approach [24]. As a matter of fact, field experiments are quantitative experimental evaluations that are conducted out in the field, drawing from aspects of both qualitative field studies and lab experiments. They take advantage of both qualitative and quantitative studies. On the one hand it involves real users in an activity that occurs in the real world. On the other hand, we can control variables and have different experimental conditions. In order to conduct such a field experiment, we decided to use a collaborative mobile game for three major reasons. The first one is because a game, especially a mobile computing one, involves participants in a real context (the physical world) with a certain ecological validity. A game in public space indeed creates a certain kind of complexity with passers-by or real-world features; for example participants are not free since they have to take the environmental topology into account; they also have to pay attention to systems uncertainties (disconnection, network availabilities…) as in the real world. Second, the task domain in games is easier for both the participants and the experimenters (compared to firefighters emergency missions for instance). The learning curve is way softer. Finally, it is better to make participants doing a game than a really complex task they will never carry out. Then, we expected participants of this game to have a better implication than in a complex task.

The empirical study presented hereafter is an exploratory investigation that engages participants to collaborate in the achievement of a spatial coordination task. The presence or absence of the location-awareness tool constitutes the experimental conditions of the study.

3. Methodology

3.1. A pervasive game as a testing platform: CatchBob!

CatchBob! is a mobile game in which groups of 3 teammates have to find a virtual object on our campus at EPFL in Lausanne. The dimensions of this 'field' are 850x510meters. Completing the game requires the players to surround the object with a triangle formed by each participant's position in the real space. To reach this goal, they employ an application running on Tablet PCs as depicted on Figure 1.

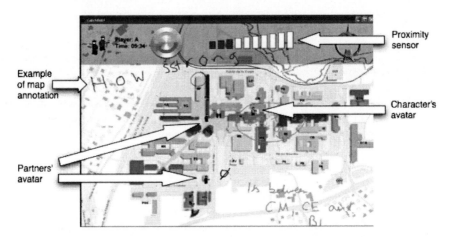

Figure 1. CatchBob! interface as seen by one player. This snapshot depicts the interface with the location-awareness tool: Avatars of other players are displayed. In the condition without the location-awareness tool, the interface only displays the character's avatar.

Another meaningful piece of information given by the software is an individual proximity sensor. It indicates whether the user is close or far from the object through the number of red bars displayed at the top of the interface. There is actually no object on the field; it only appears on the screen when the users are close to it. In addition, the tool also enables communication: Players can synchronously annotate the map with the stylus. The annotations slowly fade out until they become completely invisible (after 4 minutes). This leads to very simple acts of communication and dialogues; for instance a player asks his or her teammate to move to a specific direction with an arrow with the message "go there" and the partner acknowledge this advice. When the players are close to the object, the triangle they have to form appears on the display; they then have to adjust it in a proper way.

In the experimental condition "without the location-awareness tool", players just see their own character as an avatar on the campus map. In the condition "with location awareness", player could update his or her partners' positions by clicking on a refresh button.

Even though finding the object could be carried out alone, the collaboration in this game lies in the fact that players have to coordinate to form the triangle surrounding the virtual object. It is not possible to complete the game without collaborating. We hence avoid the free rider effect.

All the players' interactions with the applications (positions, annotations, getting others' positions, connection loss) are logged on a server. We also developed a replay tool that allows to show the paths of each player. This application allows us to confront the players to a replay of the path they took during the game, as well as the actions they performed.

3.2. Procedure and participants

Sixty students of the Ecole Polytechnique Fédérale de Lausanne (age range: 19-27; mean: 22.8) participated in this experiment. We had 10 groups of 3 persons in the condition "with awareness tool" and 10 groups in the condition "without awareness tool". All the group members knew each other because different levels of knowledge between partners may impact the representation each of them have about their teammates. Players were also all familiar with the campus. Experiments lasted approximately one hour and were conducted in French. The experiments were run on our campus, one group at a time.

Participants were asked to find the virtual object and surround it with a triangle made by their position with one constraint in mind: They should take the shortest path to it. We also told them that the goal was not to find the object in the smallest amount of time.

After presenting the game instructions at the lab, players were given 3 minutes to plan their strategy on a map. Players were then led to the common starting point at the centre of the campus. They had 30 minutes to complete the task, which is quite sufficient to achieve the goal without a too tight time-pressure, judging from the pretest we ran. After completing the game (or playing 30 minutes), players returned to our lab and filled a post-game questionnaire during 10 minutes. This questionnaire provided participants with 3 maps of the campus on which they had to draw their path as well as paths followed by the 2 partners. Players were also asked questions about how was the collaboration, if it was balanced or not, whether they had fun playing the game and if they understood their partners' intents during the joint task. The last part of the study is a structured interview, during which players are confronted to a replay of their activity; the group had to answer questions about coordination strategies, communication acts, the paths they took, the tactics they deployed as well as describing the misunderstandings and negotiations that happened. The replay tool functions like a basis to foster players' verbalizations; it shows the players' paths and their annotations on a map of the campus.

We controlled several variables like the number of participants among the group, the fact that they knew each other as well as the field, they had the same gear (a Tablet PC, no cell phone, no walkie-talkie) and they had all the same starting point. In addition, we used two different positions of "Bob". There is the same number of games with these 2 positions in each of the conditions. The distance between the starting point and Bob is the same in these 2 scenarios. We controlled that the position of 'Bob' had no effect on the dependent variables presented in the next section; which was not the case.

3.3. Extracted data

The CatchBob! platform allows us to collect a wide set of data ranging from quantitative measures to players' interview and account of the game. Quantitative data refers to both task performance and collaborative process indexes. Measuring performance is done through the sum of the path length over all players in a group. We did not choose time as a performance variable since we did not want players to run on the campus with Tablet PC and because finding a proper path was better suited to the discussion of a relevant strategy. With regards to the socio-cognitive processes involved, we measured three kinds of variables:

- The frequency and the content of annotations written on the Tablet PC reflect the communication among the group (no audio communication occurred since the only way to interact was using map annotations). The coding scheme adopted to describe the annotations content is explicated in section 4.2.
- The number of errors they made while drawing the path of their partners after the game is an indication of how each player modelled the activity of their partners. We indeed asked players to draw their path on a paper map as well as the paths of their partners, as described earlier. We could hence make comparisons between the path player A drawn about B or C to B or C's real paths. This comparison, measured by the number of mistakes, represents the quality of A's representation of B and C's behaviour in space. This is a measure of the 'mutual modeling', that is to say the inferences made by each of the individual about their teammates' whereabouts. Asking one person to draw his or her own path is a way to judge the competence to draw a trajectory.

On the other hand, the qualitative data we get range from the coding of map annotations to players' verbalizations when confronting to the reply tool after the game. Those data allow us to reconstruct the game experience and to give more sense to the three players' actions in the various phases of the game.

4. Results

4.1. Performance and modeling the partners' trails

Since it was a collaborative game, we analyzed the task performance at the group level, which corresponds to the group travel distance. As depicted on Figure 2a, groups in both conditions have a very close performance; the only difference lies in the dispersion that is higher for players without the automatic display of the partners. A oneway-ANOVA test did not show significant differences ($F = 0.07, p = .78$).

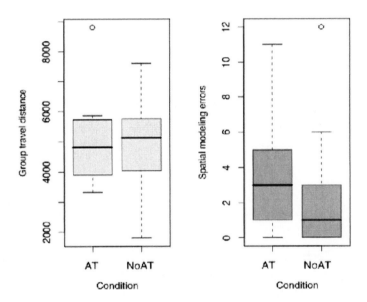

Figure 2. (a) group travel distance in the two experimental conditions (AT: with the location awareness tool; NoAT: without the location awareness tool) (b): number of errors made by each participant during the post-test (while drawing the path of the partner) in the two experimental conditions.

As mentioned in the section about the experiment procedure, we measured the number of errors between the path player A drawn about B or C to B or C's real paths. This mutual modeling index represents the quality of A's representation of B and C's behavior in space. We did that for each player. Figure 2b shows the number of errors in each condition. This variable has been analyzed at the group level. As described by [25] we checked the non-independence of the results through the computation of intraclass correlation ($r = .39$), which is significant ($p = .01$). That expresses the non-independence of the results among groups. It means that the number of errors made by the subjects is dependent on the number of errors did by the partners (e.g. if one player made a lot of errors about his/her path, the same goes for the partners). Then the unit of analysis is the group. Players without the location-awareness tool make two times fewer errors than those who had it as attested by the Wilcoxon test we conducted (because data were not distributed normally): $W = 81, p = .02$. In other words, people among groups <u>without the display of location information</u> better recalled their partners' trails: their mutual modeling of their partners were better. This result, which is quite surprising, will be explained by the next findings.

4.2. Communication through map annotations

4.2.1. Annotations frequency

Map annotations have been investigated both by quantitative measures like the frequency and qualitative dimensions such as the content or the pragmatics of the messages. This variable has been studied at the individual level since the intraclass correlation among the group is not significant ($r = -0.21$ $p = .87$). Figure 3 shows the frequency of messages sent by each player in both experimental conditions. The frequency of messages is higher in the "without the location-awareness tool" condition. A Wilcoxon statistical test shows that this difference is significant: $W = 55.56$, $p < .01$. We used a non-parametric test because data were not distributed normally (Wilcoxon's test).

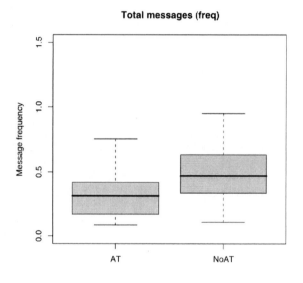

Figure 3. Frequency of map annotations written on the Tablet PC by each individual.

4.2.2. Annotations coding scheme

We developed our own coding scheme to categorize map annotations depending on the content of the messages (position/direction/strategy/proximity to the object/off-task/corrections) and also their pragmatics (announcement, order, question, and acknowledgement). Figure 4 presents examples of the aforementioned categories. We analyzed these annotations at the individual level. Inter-judge reliability of the coding system showed a Cohen's Kappa [26]of 0.89 for the content variable, a kappa of 0.86 for the pragmatics variable. The content analysis revealed that the frequency of messages about position ($W = 203$, $p < .01$) direction ($W = 292$, $p = .01$) and strategy ($W = 269$, $p < 0.01$) was higher in the condition without the awareness tool. There were not differences for messages about proximity to the object, off-task notes and corrections. In terms of pragmatics, players without the location-awareness tool sent more announcement ($W = 253$, $p < .01$) and more questions ($W = 228.5$, $p < .01$). There were no significant differences concerning the number of orders or acknowledgements. In addition, we found a negative correlation between the frequency of messages about strategy and the number of errors made by the individual when drawing their partners' path: Pearson bivariate correlation $r = -.51$ (significant $p < .001$).

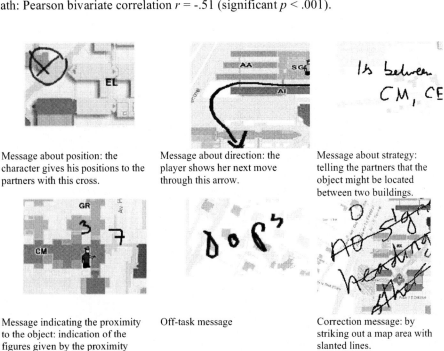

Message about position: the character gives his positions to the partners with this cross.

Message about direction: the player shows her next move through this arrow.

Message about strategy: telling the partners that the object might be located between two buildings.

Message indicating the proximity to the object: indication of the figures given by the proximity sensor.

Off-task message

Correction message: by striking out a map area with slanted lines.

Figure 4. Examples of messages of each categories described in the coding scheme.

4.2.3. Post-hoc analysis

We performed a post-hoc split of groups into two kinds of participants accordingly with the repartition of errors made by a player to draw their partners' trails (i.e. the mutual modeling index). For that matter, the split point was the mean of errors. This split showed that persons who had a good representation of their partners' whereabouts sent more messages about strategy ($W = 725$, $p < .0001$), more questions ($W = 614$, $p = .03$) and orders ($W = 664.5$, $p = .0003$). We also found an interaction between the experimental variable (awareness tool presence), the number of errors and the strategy messages as represented on figure 5 ($F = 7.2626$, $p = .009277$). Players without the awareness tool wrote more strategy messages and so did those who had a more accurate mutual model (i.e. those who better recalled their partners' trails).

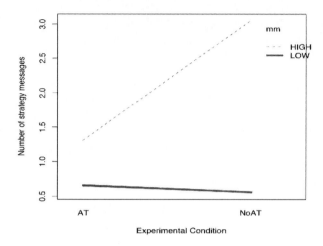

Figure 5. Interaction plot between the number of strategy messages, the two groups split according to the mutual modeling index (i.e. the repartition of errors made by a player to draw their partners' trails) and the experimental condition (with our without the awareness tool).

Simple effects of the interaction showed that the differences were significant for both experimental conditions: for groups with the AT, those who had a les accurate mutual model of their teammates (i.e. who did not recall the path of their partners very well) wrote less messages about strategy than those with a high mutual model ($p = .01$). The same goes for groups without the location-awareness tool ($p = .0001$). In addition, for people with a more accurate mutual model, the number of messages about strategy was higher in the condition without the location-awareness tool. And this is not the case for groups with the tool. In sum, removing the automatic display of partners' positions only impacted groups with a high mutual model of their teammates and not the others who did not recall their path very well. Besides, the difference between the number of messages about strategy sent by players without the AT might explain the wide dispersion about their performance (as seen on Figure 1).

Moreover, a post-hoc split of participants into two groups depending on the number of strategy messages sent by each participant showed that there is a significant difference in terms of errors. People who wrote a lot of strategy messages made fewer errors ($W = 465.5, p < .001$), which is not too much of a surprise since we found a high negative correlation between the number of errors and the number of frequency messages. There is no interaction between the experimental condition, the two classes of individuals (depending on the number of strategy messages they sent) and the mutual modeling index represented by the number of errors. Unlike players with a high mutual model, player who did lots of errors while drawing their partners' path sent few messages about strategy.

This means that the mutual modeling process depends both on the number of strategy messages sent by players and the absence of the location-awareness tool. But it seems that the most important factor is the exchange of messages about strategy since the presence of the awareness tool inhibited the writing of those annotations.

5. Discussion

Our study has revealed the underwhelming effects of automating location-awareness of others in a mobile collaboration context. As a matter of fact, we found that participants who were automatically aware of their partners' location did not perform the task better than other participants. In addition, people among groups without the location information built a more accurate mutual model since they made fewer errors when drawing the path of their partners after the game. A good mutual model is also shared among the group: when one of the teammates had a good representation of the others' whereabouts, it also held for the partners. These results can be explained by the messages exchanged. First the amount of messages is more important in the group without the location-awareness tool: players had then more traces to rely on in order to recall the others' trails. And when we look at the content, we see that players without the location-awareness tool sent more messages about position, direction or strategy. They also wrote more questions. Strategy was certainly the most important factor for the construction of the mutual modeling as attested by the post-hoc analysis. Finally, a very intriguing result is the fact that the presence of the awareness tool inhibited the writing of those annotations. By 'underwhelming', we refer to the fact that automating the location-awareness process not only undermines the exchange of messages about position but also about other kinds of information such as strategy or direction. As a consequence, the automatic awareness tool seems to make users more passive.

It appears that players without awareness tool took better advantage of the annotation capabilities, using it to express their path and their strategy. The players with the awareness tool were able to annotate as well but did not use this opportunity. There seems to be a certain inertia caused by the presence of location awareness information. We can then conclude that in the context of this experiment it was better to leave users without the location-awareness tool, with a broad channel of communication. They chose the information they perceived as relevant (position, direction and strategy) and sent them to their partners at the moment they wanted it to be known by the others. This is ostensive communication as described by [27]: the self-expressed position is both an attractor for others' attentions and a way to show the communicator's intent through messages about strategy or directions. Users could indeed express what they found relevant for the current task: with regard to the content (their position, direction, strategy messages) and to the pragmatic level (questions). This finding confirmed what [14] revealed: self-reported positioning could be reliable low-tech alternative to automated systems like GPS. However, our findings goes further by proving that letting user declare themselves their position is better with regard to various processes like communication or the construction of a mental model about the partners. These results also means that CatchBob! players anticipated something: they had to send more information otherwise the interpretation space for the others would be too small. That is why they sent messages about their direction and about strategy: the other teammates can then better infer what to do, and consequently build a more accurate mutual model.

Apart from issues regarding the field experiment paradigm, one of the limits of our study is that each group played only one game, which might be an issue in terms of interface learning. One possible response to see whether the results still hold over time is repeated play as described in [16] or a crossed experiment in which players from one condition play a second game in the other condition. Another critique is that, in this paper, we considered the task as a whole; there are actually different phases in which the effects of the location-awareness tool might be different: the exploration part, the rendezvousing moment and then the triangle formation. There might be some positive effects of the tool depending on both subtasks features and specific moments of the game.

That is the reason why future work will be directed towards the analysis of the three phases players has to achieve to complete the game. The point would then be to discriminate different impacts of the location-awareness features depending on the subtasks characteristics. Moreover, we will also investigate other collaborative processes impacted by the tool such as the division of labor among the group or the coordination strategies used over time.

6. Impacts for mobile and collaborative application practitioners

Despite the potential limitations of this study, it already surfaces key problems with location-awareness usage. Our field experiment shed some light on the idea that automatically broadcast information about whereabouts should be used carefully. It might indeed be detrimental to some collaborative processes such as mutual modeling or communication. The main lessons for practitioners are twofold.

First, automating a process such as location-awareness is not always fruitful. Letting people build their own representation of the spatial information appears to be more efficient than broadcasting mere location information. To some extent, not giving location-awareness information can be a way to support collaboration more effectively; since players may communicate more and better explain their activity and intents. Self-disclosure can hence be more effective since users could express both information about their intents relevant for the task context and their location. They could also send it whenever they want to express either their current or past positions or the intended places they are heading to. Another interesting benefit of letting the users express their position is to give them the control of privacy issues, one of the major issue related to LBS usage. They have indeed the choice to disclose information about their whereabouts, which is of tremendous importance to avoid the users' perception of privacy invasion as revealed in [13].

Additionally, though location-awareness is an important issue for mobile collaboration, it should certainly not be limited to a simple broadcast of people's position. The field experiment showed that communication about strategy was more important than automatic location-awareness for building a good mutual model. During this spatial coordination task we saw that players without location-awareness tool built a more accurate representation of their partners' paths partly thanks to these messages. They also facilitated knowledge elicitation: without the automatic location-awareness, subjects were more articulate about their strategy. It was as if the tool created certain inertia among the group, with regard to communication. Participants who relied on the automatic positioning wrote few messages, which lead them to be less explicit the situation and how they could deal with it.

References

[1]   J. Pascoe, D.R. Morse, and N.S. Ryan, Developing personal technology for the field. *Personal Technologies* **2**(1)(1998), 28–36.
[2]   K. Cheverst, N. Davies, K. Mitchell, A. Friday and C. Efstratiu, Developing a context-aware electronic tourist guide: some issues and experiences. *Proceedings of the CHI'00 Conference on Human Factors in Computing Systems,* 1-6 April 2000, pp. 17–24.
[3]   S. Benford, *Future Location-Based Experiences.* JISC Tech Report (TSW0501), 2005.
[4]   P. Dourish, and V. Bellotti, Awareness and coordination in shared workspaces, in J. Turner & R. Kraut (eds.), *Proceedings of ACM CSCW'92 Conference on Computer Supported Cooperative Work,* Toronto, Canada, 1992, pp.107-114.
[5]   C. Gutwin, and S. Greenberg, S., A Descriptive Framework of Workspace Awareness for Real-Time Groupware, *Computer Supported Cooperative Work* **11**(3) (2002), pp. 411-446.
[6]   P. Dillenbourg and D. Traum, The role of a whiteboard in a distributed cognitive system. Paper presented at the Swiss workshop on collaborative and distributed systems. (Lausanne, Switzerland, May 1st   1997),   Retrieved   from   the   Internet   (October,   17,   2005) http://agora.unige.ch/conferences/Lausanne97/dillenbourg/
[7]   N. Nova, T. Wehrle, J. Goslin, Y. Bourquin and P. Dillenbourg, P. The Impacts of Awareness Tools on Mutual Modelling in a Collaborative Video-Game, in *Proceedings of the 9th International Workshop on Groupware,* Autrans, France, September 2003, pp. 99-108.
[8]   P. Dillenbourg, What do you mean by collaborative learning?, in P. Dillenbourg (Ed) , *Collaborative-learning: Cognitive and Computational Approaches,* Oxford: Elsevier, 1999, pp.1-19.
[9]   I. Arminen, Location: a Socially Dynamic Property - A Study of Location Telling in Mobile Phone Calls, in L. Haddon et al. (eds.) *The Good, the Bad and the Irrelevant: The User and the Future of Information and Communication Technologies Conference Proceedings,* Helsinki, 2003.
[10]   A. Weilenmann, "I can't talk now, I'm in a fitting room": Availability and Location in Mobile Phone Conversations. In *Environment and Planning* A volume 35, (9) September, pp. 1589 - 1605, special issue on Technology and Mobility, ed. E. Laurier, 2003.
[11]   E. Laurier, Why people say where they are during mobile phone calls, *Environment and Planning D: Society & Space* **19**(4)(2001), 485-504.
[12]   J. Axup, S. Viller, and N. Bidwell, Usability of a Mobile, Group Communication Prototype While Rendezvousing, in *Proceedings of the Symposium on Collaborative Technologies and Systems - Special Session on Mobile Collaborative Work,* St. Louis, MO, USA, May 15-20, 2005.
[13]   I. Smith, S. Consolvo, A. LaMarca, J. Hightower, J. Scott, T. Sohn, J. Hughes, G. Iachello and G.D. Abowd, Social Disclosure Of Place: From Location Technology to Communication Practices, in *Proceedings of Pervasive 2005,* Munich, Germany.
[14]   S. Benford, W. Seager, M. Flintham, R. Anastasi, D. Rowland, J. Humble, D. Stanton, J. Bowers, N. Tandavanitj, M. Adams, J. Row-Farr, A. Oldroyd, and J. Sutton, The Error of Our Ways: The Experience of Self-Reported Position in a Location-Based Game, in *Proceedings of Ubicomp 2004 Conference on Ubiquitous Computing,* Nottingham, UK, 2004, pp. 70-87.
[15]   S. Benford, D. Rowland, D. Flintham, A. Drozd, R. Hull, J. Reid, J. Morrison, and J. Facer, Life on the edge: supporting collaboration in location-based experiences. In *Proceedings of CHI 2005 Conference on Human Factors in Computing Systems,* Portland, USA, 2005, pp. 721-730.
[16]   L. Barkhuus, M. Chalmers, P. Tennent, M. Hall, M. Bell, and B. Brown, Picking Pockets on the Lawn: The Development of Tactics and Strategies in a Mobile Game. In *Proceedings of Ubicomp 2005 Conference on Ubiquitous Computing,* Tokyo, Japan, 2005, pp. 358-374.
[17]   M. Chalmers and A. Galani, Seamful interweaving: heterogeneity in the theory and design of interactive systems, in *Proceedings of the Conference on Designing Interactive Systems* 2004, Cambridge, USA, pp. 243-252.
[18]   C. Licoppe and Y. Inada, "Seing" one another onscreen and the construction of social order in a mobile-based augmented public space: The uses of a geo-localized mobile game in Japan, in *Proceedings of Learning in the Mobile Age Conference,* Hungarian Academy of Sciences, April 28–30, 2005.
[19]   B. Brown, I. McColl, M. Chalmers, A. Galani, C. Randell, and A. Steed, Lessons from the lighthouse: Collaboration in a shared mixed reality system. In *Proceedings of the CHI 2003 Conference on Human Factors in Computing Systems,* Fort Lauderdale, Florida. ACM Press: NY, 2003, pp. 577–584.
[20]   D. Dearman, K. Hawkey, and K.M. Inkpen, Effect of location-awareness on rendezvous behaviour. *CHI Extended Abstracts,* 2005, 1929-1932.
[21]   G.D. Abowd, C.G, Atkenson, J. Hong, S. Long, R. Kooper, and M. Pinkerton, Cyberguide: a mobile context-aware tour guide. *Wireless Networks* **3**(5) (1997), 421–433.

[22] S. Antifakos, A. Schwaninger, and B. Schiele, Evaluating the Effects of Displaying Uncertainty in Context-Aware Applications, in *Proceedings of the Ubicomp 2004 Conference on Ubiquitous Computing*, Nottingham, UK, pp. 54-69.

[23] L. Takayama, L. Leung, X. Jiang, and J. Hong, You're Getting Warmer! How Proximity Information Affects Search Behavior in Physical Spaces. In *Extended Abstracts of the Human Factors in Computing Systems: CHI2003*, April 5-10.

[24] J. Goodman, S. Brewster, and P. Gray, P., Using Field Experiments to Evaluate Mobile Guides, in Schmidt-Belz, B. and Cheverst, K., (eds.), *Proceedings of HCI in Mobile Guides*, workshop at Mobile HCI 2004, Glasgow, UK, Sep 2004.

[25] D.A. Kenny, D. Kashy and N. Bolger, Data analysis in social psychology, in D. Gilbert, S. Fiske, & G. Lindzey (eds.) *Handbook of Social Psychology*, vol. 1, Boston: McGraw-Hill, 1998, pp. 233-265.

[26] J. Cohen, Weighted kappa: Nominal scale agreement with provision for scaled disagreement or partial credit. *Psychological Bulletin* **70** (1968), 213--220.

[27] D. Sperber and D. Wilson. *Relevance: Communication and cognition*, Blackwell, Oxford, 1986

Cooperative Systems Design
P. Hassanaly et al. (Eds.)
IOS Press, 2006

A Practical Sense of Knowing: Exploring Awareness Strategies in a Mobile Workplace

Carljohan ORRE[a1] & Leon A. WATTS[b2]

a Department of Informatics, Umeå University, Sweden
b Department of Computer Science, University of Bath, UK.

ABSTRACT. This paper presents and discusses strategies used by homecare workers to establish and maintain awareness in a mobile workplace. It capitalizes on data derived from a longitudinal translocal ethnographic study of homecare and the utilization of mobile technology. The study exposes two distinct dimensions of the work context, denoted the Case and Base dimensions, which are used as vehicles to describe situations of collaborative practice that occur (1) in a coordination meeting, (2) on a homecare visit, and (3) in an on-the-fly 'illicit' use of mobile technology. We propose a new conception of collaborative awareness as a 'practical sense of knowing'. Findings from the ethnographic study are consistent with a well-worn distinction between "knowing that", declarative knowledge, and "knowing how", procedural knowledge. Conventional structures of organizational control, encoded both procedurally and as declarations of responsibility, are routinely broken and reformed. This happens as workers devise new strategies in order to maintain the keen sense of their collaborative situation required to sustain an orderly workplace.

Keywords: Homecare work, Cooperative work, Awareness, Mobile technology, Control, Autonomy

Introduction

Awareness, in all its varieties, is a well-known and much-discussed concept in HCI and CSCW research; it is a core concept for ambient displays [14][26], for media spaces [8][7], for video conferencing [30][31], and for shared-workspace technologies [9][13]. However it may seem, awareness is something of an enigma in CSCW research. Schmidt has described it as an "elastic" concept that constantly threatens to slip through the fingers of designers who wish to support it [27]. Heath et al [11] stress the need to unpack the concept of awareness and take the domain seriously in order to provide enough guidance and knowledge when building systems that aim to support collaboration among distributed individuals (p. 345). Mobile collaborative systems bring a new dimension to the problem. This paper seeks to expose some of the challenges that attend the advent of mobile collaborative work and to bring a fresh

1 Work supported by the Swedish Foundation for International Cooperation in Research and Higher Education, STINT, FS2005-6008.
2 Work supported by the UK Engineering and Physical Sciences Research Council, EPSRC GR/S11404/01

perspective to the concept of awareness among collaborators. It does so through the lens of a four-year ethnographic case study of mobile homecare work teams.

According to Moran & Anderson [18], an approach to the relationship between awareness and work activities is important for the introduction of cooperative technology. They place *fluidity of action* at the center of the problem, asserting that collaborative practices inherently rely on a *keen sense* of who and what is around when they are needed. They write: "[it is] how people slide to and fro between the formal and informal in doing the things they do within the daily round of work. This fluidity is a fundamental feature of work activity, and we need to be attuned to how technologies of various kinds can play a role here..." (p. 386). Addressing awareness more directly, they observe that: "...people are very aware of what goes on in their environment; without such awareness they would feel isolated....the environment needs to signal the availability of these things by tapping on people's ability to peripherally process the non-attended parts of the environment so that they can redirect their attention when appropriate..." (p. 386).

Moran and Anderson were addressing work activity in office environments. Fluidity of action takes on a new significance with the loss of collaborators' attentional cues and the loosening of environmental bonds inherent in mobile work. The nature of the challenge we see here is to move away from the prevailing notion of office work as a baseline condition for unpacking awareness. That is not to say that office work is less important, as is evident in the studies reported by Belloti [3] which focus on local mobility within the office. Rather, office work is associated with such an abundance of proximal information that it can be hard to distill out the "keen sense" of collaborative practice.

This paper reports a longitudinal case study of mobile collaborative work, and the practice-based utilization of mobile technology. It is in set within a context of homecare work; thus, people not artifacts are the main concern of the practice. We focus on a team of homecare workers who conduct home visits to elderly people. Despite the ostensibly solitary nature of their work tasks, the day-to-day duties of team members depend on close collaboration of activities for which they take collective responsibility. We begin by introducing prior research on the provision of technological support for distributed groups and for homecare work. We then describe the sociotechnical context of our study. We go on to present our analysis of homecare work in practice, distinguishing Case and Base work contexts through the use of three vignettes: (1) in a coordination meeting, (2) on a home care visit, and (3) in an on-the-fly unauthorized use of mobile technology. Each vignette is drawn from observations, field notes and interviews.

1. Coping with mobility and achieving an orderly workplace

Mobility is a dimension of cooperative work in which awareness plays a central role, as recent work exploring mobility and mobile work clearly demonstrates. Sherry & Salvador [28] describe the use of mobile devices to support mobile work as something akin to jazz-like improvisation, where the work performed owes to a constant interplay between unplanned and planned activities. In their study of mobile workers, Churchill & Wakeford [6] identify the access of information and access of others as core elements of mobile collaborative practice: both are aspects of potential awareness. Laurier [15] focuses on how mobile work can be discussed as socio-technical accomplishment, where the awareness given through the use of mobiles makes possible the reconfiguring of spaces so that they are made suitable for work activities. Weilenmann's [32] analysis of shared technology led to a conception of awareness of others that focused on the need to negotiate the context or frame within which collaborators act. Most of these studies concern mobile workers who are engaged in collaborative activities which occur in office environments or result in the joint production of documents. Whether working as consultants, sale representatives or engineers, the nature of their work is ingrained with "the office". Sherry & Salvador argue that exploring remoteness from an office or from a home base is a place of richer resources for the researcher [28].

These studies are of mobile devices actually give the people the means to handle collaboration at a distance by transforming shared work into coordinated individual work. They are in consequence less concerned with intense collaboration. However, work even when notionally delegated can often retain a shared character. Belotti [3] showed that office workers frequently engage in a kind of "social browsing", strolling around, chatting, and picking up crucial information that was needed in order to make decisions in their own individually delegated work. Orr [20] and Wiberg [33] similarly address loosely coupled collaboration, where individual workers took steps to jointly establish a support for similar aspects of awareness by establishing conventions for meeting in places such as restaurants and cafés, or local offices. These locations played a crucial role in the workers' *strategies* for establishing social interaction and exchanging experiences and troubleshooting stories.

Pinell & Gutwin have explored mobile collaborative work in a similar context to that which we shall go on to describe [25] [23] [24]. They have focused on the design and development of technological support for the coordination requirements they have identified for loosely coupled groups. They provide a well-founded design framework that capitalizes on the characteristics of multidisciplinary homecare practice in Canada. However, homecare differs in scope and meaning depending on the social system of which it is a part. It even differs between municipalities and districts within the same country. One of the differences between different cases is the degree of coupling between the activities of team members. Pinell & Gutwin's design framework concerns loosely coupled groups beyond the world of homecare work. The activities of the team we report in this paper vary widely in degree of coupling from tight to loose.

Nilsson & Hertzum [19] report their analysis of homecare and mobile collaborative work in terms of coordinating rhythms. They describe how major temporal organization is furnished by individual, collective and social rhythms, which collectively bring about the collaborative flow of activities. The individual worker', collective and social rhythms raise questions of which "drummer" workers should listen to, and to which tempo of reverberations the care receivers should be attuned. The multitude of rhythms is noteworthy, since it is illustrative of the constraints on the time, location and activity of homecare workers the difficulties of articulating work schedules. Their focus on rhythms and tempo aligns well with our concern for the fluidity of practice, which is perhaps the dominant factor, adding the character and variation of the activities during a day of work. When comparing these studies, and while considering the overall trend of ICT-based support for homecare work, it is clear that there is more work to do in order to understand the nature of collaborative practice in homecare settings.

Paying attention to awareness as it is exposed in mobile work practice has the potential to guide design towards feasible solutions, not only for mobile collaborative systems but also for more general support for collaboration work. There is a particular value in examining settings involving mobile collaborative work practice where information and interactive aspects of the work are distributed in and through a multitude of devices. There is a real need to examine the assumption that it is a simple matter to integrate traditional administrative-oriented use of information technology and the use of mobile technology, where the mobile activities do not primarily concern administration and document management.

2. A socio-technical perspective on the mobile workplace in homecare

2.1. Technical context

The homecare workers in this study had two technologies at their disposal. These were a conventional mobile phone (for use in emergencies) and JoLiv, a purpose-build mobile system. JoLiv, contains two separate modules, a desktop application and an application that runs on PDAs. These applications are interlinked by asynchronous connections through a docking cradle (see Figure 1). Docking allows the information in either of these components to be synchronized. The information held by the system is centrally stored in a remote database that can be accessed by all the local homecare groups in the organization. The concept of the system is quite simple. The main application functions as a diary for the homecare workers. The application is used to manage the administration of care work to be done for the elderly under the responsibility of the homecare organization, and of the care workers themselves.

Figure 1: The morning meeting place (Left). And the JoLiv PDA and desktop (Right): Base setting

The application allows the workers to access information about planned actions and information about those under care, and consequently to see what remains to be done, and which of their colleagues is responsible for certain tasks. In principle, these features can help to inform individual homecare workers about the general scheme or collaborative context within which their own individual tasks are to be carried out.

2.2. Organizational context: Direct and indirect objectives of homecare work

Organizational procedures enforce a fundamental distinction between two aspects of the work place. This is due to the direct and indirect objectives and goals that the practice holds. The indirect objectives concern preparatory activities such as articulating the division of labor, administrative tasks and activities that occur in the homecare office environment. The direct objective in home are work is to tend to the elderly. The duties comprised in this activity are carried out in the homes of the elderly and force the personnel to adjust and acclimatize to new physical conditions for each and every visit. Every location has its specific features. For each and every house call the personnel have to adjust to someone else's organization of things, such as the use of household commodities, including plates and cups, towels, furniture, vacuum cleaners and more, and has to be treated according to and within those restrictions that each and every elderly person imposes on their own environment.

The health condition of the elderly person is another factor that heavily influences actions and the completion of scheduled tasks. The physical or psychological condition of the elderly has a strong bearing on the strategies that each homecare worker devises and adapts before and during a visit. The goal for each visit is to both see that the elderly was going to cope with the situation until the next visit, and at the same time to use the situation as a preparatory stage for the next visit. Of course, there is a difference in level of detail in strategies from person to person, but the key aspect is that these strategies are determined from shared knowledge which is generated through practice and which aims for the best solution for the team to provide the best possible care.

These strategies are often a result of, and an elaboration on, the information given during the morning discussion and coordination activities. Administrative tasks, which keep track of every action and record these for future evaluation, are intended to help meet the indirect objectives of homecare. This work is carried out in a locale that multifunctions as an office, dining room and as a meeting room (see Figure 1). Almost all the social activities carried out during work hours by the whole group take place here. Consequently, it is also the place where all document repositories are kept in a state of continuous maintenance and update. Paper files are created and, depending upon the sensitivity of the information these files contain, they are filed in locked archives or are kept on bookshelves.

2.3. Rationale, structure and system usage

System procurements depend on a rationale for their deployment, which crystallizes the long-term goal of what is to be achieved. This rationale is inscribed on the design of the system, and thus generally prescribes the work to be carried out with it. According to Berg [4], ICT support always embeds an inner logic of the work to be done in a way that strives to guide those that use the system. Agre [1] describes this in terms of a grammar which is related to the activity supported by a specific architecture. JoLiv mobile care™ is a system designed to support a homecare organization as a whole. Thus, the system will give the organization a mechanism for inspection, to attain a "full picture" of what the organization does, what resources are used where and when, to assess the quality of work by a number of formerly unattainable variables, and to employ powerful tools that will assist planning and budgetary work. However, the organization's main concern is to tend to those under its care. The workers need to be mobile and operate in a vast working area. The resources to be measured are found in the mobile work place, in the homes of the elderly. It is this work that is supposed to supply the system with data through which measures such as planning and budgeting can be made to work.

This general rationale for the system, and the user behavior it promotes, can be formulated as support for documenting the work while the work is being performed. The user can access a computer anytime and anywhere through the utilization of the mobile devices. In relation to the context in which the technological system is used, the rationale of the system prescribes certain ways of involving the technological support in practice. This system implies that work is carried out according to sequences based on the notion of a diary metaphor: one house call at the time, where the following house call adds to the sequence of actions and so forth. In other words, the ICT support formalizes aspects of practice, where the starting and stopping of activities is imposed, and a formalization is attained that loses the fluid character of house calls in general. Recall the importance ascribed to fluidity in office settings by Moran & Anderson [18].

Information about the group and work in general is found not only in the archival form of the repositories; in addition, a vast amount of information is posted on the closet cupboard doors and on different bulletin boards. The work in the homes of the elderly is not possible without the daily meetings. In this situation they have a mutual relationship that continuously evolves and the connection between these mobile and static components of their duties and work are a critical achievement for the workers. We denote these activities as Base activities. The others, discussed as the Case dimension, comprise those activities which are not carried out at a fixed location. There are crucial differences between the continuous change of contexts and situation while on the move and Base work activities carried out in a local office, or "Base". These dimensions have emerged from the longitudinal study of how the mobile support system gradually becomes interwoven with practice. The move from a Base to Case dimension is one which tools utilized in mobile cooperative work needs to address.

Base and Case dimensions are mutually dependent and the connections between them are crucial linkages which need to be acknowledged. However, our knowledge of these connections is under-researched and poorly understood. Ethnographic analysis of the relationships betweens these linkages promise to reveal how and why current designs are exploited to bridge these dimensions of mobile collaborative work.

3. Homecare Work In Practice

Over a period of four years, and with the advent of the JoLiv system, the work practices of homecare workers have been subject to ethnographically informed investigations to understand their functioning and evolution (see Orre [21, 22]). The fieldwork, which commenced during the autumn of 2001, has a translocal connection to related projects and sites that share a similar focus, exploring the utilization of mobile technology in mobile practices (see Hedestig et al [12]). How the research activities have unfolded during these years of prolonged fieldwork is found in the strategies that construct the multi-sited ethnography of Marcus [16]. Similar approaches are discussed in work by Weilenmann [32] and in Harper [10]. First and foremost we have *followed the people* and their situation while working in the sites outlined below. We have been supported in field activities by using a strategy where we have *followed the object*. The strategy [16] implies that the researcher follows an artifact in and out of the various contexts through which it travels. More specifically, we follow a mobile device, along with other means of supporting cooperative work, through the activities engaged in by mobile workers, as is the case for this study.

Our data collection methods consisted of participant observation, active involvement in work activities, and interviews both with groups and individuals. In addition, we drew upon both official and un-official organizational documents. Most interviews and video recordings were transcribed, and the remainder have been catalogued and cross-referenced with the notes taken during interviews and video sessions. Interview data allows a plausible reconstruction the flow of thoughts and rationale behind observed actions. For this paper, we have constructed three vignettes from our corpus of data. Each vignette represents a realistic account of what actually happens in practice (see Van Maanen [29]).

3.1. Base work vignette

The first vignette embraces the local office – the coordination hub for the homecare workers' activities. It describes the use of some of the artifacts that connect the different places for the primary, secondary and preparatory tasks of the care workers. Several studies, including those by Wiberg [33], Orr [20] and Brown et al [5], have pointed out the importance of place for providing recurrent opportunities for social interaction and the development of a mutual understanding. Every agent has an articulated need to socialize and exchange experience of the past day's work and the day yet to come. For this activity, the place is a big table around which all the homecare workers sit. The table serves many purposes. During the morning meeting, besides the coffee mugs and occasionally sandwiches, homecare workers use the table as a focal point to plan their activities for the day, and to get enough information from colleagues about the elderly they themselves are to visit. It is a multipurpose table and most of the resources found among binders and diaries, and the desktop computer are usually covering most of the space (lower left-hand corner, Figure 1). The large group diary is a particularly important artifact, containing specific case information that carries over from previous home visits. The discussions and the uses of technology are interwoven in a complex web of tools and gestures that often hold parallel threads of topics and concerns. The numbers in the Base vignette are codenames used in this practice to maintain the anonymity of elderly clients, in case aspects of work and house calls are discussed in public spaces in the village.

"...The morning meetings are one of those highlights that Anne looks forward to every morning. When someone asks her the main reasons for her staying and working in the homecare business, even though she often complains about the salary and the irregular working hours, her answer is always the satisfaction of being in contact with the elderly and in the team work with her colleagues. The morning meeting is one of the few opportunities for the whole group to meet before they carry out their daily activities. As she came into the room, she shared a joke with Agneta about their night out the previous week. Yesterday, she promised elderly 516 to book an appointment with the hairdresser. The time was set for Friday 3pm and she sticks the hairdresser's business card with all the necessary information into the diary at the table in the meeting room. -*Now, I will not forget to take her there, I have booked the time for 516 hair on Friday....Carrie- you will work on Friday won't you?* Carrie who was sitting right beside her replied – *yes I will, was it about 516?...She mentioned something about it earlier this week...no problem..*

The meeting usually takes an hour and during this time they all have time to catch up with most of the important events that unfolded the day before. They also divide the tasks that are to be carried out during the day. Eva and Margret, who worked the evening before had added the note that 576 would need a reevaluation of his service plan since his condition had got much worse the last couple of days. *–Perhaps it is time to get the process started to get him a room at Råbocken,* (one of the old peoples' home in the village) *- if he continues to be this weighty in future...*(Carrie added to the concerns that Eve and Margret were expressing)...*-we cannot have 5 visits a day much longer than for one single person...*

There is also time to go through those records and files that concerned the elderly people who she is about to visit. Usually, it is not necessary to go through those files in detail, since almost all information that would be helpful is discussed during the morning, but one cannot be too sure, better safe than sorry as usual. Fortunately she found out that elderly 413 were staying with relatives during the whole week. *-Someone must have missed writing the note about 413 and the fact that he will be away for the whole week...*she immediately made the correction to the information on the desktop computer

Agneta was very concerned about 534 and the rapid change of her health condition: *-She was not looking well at all yesterday afternoon. Her eyes where blurry and she had fever. -We consulted DSK* (the primary care unit), *and they agreed too that we give her the medicine she has been subscribed* (Eve added more information about the case, and continued). *-We have to observe her condition close today. -By the way, who will take her today? – I can do that,* Susan quickly answered, *-I will have to go to 489 anyway, and it is on the same route.* Susan asks if there are anything more that I should consider regarding the visit to 534, Susan added... *– If her condition is worse, just contact DSK,* Agneta added...*-next 587...-who will assist him today...*" (The meeting prolongs through the articulation of work and simultaneous discussion about the care receivers continues).

The Base vignette demonstrates the collective management of parallel information which accompanies a shift change. Similar information is kept in a multitude of locations, which involves a lot of work to maintain attention and consolidate for any set of visits. Most of the situations from late in the previous day that the homecare workers felt to be of sufficient importance are recorded in any of the information tools during the morning meeting. Thus, each assistant contributes information they think relevant to the whole meeting or to specific colleagues. This socially concerted aspect of awareness work involves a number of interesting components.

During the day shifts the workers often choose to take on house calls where the situation of the elderly client suits the skills or interests of a particular worker. These interests do not result in 'cherry picking', or choosing work tasks that would mean an easier case load for the individual worker. The choice criteria can also include for example the fact that a particular worker may have had an argument with one of the elderly clients, or that it has been a long time since an elderly person was handled by the particular worker.

Since responsibility for every elderly person is handed over every morning, each meeting also requires that the handover process is a person-to-person interaction as well as adding all the relevant information to the computerized history of the specific elderly client. These stories or fragments of information are identifiable in the tools, which hold these currents of information in the mobile work place. One such repository is the group diary. It is here that workers can find the information that concerns crucial details, often as a result of encounters that colleagues have had with the elderly during house calls. It is also a tool which is browsed through several times during a day, even if the person browsing does not add any information to it. The design of the digital diary did not quite fit the custom and practice of the homecare workers, a fact they repeatedly remarked upon during observations and interviews. Although its role is to communicate case-specific information for specific care workers, its circulation also contributes: (i) knowledge of ongoing case history (medium-to-long term), (ii) situational case knowledge (yesterday and today, short-term history) and (iii) colleagues' responsibilities and dispositions for the day. In short, the way it is used fosters a generalized sense of awareness in the work place, both of collaborators' activities and the objects of collaborative work. In order to understand the linkages materialized in the diary, we next turn to the activities of Case practice as they are actually performed outside the walls of the Base.

3.2. Case work vignette

Case work is performed in the homes of the elderly. Most municipal homecare organizations are concerned with Case work while discussing the efficiency and quality of the services they offer. It is especially notable in the argument that high quality care is typically associated with spending as many hours as possible in the homes of the elderly. There are actually incentives that, as a direct consequence, sweep away Base activities, since they are seen to be unproductive. The mobile workplace is a vast geographical area through which the workers move, by bicycle, foot and car, making their way to the homes of the elderly, and traveling back and forth to the Base locale. In all weathers, day and night, homecare workers must get from A to B and know how best to do so, given the opportunities for travel at their disposal. It is also in the Case dimension that we can identify the sources that hold the information carried in the dairy and which are articulated through discussions. The sources for these discussions are found in the case dimension.

Case work usually involves six to ten house calls a day for each and every worker. A number of these house calls involve concerted collaboration in that they require attendance in pairs. The work is physically demanding and is governed by health and safety laws, union agreements and organizational directives. These impose significant coordination demands on the assistants; it is not an easy task to go through a list of given assignments one after the other. While undertaking care of the elderly, mobile technology does not have any particularly important role for the actions. The main objective has the full focus. The situation where the system is used is to sign off a task, or check who will be visited next. We will follow Anne to this morning's first assignment, and perhaps more interestingly, follow and see the links of information which give awareness in the workplace.

"...Her first task for the day was to tend to 513 and see to that she took her medicine and was up on her feet. Her experience told her that this type of visit would normally take about 15 minutes. Including conversation! However, as usual, things didn't go quite as planned. 513 was in a tricky mood. She was not very keen on taking her pills, even though the doctor had prescribed them, and the task required that Anne saw with her own eyes that 513 really swallowed without keeping the pills in her hand or spitting them out afterwards. But 513 insisted on talking about the construction work by the library, using the time to her advantage. Anne knew the lady was lonely, and for sure wanted more of Anne's attention if possible. The visit had overrun by 10 minutes when Anne made a note in the medicine list posted on the cupboard door in 513's kitchen before she left. When she got outside, she rang Maria to tell her about the delay, unfortunately without any success. She was supposed to meet Maria for the next visit; the second task for the day was to tend to elder 562.

Actually, "562" meant attending to two people. Anne looked forward to this meeting every day. The lady suffered from dementia and had difficulties with her mobility, and her husband undertook the heavy lifting of her every day, even though he was several years older than her. The task involved helping the lady with washing and dressing. The husband needed to get his frustration off his chest at the same time, blaming him self for not doing enough. This was one of the cleaning days. The regulation implies that Anne does not undertake cleaning tasks or heavy lifting by herself. There are usually two assistants on these tasks and Maria had already started to assist the lady in the bathroom when Anne arrived. The husband opened the door and they talked about what had happened since the last visit. Maria had for certain heard the story when she came, but the bottom line was that the night had been calm without any mishaps. Anne went to the kitchen to fetch a small broom and a dust cloth. While in the kitchen she went through the medicine list posted on the fridge…"

Before each house call, the workers need to (i) to prepare for the situation they might find hiding behind the care receiver's front door. While being delayed from earlier house calls, rushing in to a completely new environment is a usual scenario. The information given through the diary and the day-to-day ongoing discussions is a support in these situations since it often signals when unexpected situations may occur. Such information is also given in everyday stories of a specific house call, or through the diary where the note gives similar advice. Discussion about the specifics of every activity is part of the culture and emphasizes participation in activities which would otherwise be conducted in isolation. The way specific tools are used generates a vital sense of what is going on, helping to attune workers to the circumstances: here the diary, computer, and the continuing discussions play an important role through which information can be shared.

While indoors, the workers need to (ii) adapt to the home of the care receiver, meaning that one needs to learn and be aware of routines and habits that a care receiver appreciates or is accustomed to. When adapting to such circumstances, it is unavoidable that the workers get involved in their care receiver's life. This involvement is also visible in the discussions that the workers have when the orderliness of a care receiver is affected. The care receiver's health might of course be as such that it is difficult to discuss what is appreciated. Here, maintaining or establishing habitual patterns is a factor which helps both the care receiver and the workers. The method is often applied when the care receiver is suffering from dementia, which is a common reason why homecare is involved if the elderly person is able to continue living in his/her home. It also helps the workers to perform as if they were one carer and also ensures that the service plan approved by the assistant officer is carried out. The social dimension of homecare, such as chatting over a cup of coffee, is another important mechanism which allows the worker to uncover health information as part of the awareness process. It is often through such conversations that crucial information emerges which is later reflected in discussions and in the diary.

Most of the care receivers are on medication. It is also an element that connects homecare and primary care. The homecare workers are (iii) delegated to give medicine by injection if necessary, or carry out care procedures delegated by the primary care unit. The intake of prescription medicine is often closely watched. Medication is regarded among care receivers with suspicion, and some house calls only have the role of regularly watching that subscribed medicine is taken properly. In the majority of the care receivers' homes, one will find an information hub where the information about the medication and the routines are kept. Usually these hubs are kept somewhere in the kitchen area, since the medicine is stored either in cupboard that is not easily accessible or the fridge if it needs to be kept cold. The arrangement also helps family members who share their time helping the care receiver. All intake of medication is carefully recorded in a list. Routinely checking the information hubs and ensuring that the right amount of medication is taken provides information about the health status of the care receiver, and should there be doubts, this is reported and shared amongst the team members.

3.3. Transport, weather, ill health: Contextual factors enforce illicit case coordination

The work involved in keeping up a reasonable level of orderliness is the other side of case work and it concerns efficient articulation and coordination of tasks, transport and time. The only factor among these three that constantly increases is the number of tasks. Transport and time are the crucial and scarce resources. The planned sequence of actions after the morning meetings is rarely valid for more than an hour. Even if most of the house calls on the rounds usually take the time stipulated by the service plan, exceptions affect a whole chain of events. At the same time, there is a general understanding that the worker should stay longer than planned if the health condition of the care receiver demands it. Even if such actions add to the work pile and generate more work in terms of re-coordinating and rescheduling planned sequences of house calls, they are worth the effort since care receivers get the care and attention the team considers appropriate. If any of the transport and supporting activities is delayed it may similarly require the chain of activities to be re-articulated.

The time needed to keep the operations going does vary with the seasons, but during the weeks and months when weather conditions do constrain the options of transport, more effort is consequently required. The geographical area over which the elderly people are distributed does, in most cases, demand the use of cars or other means of transport, e.g. bicycles, on foot, or in private cars. Yet another factor that provides constrains for case work is the teams' shared responsibility of the personal alarm each care receiver has installed in his or her home. These mobiles are, according to organizational policy, not allowed to be used for anything else than answering emergency calls and making calls connected to such circumstances. Three cars are assigned to the homecare work group, and at times when the workload is too heavy, private cars are used as well. The third vignette continues to follow Anne as her day unfolds. Here, Anne is on call for emergency calls and is entitled to use one of the homecare cars available for the team:

"...The car door closed behind Ulla, who would tend to 456 in the next 30 minutes. - *If everything goes well in the next few hours we should manage to get through the assigned house calls before lunch - if no emergency calls are made, that is,* Anne said out loud in order to get Karin's attention. The beeping noise beside her was Karin looking at, and maneuvering, her handheld computer, to check the assignment list for the whole group. – *We just have too much to do nowadays, how will we manage this with the numbers of staff we have, we should at least be allowed to call in more replacements.* This was one of the heated discussions of the moment. Some of the staff had recently been talking about how much they had to do. They were even forced to use their private cars frequently or they would not have managed to get it all together. Anne usually took the initiative to be assigned as the person responsible for the alarm phone – a mobile phone through which all emergency calls were to be handled. They arrived at 314 and it was time for Karin to get out. -*Then we meet at 563, in one and a half hours*, she said before she closed the door. What Karin referred to was the cleaning call by 563 which was a call squeezed into the plan this morning. It was impossible to find a time slot the same afternoon when cleaning calls were usually planned. RKF needed a service (the cars the team have at their disposal are referred to by the letters on their license plates). It was Ulla who had noticed that the summer tires were still on. It is a criminal offence to drive in winter conditions with such tires. Anne picked up the emergency phone and dialed the number to one of the repair shops she knew in the village. *–Hello John, do you by any chance have the time for our RKF this week...- Perfect...on Friday you say..Friday it is then...yes, it's the tires, you have them stored have you not?...perfect, see you then...bye.* She hangs up. The car started to gain speed again. Her first duty this morning was to prepare breakfast and coffee for 576, an older lady who had almost lost most of her hearing, but who had amazingly sharp eyes. Just before she pressed the doorbell, the alarm phone rang its hard and sharp signal in her pocket. It was not an emergency call thank God this time, as she checked the phone. If it had been an emergency call, she would have had to call some of her colleagues and say that the missed house call needed to be attended to before 10am. But it was Ulla who called saying that she had finished earlier than planned and wondered if she should sit and wait, or if she should call Birgitta and tell her that she was on her way by foot to assist her with 543 instead, - *you do not need to pick me up as we agreed, I think Birgitta took her own car so we will have to use that until lunch, if she is not there I just walk to 544, see you at lunch*...and she rang off. The breakfast was served 576 at 8.45am sharp, with fifteen minutes left until Karin was supposed to be picked up when the emergency phone rang again, *same, same* Anne said out loud - *it must be the usual toilet visit by 435.* 435 had figured that if she pushes the alarm button rather than wait until the homecare workers arrived, they will show up earlier. 435 was not the only elderly person that used the alarm this way, it was quite common. It usually ended with the assistants turning up earlier, and as always, explaining to the old lady that the button was for her own safety when it really is for real, you know. Anne called Karin that she had to go to 435, and added that there was no reply when she tried to ring her, so she had better go and check it out. *-I will be twenty minutes late at 563, you can start, I will show up in time..."*

The vignette reveals the spatiotemporal coordination complexity of homecare casework as a collaborative activity. In terms of awareness, we notice that mobile phones are used to make colleagues aware of a late arrival or if another route is chosen instead. But this is a different variety of awareness to that discussed earlier. It is rather a just-in-time delivery of awareness information, valid at a specific moment in time and space, and directed towards an immediate and proximal response. Mobile phones are routinely used as an important tool in the mobile workplace, with decisions concerning the moment-to-moment logistics of maintaining the orderliness of the workplace.

Private means are by any argument a feasible solution for any of the parties, even if the workers are compensated when no other solution is there to be found. The obvious need for smoothness in daily operations, keeping up the relative "normality of affairs", constantly invokes an illicit use of the emergency phone which should be a dedicated line. The worker with responsibility for the emergency phone suddenly gets to play the important role of mobile coordination central. This eases the logistics during days when transportation is scarce. Moreover, it also allows a culture of remote coordination through mobile phones to develop, a development not sanctioned by management or policies. The culture of keeping each other aware of how work is progressing and developing is given new means through mobile phones: in this case they form a technological infrastructure which works in parallel with the mobile support they have at hand. The observation is that the mobile support at hand is seldom used during case work as this system does not align to the activities taking place. Rather, other means offer a more adaptive architecture, providing the means to establish a just-in -time connection to their peers.

4. Discussion

This paper set out to explore the problematics of awareness in distributed groups by examining how homecare workers conduct their affairs in a mobile workplace. We propose a generalized concept of awareness: *information that is acted on by collaborators as knowledge, which is generated, given or accessed, through interaction constituting and contributing to the cooperative accomplishment of an orderly workplace.* We found it most useful to deal with the underlying concept of awareness by exposing patterns of action. Workers obtain and disseminate knowledge about changes in one anothers' whereabouts, the condition of those in their care, the daily schedules around which they coordinate their actions, and so on. We describe this aspect of their joint work as awareness strategies embedded into their collaborative work practice. Awareness is knowledge by another name; knowledge that is infrequently articulated but frequently used to determine an appropriate choice from a repertoire of practical actions. Having a "keen sense" of appropriate action, for us, means having a set of strategies to obtain and maintain a workable set of constraints on action in the face of the frequently ephemeral and transient nature of the constraining forces.

Bearing in mind that usage of technology may be involved already in established awareness strategies, how might one anticipate the value of involving additional or replacement forms technological support? The question is like the chicken and the egg; it is difficult to pinpoint why and when a particular scheme of use emerged.

What we see through our exploration of the mobile work place and workers' awareness strategies is that Base and Casework dimensions are interconnected through tools and repositories. Both can provide and enable awareness to be actively communicated. The examples provided though the case work are the mobile phone and the diary. Tools are chosen and used according to their ability to provide a form of *practical sense of knowing* what is happening in the mobile work place. Returning again to the importance of fluidity, and according to Agre [1], the transformation of institutions is about being less tied to places, with the activities becoming more fluid. This is partly a change brought about by the introduction of new technologies - technologies which have paved the way for flexible work arrangements. Moran & Anderson [18] found that fluidity is an ordinary part of everyday organization in office settings. Here, the idea of fluidity has a depth hitherto unplumbed. The work is fluid because the situation 'on the ground' is always changing. Whereas one might consider fluidity to be a normal perturbation of office procedures, it is almost the reverse in mobile homecare work. Procedure is a normal perturbation of fluidity. The ability to muster a set of tasks into a workable sequence is a practical skill that is used to counter the volatility of the elemental activities to be performed. The degree to which it is possible to do this is not only a matter of resource coordination (material, co-worker, transport) but also of a "keen sense" of the laterality for acting within and beyond the limits set by the organization. So it is also made fluid in a very different way, namely, by the degree of autonomy for deciding what to do next that has resulted from the 'abuse' of the alarm phone.

Homecare workers continuously strive to learn about each other's activities. It is a proactive articulation behavior of work place activities that the whole team adjusts to. Mark [17] sees such behavior as having a normative effect on work place conventions, proposing awareness as a learning device. It is thus surpasses implementation of awareness features, e.g. setting user modes state in a buddy list. It concerns the activities that trigger the mode setting. The proactive behavior enacted by the homecare worker is also featured in the diary, in different binders, and in computer files. Heath et al [11] identify the potential of awareness to foster learning. Or as we discussed, having or attaining *a practical sense of knowing* generates and capitalizes on the active involvement of workers, contributing to the ongoing discussion and development of the workplace. Heath et al. also discuss the potential for providing the user with automatically revealed awareness information: we could provide the users themselves with tools, allowing people to selectively generate traces of their ongoing activities and actions which are visible to others in different ways. Thus, it is a matter of consenting surveillance. However, as we have seen in the study, the reward given through sharing seems to be supplementary and is contingent on the culture of the team.

The conventions in which the use of such tools are either promoted or rejected seem to be playing a crucial role. This is especially evident when comparing the use situations of different tools. Diaries, computer applications, PDAs and mobile phones can be mapped to particular ideas of conventions of convenience and utility. Within the architecture these tools provide a freedom to act [1] which is negotiated collectively. For our homecare team, these conventions have their roots in efficiently sustaining orderliness and the well being of the elderly. They are in some sense treated as constraints that have an equivalent legitimacy to those imposed by the regulations of their institution. The autonomy enjoyed by homecare workers seems to have contributed to the flouting of a clear organizational directive: not to use the emergency mobile phone for any purpose other than an emergency. Their practice knowledge led to an understanding of the likelihood and nature of any emergency call. They were able to exploit the device by virtue of the position in which it was held in the team structure: central, always on and associated with transport. Furthermore, the fact that multiple devices (private mobile phones) could work with the emergency phone overrode the disincentive of using personal property and incurring personal expense for work. They were only able to do this since a major part of their work relies on a keen understanding of its spatio-temporal nature and, arguably, the "culture of giving" that characterized this group of healthcare workers. Part of their practice knowledge involves recurrence of route traversal, of particular people and their particular environments, and of procedures. The phasic nature of the work integrated with a phasic technology. Such mobile technology as a mobile phone has the flexibility to challenge these conventions; as a case activity tool, it is a technology which easily supports the transitions between Base and Case.

5. Concluding Remarks

A central characteristic in the homecare practice reported in this study is that the workers need to observe and take notice of what is normal, what is not considered to be a normal event, or a development that is heading towards an unwanted situation. The health condition of the care receivers and the service plan are the core markers that need to be in accord. Information is related to exceptions and when a situation goes beyond the service plan. It is common practice to inform the whole group in these cases, to put that piece of information in the diary and to use other tools which connect pieces of information to the discussion. The practice that surrounds such mnemonic tools involves everything that is a noteworthy observation after, before or during a house call and thus gives each and every worker *a practical sense of knowing*. Thus, any information connected to the health and wellbeing status of the care receivers is shared through discussions or stories triggered by what one might find written in these repositories. The information has an effect on the daily or upcoming work schedules and plans, which makes the ability to attune to the ongoing discussion even more important. There is a well-worn distinction between "knowing that", declarative knowledge, and "knowing how", procedural knowledge. Our contention that awareness in all its varieties is a manifestation of a practical sense of knowing, bridges this distinction: at least some articulated knowledge originates from knowing how to function as a member of a collaborative group. The relationship between collaborative practice and procedural knowledge is complex. Certainly, in terms of tool support for mobile collaborative work, it requires further investigation. Agre [1] and Mark [17] have variously argued that practice is tied up with local conventions for work. These conventions mediate between organizational rules ('institutions') and tools and structures ('architectures'). For us, authority and control are critical and inescapable components of the awareness concept. The reality of mobile collaborative work is that conventional structures of organizational control are broken and reformed. Change of this kind brings with it the potential for compensatory surveillance mechanisms to maintain control. Equally, as with this case study, control can be delegated to local groups to bring about a new autonomy.

References

[1] Agre, P. Changing Places: Context of Awareness in Computing. *Human-Computer Interaction, 16.* 177-192.
[2] Bannon, L. and Bødker, S. "Constructing Common Information Space". in *Proceedings of the European Conference on Computer-Supported Cooperative Work ECSCW'97*, 1997.
[3] Belotti, V. and Bly, S. Walking away from the desktop computer: distributed collaboration and mobility in a product design team. in *Conference on Computer Supported Cooperative Work*, ACM Press, Boston, Mass, 1996, 209-218.
[4] Berg, M. *Rationalizing Medical Work: Decision-Support Techniques and Medical Practices.* The MIT Press, Cambridge, Massachusetts, London, England, 1997.
[5] Brown, B., Green, N. and Harper, R. (eds.). *Wireless world: social and interactional implications of wireless technology.* Springer Verlag, 2001.
[6] Churchill, E.F. and Wakeford, N. Framing Mobile Collaboration and Mobile Technologies. in In Brown, B., Green, N., and Harper, R. ed. *Wireless world: social and interactional implications of wireless technology.*, Springer Verlag, 2001.
[7] Daly-Jones, O., Monk, A.F. and Watts, L.A. Some advantages of video conferencing over high-quality audio conferencing: fluency and awareness of attentional focus. *International Journal of Human-Computer Studies, 49* (1). 21 - 59.
[8] Dourish, P. and Bly, S. Portholes: Supporting awareness in a distributed work group. in *Proceedings of ACM CHI'92 Conference on Human Factors in Computing Systems*, 1992, 541-547.
[9] Gutwin, C., Greenberg, S. and Roseman, M., Supporting awareness of others in groupware. in *CHI'96 Conference on Human Factors in Computing Systems*, (Vancouver, Canada, 1996), ACM Press, 205.
[10] Harper, R. The Organisation of Ethnography- *A Discussion of Ethnographic Fieldwork Programs in CSCW. Computer Supported Cooperative Work* (9). 239-264.
[11] Heath, C.C., Marcus Sanchez Svensson, Jon Hindmarsh, Paul Luff, and Dirk Vom Lehn Configuring awareness. *Computer Supported Cooperative Work. The Journal of Collaborative Computing, vol.11* (no. 3-4).
[12] Hedestig, U., Kaptelinin, V., & Orre, C. J. Supporting Decentralized Education with Personal Technologies. in *Proceedings of E-LEARN 2002*, Montreal, Canada., 2002.
[13] Ishii, H., Kobayashi, M. and Grudin, J. Integration of Interpersonal Space and Shared Workspace: ClearBoard Design and Experiments. *ACM Transactions on Information Systems, 11* (4). 349-375.

[14] Ishii, H., Wisneski, C., Brave, S., Dahley, A., Gorbet, M., Ullmer, B. and Yarin, P. ambientROOM: Integrating Ambient Media with Architectural Space. in *Companion Proceedings of ACM CHI98*, ACM Press, New York, 1998, 173-174.

[15] Laurier, E. Work as a Socio-technical Accomplishment. in *In Brown, B., Green, N., and Harper, R.* ed. *Wireless world: social and interactional implications of wireless technology.*, Springer Verlag w, 2001.

[16] Marcus, G.E. Ethnography in/of the World System: The emergence of Multi-Sited Ethnography. *Annual Review Of Anthropology, Vol 24.* pp. 95-117.

[17] Mark, G. Conventions and commitments in distributed CSCW groups. *The Journal of Collaborative Computing Computer Supported Cooperative Work., vol 11* (no. 3-4).

[18] Moran, P.A., R. J., The Workaday World As a Paradigm for CSCW Design. in *Proceedings of the international conference of computer supported collaborative work, CSCW,* (1990).

[19] Nilsson, M. and Hertzum, M., Negotiated Rythms of Mobile Work: Time, Place and Work Scheduels. in *Proceedings of the 2005 International ACM SIGGROUP Conference on Supporting Group Work (Group 2005)*, (Sanibel Island, FL, US, 2005), ACM Press, New York, pp. 148-157.

[20] Orr, J. *Talking about machines- An Ethnography of a Modern Job.* Cornell University Press. Ithaca. United states of America, 1996.

[21] Orre, C.J. Keeping track of notes- implications of mobile information and communication technology in homecare practice. in Wiberg, M. ed. *The interaction Society: Practice, Theories, and Supportive technologies.*, IDEA-group Inc, 2004.

[22] Orre, C.J. Put Mobile IT into Practice; Make Information Available Across Organizational Boundaries. in *Proceedings of (IRIS 25),The 25th Information Systems Research Seminar in Scandinavia*, Bautahoj, Denmark, 2002.

[23] Pinell, D. and Gutwin, C. *Designing for loose coupling in mobile groups.* ACM Press, New York, NY, Sanibel Island, FL, US. (November 16-20, 2002), 2003.

[24] Pinell, D. and Gutwin, C., A Group Design Framework for Loosely Coupled Workgroups. in *ECSCW 2005: Proceedings of the Ninth European Conference on Compute-Supported Cooperative Work*, (Paris, France, 2005), Springer, 65-82.

[25] Pinell, D. and Gutwin, C. *Supporting colllaboration in multidisiplinary home care teams.* AMIA, Bethesd, M, 617-621, San Antonio, Texas, USA, (November 9-13, 2002), 2002.

[26] Rønby-Pedersen, E. and Sokoler, T. AROMA: abstract representation of presence supporting mutual awareness. in Pemberton, S. ed. *Proceedings of ACM CHI'97 Conference on Human Factors in Computing Systems*, ACM Press, Atlanta, Georgia. USA., 1997, 51 - 58.

[27] Schmidt, K. The problem with Awareness. *Computer Supported Cooperative Work. The Journal of Collaborative Computing, Vol. 11* (no. 3-4).

[28] Sherry, J., & Salvador, T. Running and Grimacing: the Struggle for Balance in Mobile Work. in *In Brown, B., Green, N., and Harper, R. (Eds)* ed. *Wireless world: social and interactional implications of wireless technology.*, Springer Verlag, 2001.

[29] Van Manen, J. *Tales of the field – on writing ethnography.* The University of Chicago Press, US, 1988.

[30] Vertegaal, R., Conversational awareness in multiparty VMC. in *CHI'97 Conference on Human Factors in Computing Systems*, (Atlanta, Georgia, 1997), ACM Press, 6 - 7.

[31] Watts, L.A. and Dubois, E. Managing visibility in ubiquitous multimedia communication environments. in *People and Computers XII, the proceedings of IHM-HCI2001*, New Holland, Amsterdam, 2001.

[32] Weilenmann, A. *Doing Mobility*, Department of Informatics. Gothenburg University, Sweden, 2003.

[33] Wiberg, M. *In between Mobile Meetings: Exploring seamless ongoing interaction support for mobile CSCW*, PhD-thesis, Department of Informatics, Umeå University, Umeå, Sweden, (2001). *Department of Informatics*, Umeå Univeristy, Umeå, 2001.

Cooperative Systems Design
P. Hassanaly et al. (Eds.)
IOS Press, 2006

Collaboration support by co-ownership of documents

Michael PRILLA and Carsten RITTERSKAMP
Institute for Applied Work Science, Ruhr University of Bochum
{michael.prilla, carsten.ritterskamp}@rub.de

Abstract. The concept of co-ownership well-known from real-life collaboration is a valuable means to support work with documents in groupware systems. In this paper, we present an approach leading to the practical appliance of co-ownership in a groupware system and show how this concept can be used to foster collaboration. Our efforts are supported by a review of related systems and concepts as well as a requirements analysis based on scenarios.

Keywords: Co-ownership, Groupware, Negotiation

Introduction

Considering real-life processes in which participants collaboratively work on documents, *co-ownership* is a widely-known and approved concept. Besides others, such processes[1] can be found in the joint creation of scientific papers or in the publishing of books. In the former case the participants work on their paper by jointly developing its content, in the latter case editors integrate contributions from several authors into a book. Under normal circumstances, in both process the participants finally become co-owners of the resulting documents. With regard to these documents, co-ownership supports the collaboration among co-workers by emphasising that individual work has *converged* and can now be regarded as common work resulting in common responsibility for a document's content. Co-ownership serves as a kind of *contract* in real-life processes, sustaining the agreement on a document's content. However, not only responsibilities but also certain changes in the collaboration among the participants result from co-ownership: while individuals can edit their documents on their own behalf or make them public for others, co-owners have to agree on changes of their documents. The latter process usually evokes *negotiations* among the participants. Furthermore, decisions like e.g. publishing documents depend on the agreement of at least a majority of their co-owners. In the case of conflicts individuals may also withdraw their status of being co-owner of a particular document.

To focus on the consequences of co-ownership, we distinguish between *shared ownership* and the concept of *co-ownership* as represented above. With shared ownership we refer to a situation in which the membership in a group of owners results in the assignment of additional *individual* privileges. In such situations, owners may manipulate documents irrespective of the agreement of other owners. In contrast to

---

[1] By the term *process* we refer to a set of logically interrelated activities (e.g. writing, making agreements) aiming at the creation of a specific result (e.g. documents).

shared ownership, co-ownership describes a situation in which not only documents become the property of a group but also work on the document has to be done in accordance with the group of owners. Thus, co-ownership transforms individual work on documents into a group process.

Although co-ownership can be considered as a well-established concept in real-life settings, to our knowledge no groupware system providing suitable support for co-ownership exists. Taking into account our notion that the concept can support collaboration and to sustain agreements in collaborative work with documents, in this paper we argue that groupware can be improved by supporting co-ownership. Due to the nature of co-ownership as described above, its support has to include mechanisms for the negotiation of both co-ownership itself and resulting changes in the work process. Facing the absence of co-ownership in groupware systems, this paper describes the requirements for its support and presents our approach to its implementation.

In the following sections we will examine the consequences of supporting co-ownership and show that the concept is basically made up by the two aspects of *durable expressions of co-ownership* in systems and *configurable negotiation support* for the work processes related to documents affected by co-ownership. In section 1, we give a brief overview of related approaches to group ownership and negotiations in groupware systems and contrast these approaches with the concept of co-ownership. To describe work supported by co-ownership, in section 2 we provide three different scenarios of collaborative work with documents. Section 3 describes the analysis of the scenarios and provides requirements for the support of co-ownership derived from the analysis. Next, we describe our concept for supporting co-ownership in and show its implementation and practical appliance in section 4. We conclude the paper with reflections on our concept and its implementation.

1. State of the Art

We consider the concept of co-ownership to be a valuable means for the support of collaborative work. Yet there's no groupware or document management system available that offers a suitable support for such a concept. In this paper we present the design and implementation of a groupware system allowing for co-ownership. Notwithstanding the absence of similar systems, valuable insights for our design task can be gained from the analysis of related concepts: concepts to support group ownership and negotiations are essential to the facilitation of co-ownership in groupware systems. In this section, we therefore comment on corresponding approaches and systems, pointing out their limitations with respect to co-ownership.

1.1. Shared Ownership and access control mechanisms

Shared ownership is a well-known concept in systems that aim to support collaboration. In most systems, it is supported implicitly by conferring a specific set of access rights to a group of users and is therefore closely related to the field of access control mechanisms. Different approaches to govern a user's access to system functionalities have been discussed in the literature. Amongst these, role based access control (RBAC) models are merited for providing a sophisticated, flexible and reliable means to deal with authorization in multi-user application domains [17]. Within RBAC, roles are used as a *mediating* construct that offers a specific set of access permissions to a system's functionalities [10]. They are usually described in terms of their position, associated functions and tasks [16]. To allow for a flexible and fine-grained administration of access policies, roles are granted to users in a contextualized manner, i.e. with respect to a distinct set of documents governed by the system.

One could argue that by defining the role of an owner, equipping it with adequate access permissions and assigning it to a group of users with reference to a specific set of *artefacts* (e.g. documents), co-ownership is sufficiently supported. This is only partially true: albeit the appliance of RBAC provides a means to express *shared ownership*, it lacks mechanisms to support *co-ownership*. What is important is that standard RBAC mechanisms along with other access control methods primarily concentrate on the individual appliance of privileges: a user's possibility to execute a specific operation is subject to the presence of appropriate privileges, but does not depend on whether or not other users consent with the execution of the operation in question. Considering the case of BSCW [1], access rights are granted on a per-object level using configurable roles. Although this is sufficient to facilitate shared ownership, it is not to make co-ownership work: at any time a user may perform operations she is authorized to by means of her role membership, regardless of other users agreeing to do so or not.

As we have already argued in the introduction and will see in greater detail from the scenarios presented later in this paper, *collectively* deciding upon whether or not to apply a specific function is a task often performed given the concept of co-ownership. When it comes to foster group decisions within a groupware system, support for negotiations is a natural means. We will comment on the appliance of negotiations in the following section.

1.2. Negotiations

Negotiation processes are a substantial part of cooperative work [5]. An early contribution by Davis and Smith approaches the issue from the field of distributed problem solving and applies the concept of negotiation to a network of "decentralized, loosely coupled knowledge sources" [4]. Here, the concept of negotiation is characterized as a central element to problem solving in such networks and described as a "fundamental mechanism for interaction". Derived from appliances in requirements engineering, where computer-support for negotiations has been used to "get through routine cases of agreement, abstention, or simple modifications of proposals as quickly as possible in order to determine efficiently which proposals require a more intensive communication process" [19], the concept is generally applied for accomplishing coordinative tasks, for developing a shared understanding of a topic or for resolving conflicts [6]. Other approaches use negotiations to share perspectives in collaborative learning scenarios [7], to foster decision making [5] or to augment access control mechanisms in groupware [20].

One can generally classify groupware systems with negotiation support by the degree to which the process of negotiating itself is central to the system's application domain. The scale varies from sophisticated systems, whose primary or sometimes even sole concern is the support of complex real-life negotiation processes [2], to applications in which negotiations act as one instrument amongst others to foster cooperation. So-called *decision support systems* [5] and *negotiation support systems*

[2] are of the former kind, whereas approaches modelling negotiations as a voting process (e.g. PoliTeam [20]) belong to the latter.

From a process-related point of view, it is necessary to have a closer look at the nature of the outcomes a negotiation process may have. We differentiate between negotiations in terms of whether they entail consequences internal or external to the corresponding groupware system:

- A negotiation may lead to activities that are not carried out within the groupware system. We refer to this as *system-external behaviour.* For an example, take a group of people negotiating where to go on vacation: if they have mutually agreed upon a destination, subsequently it is usually not the system but the people going on a journey.

- A negotiation may have effects on the configuration, the content of or the activities within a groupware system and thus lead to an *internal state transition* within this system. For an example, imagine a group of people negotiating whether or not to allow additional users to view a shared document. If a majority agrees upon the proposal to extend the group of the document's recipients, the negotiation process results in corresponding changes performed by the system.

It is a commonality of most systems offering negotiation support to pay only little attention to the case that a negotiation may have effects on the system's future behaviour or configuration (internal state transitions): the possibility to let the execution of a system's functionalities become subject to a computer-supported negotiation process is present in only a few systems, none of them tailored to fully support the collaborative processes that come along with co-ownership. For example, in PoliTeam [20], access control mechanisms are extended with negotiations. Here, the application of negotiations is limited to the (momentary) adaption of access policies, i.e. the temporary *assignment* of privileges that are not covered by access permissions available to a user. The task of negotiating whether or not a function available to a group of users and subject to their authorisation shall be applied remains unaddressed. However, exactly this is a necessity to the support of co-ownership. We can identify a similar limitation in WebGuide [19] and its successor BSCL [18]. Although these systems both incorporate the concept of perspectives providing a means to collectively share artefacts and furthermore both provide for negotiation mechanisms mediating the use of commonly owned objects, they still fall short of supporting co-ownership due to their limited use of negotiations. In both systems, negotiations are merely used for deciding whether or not an artefact shall be accessible to a larger audience, e.g. by moving it from a perspective only shared by a small group of collaborating learners to the shared perspective of the whole course. Though letting the decision of whether or not to publish a shared artefact become subject to negotiation surely is an important aspect when supporting co-ownership, it is not sufficient: for example, co-owners also have to collectively decide whether or not to perform changes on collaboratively owned artefacts. The scenarios presented in the forthcoming section underpin that negotiations have to be applied in a much broader sense, ultimately as a means to mediate the execution of arbitrary functionalities of a groupware system.

2. Scenarios

Before we present our approach to support co-ownership in groupware systems, we describe requirements for its implementation. To get a deeper understanding of these affordances we use a scenario-based approach [3] to get an insight on appliances of co-ownership in the context of collaborative work with documents in groupware[2]. Scenarios are a well-known means to "capture valuable information about how users actually go about doing their work". The usage of such scenarios enables us to find characteristic elements of such work and, as Caroll puts it, "orients design and analysis toward a broader view (...)" [3]. Our scenarios are therefore intended to establish a basis for an analysis of requirements for the support of co-ownership in groupware systems. Beyond their usage for this analysis we will use the scenarios to illustrate our further considerations in the following sections as well.

Deriving requirements from scenarios is a task in which scenarios are "used as sources of information about the objects in the domain and how they interact" [14]. By carefully examining interactions, artefacts and state transitions, analysts can identify mechanisms and their characteristics that can be regarded as requirements for the support of the processes described in scenarios. Caroll [3] describes several methods to derive requirements from scenarios. Without going into details, we will use a slightly adapted combination of two of the methods in our analysis presented later on: *scanning for causes and effects* and *questioning stages of actions*.

Regarding the characteristic elements of scenarios described in [3], our scenarios share the same setting and main objective. The base setting is made up by a groupware system in which the work is taking place and the main objective is the joint creation and manipulation of documents. Before we describe activities in the scenarios, we briefly sketch their context. The scenarios themselves will be told in the form of three users (Kent, Mary and Ward) working on their respective task.

2.1. Reaching consensus in collaborative learning

Collaborative learning is based on the paradigm of constructivism, in which learning is regarded as an active process of constructing rather than acquiring knowledge. Therefore, Computer Supported Collaborative Learning (CSCL) systems support learners in constructing knowledge in interaction with other learners in order to reach a common understanding [7].

In this scenario our users Kent, Mary and Ward learn some basics of agile development methods in software engineering and have to keep a record of their learning progress by creating shared documents. To start off with the learning process they are provided with some material on the topic in a CSCL environment. The users afterwards start to work on the material provided and also begin some inquiry on their own including looking for external resources, providing excerpts and discussing the material. After a certain amount of time Mary proposes that the three of them should come to an end of the learning process and try to find a common understanding of the learning topic. For example, to confirm and objectify their understanding they agree on

---

[2] To our knowledge, there are only a few specialised studies dealing with co-ownership, none of them providing suitable input for its support in groupware systems. Therefore, to provide our design considerations with a broad context, they are based on scenarios. However, empirical studies may help to refine our approach with respect to specific usage scenarios.

a document written by Mary to express their common understanding of the topic. As a result of these agreements and mediated by a corresponding negotiation, they become co-owners of this document. Alternatively, our users might have agreed upon the co-ownership on a folder containing documents. They would have then negotiated whether documents should be added to this folder or not. In the following learning process, Ward may propose to add some information to the document they have previously agreed upon. Accordingly, this proposal leads to another negotiation process mediating whether or not they agree to Ward's proposal. Assuming that Kent and Ward support the proposal and Mary does not, they have to jointly find a solution to the problem by e.g. discussing it. If no solution can be found, they may repeat the negotiation process with different proposals. Ultimately, Ward may withdraw his ownership on the document to express that without one of the proposed changes he disagrees with its content. However, if all of them agree to a proposal, the changed document remains an expression of their common understanding.

2.2. Agreeing in quality management issues

Quality management is a field of work in which co-workers evaluate certain properties of a particular product. Whereas in industry processes the quality of a product can be measured by single experts using more or less strict criteria, there are cases in which this can not be done easily in such a formalized manner. Such cases include the evaluation of the quality of software architectures. For this purpose several approaches and experts exist but none of the approaches can be taken as an absolute measurement tool. Thus, the evaluation of software architectures becomes a collaborative task fulfilled by several experts that jointly have to come to a conclusion.

In the quality management scenario, Kent, Mary and Ward are experts for software architectures and are hired to evaluate a complex architecture for their customer. At the beginning of the process they are provided with information on the software product. Thereafter they start to work individually on the evaluation regarding the criteria the architecture has to meet according to their expertise. Finally, they have to produce a joint report surveying the quality of the customer's architecture. Therefore, they have to either agree to one of the individual opinions or make a compromise. Let's assume that according to the collaborative learning scenario presented above they agree on a report and collaboratively edit it: while they are jointly working on the report in privacy, their customer does not know its content. Once Kent thinks that their work is done, he proposes to make the report available to the customer, telling the others why he thinks so. As this will cause their work to become public, our users being co-owners of the report have to negotiate on Kent's proposal. In case that Ward is the first of them to vote in the negotiation, he may vote *preliminary* and wait on the others' votes before he confirms or changes his vote. Once again, Mary might disagree with the proposal and accordingly refuse it. In contrast to the preceding scenario, Kent and Ward may outvote Mary, as their opinion holds the majority. Later on, they may publish the report to the customer, as publishing does not cause any change in the report's content.

2.3. Collaborative editing

Collaborative editing is a common task when a publication consists of chapters written by different authors who are regarded as experts in particular fields. The editing task thus is one of bringing the contributions of authors together, synchronize and review them and afterwards bring them into a reasonable order.

In the collaborative editing scenario Kent, Mary and Ward are the editors of a book. Several experts are contracted and contribute to the book by providing single chapters. At the beginning of the editing process Kent provides a workspace in a groupware system in which the contributions are stored. For the purpose of review and layout changes, our editors become co-owners of each of the chapters provided. Changes in the content of a chapter have to be negotiated among the editors and the initial owner of the chapter, who originally wrote the chapter and can therefore determine whether changes should take place by her right of veto. In contrast to changes on the content, modifications concerning editorial tasks like spelling or layout changes can be done individually by one of the editors, because they affect the presentation but not the content of the chapter.

To finish the editing activities, Kent, Mary and Ward announce a deadline for changes, after which the book will be published (and thus changes of chapters will not affect the book's content after the deadline has expired) and start a corresponding negotiation on the co-ownership. Until the expiration the experts can agree to become co-owners of the book to express their agreement with its publication. Otherwise, due to their status of being contractors, the experts have to finish their editing work before this deadline expires anyway. In this negotiation process, the votes of editors and experts have to be interpreted differently. If there are some experts who refuse to become co-owners, this conflict is not supposed to block the publishing of the book. In this case, the editors are in charge of the publication and therefore decide whether the book can be published. The votes of the contractors result in co-ownership, which in this case does not determine the publishing process due to the experts' role in the process.

3. Analysis: Requirements for the support of co-ownership

To provide a basis for the design and implementation of support for co-ownership described later on, we use the scenarios presented above to derive requirements. In the following sections we refer to the scenarios and combine their analysis with the description of resulting requirements. Our analysis addresses basic requirements first and afterwards describes more specific demands. It also includes additional constraints, which can not be derived directly from our scenarios but are essential to the subsequent design.

3.1. Basic requirements: Enabling co-ownership

The appliance of co-ownership in groupware systems depends on a systems' capability to manage user roles. Furthermore, these roles have to be managed contextually, that is, roles have to be assignable to users with respect to single documents. Otherwise, co-ownership can not be applied to express and sustain agreements on particular content of a system. Rather than a requirement, the support for *contextualized role management* can be regarded as a precondition for the appliance of co-ownership in groupware.

Each of the scenarios in section 2 deals with the establishing of co-ownership on documents. Furthermore, in all of the scenarios negotiations serve as a mediating mechanism for co-ownership. Thus, the two basic requirements derived from our scenarios contain a mechanism for the *support of multiple owners* for documents and the usage of *negotiations to enable co-ownership*. Analysing the changes in the work processes described in the scenarios and the different appliances of negotiations in these processes, one can identify several demands to support these changes. In the next section, we provide a closer look at these additional requirements.

3.2. Specific requirements: Consequences of applying co-ownership

Our scenarios show different appliances of co-ownership in collaborative work with documents such as agreeing on a shared understanding or creating and publishing a book. Accordingly, the requirements derived from these scenarios differ. Nevertheless, these requirements can be grouped into two categories. The first category encapsulating a set of requirements deals with the *changes in the work process* caused by co-ownership. The second category describes demands concerning the *configuration of a negotiation mechanism* to mediate co-ownership and its consequences.

Referring to our scenarios co-ownership transforms the work on affected documents to be determined by group decisions. In the collaborative learning scenario from section 2.1, our users have to commonly agree upon changes in their document. Accordingly, in the editing scenario our users jointly have to decide whether to publish the book they edit. On a requirements level, the need for group decisions results in the demand for a negotiation mechanism managing the execution of *system-internal functionalities* like editing a document or publishing it. Furthermore, as can be seen when our users make their report available to their customer in the scenario of quality management, such a negotiation mechanism has to mediate *changes in the internal state* of a groupware system by e.g. assigning read privileges to the customer.

In the collaborative learning scenario, Kent ultimately wished to withdraw his ownership in order to express his disagreement with the content of a particular document. Taking into account that co-ownership is based on voluntary participation, a mechanism for its support has to allow user to *revoke their ownership* for certain documents. A negotiation mechanism has to be able to support this system function as well.

Besides the conflict resolved by recursive negotiations (cf. section 2.1) or by a user withdrawing her ownership on a certain document, several other conflicts might occur when co-ownership is supported. In the scenario of quality management, our users cannot agree whether to publish their report or not. In this case, the negotiation is determined by the majority of votes. In contrast, the negotiation on the editing of a document in the collaborative learning scenario has to be decided unanimously. As a result, the negotiation mechanism needed for co-ownership has to be *configurable in terms of its decision mode*. Additional conflicts might occur when participants in a negotiation hold different roles like in the editing scenario. In this case, our users being editors instead of contractors decide whether to publish the book or not. Accordingly, co-ownership needs a *role-based* negotiation mechanism.

Conflicts are only one of the reasons for *high configurability* of negotiations for co-ownership. Depending on the work setting, users may be allowed to *revoke their votes*, and can thus *vote preliminary* like Ward in the quality management scenario or have the *right of veto* like the experts in the editing scenario. The former case affects the commitment of a single vote. In the latter case, another requirement is to *remember the originator* of a document to e.g. prevent take-overs by other co-owners. Other examples for the configurability of the negotiation mechanism can be found in Kent telling the others why they should vote positive in the quality management scenario or in our users announcing a deadline for the negotiation process in the editing scenario. The former example describes a demand to *add explanatory comments* to a negotiation; the latter requires a *deadline for negotiations*. Such expiry dates must be *limited by certain boundaries* to guarantee an appropriate duration for negotiations (cf. [19] for corresponding problems).

Configurability has to provide even more complex options. Remembering the editing scenario, when changes in the content had to be negotiated whereas editorial changes like corrections to the layout could be performed individually by the editors, the negotiation mechanism needs to be configurable in terms of the context an action is executed in. Therefore, in some case the mechanism may *relax the condition of co-ownership to shared ownership* as described above [3]. The collaborative learning scenario indicates that in some cases it is necessary to negotiate on changes to *collections* of documents. If Kent, Mary and Ward would have used a commonly owned folder, changes to its content like e.g. adding documents would have become subject to negotiations.

3.3. Additional constraints for the design

Despite the multitude of requirements that can be extracted directly from our scenarios, we have to think of additional requirements for the implementation of a mechanism supporting co-ownership. While the scenarios can provide information on interactions and mechanisms supporting the interaction, due to their focus they cannot provide information on the usage and representation of such negotiations. Thus, derived from design considerations concerning groupware systems in general, we provide additional constraints for the support of co-ownership.

Our first considerations are concerned with the representation of negotiations in a groupware system. As we apply negotiations to support co-ownership on documents, we need to contextualize the representation of each negotiation. Thus, like the concept of contextual communication with annotations in [12], *negotiations have to be attached to the representation of the document they refer to*. As multiple changes on a document may cause multiple negotiations, we state that the *visualisation* of negotiations in a groupware system has to be *volatile*. This means that after a negotiation has been finished it should not be visible in the system by default. Of course, users have to be aware of *current* – and therefore visible – negotiations affecting them. Thus, besides the appliance of awareness mechanisms [8], a mechanism to *directly address negotiations to users* is needed.

Negotiations need discussions among participants [19]. Therefore, negotiations for co-ownership require the ability of users to *discuss whether to accept or refuse* their proposal. Consistency is another issue when dealing with negotiations. Once a negotiation is started, *no further changes on the document affected by the negotiation* can be made or proposed to avoid inconsistencies resulting from parallel changes. Furthermore, during the negotiation process transparency mechanisms have to *inform participants about the status* of the negotiation. Taking into account the need to directly address negotiations to users, *notification mechanisms* are needed. Such

---

[3] There are other options to relax the condition of co-ownership such as weighting the votes of participants. Without going into details, such a weighting can be found in the role-based negotiation mechanism required for co-ownership.

mechanisms may be based on system-internal messages and communication tools such as email or instant messaging.

4. From concept to implementation: Co-ownership in action

Our concept of supporting collaboration by co-ownership aims at being applicable to groupware systems in general. Based on the requirements described above, this section covers the concept and exemplifies it by the implementation of co-ownership in the web-based groupware system Kolumbus 2[4]. Before we show how our implementation can be applied to one of the scenarios presented earlier, we briefly sketch our concept to show that it fulfils all of the requirements.

4.1. A concept to apply co-ownership

The integration of support for co-ownership in Kolumbus 2 both involved conceptual and technical considerations. While we will elaborate on the conceptual level in greater detail in this section, technical aspects will only be described to provide information on the background of our work.

When we started to conceptualize the support for co-ownership in Kolumbus 2, the system was already using a role-based access control mechanism providing contextual role management. Thus, we only had to extend this mechanism to allow for multiple owners of a document. The main design task therefore was to develop a concept for a negotiation mechanism mediating the appliance of co-ownership.

Derived from the specific requirements presented in section 3.2, this mechanism had to both enable co-ownership and support the changes in the further work process. The latter demand aims at the mediation of system functions [15] and internal state transitions. With regard to the system functions, we could easily define a set of them affected by co-ownership, as from our scenarios we saw that these functions were all concerned with manipulations of documents. Thus, we built a negotiation mechanism controlling the execution of these functions in Kolumbus 2. On a technical level, mediating system functions depends on their proper encapsulation and monitoring. In the case of Kolumbus 2, a redesign of system functions turned out to be necessary: we extracted these functions and encapsulated them into so-called *actions*. Based on this design we implemented a mechanism observing the execution of actions at run-time and letting them become subject to negotiation if required.

As internal state changes such as changes in the role assignments within Kolumbus 2 are performed by system functions, this approach also supports their mediation. This includes both establishing co-ownership on a document and actions like withdrawing ownership.

Configurability is critical to co-ownership, as different settings of its appliance might cause different modes of negotiations. To fulfil the requirements related to this issue, our mechanism leaves most of the configuration to the user initiating a negotiation. The user can thereby determine whether e.g. votes can be set preliminary. Furthermore, it is up to the user to add her proposal to the negotiation and set a proper deadline within certain boundaries. From a technical point of view, the multitude of possible user configurations (e.g. allowing for preliminary votes, demanding a secret

---

[4] For further information on Kolumbus 2 please refer to http://www.kolumbus2.de.

poll or commenting on the negotiation) has to result in a generic implementation of the negotiation mechanism. In Kolumbus 2, basic tasks of negotiation support are handled by an abstract mechanism leaving the details of a negotiation's execution to user configuration.

While there are several options determined by users, the negotiation mechanism provides additional features such as identifying the originator of a document in order to provide her with the right of veto. Furthermore, we included certain presets for the mechanism to e.g. determine the decision mode of negotiations depending on the action currently negotiated. Within certain boundaries, the decision mode may also be configured by a user. Our presets also address *organizational settings like relaxing* negotiation demands to the mode of shared ownership and therefore not initiating a negotiation on corresponding actions, e.g. when performing editorial changes in documents. Technically, this requires the negotiation mechanism to be generic in terms of the system function to be negotiated as well. In Kolumbus 2, we use different configuration sets allowing for action-dependent negotiation modes.

4.2. Applying co-ownership

We have practically applied the concept described in the preceding section to Kolumbus 2. As we described above, the system is equipped with a role based access control subsystem which among other things is capable to express which users hold the ownership and which users are recipients of a document. According to our concept we extended this subsystem and developed a generic negotiation mechanism to enable co-ownership in Kolumbus 2.

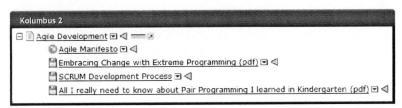

Figure 1: Initial material for the collaborative learning scenario.

Besides being applicable to other domains, the system supports learning processes similar to the one described in section 2.1. To illustrate how the appliance of our concept in Kolumbus 2 supports processes related to co-ownership, we turn back to this scenario and assume that Kent, Mary and Ward use Kolumbus 2 for their learning efforts. They start the learning process with some initial material. Figure 1 shows the initial content our users are provided with, represented by a tree of artefacts like e.g. documents in Kolumbus 2. The disk icons in Figure 1 indicate binary content like e.g. PDF-Files, the arrow icon depicts a hyperlink to an external resource and the sheet represents an editable text document.

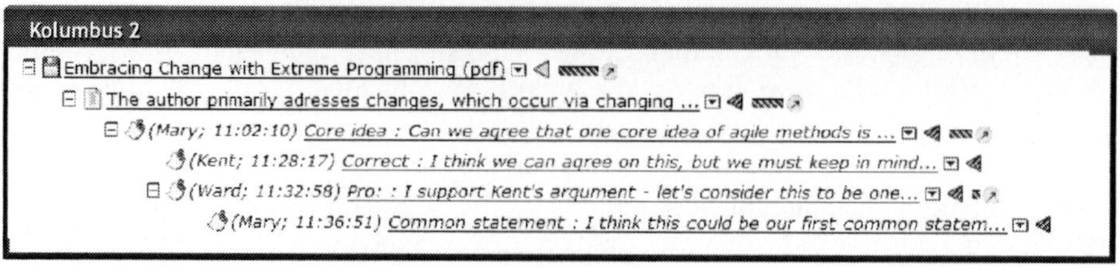

Figure 2: Learners discussing a document.

According to the description provided in the scenario, our users start to work with the material provided. During the process they discuss particular documents. One of these discussions is shown in Figure 2, when our users discuss whether or not Mary's opinion reflects the others' understanding of the topic. Here, each discussion statement consists of a so-called *annotation* in Kolumbus 2. Such annotations are represented by an icon showing a yellow sticky note. As can be taken from Mary's last annotation Kent and Ward implicitly agree that her prior statement reflects the group's common understanding. Thus, in her last annotation Mary also proposes to write down their understanding and Kent and Ward to become co-owners of the resulting document, taking responsibility for its content.

As can be seen in Figure 3, Mary accordingly initiates a negotiation (represented by the face-to-face icon) that invites Kent and Ward to become co-owners and will lead to a corresponding change in the set of owners in case of positive completion. The negotiation is attached to the corresponding document as demanded in section 3.3 and system-internal notification messages are sent to Kent and Ward. In accordance with the requirements presented in section 3, Mary can now configure this negotiation. As depicted by Figure 4, she provides a name and proposal for the negotiation and sets its expiry date to the day after. Furthermore, she decides that Kent and Ward may not revoke their votes. With respect to the demand for transparency, the configuration dialogue contains information on e.g. the decision mode. In this case, a majority decision is used, according to the original scenario a unanimous decision could be configured as well.

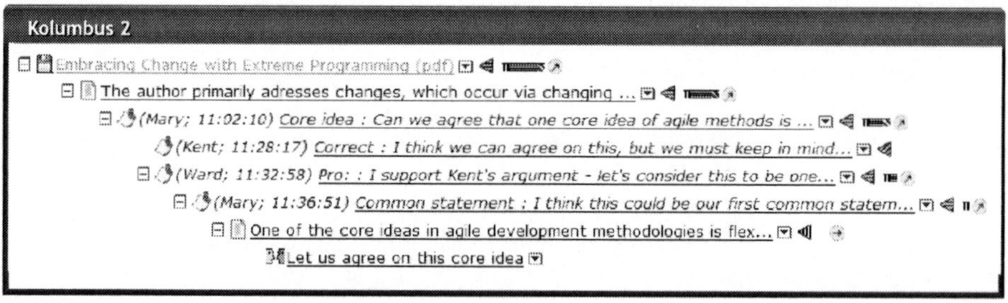

Figure 3: Negotiating co-ownership to express common understanding.

Referring to the conceptualization of negotiations as a voting process described section 1.2, Kent and Ward can either accept or decline Mary's proposal. Sharing the understanding expressed by her document, in this case they accept the proposal and become co-owners of the text. Figure 5 shows the resulting change in ownership. As can be seen at the bottom of the figure, Kent, Mary and Ward share the ownership of

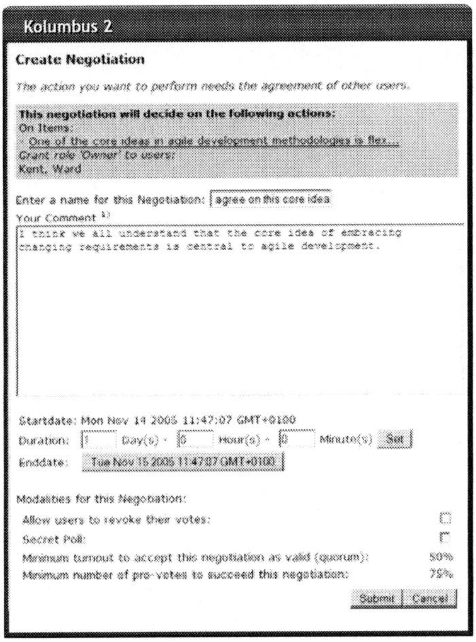

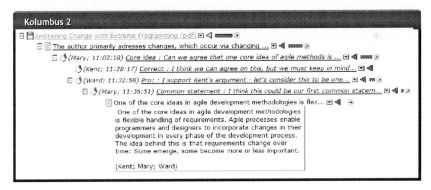

Figure 4: Negotiation configuration dialogue.

the text originally written by Mary. As we have demanded in section 3.3, after its completion the negotiation is no longer visible by default.

In our scenario, Kent, Mary and Ward have now agreed on a shared understanding representing a certain amount of their knowledge on the learning content. As learning and understanding evolve over time, later on in the scenario Ward proposes to alter the co-owned text. According to the concept of co-ownership, he can not change the text without Mary and Ward agreeing to his proposal. Therefore, the proposal and thereby the co-ownership on the altered text are subject to another negotiation process. In our scenario the users cannot agree on the proposal, resulting in further negotiations or even the withdrawal of co-ownership by one of them.

Figure 5: Co-ownership on a document.

Considering the different work settings described by the other scenarios of section 2, our mechanism is also capable of remembering a document's originator and supplying her with the right of veto. In case of the collaborative learning scenario, Mary would be provided with the right of veto when our users negotiate whether or not to become co-owners of her document. Furthermore, if Ward would have proposed to correct the document's *spelling* rather than its *content*, the negotiation subsystem would have relaxed the situation to shared ownership conditions. In this case, Ward would have been allowed to perform the change individually. Situations in which the system may relax co-ownership are subject to the configuration of the mediating mechanism described in section 4.1.

5. Summary

In this paper, we have identified co-ownership to be a common concept to real-life processes concerned with collaborative work on documents. Inspired by this finding, we believe this concept to be valuable to the support of collaborative work in groupware. As we have shown, current approaches and groupware applications fall short of supporting co-ownership. Therefore, we developed a mechanism to support co-ownership applicable to groupware systems in general. The corresponding design task was guided by a scenario-based approach that enabled us to derive a multitude of requirements from different work settings. Referring to one of these scenarios we illustrated how our implementation of the mechanism can be applied to foster collaborative work with documents in the groupware system Kolumbus 2.

So far, we have practically applied co-ownership in small test settings and are currently preparing to examine its effects in large-scale settings of collaborative learning. We are looking forward to confirm our first impressions by empirically scrutinizing the appliance of co-ownership in groupware. From these studies, we also expect to gain information on how to optimize the support of co-ownership.

Besides other improvements, this optimization has to deal with possible delays caused by negotiations (cf. [19] for further details). Especially when system functions become subject to negotiations, collaborative work may be inadequately slowed down when e.g. deadlines are not properly set. Therefore, our examination aims at a compromise between preventing delays by adequate boundaries for deadlines and leaving enough time for users to participate in negotiation processes. For instance, the use of instant messaging agents to inform users about negotiations may serve well in speeding up the negotiation process.

Another challenge lies in extending our concept to support co-ownership on collections of documents. In such cases, the scope of the negotiation mechanism has to be extended: when referring to a single document the decision whether to start a negotiation or not solely depends on co-ownership. In contrast, when dealing with collections the decision whether a document should be added depends on the context made up by the documents forming a collection. Suitable negotiation support for this task has to make this context explicit.

6. Acknowledgements

The authors would like to thank the rest of the Kolumbus 2 development team – Hans Nix and Peter Schyma – for their efforts in implementing the functionalities described in this paper.

References

[1]   Bentley, R.; Appelt, W.; Busbach, U.; Hinrichs, E.; Kerr, D.; Sikkel, Trevor, J. and Woetzel, G., Basic Support for cooperative work on the World Wide Web, *International Journal of Human Computer Interaction. Special issue: innovative applications of the World Wide Web.* Volume 46, Issue 6 (June 1997), Duluth, MN, USA: Academic Press, Inc., 827-846.

[2]   Bui, T.; Kertsen, G. and Ma, P., Supporting Negotiation with Scenario Management, *Proceedings of the 29th Annual Hawaii International Conference on System Sciences* (1996). Los Alamitos: IEEE, 209-218.

[3]   Caroll, J. M., *Making Use: Scenario-Based Design of Human-Computer Interactions* (2000). Cambridge: MIT Press.

[4]   Davis, R. and Smith, R. G., Negotiation as a Metaphor for Distributed Problem Solving, *Artificial Intelligence 20* (1983), 63-109.

[5]   DeSanctis, G., and Gallupe, R. B., A Foundation for the Study of Group Decision Support Systems, Management *Science*, 33, 2 (1987), 589-609.

[6]   Dillenbourg, P. and Baker, M., Negotiation Spaces in Human-Computer Collaborative Learning, *Proceedings of the International Conference on Cooperative Systems* (1996), France, 187-206.

[7]   Dillenbourg, P., Over-scripting CSCL: The risks of blending collaborative learning with instructional design, Kirschner, P. A. (ed.), Three *worlds of CSCL. Can we support CSCL?* (2002) Heerlen, Open Universiteit Nederland, 61-91.

[8]   Dourish, P. and Bellotti, V., Awareness and Coordination in Shared Workspaces, Turner, J. and Kraut, R. (eds.), *CSCW '92. Sharing Perspectives. Proceedings of the Conference on Computer-Supported Cooperative Work* (1992), Toronto, ACM/SIGIOS, 107-114.

[9]   Erickson, T. and Kellogg, W. A., Social Translucence: An Approach to Designing Systems that Support Social Processes, *ACM Transactions on Computer-Human Interaction*, Vol. 7 (2000), No. 1, 59-83.

[10] Ferraiolo, D. F.; Cugini, J. A. and Kuhn, D. R., Role-Based Access Control (RBAC): Features and Motivations, *Proceedings of 11th Annual Computer Security Applications* (1995), 241-248.

[11] Herrmann, T., Learning and Teaching in socio-technical environments, Van Weert, T. J. and Munro, R.K. (ed.), *Informatics and the Digital Society. Social, Ethical and Cognitive Issues* (2003), Boston, Kluwer, 59-72.

[12] Kienle, A. and Herrmann, T., Integration of communication, coordination and learning material – a guide for the functionality of collaborative learning environments, *Proceedings of the 36th Annual Hawaii International Conference on System Sciences* (2003), 33-42.

[13] Nardi, B., Some reflections on scenarios, Caroll, J. M. (ed.), *Scenario Based Design: Envisioning Work and Technology in System Development* (1995), New York, Wiley & Sons, 387-399.

[14] Robertson, S. P., Generating Object-Oriented Design Representations via Scenario Queries, Caroll, J. M. (ed.), *Scenario Based Design: Envisioning Work and Technology in System Development* (1995), New York, Wiley & Sons, 279-308.

[15] Roschelle, J.; Teasley, S. D., The Construction of Shared Knowledge in Collaborative Problem Solving, O'Malley C. E. (ed.), *Computer Supported Collaborative Learning* (1995), Heidelberg, Germany, Springer, 69-97.

[16] Sandhu R.; Coyne, E.; Feinstein H. and Youman, C., Role-based access control models, *IEEE Computer* (1996), Vol. 29, 38-47.

[17] Sandhu, R. S.; Ferraiolo, D. and Kuhn, R., The NIST Model for Role-Based Access Control: Towards a Unified Standard, *Proceedings of 5th ACM Workshop on Role-Based Access Control* (2000), New York, ACM Press, 47-63.

[18] Stahl, G., Knowledge Negotiation in Asynchronous Learning Networks, *Proceedings of the 36th Annual Hawaii International Conference on System Sciences* (2003), 3.

[19] Stahl, G. and Herrmann, T., Intertwining Perspectives and Negotiation, Hayne, S. C. (ed.) , *Proceedings of the Group '99 International Conference on Supporting Group Work* (1999), New York, ACM, 316-325.

[20] Stiemerling, O. and Wulf, V., Beyond 'Yes or No' – Extending Access Control in Groupware with Awareness and Negotiation, Darses, F. and Zaraté, P. (ed.), *Proceedings of COOP '98* (1998), Cannes, 111-120.

Cooperative Systems Design
P. Hassanaly et al. (Eds.)
IOS Press, 2006

To Share or Not to Share – Distributed Collaboration in Interactive Workspaces

Hillevi SUNDHOLM[1]
Dept. of Computer and Systems Sciences
Stockholm University/Royal Institute of Technology, 164 40 Kista, Sweden
E-mail: hillevi@dsv.su.se

Abstract. We followed an international research network that holds regular meetings in technology-enhanced working environments. The team is geographically distributed and uses a set of technical artefacts to support their collaborative work, including a videoconferencing system and a media space. We have been studying how mutual understanding is created between the team members and the role that visual representations play in this work. Our approach has been to analyse the initiatives and responses made by the team members. The meeting situation is complex because the team members are participating either in both video and audio, or audio only. In this multi-channel setting it often has to be clarified who is attending, and there is also a risk of team members being forgotten when they are present only on audio. The communication space is limited; when many want to participate in the communicative activity, it becomes harder to make successful initiatives; moreover, the roles of the team members seem to become accentuated in the distributed setting. The media space is restricted in that it only allows one person to be active at the time; this causes problems when several persons want to contribute simultaneously. Some of these limitations in the system are overcome through verbal articulations of actions.

Keywords: Common ground, Awareness, Distributed collaboration, Shared workspace, Interactive spaces

Introduction

For some time now, distant collaboration has been suggested as an alternative to travelling and face-to-face meetings; it is now seen increasingly often, driven partly by technological improvements and partly by globalisation. It is also a consequence of workers belonging to several teams at the same time, making it physically impossible to be co-located with all of them, all the time [36]. Although current technologies offer many different possibilities for communicating, interacting, and sharing information simultaneously at a distance, people still prefer to work at the same place using a common collaborative space [39]. It is also known that the frequency and quality of communication declines when the distance increases between participants' offices [23]. This finding has been supported recently in an experimental study [7], where the

---

[1]This work was conducted at EDF R&D, Laboratory of Design for Cognition (LDC), 1, avenue du Général de Gaulle, 92141 Clamart cedex, France.

authors concluded that those in the field of Computer-Supportive Cooperative Work (CSCW) need to pay more attention to the design of technology to overcome social and geographical distance.

Our work focuses on collaboration in so-called interactive spaces, and more precisely on the role of visual representations when conducting teamwork and the ways that team members come to contribute and express ideas in such environments. In previous research we studied co-located collaboration in an interactive space. We found that even peripherally-located team members can have an immense impact on the overall work and that their ideas could be captured and followed up later on even if they were given no attention during the interaction [43]. We have also reported on the role of large interactive screens for communicating, expressing, and negotiating ideas [3, 43, 44].

In this paper we present a case study with a group of researchers who regularly engage in geographically distributed meetings in interactive spaces. The team uses a set of technical artefacts to support their collaborative work, including a videoconferencing system and a media space. In this area of research many studies focus on systems and users, and on the specific design of shared tools for distributed collaboration (cf. [11, 17, 28, 38, 47]). However, we see a lack of long-term empirical studies that are aiming at furthering our understanding regarding teamwork in these settings. Our particular interest is how team members create mutual understanding about the current situation, how available artefacts mediate the collaboration, and what role the visual representations play. An important characteristic of the setting is that both video- and audio conferences have been used as communication channels, which adds complexity to the meeting situation and makes our study more interesting. To investigate these issues we have looked at turn-taking both between the team members and when using the shared media space, in addition to which communication channel (i.e. video and/or audio) they use. Initiative-Response Analysis [29] helped us study the turn-taking.

1. Related Work

A shared view of the collective work is fundamental in order to be able to coordinate activities, and it is critical for the collaboration itself [10]. What Dourish and Bellotti [10] refer to as 'awareness', we here call *shared view*. They define it as an "understanding of the activities of others", which in turn provides a "context for your own activity" ([10], p. 107). An important part of all collaborative work is to maintain both a shared view and a shared understanding at least to some degree, so that the team members can perform the work and reach common goals. Collaborating teams continuously face the task of constructing a common cognitive environment; that is, team members must determine and represent relevant information that enables them to have a shared vision of the work situation [22]. In long-term collaborative activities the team members must establish and maintain a shared awareness of their actions, plans, goals and activities [34]. *Mutual knowledge* refers to knowledge that the team members both share and know that they share [22].

Demonstrating the activity to the other team members is an efficient mechanism for establishing a shared understanding within the group [13]. The visual information that is presented to the other team members "provides a situational awareness that may change both the structure (e.g. who is speaking) and the content (e.g. what is said when) of the interaction" ([13], p. 488), and the use of visual tools may even reduce the need for some language.

The main advantage of visual information is that it allows the team members to have a shared view of the work, and this has been shown to be more important than seeing each other. Still, we do not know enough about the mechanisms and features that improve the performance in a shared visual space [24].

1.1. Grounding for Reaching Mutual Understanding

The process of accomplishing *mutual understanding* between people is called *grounding* (cf. [8]); this is an interactive process in which individuals maintain and construct a common ground. The concept has roots in linguistics and cognitive psychology, and focuses on the use of language to reach mutual understanding. The language use is described as a joint action carried out by people acting in coordination with each other and it consists of both individual and social processes [40]. However, rather than focusing solely on the language, the approach also looks at the ways in which people organise interactions in order to create mutual understanding [40]. The environment is also part of this process at it provides the team members access to the same information; it allows them to see and hear the same things [9].

Grounding is part of a "refinement process" through which the actors refine and become more and more exact in what they mean over time [4]. The common ground is augmented when new related information is added, either through the tools, the goal, the setting, or the individuals themselves [6]. Constraints and "costs" change in the collaborative situation depending on which medium is used; to different extents each medium supports *co-presence* (ability to see the same things), *co-temporality* (ability to receive messages at the same time they are sent), *simultaneity* (whether all parties can send messages at the same time or must take turns) and *sequentiality* (whether the turns can be kept in a sequence) [6]. But collaborative work is not only dependent on the available media; the composition and the dynamics of the group shape the collaborative work. People also use social representations [33] – socially and shared knowledge – to guide and orient their actions and social relationships [1].

1.2. Shared Work Environments

The work environments we are studying are characterised as supporting collaborative work, co-located as well as distributed, where there are public and private displays, and where it is possible for team members to share information in several ways. We have chosen to call these kinds of environments *interactive spaces*, to stress the possibility of conducting teamwork in a more flexible way. When designing and constructing such environments it is important to have a global vision, and part of this is that the users are not interacting with single objects but with the environment as a whole. This way of viewing technology and of interacting with resources leads to a broader way of thinking about design (cf. [30, 45]). Prototypes of environments that implement, demonstrate and exemplify those ideas can be found in [19, 25, 27, 38, 40, 42, 46].

In this paper we focus on geographically distributed meetings, which take place in workspaces characterised by large displays and tools for sharing information. During the meetings the team members are present in video and audio or in audio only. Several studies have explained the role of audio only in a distributed setting [16], the role of video for remote collaboration [18], and how large displays supports teamwork [32]. Mantei et al. [31] have studied the use of a media space that integrates video, audio and a shared tool for collaborating at a distance. They looked at the technical obstacles, and the social and psychological impact of the technology. One of their conclusions was that they see a relationship between the size of the video image and how the other team members perceived each other. The team members who were presented with small images were less effective in the conversation. Olson et al. [35] studied teams of three people who were conducting a design task during a 90-minute period, first co-located and then remotely. To accomplish the task they used a software tool that enabled them to the share workspace, and to communicate verbally at a distance they used either video and audio, or audio only. They found that with video the quality of work was the same as in the co-located situation, but that using audio alone made the work slightly but significantly worse compared to working co-located.

2. Method

2.1. General Description of Corpus

Between April and December 2004 we followed nine meetings of an international research network that consists of ten laboratories spread out across Europe and North America, and about twenty team members are part of the network. All the laboratories have access to interactive workspaces. The teams are not working on a common project but they do exchange ideas and knowledge between the labs on a regular basis. Every month they have a geographically distributed meeting.

They use a multiplex videoconferencing system to transmit video and audio; an audio conference system is available in case the video link fails (or if someone who is away from the office wants to connect). They have also access to a shared media space and a wiki[2] website to share information; both are accessible on the Internet. They use the wiki site mainly to store internal information about the team members and the labs, along with meeting dates and agendas; this information is primarily used between the meetings. General information is available to individuals who visit the page. The media space on the other hand is used as an information resource, a place to where they can upload and download documents such as their presentations and working documents. The media space is used during the meetings and functions as a shared virtual workspace where everyone who is logged in can work simultaneously. One restriction is that only one person at a time can manipulate a document. To handle meta-communication and silent support during the meetings the team members use an instant messenger, to which they log on before the meetings begin.

Normally the laboratories use two screens to display different information: one shows the team members who are present on video and the other displays the shared media space, where usually at least one of the screens is large. Figure 1 shows the meeting situation at Laboratory of Design for Cognition (LDC); the video connections are shown on the left screen and the shared media space on the right one.

---

[2] Wiki is a type of server software that allows invited users to create, add and remove web page content while using any browser (http://wiki.org/wiki.cgi?WhatIsWiki)

The meetings are divided into two parts. During the first part, for which 45 minutes is reserved, all the labs are to be connecting and technical issues are discussed. The second part, which lasts about an hour, is the research seminar: network activities and research is presented and discussed.

Figure 1. Meeting situation

2.2. Data Collection

We recorded all the meetings from LDC. We used two to four fixed cameras in order to cover different angles in the meeting space: one camera for the shared media space, one for the screen that shows the videoconference picture, and finally one or two for the local space. We also used a 360° angle camera and ceiling cameras to position the local participants, and at two of the meetings one of the participants used a wearable camera ([26] describes the wearable camera), but we do not include data from those cameras in this analysis. The data collection consists of about 18 hours of video recordings.

Before and after the meeting questionnaires[3] were handed out or e-mailed. The analysis reported on here draws on one of the questions, addressing the personal objectives of the team members in attending the meetings.[4]

2.3. Data Analysis

Interaction Analysis (IA) [20] has inspired our analysis, but we did not use it exclusively. IA is a useful guide for studying the interactions between humans and their resources, and it concretely describes how to approach video material. In this analysis the collaborative viewing or reviewing sessions have been somewhat limited; in IA they represent a core activity.

Our work is based on Initiative-Response Analysis [29], which discusses the dialogue or multiparty communication – a neutral term is 'communicative activity'

---

[3] Valery Nosulenko and Lena Samoylenko have created the questionnaires in cooperation with LDC.
[4] This was asked in the pre-meeting questionnaire.

([29], p. 7) – in terms of initiatives and responses. We have focused especially on how people make an initiative to introduce a new episode [21]. The unit of analysis is the *turn*, and it is a useful model for understanding the global aspects of communicative activities in which the turns are relatively short. The initiative is an attempt to request, claim or dominate and it refers forwards; the response refers backwards, and can be more or less immediate. In contrast to many other theorists, as e.g. [41], Linell and Gustavsson [29] do not talk about 'follow-up moves' or evaluation of utterances. They mean that all utterances could be defined as either an initiative or a response. A 6-level system is developed to evaluate how strong or weak the initiatives and responses are; ranging from a free and demanding initiative to an inadequate response [29]. For our purposes we have restricted the analysis to the following four levels: *strong initiative* (introducing a new topic and explicitly requesting a response), *weak initiative* (introducing new content by claming something that possibly requests a response), *extended response* (response which adds new content to the preceding turn, or implicitly asks for a response) and *minimal response* (response without any initiative).

Five of the meetings were transcribed with regularly indicated time stamps. During the transcription and analysis, we have noted the most interesting episodes. The notes covered a wide range, from what was monitored or manipulated on the displays to social interaction between the team members. Our main foci for analysis were (in line with [20]): 'Beginning and Endings', 'Turn-taking', 'Trouble and Repair', and 'The Spatial Organization of Activity'. The latter three categories are particularly useful for understanding how the workspace supports the participants.

We re-transcribed the parts we thought to be most interesting, adding detailed information, including the exact time stamps for beginnings and endings. We divided the excerpts following the work of [37], but modified the format slightly. The 'Transcript of Interaction' does not indicate the times of pauses in the talk; instead some actions have been added in brackets. The 'Characteristics of Action' clarify the action in a more abstract way where we have identified a number of categories relevant to the communication: information request, information delivery (positive/negative), confirmation/accepting, action request, accepting request, refusing request, action verbalisation, social interaction, interaction management and situation verbalisation. We also added a column for comments regarding the utterance: whether it was an initiative (I) or a response (R), and to which line (L) each turn referred. In the excerpts presented in the results all names and personal information were changed or replaced by 'x'.

3. Results and Analysis

In this section we focus on how team members create shared understanding and how the shared workspace supports their work. A short description of the work process and the activities of the team, provided in 3.1, will help to understand the results and the analysis.

3.1. Character of the Meetings and Meeting Activities

The meetings are a blend of formal and informal aspects. They are formal in the sense of having a clear meeting time, a chair, an agenda, and a procedure for getting connected. But they are also informal: the team members – specially the lab managers – know each other very well and the meetings function as a way to keep in touch. The number of participating teams may differ from one meeting to the next, but generally 4 to 7 teams are present in at a given videoconference, and sometimes one or more teams are present in audio. Anywhere from 11 to 19 team members have participating in various meetings.

In the first meeting we studied, in April, most of the team members were present at one conference venue (i.e. outside the laboratories), and only two teams (three participants) were present on video from their labs (a third lab was connected to handle the technical support). This meeting differed from the others because it was more like a co-located meeting that uses a videoconferencing system to connect a few distant team members (including a shared media space). In the other meetings the labs were geographically distributed from each other: in these situations the difference was instead whether the teams were present on video and audio, or only on audio.

As mentioned earlier the network uses these occasions to share information and expertise, through both discussions and presentations. The items they have discussed over time include isolated items like preparations for a workshop or conference, and more long-term issues like technical solutions essential to their work and ways to improve the meeting situation. The research presentations were made either by someone within the network or by an invited researcher.

3.2. Sharing Resources and Taking Turns

The setting of the meetings includes several technical resources that make the meetings possible; the video- and audio conference systems, the shared media space, the instant messenger (IM), and the wiki site (which is mainly used between the meetings). The labs also use large screens so that all participants at a given site have the same view.

Using the media space requires a few instructions, but after that participants encounter few problems. The media space is mainly used to show presentations, and when a page is turned in a document it is turned for everyone who is logged in. During the June meeting they have decided to use an instant messenger to handle meta-communication; Section 4.4 describes how the decision was made. Excerpt 1 is an introduction to Excerpt 2, where they changed the focus from downloading the IM and creating a user account to making the usernames available to the others.

Excerpt 1. June meeting: From talking to action

Time 0:26:14	Person, team, mode	Transcript of Interaction	Characteristics of Action	Comments
1	Olivier, #1, video	"Jenny, do you have, you have your name?"	Information request	Strong I
2	Jenny, #3, video	"Almost."	Information delivery (negative) (indirect verbalisation of action)	Minimal R to L1
3	Olivier, #1, video	"Okay."	Confirmation	Minimal R to L2
4	Jenny, #3, video	"Maybe… ah okay [*typing sound*]. Okay… Okay, my screen name is jenny-s-d."	Information delivery (positive), Action verbalisation	Extended R to L1
5	Peter, #2, video	"Can you type it into the, the, into the x server, there is the document opened,	Information request + Action request (action verbalisation)	Strong I (to subtask)

		that I just opened up on the x server, where you just showed your presentation."		
6	Jenny, #3, video	"Okay."	Accepting	Minimal R to L5

End of Excerpt: 0:27:06

In Excerpt 1 Olivier took a strong initiative (line 1) by asking Jenny about her username. A few turns later Peter also took a strong initiative (line 5) to make this information visible to all team members by opening an Excel file where they could collect the usernames (since this information was of interest to everyone). In the continuation, in Excerpt 2, we see that this led to a conflict over taking turns when several team members wanted to type into the document simultaneously. The excerpt also shows how human communication can help to overcome the limitations imposed by the technology. Note that Andy is participating only on audio.

Excerpt 2. Direct continuation of Excerpt 1: Taking turns in the shared media space

Time 0:27:06	Person, team, mode	Transcript of Interaction	Characteristics of Action	Comments
7	Peter, #2, video	"Andy, can you do that too?"	Action request	2nd (strong)[5] I (to subtask)
8	Andy, #9, audio	"So, okay… [typing sound] [pause] I'm trying to type, it is not taking it." [typing sound]	Confirming/accepting Action verbalisation	Extended R to L7
9	Eric, #4, audio	"Maybe too many people are trying to type?"	Information delivery	Weak I (problem identification from L8)
10	Olivier, #1, video	"Here is mine, okay?"	Information delivery Action verbalisation	Extended R to Peter's I in L5 and L7
11	Andy, #9, audio	"Sorry, I just deleted it!"	Information delivery Action verbalisation	Extended R to L10
12	Olivier, #1, video	"Hey, it's okay! [laughs] I'll finish it and give you back the hand."	Accepting Interaction management	Expended R to L11 (organising the turns)
13	Andy, #9, audio	"Okay, thank you."	Confirmation/accepting	Minimal R to L12
14	Eric, #4, audio	"Okay, who's next?"	Accepting and interaction management	Weak I
15	Andy, #9, audio	"Okay, I'll do mine next."	Interaction management	Extended R to L14
16	Eric, #4, audio	"Okay."	Confirmation/accepting	Minimal R to L15

End of Excerpt: 0:27:48

Excerpt 2 illustrates several things. First, it shows how a conflict can arise in turn-taking in the shared media space if more than one person tries to type simultaneously (Olivier and Andy, in lines 8 and 10). Eric recognised this problem and informed the others (line 9), but no one was paying any (explicit) attention to this. When only one person can be active at a time, the turns have to be organised so members can complete their tasks (lines 14-16). The way the team solved the conflict was by letting everyone

---

[5] Since this is a repeated request it is less strong, but on the other hand it is directed to another person.

provide his or her usernames to Jenny, who typed them into the document. But as we will see later on in the meeting (see Excerpt 6 in Section 3.4), they did not complete the task of collecting usernames.

The turn-taking conflict is probably related to the fact that the participants do not share the same physical space. In the two excerpts we see that the participants were verbalising their actions (indirectly as in lines 2 and 5 and directly as in lines 4 and 10-12); in this way they overcame the difficulties of not being able to see what was happening in the media space. This illustrates the need to support the action in a shared, but geographically distributed, space. In the following section we will see other effects of not sharing the same physical space.

3.3. Sharing the View – Understanding the Situation as a Whole

Each team member can only completely view his or her own local situation; that is, they can tell who is attending locally, what they have access to (media space, IM) and the quality of sound and picture. The lab that is organising the meetings as well as connecting the other labs using video and/or audio is the one that can best understand the whole situation. Normally the chair explicitly shares his knowledge about the presence of the participants with the other team members (compare this to Excerpt 5, lines 1-3, in Section 3.4). They also use the IM to share the fact of their presence and other relevant information (e.g. connection problems). To be recognised as present is especially important to the participants in an audio conference, but those in the videoconference also need to know who is present only on audio. In Excerpt 3 we will see a somewhat different situation as one team member, Wolfgang, explicitly asked for confirmation of a particular person's presence in one of the other labs.

Excerpt 3. November meeting: Checking presence

Time: 0:04:12	Person, team, mode	Transcript of Interaction	Characteristic of action	Comments
1	Wolfgang, #4, video	"In the middle of the table [*directed to team 1*] do I see John?"	Information request	Strong I (clarifying vision)
2	John, #1, video	"Yes, you do!"	Confirmation	Minimal R to L1
3	Wolfgang, #4, video	"Oh, hello! How are you?"	Social interaction	Minimal R to L2 + weak I
4	John, #1, video	"I'm fine. How are you?"	Social interaction	Extended R to L2 + weak I
5	Wolfgang, #4, video	"I'm well. I can't complain. I have also been to Paris recently."	Social interaction	Minimal R to L4 + weak I
6	John, #1, video	"Oh, good."	Social interaction	Minimal R to L5

End of Excerpt: 0:04:26

Wolfgang asked that question not only to get a clarification because the picture might be fuzzy, but also because he had not expected to see John on Team #1: John is part of Team #3. Such clarifications are not rare; at most meetings people want to clarify how is present. But it is not only a question of who is there and who is not; people also need to understand who has access to the shared media space and be sure that everyone can see and hear well. Some amount of time in each meeting time must be devoted to handling such issues, although the amount has decreased with experience. Excerpt 4 illustrates how the chair, Olivier, ensured that the other team members could see and hear before he started his presentation.

Excerpt 4. November meeting: Seeing and hearing well

Time: 0:10:42	Person, team, mode	Transcript of Interaction	Characteristic of action	Comments
1	Olivier, #1, video	"I will start today's presentation. And it's, it's about eh… [opens the presentation in the media space] All right. Can everybody clearly see what I am presenting?"	Interaction management Information request	Weak I Strong I
2	Wolfgang, #4, video	"Yes, could you…?"	Information delivery (positive), and information request	Minimal R to 2nd part of L1, tries to make an strong I
3	Olivier, #1, video	Does everybody hear me correctly?"	Information request	Strong I
4	Nils, #7, audio	"Yes."	Information delivery (positive)	Minimal R to L3
5	Jenny, #3, video	"Yes."	Information delivery (positive)	Minimal R to L3
6	Wolfgang, #4, video	"Yes, could you speak slowly?"	Information delivery (positive) and information request	Minimal R to L3, and 2nd trial to make a strong I (1st try in L2)
7	Olivier, #1, video	"I will speak slowly.	Information delivery (positive)	Minimal R to L6

End of Excerpt: 0:11:15

Once Olivier had gotten the confirmations from each team member about the acoustic and visual conditions he started his presentation.

3.4. Physical Space Matters – What does it Mean to Participate in Audio?

The following two excerpts are taken from the same meeting: the team members discussed how to handle the communication between the labs when both the video and audio channels fail. A solution has been raised at an earlier meeting: use an instant messenger. Peter, who was present on video, was proposing different possibilities – including using AOL [2] – but he had not received any clear response. Excerpt 5 illustrates that when a team member is present only on audio he can shift quickly, not only from unknown to known, but also from unknown to leader of the discussion.

Excerpt 5. June meeting: Going from periphery to main actor

Time 0:19:45	Person, team, mode	Transcript of Interaction	Characteristic of action	Comments
1	Olivier, #1, video	"I, I think hmm… Andy? Did you join us, Andy?"	Information request	Strong I
2	Andy, #9, audio	"Yes, yes I am here."	Information delivery (positive)/confirmation	Minimal R to L1
3	Olivier,#1,	"Yes, you are here, okay…	Situation verbalisation	Extended R

	video	because the others were not aware that, that you had come in, so… I was the only one to know so I share the news."		to L2
4	Andy, #9, audio	"Well, thank you. Although I sent, sent both you and Peter my AOL screen name. So since AOL is free and accessible I would recommend that a simple e-mail message with everybody's AOL screen name on would be really handy."	Social interaction Information delivery	Strong I
5	Olivier, #1, video	"Okay."	Accepting request	Minimal R to L4
6	Peter, #2, video	"Yeah."	Confirmation	Minimal R to line 4
7	Olivier, #1, video	"That's, well that, that would be the same thing as Peter's suggestion, right?"	Information request	Weak I (clarifies the statement of Andy, L4)
8	Andy, #9, audio	"Yes, that's basically the same."	Information delivery (positive)	Minimal R to L7
9	Olivier, #1, video	"Correct."	Confirmation	Minimal R to L8
10	Andy, #9, audio	"Although we could, we could do it in five minutes."	Interaction management and Action request	Strong I

End of Excerpt: 0:20:26

The above example shows how Andy very effectively used the door that Olivier opened to him (lines 1 and 3). As we see, being "invisible" does not automatically mean that it is more difficult to influence the group; perhaps it is a question of how things are said and who is saying them. In this case Olivier made a strong initiative to introduce Andy, who immediately continued on the same topic as Peter, who had been arguing unsuccessfully to choose AOL, just before Andy was introduced. But once Andy entered the stage, he started (line 4) by stressing that he had already taken an action (sending out his AOL user name to the others). Andy was recommending this action without arguing for it (lines 4 and 10), and Peter supported him (line 6). In line 7, Olivier took a step back to compare Andy's statement to what Peter had said earlier. In this way Andy actually led the group to choose AOL, although they did not make a formal decision, in the sense of all team members agreeing upon this particular service. In fact, after this episode the team members who did not have an AOL user account got one and then they collected the usernames in a document (illustrated in Excerpts 1 and 2, Section 3.2). This activity however, did not take the "five minutes" that Andy estimated (line 10), but rather about 25 minutes of meeting time.

In Excerpt 6 we illustrate how a team member, who is participating only on audio and who has "been forgotten", has invisibly contributed to the overall goal of the team (to collect the usernames).

Excerpt 6. June meeting: Forgotten in the audio

Time 0:46:42	Person, team, mode	Transcript of Interaction	Characteristics of Action	Comments
1	Olivier, #1, video	"By the way, Thomas, are you still there?"	Information request	Strong I

2	Thomas, #5, audio	"I am still here, yeah."	Confirmation	Minimal R to L2
3	Olivier, #1, video	"Okay, because I realized we have forgotten you for a while, nobody has asked you for your, you know, AOL name."	Interaction management	Weak I
4	Thomas, #5, audio	"Well, I've put it in the list."	Information delivery	Extended R to L3
5	Olivier, #1, video	"Oh!"	Accepting	Minimal R to L4

End of Excerpt: 0:46:56

Olivier, the chair of the meeting, realised that Thomas had been forgotten (line 1), and specifically asked for his username, but Thomas had already typed it into the shared document, just after the others had finished doing so. This initiative was "invisible" in two ways. Thomas was literally not visible to the others because he was present only on audio, and the shared media space did not indicate that someone was using it.

4. Discussion

In this paper we have focused on the role of visual representations during geographically distributed meetings in shared interactive spaces, and on the ways that team members create mutual understanding about the situation. Our approach has been to analyse the initiatives and responses made by the team members.

In the first two excerpts we saw how the team used the media space to share information easily with the other team members. Hindering the process is in fact that only one person can work actively at a time. That fact led them to organise the turns, which both interrupted the meeting and inhibited the sharing of information. This conflict revealed a gap between the individual and the system (the lack of any indication that someone else is using it at any given moment) and therefore also between the team members (see Excerpt 2, lines 8-11). This illustrates that the system does not give the users enough feedback for them to understand the activities of the others [10], or a shared view of what is happening in the system. The workspace should "communicate who is working in the space and what they are doing" ([36], p. 70), which clearly did not happen here. This finding might help explain why Thomas, Excerpt 6, contributed after the others; it would have taken too much effort to intervene whilst the others collected their user names. If this is the case it confirms that what the medium allows us to see and do affects how we communicate and interact [12].

We also noted in the first two excerpts that the participants complemented their actions by articulating what they were doing (indirectly in lines 2 and 5, and directly in lines 4 and 10-12).[6] In this way they helped the other team members to remain aware of the ongoing action [34]. This would probably also happen to some extent in a co-located setting, but we think this is an effect of not having a sufficient overview of what is taking place in the shared and geographically distributed workspace. This same problem of not sharing the physical space underlies the repeated questions about who is

---

[6] [15] also has identified that participants compensates for the shortcomings of the system by spoken account.

present and who can hear and see well (as illustrated in Section 3.3), which is a basic requirement for creating a common ground between collaborating people. We think this problem is exacerbated by the fact that they are not all co-present [6]; some participants are connected via audio and video and some via audio only. This *blended* quality makes the meeting situation more complex and cognitively more demanding for both the chair and the other participants.

We also see a limitation on how many people can be active in the communication space at the same time in this distributed setting. In Excerpts 2 and 4 we saw team members have trouble making their voices heard when too many were trying to make contributions simultaneously. In Excerpt 2, line 9, Eric was making a weak initiative without getting his voice heard; his polite request in line 14 can be interpreted the same way. We can see this request as the result of his participation in turn-taking, but he does want to share his usernames with the others. We interpret his request in this way because later on, 10 and 11 turns after the end of the excerpt, he tried again, asking "Okay, is it my turn, Olivier?" and "Is it my turn now?" In Excerpt 4 we see how Wolfgang tried to make a weak initiative and succeeded after his second attempt (lines 2 and 6). As long as only two or three people are interacting there is no problem (as in Excerpts 1, 3, 5 and 6), but when more than three try at once, it is apparently more difficult. Obviously it is also easier to enter the communicative space when someone is making a direct request (strong initiative), as we see in Excerpt 2, lines 7-8, and in Excerpts 3 and 6.

In our earlier study in a co-located setting we saw how team members used different interactive resources to contribute to the common work [43]. In addition we noticed that the team members preferred different ways of expressing ideas and contributing to the work. This in turn indicated that this kind of environment even might lead to equalising the roles of the team members. The teams also had many ad hoc discussions, and in several situations non-linear relationships developed between initiatives and responses. This was illustrated by the fact that even peripheral team members could make major contributions to the overall work although they had initially been given no attention. We have not, yet, been able to see these phenomena in this corpus. These phenomena might not have occurred because the meetings had agendas and were more structured; however we also think this is an effect of the distributed setting. Instead of the roles each team member becoming more equalised, they become accentuated in the distributed setting, as each initiative and response is received either more weakly or more strongly than it would be in a face-to-face situation. This is probably also related to the status or the role of the team member in the group.[7] If this is so, it supports [5] in that material resources are part of the determination and distribution of roles between the participants. It would also support the work of [14], who suggest that team members can communicate and exchange information more effectively if community systems were to support role-mechanisms (e.g. role-assignment, role-taking and role-making).

As these examples show, two key elements of grounding [6] – the lack of feedback on the others' situation, and the inability to monitor the state of one's own team members – create problems in developing mutual understanding. Thus, it is not enough to allow participants to see the actions of the others; they also need too know what

---

[7] Other relevant aspects include intonation and the way something is said, but those are not our focus in this work.

remote participants can see in the shared workspace [13]. Excerpt 6 illustrated one consequence of this when a team member was forgotten, probably because he was present only on audio and not in the videoconference. Not only is this important for creating a mutual understanding between the team members; we also see another, more pragmatic, issue. The repeated questions about who is present and who sees what take energy, focus, and time from the main objective of the meetings. Kraut et al. [23] reported that it is more important to share the view of common objects than to see each other, but we would modify this: depending on the setting it is also essential to also a view of all the participants and not only of the shared objects. In our specific case this might be related to the number of participants, or number of teams, or the fact that using audio conferencing as a backup confuses the situation. On the other hand we also saw in Excerpt 5 that this does not by default make major contributions more difficult, though we point out the great value of ensuring that an audio participant is introduced to the others at the beginning.

We will continue to study turn-taking and making initiatives in relation to the mode of presence (through video and audio, or audio only). In particular we will look at a situation when a large part of the group is located in the same place. We will also look more deeply into how the team members develop the social conventions they need to work in a shared but distant interactive workspace.

Acknowledgements

This work was partly sponsored by EDF R&D and the European Commission through a Marie Curie Fellowship in Social Representation and Communication. I want to thank Saadi Lahlou, Henrik Artman and Robert Ramberg for helpful comments on an earlier draft, and Michael Baker for fruitful discussions regarding the analysis. Finally, I want to thank the researchers in the RUFAE network who have allowed me to observe and take part in their meetings.

References

[1]   Abric, J.-C. (1994). Les représentations sociales: Aspects théoretiques. In Abric, J.-C. (Ed.) *Practiques socials et representations*. Paris: PUF, pp. 11-35.
[2]   www.aim.aol.com
[3]   Artman, H., Ramberg, R., Sundholm, H. and Cerratto-Pargman, T (2005). Action Context and Target Context Representations: A Case Study on Collaborative Design Learning. In: Koschman, T., Suthers, D., & Chan, T.W., (Eds.), *Computer Supported Collaborative Learning 2005: The Next 10 Years!* Mahwah, NJ: Lawrence Erlbaum Associates.
[4]   Baker, M.J. (1995). Negotiation in Collaborative Problem-Solving Dialogues. In Beun, R.J., Baker, M.J. & Reiner, M. (Eds.), *Dialogue and Instruction: Modelling Interaction in Intelligent Tutoring Systems*. Berlin: Springer-Verlag, pp. 39-55.
[5]   Baker, M.J. (2002). Forms of cooperation in dyadic problem-solving. *Revue d'Intelligence Artificielle*, 16, N°4-5, pp. 587-620.
[6]   Baker, M.J., Hansen, T., Joiner, R. & Traum, D. (1999). The role of grounding in collaborative learning tasks. In P. Dillenbourg (Ed.), *Collaborative Learning: Cognitive and Computational Approaches*. Amsterdam: Pergamon / Elsevier Science, pp. 31-63.
[7]   Bradner, E. and Mark, G. (2002). Why Distance Matters: Effects on Cooperation, Persuasion and Deception. In *Proceedings of Computer Supported Cooperative Work* (CSCW 2002), November 16-20, 2002, New Orleans, Louisiana, USA. New York: ACM Press, pp. 226-235.

[8]   Clark, H.H. and Brennan, S.E. (1991). Grounding in Communication. In Resnick, L.B., Levine, J.M. and Teasley, S.D. (Eds.), *Perspectives on Socially Shared Cognition*, Washington DC., APA Press, pp. 127-149.

[9]   Dillenbourg, P. and Traum, D., (1999). The long road from a shared screen to a shared understanding. In Hoadley, C. and Rochelle, J. (Eds.), *Proceedings of Computer Supported Collaborative Learning* (CSCL 1999), December 12-15, 1999, Stanford, California, USA.

[10]   Dourish, P. and Bellotti, V. (1992). Awareness and Coordination in Shared Workspaces. In *Proceedings of Computer Supported Cooperative Work* (CSCW 1992), November 1-4, 1992 Toronto, Ontario, Canada, pp. 107-114.

[11]   Geyer, W., Richter, H., Fuchs, L., Frauenhofer, T., Daijavad, S. and Poltrock, S. (2001). A team collaboration space supporting capture and access of virtual meetings. In *Proceedings of the 2001 International ACM SIGGROUP Conference on Supporting Group Work,* September 30 - October 3, 2001, Boulder, Colorado, USA. pp. 188-196.

[12]   Gaver, W. (1992). The Affordances of Media Spaces for Collaboration. In *Proceedings of Computer Supported Cooperative Work* (CSCW 1992), November 1-4, 1992, Toronto, Ontario, Canada, pp. 17-24.

[13]   Gergle, D., Kraut, R.E. and Fussell, S.R. (2002). Action as Language in a Shared Visual Space. In *Proceedings of Computer Supported Cooperative Work* (CSCW 2002), November 6-10, 2004, Chicago, Illinois, USA, pp. 487-496.

[14]   Herrmann, T., Jahnke, I. and Loser, K.-U. (2004). The Role Concept as a Basis for Designing Community Systems. In Darses, F., Dieng, R., Simone, C. and Zacklad, M. (Eds.), *Cooperative Systems Design, Scenario-based Design of Collaborative Systems*. Amsterdam, IOS Press, pp. 163-178.

[15]   Hindmarsh, J., Fraser, M., Heath, C., Benford, S. and Greenhalgh, C. (1998). Fragmented Interaction: Establishing Mutual Orientation in Virtual Environments. In *Proceedings of ACM Conference on Computer Supported Cooperative Work* (CSCW 1998), November 14-18, 1998, Seattle, Washington, USA, pp. 217-226.

[16]   Hindus, D., Ackerman, M., Mainwaring, S.D., Starr, B. (1996). Thunderwire: A Field Study of an Audio-Only Media Space. In Olson, G.M., Olson, J.S., and Ackerman, M. (Eds.), *Proceedings of the 1996 ACM conference on Computer supported cooperative work* (CSCW 1996), November 16 - 20, 1996, Boston, Massachusetts, USA, pp. 238-247.

[17]   Isaacs, E.A., Morris, T. and Rodriguez, T.R. (1994). A forum for supporting interactive presentations to distributed audiences. In *Proceedings of the 1994 ACM Conference on Computer Supported Cooperative Work* (CSCW 1994), October 22-26, 1994, Chapel Hill, North Carolina, USA, pp. 405-416.

[18]   Isaacs, E. and Tang, J.C. (1994). What Video Can and Cannot Do For Collaboration: A Case Study. In *Multimedia Systems*, 2(2), pp. 63-73.

[19]   Johanson, B., Fox, A. and Winograd, T. (2002). The Interactive Workspaces Project: Experiences with Ubiquitous Computing Rooms. *IEEE Pervasive Computing Magazine 1(2),* April-June 2002, pp. 67-75.

[20]   Jordan, B. and Henderson A. (1995), Interaction Analysis: Foundations and Practice, *The Journal of the Learning Sciences* 4(1). Lawrence Erlbaum Associates, Inc., 1995, pp. 39-103.

[21]   Korolija, N. (1998). *Episodes in Talk: Constructing Coherence in Multiparty Conversation*. Doctoral thesis, Department of Theme Research, Linköping University, Sweden.

[22]   Krauss, R.M. and Fussell, S.R. (1990). Mutual Knowledge and Communicative Effectiveness. In Galegher, J., Kraut E.K. and Egido C. (Eds.), *Intellectual Teamwork: Social and Technological Foundations of Cooperative Work*, Lawrence Erlbaum Associates, Hillsdale, New Jersey, pp. 111-145.

[23]   Kraut E.K., Egido, C. and Galegher, J. (1990). Patterns of Contact and Communication in Scientific Research Collaborations. In Galegher, J., Kraut E.K. and Egido C. (Eds.), *Intellectual Teamwork: Social and Technological Foundations of Cooperative Work*, Lawrence Erlbaum Associates, Hillsdale, New Jersey, pp. 149-171.

[24]   Kraut, R.E., Gergle, D. and Fussell, S.R. (2002). The Use of Visual Information in Shared Visual Spaces: Informing the Development of Virtual Co-Presence. In *Proceedings of Computer Supported Cooperative Work* (CSCW2002), November 16-20, 2002, New Orleans, Louisiana, USA, pp. 31-40.

[25]   Krogh P. and Grønbæk. K. (2001). Roomware and Intelligent Buildings – Obejcts and Buildings become Computer Interfaces. Conference on Architectural Research and Information Technology, Nordic Association for Architectural Research, Århus School of Architecture, Århus, Denmark, April 27-29, 2001, pp. 63-68

[26]   Lahlou, S. (1999). Observing Cognitive Work in Offices. In Streitz, N., Siegel, J., Hartkopf, V. and Konomi, S. (eds.) *Cooperative Buildings. Integrating Information, Organisations and Architecture*. Heidelberg: Springer, Lecture Notes in Computer Science, 1670, pp. 150-163.

[27] Lahlou, S. (2005). Cognitive Attractors and Activity-Based Design: Augmented Meeting Rooms. In *Proceedings of Human Computer Interaction International* (HCII 2005), July 22-27, 2005, Las Vegas, NA, USA.

[28] Liao, C., Liu, Q., Kimber, D., Chiu, P., Foote, J., and Wilcox, L. (2003). Shared Interactive Video for Teleconferencing. *Proc. ACM Multimedia 2003*, November 2-8, 2003, pp. 546-554.

[29] Linell, P and Gustavsson, L. (1987). *Initiative and Respons: Tthe Dynamics, Dominance and Coherence of the Dialogue*, Department of Theme Research, Linköping University, Sweden, SIC 15. [*in Swedish*]

[30] Mackay, W.E. (1998). Augmented Reality: Linking real and virtual worlds. In *Proceedings of ACM AVI '98, Conference on Advanced Visual Interfaces*. L'Aquila, Italy: ACM. Keynote address. pp. 1-9.

[31] Mantei, M., Baecker, R.M., Sellen, A.J., Buxton, W., Milligan, T., and Wellman, B. (1991). Experiences in the Use of a Media Space. In Robertson, S.P., Olson, G.M., Olson, J.S. (Eds.), *Proceedings of the ACM CHI 91 Human Factors in Computing Systems Conference*, April 28 - May 5, 1991, New Orleans, Louisiana, USA, pp. 203-208.

[32] Mark, G., Kobsa, A. and Gonzalez, V. (2002). Do four eyes see better than two? Collaborative versus individual discovery in data visualization systems. In *Proceedings of IEEE Sixth International Conference on Information Visualization (IV'02)*, London, July 10-12, 2002. IEEE Press, pp. 249-255.

[33] Moscovici, S. (1976). *La Psychanalyse, son image et son public*. Paris: PUF.

[34] Neale, D.C., Carroll, J.M. and Rosson, M.B. (2004). Evaluating Computer-Supported Cooperative Work: Models and Framworks. In *Proceedings of Computer Supported Cooperative Work* (CSCW2004), November 6-10, 2004, Chicago, Illinois, USA, pp. 112-121.

[35] Olson, J.S., Olson, G.M., Meader, D.K. (1995). What Mix of Video and Audio is Useful for Small Groups Doing Remote Real-Time Design Work? In Katz, I.R., Mack, R.L., Marks, L., Rosson, M.B., Nielsen, J. (Eds.), *Proceedings of the ACM CHI 95 Human Factors in Computing Systems Conference*. May 7-11, 1995, Denver, Colorado, USA, pp. 362-368.

[36] Poltrock, S.E. and Engelbeck, G. (1997). Requirements for a Virtual Collocation Environment. In *Proceedings of GROUP 97*, November 16-19, 1997, Phoenix, Arizona, USA, pp. 61-70.

[37] Pomerantz, A. & Fehr, B.J. (1997) Conversation Analysis: An Approach to the Study of Social Action as Sense Making Practices. In van Dijk, T. A. (Ed.), *Discourse as Social Interaction*. London: Sage Publications, pp. 64-91.

[38] Rogers, Y., Brignull, H. and Scaife, M. (2002). Designing Dynamic Interactive Visualisations to Support Collaboration and Cognition. In *First International Symposium on Collaborative Information Visualization Environments* (IV 2002), London, July 10-12, 2002, IEEE, pp. 39-50.

[39] Rosenberg, D., Foley, S., Kammas, S. and Lievonen, M. (2003). Interaction space theory: a framework for tool development. In *Proceedings of the 1st international symposium on Information and communication technologies*, September 24-26, 2003, Dublin, Ireland, pp. 427-432.

[40] Scholz, J.B., Grigg, M.W., Prekop, P. and Burnett, M. (2003). Development of the Software Infrastructure for a Ubiquitous Computing Environment: the DSTO iRoom. In *ACSW Frontiers*, 2003, pp. 169-176.

[41] Sinclair, J. McH. and Coulthard, M. (1975). *Towards an Analysis of Discourse: The English Used by Teachers and Pupils*. London: Oxford University Press.

[42] Streitz, N.A., Geißler, J., Holmer, T., Konomi, S., Müller-Tomfelde, C., Reischl, W., Rexroth, P., Seitz, P., and Steinmetz, R. (1999). i-LAND: An interactive Landscape for Creativitiy and Innovation. In *Proceedings of ACM Conference on Human Factors in Computing Systems (CHI '99)*, Pittsburgh, Pennsylvania, USA, May 15-20, 1999, ACM Press, New York, 1999, pp. 120-127.

[43] Sundholm, H., Artman, H. and Ramberg, R. (2004). Backdoor Creativity – Collaborative Creativity in Technology Supported Teams. In Darses, F., Dieng, R., Simone, C. and Zacklad, M. (Eds.), *Cooperative Systems Design, Scenario-based Design of Collaborative Systems*. Amsterdam, IOS Press, pp. 99-114.

[44] Sundholm, H., Ramberg, R. and Artman, H. (2004). Learning Conceptual Design: Activities with Electronic Whiteboards. In Agger Eriksen, M., Malmborg, L. and Nilsen, J. (Eds.), *CADE2004 Web Proceedings of Computers in Art and Design Education Conference*, Copenhagen Business School, Denmark, and Malmö University, Sweden, 29 June – 1 July 2004. asp.cbs.dk/cade2004/proceedings/

[45] Weiser, M. (1991). The Computer for the 21st Century. *Scientific American*, vol. 265, pp. 94-104.

[46] Werle, P., Kilander, F., Jonsson, M., Lönnqvist, P. and Jansson, C.G. (2001). A Ubiquitous Service Environment with Active Documents for Teamwork Support. In *Proceedings of Ubicomp 2001*, Atlanta, Georgia, USA, pp. 139-155.

[47] Yankelovich, N., Walker, W., Roberts, P., Wessler, M., Kaplan, J. and Provino, J. (2004). Meeting Central: Making Distributed Meetings more Effective. In *Proceedings of Computer Supported Cooperative Work* (CSCW 2004), November 6-10, 2004, Chicago, Illinois, USA, pp. 419-428.

Cooperative Systems Design
P. Hassanaly et al. (Eds.)
IOS Press, 2006

Author Index